ENGLISH-GERMAN
GERMAN-ENGLISH
DICTIONARY

ENGLISH-GERMAN
GERMAN-ENGLISH
DICTIONARY

BARNES & NOBLE BOOKS
A DIVISION OF HARPER & ROW, PUBLISHERS
New York, Evanston, San Francisco, London

This book is published by arrangement with
Ottenheimer Publishers, Inc.

ENGLISH-GERMAN GERMAN-ENGLISH DICTIONARY.
Copyright © 1967 by Bancroft & Co. (Publishers) Ltd. All rights reserved. Printed in the United States of America. No part of this book may be used or reproduced in any manner without written permission except in the case of brief quotations embodied in critical articles and reviews. For information address Ottenheimer Publishers, Inc., 1632 Reisterstown Road, Baltimore, Md. 21208.

First BARNES & NOBLE BOOKS edition
published 1974.
STANDARD BOOK NUMBER: 06-465028-6

ENGLISH-GERMAN
DICTIONARY

Abbreviations	6
Pronunciation	6
German Grammar	8
Irregular Verbs	12
German Phrases	18
Dictionary	23

ABBREVIATIONS

adj.	adjective	*pp.*	past participle
adv.	adverb	*prep.*	preposition
art.	article	*pron.*	pronoun
conj.	conjunction	*rel.*	relative
etw.	etwas	*s.*	substantive
f.	feminine	*sing.*	singular
fig.	figurative	*s.o.*	someone
inf.	infinitive	*sth.*	something
int.	interjection	*v.a.*	active verb
jm.	jemand	*v.a.&n.*	active and neuter verb
m.	masculine	*v.aux.*	auxiliary verb
pl.	plural	*v.n.*	neuter verb
poss.	possessive	*	irregular verb

German Pronunciation

We give below a short guide to German pronunciation, describing German sounds by the nearest English ones. Vowels or consonants that are equivalent to the English ones are not indicated in this list.

Letters	Description
a	as *a* in *father*.
ai, ay	as *i* in *mine*.
au	as *ow* in *fowl*.
äu	as *oy* in *boy*.
ä	as *a* in *fate*.
c	as *ts* in *waits* before *i, e, ü, ö, ä;* as *k* elsewhere.
ch	as *ch* in Scottish *loch* after *a, o, u, au;* as an exaggerated *h* in *hue* before *i, e, ü, ö, ä.*
e	when short as *e* in *get;* when

	long (also spelled *eh* and *ee*), like Northern English *a* in *cake*.
ei, ey	same as *ai* and *ay* above.
eu	same as *äu* above.
h	aspirated as the *h* in *half*.
i	as *i* in *fit* when short; as *i* in *machine* when long (also spelled *ih, ie, ieh*).
j	as *y* in *you*.
ck	=*kk*.
l	as *l* in *long*.
o	when short, as *o* in *not;* when long as Scottish *o* in *no*.
ö	when short, like the *ir* sound in *sir;* when long, like a close *e* pronounced with lips pouted, similar to *ea* in *learn*.
ph	=*f*.
qu	=*kv*.
r	rolled on the tongue.
s	The letter *s* is pronounced like English *z* in *zeal*. Used initially, as in *sonnig, sehen,* and in the interior of a word between vowels, as in *lesen, weise,* it is pronounced like English *z*. In the interior of a word before consonants it is pronounced like our *s* in *soap*. It is used in combination with *p* and *t* and is then pronounced *shp* and *sht* when initial; and *sp* and *st* in the interior of a word, as in English. The *ß* is always pronounced like English *s*. The *ss* is always pronounced as English *s* in *soap*.
sch	as *sh* in *short*.
t, th, dt	as *t* in English.
u	when short as *u* in *put,* when long (spelled also *uh*) as *oo* in *moon*.
ü	There is no such sound in English; prounounce *lee* with lips well pouted.
	as *f* in English.
	as *v* in English.
	as German *ü* in Greek loanwords; otherwise like German *i*.
z	as *ts* in *waits*.

German Grammar

Declension of the Articles
Definite Article

Singular

	Masc.	Fem.	Neut.
Nom.	der	die	das
Acc.	den	die	das
Gen.	des	der	des
Dat.	dem	der	dem

Plural
All genders

Nom.	die
Acc.	die
Gen.	der
Dat.	den

Words declined like the above are: *dieser, diese, dieses; jener, jene, jenes; welcher, welche, welches; solcher, solche, solches; mancher, manche, manches; aller, alle, alles*.

Indefinite Article

Singular

	Masc.	Fem.	Neut.
Nom.	ein	eine	ein
Acc.	einen	eine	ein
Gen.	eines	einer	eines
Dat.	einem	einer	einem

Plural
All genders

Nom.	keine
Acc.	keine
Gen.	keiner
Dat.	keinen

As *ein, eine, ein* has no plural, *kein* is delined like *ein=*not a

Declension of the Noun

Singular

a) Feminine nouns have no case endings in the singular: N. *die* **Frau** A. *die* **Frau** G. *der* **Frau** D. *der* **Frau**.

b) Masculine and Neuter nouns are declined as follows: N. *der* **Tisch** A. *den* **Tisch** G. *des* **Tisches** D. *dem* **Tisch(e)**.

The Dat. ending -*e* is becoming old-fashioned and is frequently omitted.

c) A group of Masc. nouns, add -*n* or -*en* to form the Acc., Gen. and Dat. e.g.: N. *der* **Knabe** A. *den* **Knaben** G. *des* **Knaben** D. *dem* **Knaben**.

For these not only the plural form but also the ending (- en) of the Gen. singular is given in the body of the dictionary.

Plural

a) The great majority of Fem. nouns add -*n* or -*en*.

b) The Nom., Acc., and Gen. of all Plurals are alike.

c) The Dat. Plural always ends in -*n*.

Plurals can be classified as follows:

I. Those which add -*n* or -*en*; *die Frau — die Frauen*;

II. Those which add nothing: *das Mädchen — die Mädchen*.

III. Those which add -*e*; *der König — die Könige*;

IV. Those which add -*er*; *das Glas — die Gläser*.

In the body of the dictionary German entries are followed by an abbreviation *(m., f.)* showing the gender of the noun, and an indication of the plural form of the entry word, in brackets, e.g. **Inhalt.** *m.* (-e); **Fach,** *n.* (⸚ er). The swung dash (-) stands for the entry-word. The modification (Umlaut) of the vowel sounds *a, o, u* and *au* into *ä, ö, ü* and *äu* is indicated by two dots placed above the swung dash

(⸚). Plurals, other than the above, are also indicated, e.g. **Ministerium,** *n.* (-rien), i.e. Ministerien; or written out in full: **Nuß,** *f.,* (Nüsse). Plurals of compounds are not given, since compound nouns take the gender and plural form of the last component: **Reisepaß** 7.

Declension of the Adjective

The adjective is invariable when it forms part of the predicate. If the adjective qualifies the noun, it is inflected. There are three declensions:

I. Weak, when the adjective is preceded by the *definite article* or a word of similar declension, like *dieser, jener, welcher, jeder,* etc.

II. Mixed, when the adjective is preceded by the *indefinite article,* a *possessive adjective* or *kein.*

III. Strong, when the adjective precedes a noun *without* any article or other limiting word, e.g. red wine.

I. Weak
	M.	F.	N.	P.
N.	-e	-e	-e	-en
A.	-en	-e	-e	-en
G.	-en	-en	-en	-en
D.	-en	-en	-en	-en

II. Mixed
Endings of the adjective before *ein, keine, mein, dein, sein, ihr, unser, euer, Ihr*:

	M.	F.	N.	P.
N.	-er	-e	-es	-en
A.	-en	-e	-es	-en
G.	-en	-en	-en	-en
D.	-en	-en	-en	-en

III. Strong
Endings of the adjective where there is *no* article or possessive adjective.

	M.	F.	N.	P.
N.	-er	-e	-es	-e
A.	-en	-e	-es	-e
G.	-en	-er	-en	-er
D.	-em	-er	-em	-en

Comparison of Adjectives

Add *-er* to the Positive for the Comparative, and *-st* or *-est* for the Superlative. E.g. *lang, länger, der, die, das längste.*

The Adverb

In German the adverb has the same form as the adjective, but it is not declined. The adverb is compared in the same way as the adjective.

Personal Pronouns

Singular
	1st Pers.	2nd Pers.
N.	ich	du, Sie
A.	mich	dich, Sie
G.	meiner	deiner, Ihrer
D.	mir	dir, Ihnen

	3rd Pers.
N.	er, sie, es
A.	ihn, sie, es
G.	seiner, ihrer, seiner
D.	ihm, ihr, ihm

Plural
	1st Pers.	2nd Pers.
N.	wir	Ihr, Sie
A.	uns	euch, Sie
G.	unser	euer, Ihrer
D.	uns	euch, Ihnen

	3rd Pers.
N.	sie
A.	sie
G.	ihrer
D.	ihnen

Possessive Adjectives and Pronouns

The Possessive Adjectives are: *mein, meine, mein* my; *dein, deine, dein* thy; *sein, seine, sein* his; *ihr, ihre, ihr* her; *sein, seine, sein* its; *unser, unsere, unser* our; *euer, eure* your; *Ihr, Ihre, Ihre* your; *ihr, ihre, ihr* their. They are declined like *ein, eine, ein*.

The three inflected forms are:

a) meiner, meine, meines; deiner, deine, deines; etc.

These are declined like *dieser, diese, dieses*.

b) der meine, die meine, das meine; der deine, die deine, das deine; etc.

These are declined like an adjective with the definite article.

Demonstrative Adjectives and Pronouns

Der, die, das is used as a Demonstrative Adjective and is declined like the definite article. *Dieser, diese, dieses*, this; *jener, jene, jenes* that; *solcher, solche, solches* such; *derjenige, diejenige, dasjenige* that; *derselbe, dasselbe, dieselbe* the same, are used as adjectives and pronouns.

Relative Pronouns

German has two relatives: *der, die, das* and *welcher, welche, welches*, both meaning who, which or that.

Singular
N. der, die, das, welcher, welche, welches
A. den, die, das, welchen, welche, welches
G. dessen, deren, dessen, dessen, deren, dessen
D. dem, der, dem, welchem, welcher, welchem

Plural
N. die, welche
A. die, welche
G. deren, deren
D. denen, denen

Prepositions

a) Those governing the accusative only, are: *bis* up to; till; *durch* through; by; *für* for; *gegen* against, toward, about; *ohne* without; *um* around, at; *wider* against, in opposition to.

b) Those governing the dative only are: *aus* out of, from; *bei* at, near; *mit* with; *nach* after, according to; *seit* since; *von* of, from, by; *zu* to at.

c) The prepositions shown below govern both the accusative and dative. If it answers the question *who? where?* the dative is used; If it answers the question *wohin?, whither, where to?* then the accusative is used:

an at, to; *auf* on; *hinter* behind; *in*, in, into; *neben* beside, near; *über* over, above; *unter* under, below; *vor* before, in front; *zwischen* between.

d) Prepositions taking the genitive are: *anstatt* or *statt* instead of; *trotz*, in spite of; *während* during; *wegen* on account of; *um . . . willen* for the sake of.

The Verb

Before discussing the conjugation of the verbs, we shall do

well to state some important points.

The **Infinitive** ends in -en. The **Present Participle** is both adjectival and verbal. It is formed by adding -d to the Infin.: *lieben, liebend.* The **Past Participle** is both adjectival and verbal. It is formed by prefixing ge- to the stem and adding -t in the case of *Weak Verbs* or -en (with vowel change) for *Strong Verbs: lieben,* **ge***liebt, sprechen,* **ge***sprochen.*

The **Present Indicative** is formed by adding -e, -(e)st, -(e)t, -en, -(e)t, -en to the stem.

The **Imperfect** is formed by adding -te, -test, -te, -ten, -tet, -ten to the stem of *Weak Verbs; Strong Verbs* show the past by vowel change in the stem and by adding -st in the 2nd pers. sing. and -en, -t, -en in the plural.

The **Compound Tenses** are: the *Perfect,* the *Pluperfect,* the *Future,* the *Conditional,* the *Future Perfect,* the *Past Conditional.*

In the case of transitive and reflexive verbs the auxiliary **haben** is used to form the compound past tenses: *Ich* **habe** *(hatte) gelernt.*

With instransitive verbs indicating a change of position or state, and a few others, **sein** is the auxiliary. *Ich* **bin** *gegangen.*

The *Future* is formed by the present of *werden* plus the *Infin.* of the verb: *ich* **werde** *lernen.*

The *Conditional* is formed by the *Past Subjunctive* of *werden* plus the *Infin.* of the verb: *ich* **würde** *lernen.*

The **Subjunctive Mood** is formed by adding to the stem -e, -est, -e, -en, -et, -en. The *Imperfect Subj.* of *Weak Verbs* has exactly the same form as the Imperfect Indicative. In *Strong Verbs* it is formed by modifying the vowel of the Imperfect Indicative and adding -e, -(e)st, -e, -en, -(e)t, -en.

The **Imperative** is formed for both *Weak Verbs* and *Strong Verbs* by adding -(e) for the 2nd pers. sing. and -t for the plural.

WORD ORDER

In German the finite verb, i.e. the inflected verb agrees with the subject.

In principal clauses the normal order is: 1. **subject**: 2. **finite verb**; i.e. all that comes within the scope of the verb: *the objects,* direct and indirect, the *adverbs,* and lastly those words closely linked with the finite verb, such as the Infinitive, Past Part., separable participle, predicative adjective.

IRREGULAR VERBS

Infinitive	3rd Sing. Pres. Ind.	3rd Sing. Imp. Ind.	Past Participle
backen	bäckt	backte	gebacken
befehlen	befiehlt	befahl	befohlen
beginnen	beginnt	begann	begonnen
beißen	beißt	biß	gebissen
bergen	birgt	barg	geborgen
betrügen	betrügt	betrog	betrogen
bewegen	bewegt	bewog, bewegte	bewogen, bewegt
biegen	biegt	bog	gebogen
bieten	bietet	bot	geboten
binden	bindet	band	gebunden
bitten	bittet	bat	gebeten
blasen	bläst	blies	geblasen
bleiben	bleibt	blieb	geblieben
braten	brät	briet	gebraten
brechen	bricht	brach	gebrochen
brennen	brennt	brannte	gebrannt
bringen	bringt	brachte	gebracht
denken	denkt	dachte	gedacht
dreschen	drischt	drosch	gedroschen
dringen	dringt	drang	gedrungen
dünken	es dünkt, deucht mich, mir	dünkte, deuchte	gedünkt, gedeucht
dürfen	darf	durfte	gedurft
empfangen	empfängt	empfing	empfangen
empfehlen	empfiehlt	empfahl	empfohlen
empfinden	empfindet	empfand	empfunden
erwägen	erwägt	erwog	erwogen
essen	ißt	aß	gegessen
fahren	fährt	fuhr	gefahren
fallen	fällt	fiel	gefallen
fangen	fängt	fing	gefangen
fechten	ficht	focht	gefochten
finden	findet	fand	gefunden
flechten	flicht	flocht	geflochten
fliegen	fliegt	flog	geflogen
fliehen	flieht	floh	geflohen
fließen	fließt	floß	geflossen
fressen	frißt	fraß	gefressen
frieren	friert	fror	gefroren

gären	gärt	gor, gärte	gegoren, gegärt
gebären	gebiert, gebärt	gebar	geboren
geben	gibt	gab	gegeben
gedeihen	gedeiht	gedieh	gediehen
gehen	geht	ging	gegangen
gelingen	gelingt	gelang	gelungen
gelten	gilt	galt	gegolten
genesen	genest	genas	genesen
genießen	genießt	genoß	genossen
geraten	gerät	geriet	geraten
geschehen	geschieht	geschah	geschehen
gewinnen	gewinnt	gewann	gewonnen
gießen	gießt	goß	gegossen
gleichen	gleicht	glich	geglichen
gleiten	gleitet	glitt	geglitten
graben	gräbt	grub	gegraben
greifen	greift	griff	gegriffen
haben	hat	hatte	gehabt
halten	hält	hielt	gehalten
hängen	hängt	hing	gehangen
hauen	haut	hieb	gehauen
heben	hebt	hob	gehoben
heißen	heißt	hieß	geheißen
helfen	hilft	half	geholfen
kennen	kennt	kannte	gekannt
klingen	klingt	klang	geklungen
kommen	kommt	kam	gekommen
können	kann	konnte	gekonnt
kriechen	kriecht	kroch	gekrochen
laden	lädt	lud	geladen
lassen	läßt	ließ	gelassen
laufen	läuft	lief	gelaufen
leiden	leidet	litt	gelitten
leihen	leiht	lieh	geliehen
lesen	liest	las	gelesen
liegen	liegt	lag	gelegen
löschen	lischt	losch	geloschen
lügen	lügt	log	gelogen
mahlen	mahlt	mahlte	gemahlen
meiden	meidet	mied	gemieden
messen	mißt	maß	gemessen
mögen	mag	mochte	gemocht, mögen
müssen	muß	mußte	gemußt
nehmen	nimmt	nahm	genommen
nennen	nennt	nannte	genannt

pflegen	pflegt	pflegte, pflog	gepflogen, gepflegt
preisen	preist	pries	gepriesen
raten	rät	riet	geraten
reiben	reibt	rieb	gerieben
reißen	reißt	riß	gerissen
reiten	reitet	ritt	geritten
rennen	rennt	rannte	gerannt
riechen	riecht	roch	gerochen
ringen	ringt	rang	gerungen
rinnen	rinnt	rann	geronnen
rufen	ruft	rief	gerufen
salzen	salzt	salzte	gesalzen, gesalzt
saugen	saugt	sog, saugte	gesogen, gesaugt
schaffen	schafft	schuf, schaffte	geschaffen, geschafft
scheinen	scheint	schien	geschienen
schelten	schilt	schalt, scholt	gescholten
schießen	schießt	schoß	geschossen
schinden	schindet	schund	geschunden
schlafen	schläft	schlief	geschlafen
schlagen	schlägt	schlug	geschlagen
schleichen	schleicht	schlich	geschlichen
schleifen	schleift	schliff	geschliffen
schließen	schließt	schloß	geschlossen
schmeißen	schmeißt	schmiß	geschmissen
schmelzen	schmilzt	schmolz	geschmolzen
schneiden	schneidet	schnitt	geschnitten
schreiben	schreibt	schrieb	geschrieben
schreien	schreit	schrie	geschrie(e)n
schreiten	schreitet	schritt	geschritten
schweigen	schweigt	schwieg	geschwiegen
schwellen	schwillt	schwoll	geschwollen
schwimmen	schwimmt	schwamm	geschwommen
schwinden	schwindet	schwand	geschwunden
schwören	schwört	schwor	geschworen
sehen	sieht	sah	gesehen
sein	ist	war	gewesen
senden	sendet	sandte, sendete	gesandt, gesendet
singen	singt	sang	gesungen
sinken	sinkt	sank	gesunken
sinnen	sinnt	sann	gesonnen
sitzen	sitzt	saß	gesessen

sollen	soll	sollte	gesollt
speien	speit	spie	gespie(e)n,
spinnen	spinnt	spann	gesponnen
sprechen	spricht	sprach	gesprochen
springen	springt	sprang	gesprungen
stechen	sticht	stach	gestochen
stecken	steckt	stak	gesteckt
stehen	steht	stand	gestanden
stehlen	stiehlt	stahl	gestohlen
steigen	steigt	stieg	gestiegen
sterben	stirbt	starb	gestorben
stinken	stinkt	stank	gestunken
stoßen	stößt	stieß	gestoßen
streichen	streicht	strich	gestrichen
streiten	streitet	stritt	gestritten
tragen	trägt	trug	getragen
treffen	trifft	traf	getroffen
treiben	treibt	trieb	getrieben
treten	tritt	trat	getreten
trinken	trinkt	trank	getrunken
trügen	trügt	trog	getrogen
tun	tut	tat	getan
verderben	verdirbt	verdarb	verdorben
vergessen	vergißt	vergaß	vergessen
verlieren	verliert	verlor	verloren
verwirren	verwirrt	verwirrte	verwirrt, verworren
wachsen	wächst	wuchs	gewachsen
wägen	wägt	wog	gewogen
waschen	wäscht	wusch	gewaschen
weben	webt	webte, wob	gewebt, gewoben
weichen	weicht	wich	gewichen
weisen	weist	wies	gewiesen
wenden	wendet	wandte, wendete	gewandt, gewendet
werben	wirbt	warb	geworben
werden	wird	wurde	geworden
werfen	wirft	warf	geworfen
wiegen	wiegt	wog	gewogen
winden	windet	wand	gewunden
winken	winkt	winkte	gewinkt
wissen	weiß	wußte	gewußt
wollen	will	wollte	gewollt
ziehen	zieht	zog	gezogen
zwingen	zwingt	zwang	gezwungen

NAMES

Abyssinia, Abessinien *n*.
Adria, Adria *f*.
Africa, Afrika *n*.
Albania, Albanien *n*.
Algeria, Algerien *n*.
Algiers, Algier *n*.
Alps, Alpen *pl*.
America, Amerika *n*.
Andrew, Andreas *m*.
Anne, Anna *f*.
Anthony, Anton *m*.
Antwerp, Antwerpen *n*.
Apennines, Apenninen *pl*.
Arabia, Arabien *n*.
Argentine (the), Argentinien *n*.
Asia, Asien *n*.
Assyria, Assyrien *n*.
Athens, Athen *n*.
Atlantic, Atlantischer Ozean.
Australia, Australien *n*.
Austria, Österreich *n*.

Balkans (the), Balkan (der).
Baltic, Ostsee *f*.
Bavaria, Bayern *n*.
Belgium, Belgien *n*.
Belgrade, Belgrad *n*.
Bermudas, Bermuda-Inseln *pl*.
Bohemia, Böhmen *n*.
Bolivia, Bolivien *n*.
Brazil, Brasilien *n*.
Britannia, Britannien *n*.
Brittany, Bretagne *f*.
Brussels, Brüssel *n*.
Bulgaria, Bulgarien *n*.
Burma(h), Birma *n*.

Cairo, Kairo *n*.
California, Kalifornien *n*.
Canada, Kanada *n*.

Capetown, the Cape, Kapstadt *n*.
Carpathians, Karpaten *pl*.
Caspian Sea, Kaspisches Meer.
Channel (the), Ärmelkanal *m*.
Charles, Karl *m*.
Chile, Chile *n*.
China, China *n*.
Christopher, Christoph *m*.
Clara, Klara *f*.
Cleopatra, Kleopatra *f*.
Cologne, Köln *n*.
Copenhagen, Kopenhagen *n*.
Corea, Korea *n*.
Corsica, Korsika *n*.
Cracow, Krakau *n*.
Crimea, Krim *f*.
Croatia, Kroatien *n*.
Cyprus, Cypern *n*.
Czechoslovakia, Tschechoslowakei *f*.

Dalmatia, Dalmatien *n*.
Danube, Donau *f*.
Denmark, Dänemark *n*.
Dorothy, Dorothea *f*.
Dunkirk, Dünkirchen *n*.

Ecuador, Ekuador *n*.
Egypt, Ägypten *n*.
Elizabeth, Elisabeth *f*.
Emily, Emilie *f*.
England, England *n*.
Ethiopia, Äthiopien *n*.
Europe, Europa *n*.
Eve, Eva *f*.

Finland, Finnland *n*.
Flanders, Flandern *n*.
Flora, Flora *f*.
Florence, Florenz *f*.
France, Frankreich *n*.

Gascony, Gascogne *f.*
Gaul, Gallien *n.*
Geneva, Genf *n.*
Great Britain, Großbritannien *n.*
Greece, Griechenland *n.*
Greenland, Grönland *n.*

Hague (the), (der) Haag *m.*
Hanover, Hannover *n.*
Helen, Helene *f.*
Henry, Heinrich *m.*
Holland, Holland *n.*
Hugh, Hugo *m.*
Hungary, Ungarn *n.*

Iceland, Island *n.*
India, Indien *n.*
Indies, *pl.* Indien *n. East* ~ Ostindien *n., West* ~ Westindien *n.*
Iraq, Irak *m.*
Ireland, Irland *n.*
Italy, Italien *n.*

Jack, Hans *m.*
Jamaica, Jamaika *n.*
Jane, Johanna *f.*
Japan, Japan *n.*
John, Johannes *m.*
Joseph, Joseph *m.*
Jugoslavia, Jugoslavien *n.*

Lapland, Lappland *n.*
Latvia, Lettland *n.*
Lisbon, Lissabon *n.*
London, London *n.*
Louis, Ludwig *m.*
Lyons, Lyon *n.*

Manchuria, Mandschurei *f.*
Marseilles, Marseille *n.*
Mary, Marie *f.*
Moscow, Moskau *n.*
Munich, München *n.*

Netherlands, Niederlande *pl.*

Newfoundland, Neufundland *n.*

New Zealand, Neuseeland *n.*

Nile, Nil *m.*
Normandy, Normandie *f.*
Norway, Norwegen *n.*
Nuremberg, Nürnberg *n.*

Ostend, Ostende *n.*

Palestine, Palästina *n.*
Peking, Peking *n.*
Pennsylvania, Pennsylvanien *n.*
Persia, Persien *n.*
Peter, Peter *m.*
Poland, Polen *n.*
Portugal, Portugal *n.*
Prague, Prag *n.*
Prussia, Preußen *n.*
Pyrenees, Pyrenäen *pl.*

Rhine, Rhein *m.*
Rome, Rom *n.*
R(o)umania, Rumänien *n.*
Russia, Rußland *n.*

Sarah, Sara *f.*
Sardinia, Sardinien *n.*
Saxony, Sachsen *n.*
Scandinavia, Skandinavien *n.*
Scotland, Schottland *n.*
Serbia, Serbien *n.*
Siberia, Sibirien *n.*
Sicily, Sizilien *n.*
Silesia, Schlesien *n.*
Singapore, Singapur *n.*
Soviet Union, Sowjetunion *f.*
Spain, Spanien *n.*
Sweden, Schweden *n.*
Switzerland, Schweiz *f.*
Syria, Syrien *n.*

Thuringia, Thüringen *n.*
Tokyo, Tokio *n.*
Tunis, Tunesien *n.*

Warsaw, Warschau *n.*

Zurich, Zürich *n.*

PHRASES

Yes. No.	Ja. Nein.
Good morning.	Guten Morgen.
Good afternoon.	Guten Tag.
Good evening. Good night.	Guten Abend. Gute Nacht.
Good-bye.	Auf Wiedersehen.
Excuse me please.	Entschuldigen Sie bitte.
I am sorry.	Verzeihen Sie.
Can I help you?	Kann ich Ihnen behilflich sein?
Help yourself!	Bedienen Sie sich!
How are you?	Wie geht es Ihnen?
Very well—and you?	Sehr gut und Ihnen?
Allow me to introduce you to...?	Darf ich Ihnen ... vorstellen.
Delighted to meet you.	Sehr angenehm.
Congratulations.	Glückwünsche.
Am I disturbing you?	Störe ich?
It's all the same to me.	Es macht mir nichts aus.
Your good health.	Prosit.
Thank you for your hospitality.	Vielen Dank für Ihre Gastfreundschaft.
We had a very good time.	Es hat uns sehr gefallen.
I do not speak German.	Ich spreche nicht deutsch.
Can anyone speak English?	Spricht jemand englisch?
I do not understand.	Ich verstehe nicht.
Will you please speak more slowly?	Bitte sprechen Sie langsamer!
Write it down, please!	Bitte schreiben Sie es auf!
I have lost....	Ich habe ... verloren.
I will give you my address.	Ich gebe Ihnen meine Adresse.
What is your name?	Wie heissen Sie?
What is your address?	Wo wohnen Sie?
Is this the right way to...?	Komme ich auf diesem Wege nach...?
Please can you tell me?	Bitte, können Sie mir sagen?
Keep straight on.	Immer geradeaus.
First on the right.	Die Erste rechts.
Second on the left.	Die Zweite links.
Where is the W. C.	Wo ist die Toilette?
You are mistaken.	Sie haben sich geirrt.
It is very annoying.	Es ist sehr ärgerlich.

It has nothing to do with me.	Das geht mich nichts an.
I have already paid you.	Ich habe bereits bezahlt.
Where is the Police Station?	Wo ist die Polizeiwache?
Where is the British Consulate?	Wo ist das englische Konsulat?
Look down there (up there).	Sehen Sie dort unten (dort oben).
On this side. On the other side.	Auf dieser Seite. Auf der anderen Seite.
As soon as possible.	So bald wie möglich.
Look out!	Vorsicht!
Wait a minute please.	Bitte, warten Sie einen Moment.
I am in a hurry.	Ich habe es eilig.
It is fine (bad) weather.	Es ist schönes (schlechtes) Wetter.
Things are going badly.	Es sind schlechte Zeiten.
I am bored.	Ich langweile mich.
Take it easy!	Langsam!
Attention!	Achtung!
All out (all aboard, all change)!	Alles aussteigen (einsteigen, umsteigen)!
Keep off the grass.	Das Betreten des Rasens ist verboten.
No Exit (thoroughfare, entrance).	Kein Ausgang (Durchgang, Eingang).
No smoking.	Rauchen verboten.
Keep to the right.	Rechts fahren.
Strictly forbidden.	Strengstens verboten.
What time is it?	Wie spät ist es?
Quarter to eleven	Viertel vor elf.
Eleven a. m.	Elf Uhr morgens.
Twenty past six.	Zwanzig nach sechs.
Is that clock right?	Geht diese Uhr richtig?
It is late.	Es ist spät.
How long does it take to...?	Wie lange braucht man nach...?
For some days past.	Seit einigen Tagen.
Every day.	Jeden Tag.
Last week.	Vorige Woche.
Next week.	Nächste Woche.
A fortnight on Monday.	Montag in vierzehn Tagen.
Can I lunch (dine) here?	Kann man hier zu Mittag (Abend) essen?
Waiter!	Herr Ober!
Waitress!	Kellnerin!

We don't want a complete meal.	Wir möchten keine volle Mahlzeit.
Bring me the menu (wine-list) please.	Bringen Sie mir bitte die Speisekarte (Weinkarte).
We want only a snack.	Wir möchten nur einen Imbiss.
Please serve us quickly, we are in a hurry.	Bitte bedienen Sie uns schnell wir haben es eilig.
We would like black coffee (white coffee).	Wir möchten schwarzen Kaffee (Milchkaffee).
Can you recommend a good (cheap) local wine?	Können Sie einen guten (billigen) Wein aus der Umgegend empfehlen.
Bring us two rolls each with some butter, please.	Bringen Sie uns bitte je zwei Brötchen und Butter.
Bill, please.	Zahlen bitte.
Keep the change.	Das stimmt so.
I made a mistake. I beg your pardon.	Ich habe mich geirrt. Entschuldigen Sie bitte.
My car (motor-cycle) is two kilometres from here.	Mein Wagen (Motorrad) ist) zwei Kilometer von hier.
Can you send a breakdown truck?	Können Sie einen Abschleppwagen schikken?
I want some petrol (water, oil).	Ich möchte Benzin (Wasser, Öl) haben.
Can you lend me...?	Können Sie mir... leihen?
How much do I owe you?	Was schulde ich Ihnen?
I have nothing to declare.	Ich habe nichts zu verzollen.
Where is the booking-office?	Wo ist der Fahrkartenschalter?
Please write down the price.	Bitte, schreiben Sie den Preis auf.
Which is the way to the trains?	Wie komme ich zu den Zügen?
Which platform does the train go from?	Von welchem Bahnsteig fährt der Zug ab?
When does the train for.... go?	Wann fährt der Zug nach... ab?
Must I (can I) reserve a seat?	Muss ich (kann ich) einen Platz belegen?
Porter, take my luggage to the train for...	Träger, bringen Sie mein Gepäck zum Zug nach...
Is this seat taken?	Ist dieser Platz frei?

Excuse me please.	Entschuldigen Sie bitte.
Must I change trains?	Muss ich umsteigen?
Does the train go to...?	Fährt dieser Zug nach...?
What time is breakfast (lunch, tea, dinner)?	Wann gibt es Frühstück (Mittagessen, Tee, Abendessen)?
When do we arrive?	Wann kommen wir an?
Is there another train this evening?	Fährt heute abend ein anderer Zug?
Is there a plane from here to...?	Fliegt ein Flugzeug von hier nach..?
What is the fare (return)?	Was kostet es (hin und zurück)?
I want to reserve a seat in the plane leaving tomorrow morning for...	Ich möchte einen Platz in dem Flugzeug belegen, das morgen früh nach... fliegt.
I should like a cup of tea (coffee).	Ich hätte gern eine Tasse Tee (Kaffee).
Would you be so good as to direct me to...	Würden Sie so gut sein, mir den Weg nach... zu zeigen?
Can I go by (bus tram, underground)?	Kann ich mit dem Autobus (der Strassenbahn, der Untergrundbahn) fahren?
Which bus (tram) do I have to take?	Welchen Bus (welche Strassenbahn) muss ich nehmen?
I want to get off at...	Ich möchte am... aussteigen.
Go quickly I am in a hurry.	Fahren Sie schnell Ich habe es eilig.
Can you recommend a small hotel?	Können Sie ein kleines Hotel empfehlen?
Have you any rooms vacant?	Haben Sie Zimmer frei?
I want a single room (double room).	Ich möchte ein Einzelzimmer (Doppelzimmer).
What is the price of this room (these rooms)?	Was kostet dieses Zimmer? (Was kosten diese Zimmer)?
Have you anything cheaper?	Haben Sie etwas Billigeres?
How much is bed and breakfast?	Was kostet das Zimmer mit Frühstück?
What does it cost to send a letter to...?	Was kostet ein Brief nach...?

I want to send a telegram.	Ich möchte ein Telegramm aufgeben.
Where can I buy...?	Wo kann ich ... kaufen?
Can I have breakfast in my room?	Kann ich in meinem Zimmer frühstücken?
Who is there?	Wer ist da?
Wait a minute!	Einen Moment, bitte!
Come in!	Herein!
I must leave at once.	Ich muss sofort abreisen.
Will you take a traveller's cheque?	Nehmen Sie einen Reisescheck?
I am leaving tonight.	Ich reise heute abend ab.
I have been very comfortable.	Ich habe mich sehr wohl gefühlt.
Thank you and good-bye.	Danke sehr und auf Wiedersehen.
I want an English-speaking guide.	Ich möchte einen Führer, der englisch spricht.
Is this the right way to ...?	Komme ich auf diesem wege nach...?
May I photograph here?	Darf ich hier photographieren?
Would you like to dance?	Möchten Sie tanzen?
Do you know what is on at the cinema (theatre)?	Wissen Sie was im Kino (Theater) gespielt wird?
We are lost.	Wir haben uns verlaufen.
Put rubbish in the proper place!	Abfälle in den Mülleimer!

A

a, an, ein, eine, ein.
abandon, *v. a.* aufgeben; verlassen.
abate, *v. a. & n.* vermindern; nachlassen.
abbey, *s.* Abtei *f.*
abbot, *s.* Abt *m.*
abbreviate, *v. a.* abkürzen.
abbreviation *s.* Abkürzung *f.*
abdicate, *v. a. & n.* abdanken.
abdomen, *s.* Unterleib *m.*
abhor, *v. a.* verabscheuen.
ability, *s.* Fähigkeit *f.*
able, *adj.* fähig.

aboard, *adv.* an Bord.
abode, *s.* Wohnsitz *m.*
abolish, *v. a.* abschaffen, aufheben.
abominable, *adj.* abscheulich.
abound, *v. n.* reichlich vorhanden sein.
about, *adv.* (rund)herum; ungefähr; — *prep.* um; gegen, etwa; *be ~ to* im Begriff sein zu ...
above, *adv.* oben; darüber; — *prep.* über.
abroad, *adv.* im Ausland sein; ins Ausland fahren.
absent, *adj.* abwesend.
absolute, *adj.* absolut.
absolve, *v. a.* lossprechen.
absorb, *v. a.* aufsaugen.
abstain, *v. n.* sich enthalten.
abstract, *s.* Auszug *m.*, Abriß *m.*
abstraction, *s.* abstrakter Begriff; *fig.* Zerstreutheit *f.*
absurd, *adj.* absurd, albern.

abundance, *s.* Überfluß *m.;* Fülle *f.*
abundant, *adj.* reichlich.
academy, *s.* Akademie *f.*
accelerate, *v. a.* beschleunigen; *v. n.* schneller werden.
accent, *s.* Akzent *m.*
accept, *v. a.* annehmen.
acceptance, *s.* Annahme *f.*
access, *s.* Zugang *m.*, Zutritt *m.*
accessory, *s.* Zubehör *n.;* — *adj.* hinzukommend.
accident, *s.* Zufall *m.;* Unfall *m.*
accommodate, *v. a.* anpassen; *v. n.* ~ *oneself* sich anpassen.
accommodation, *s.* Anpassung *f.*, Aushilfe *f.;* Unterkunft *f.*
accompany, *v. a.* begleiten.
accomplish, *v. a.* vollenden; zustande bringen.
accord, *s.* Übereinstimmung *f.;* Einklang *m.*
according, ~ *to* gemäß, laut.
accordingly, *adv.* demgemäß; folglich.
account, *s.* Rechnung *f.;* Konto *n.;* Bericht *m.;* *on ~ of* wegen; *on no ~* auf keinen Fall; *take into ~* in Betracht ziehen; — *v. n.* halten für; ~ *for* Rechenschaft über etwas ablegen.
accuracy, *s.* Genauigkeit *f.*
accusation, *s.* Anklage *f.*
accuse, *v. a.* anklagen.
accustom, *v. a.* gewöhnen.
ache, *s.* Schmerz *m.*
achieve, *v. a.* ausführen, vollenden.

acknowledge   24.   **agree**

acknowledge, v. a. anerkennen; bestätigen.
acquaintance, s. Bekanntschaft f.; Bekannte m., f.
acquire, v. a. erwerben.
acquisition, s. Erwerbung f.
across, prep. quer, durch.
act, s. Handlung f.; Tat f.; Aufzug m.; Akt m.; Akte f.; Gesetz n.; — v. a. spielen; v. n. handeln; benehmen.
action, s. Handlung f.; Prozess m.; Gefecht n.
active, adj. tätig, aktiv.
activity, s. Tätigkeit f.
actor, s. Schauspieler m.
actress, s. Schauspielerin f.
actual, adj. wirklich.
actually, adv. tatsächlich.
adapt, v. a. anpassen; bearbeiten.
add, v. a. hinzufügen.
addition, s. Hinzufügung f.; in ~ außerdem.
address, s. Adresse f.; Ansprache f.; — v. a. anreden; adressieren.
adequate, adj. angemessen; hinreichend.
adjust, v. a. ordnen; anpassen.
administration, s. Verwaltung f.
admirable, adj. bewundernswert.
admiral, s. Admiral m.
admire, v. a. bewundern.
admission, s. Zulassung f.; Eintritt m.
admit, v. a. zulassen.
adopt, v. a. adoptieren.
adore, v. a. anbeten.
adult, s. Erwachsene m. — adj. erwachsen.
advance, v. a. befördern; v. n. vorgehen. — s. Beförderung f.; Fortschritt m.; Vorschuß m.
advantage, s. Vorteil m.
adventure, s. Abenteuer n.
adversary, s. Gegner m.
adversity, s. Not f.; Unglück n.
advertise, v. a. anzeigen; annoncieren.
advertisement, s. Anzeige f.; Annonce f.
advice, s. Rat m.; Nachricht f.
advise, v. a. (be)raten; benachrichtigen.
aerial, s. Antenne f.
aerodrome, s. Flugplatz m.
aeronaut, s. Luftfahrer m.; Flieger m.
aeroplane, s. Flugzeug n.
affair, s. Angelegenheit f.; Sache f.
affect, v. a. berühren, (er)heucheln; wirken.
affection, s. Vorliebe f.; Affektiertheit f.
affirmative, adj. bejahend; positiv.
afford, v. a. bieten; (sich) leisten.
afore-mentioned, adj. vorher erwähnt.
afraid, adj. bange; be ~ of sich fürchten vor.
after, prep. & adv. nach.
afternoon, s. Nachmittag m.
afterwards, adv. nacher; später.
again, adv. wieder.
against, prep. gegen.
age, s. Alter n.
agency, s. Agentur f.
agent, s. Agent m.; Instrument n.
aggression, s. Angriff m.
ago, adv. vor.
agree, v. n. übereinstimmen; ~ to zustimmen; ~ (up)on einig werden;

agreeable   25.   **angle¹**

~ *with (s. o.)* zuträglich sein.
agreeable, *adj.* angenehm.
agreement, *s.* Übereinstimmung *f.*; Abkommen *n.*
agricultural, *adj.* landwirtschaftlich.
agriculture, *s.* Landwirtschaft *f.*
ahead, *adj. & adv.* voraus; vorwärts.
aid, *v. a.* helfen; — *s.* Hilfe *f.*
aim, *s.* Ziel *n.*; Absicht *f.*; — *v. a. & n.* zielen; ~ *at fig.* streben nach.
air, *s.* Luft *f.*; Lied *n.*
air-conditioning, (automatische) Klimatisierung *f.*
aircraft, *s.* Luftfahrzeug *n.*
air-line, *s.* Luftverkehrs-linie *f.*
air-mail, *s.* Luftpost *f.*
airport, *s.* Flughafen *m.*
aisle, *s.* Seitenschiff *n.*
alarm, *s.* Alarm *m.*; — *v. a.* alarmieren.
alcoholic, *adj.* alkoholisch.
ale, *s.* Ale *n.*; englisches Bier *n.*
alike, *adj.* ähnlich.
alive, *adj.* lebendig.
all, *adj. & adv.* all; ganz, jeder, jede, jedes; — *pron.* alles, alle *(pl.)*; vor allem; *at* ~ überhaupt; *not at* ~ durchaus nicht.
alley, *s.* Allee *f.*
allow, *v. a.* erlauben; bewilligen.
ally, *v. a.* verbünden; — *v. n.* (sich) verbünden; — *s.* Verbündete *m., f.*
almost, *adv.* fast, beinahe.

alone, *adj. & adv.* allein.
along, *adv. & prep.* längs; entlang.
aloud, *adv.* laut.
already, *adv.* schon.
also, *adv.* auch.
altar, *s.* Altar *m.*
alter, *v. a.* (ab)ändern; — *v. n.* (sich) (ver)ändern.
although, *conj.* obgleich.
altogether, *adv.* zusammen; ganz und gar.
always, *adv.* immer.
amazing, *adj.* erstaunlich.
ambassador, *s.* Botschafter *m.*
ambition, *s.* Ehrgeiz *m.*
ambitious, *adj.* ehrgeizig.
ambulance, *s.* Krankenwagen *m.*
amendment, *s.* Verbesserung *f.*
amends, *s. pl. make* ~ *for* entschädigen.
amid(st), *prep.* inmitten.
among, *prep.* unter; zwischen.
amount, *s.* Betrag *m.*; — *v. n.* betragen; ~ *to* sich belaufen auf; betragen.
amplifier, *s. (Radio)* Verstärker.
amuse, *v. a.* unterhalten.
amusement, *s.* Zeitvertrieb *m.*; Vergnügen *n.*
an see **a**
analyse, *v. a.* analysieren.
analysis, *s.* Analyse *f.*
anatomy, *s.* Anatomie *f.*
ancestor, *s.* Vorfahr *m.*, Ahn *m.*
anchor, *s.* Anker *m.*
ancient, *adj.* alt; ehemalig.
and, *conj.* und.
anecdote, *s.* Anekdote *f.*
angel, *s.* Engel *m.*
anger, *s.* Zorn *m.*
angle¹, *s.* Winkel *m.*

angle, *v. n.* angeln.
Anglican, *adj.* anglikanisch.
angry, *adj.* zornig; *be ~ with* böse sein auf jm.
animal, *s.* Tier *n.*
ankle, *s.* Enkel *m.*
anniversary, *s.* Jahrestag *m.*
announce, *v. a.* ankündigen.
announcement, *s.* Ankündigung *f.;* Anzeige *f.*
announcer, *s.* Ansager *m.*
annoy, *v. a.* ärgern.
annual, *adj.* jährlich.
annul, *v. a.* annullieren; ungültig erklären.
another, *adj. & pron.* ein anderer; einander.
answer, *s.* Antwort *f.;* Lösung *f.;* — *v. a.* beantworten; lösen.
antibiotic, *s.* Antibiotikum *n.*
anticipate, *v. a.* voraussehen; erwarten.
antipathy, *s.* Abneigung *f.*
antiquity, *a.* Altertum *n.*
anxiety, *s.* Angst *f.;* Besorgnis *f.*
anxious, *adj.* ängstlich; besorgt; *~ to* begierig auf/zu.
any, *adj.* (irgend) ein(e), einige; etwas; *not ~* gar keine; jeder, jede, jedes; — *pron.* irgendeiner; irgendwelche; — *adv.* irgend(wie).
anybody, *pron.* (irgend) jemand; jeder.
anyhow, *adv.* irgendwie.
anyone, *see* **anybody**.
anything, *pron.* irgend etwas; jedes beliebige.
anyway, *see* **anyhow**.
anywhere, *adv.* irgendwo(hin).
apart, *adv.* getrennt; beiseite; *~ from* abgesehen von.
apartment, *s.* Zimmer *n.*
apologize, *v. n.* sich entschuldigen.
apology, *s.* Entschuldigung *f.*
apostle, *s.* Apostel *m.*
apparatus, *s.* Apparat *m.;* Vorrichtung *f.*
apparent, *adj.* offenbar; scheinbar.
appeal, *s.* Anruf *m.;* Appellation *f.;* Reiz *m.;* — *v. n.* anrufen; appellieren.
appear, *v. n.* (er)scheinen.
appearance, *s.* Äusere *n.;* Erscheinung *f.;* Anschein *m.*
appendicitis, *s.* Blinddarmentzündung *f.*
appendix, *s.* Anhang *m.;* Blinddarm *m.*
appetite, *s.* Appetit *m.*
applaud, *v. a.* applaudieren.
applause, *s.* Applaus *m.,* Beifall *m.*
apple, *s.* Apfel *m.*
appliance, *s.* Vorrichtung *f.;* Mittel *n.*
applicant, *s.* Bewerber *m.,* -in *f.*
application, *s.* Verwendung *f.;* Bedeutung *f.;* Gesuch *n.*
apply, *v. a.* anwenden; auflegen; — *v. n.* gelten (für); *~ for* antragen auf; sich bewerben um.
appoint, *v. a.* bestimmen; ernennen.
appointment, *s.* Verabredung *f.;* Ernennung *f.;* Stelle *f.*
appreciate, *v. a.* schätzen.
apprehend, *v. a.* festnehmen; begreifen.
apprentice, *s.* Lehrling *m.*
approach, *v. n. & a.* (sich)

| appropriate | 27. | assure |

nähern; — s. Annäherung f.; Versuch m.
appropriate, adj. entsprechend; angemessen.
approve, v. a. billigen.
approximate, v. a. & n. (sich) nähern; — adj. ungefähr.
apricot, s. Aprikose f.
April, s. April m.
apron, s. Schürze f.
arbitrary, adj. willkürlich.
arch, s. Bogen m.
archaeology, s. Archäologie f.
archbishop, s. Erzbischof m.
architect, s. Architekt m.
architecture, s. Architektur f.
area, s. Grundfläche f.
argue, v. a. & n. streiten; beweisen.
argument, s. Argument n.
arise, v.n. entstehen.
aristocratic, adj. aristokratisch.
arm¹, s. Arm m.; Armlehne f.
arm², s. Waffe f.
armament, s. Rüstung f.
armchair, s. Lehnstuhl m.
armour, s. Panzer m.
army, s. Heer n.; Armee f.
around, adv. (rund)herum; — prep. um ... her.
arrange, v. a. ordnen.
arrangement, s. Anordnung f.; ~s Vorbereitungen f. pl.
arrears, s.pl. Rückstände.
arrest, v. a. verhaften; — s. Verhaftung f.
arrival, s. Ankunft f.; Ankömmling m.
arrive, v. n. ankommen.
arrow, s. Pfeil m.
art, s. Kunst .
artery, s. Arterie f.
article, s. Artikel m.; Abschnitt m.
artificial, adj. künstlich; Kunst-.
artillery, s. Artillerie f.
artist, s. Künstler m.
as, adv. & conj. als; so; da; as ... as (eben) so ... wie.
ashamed, adj. beschämt.
ash(es) s. (pl) Asche f.
ashore, adv. am Ufer sein; ans Ufer kommen.
ash-tray, s. Aschenbecher m.
aside, adv. beiseite.
ask, v. a. & n. fragen; fordern; bitten; ~ about sich erkundigen nach.
aspect, s. Aussehen n.
aspire, v. a. streben.
ass, s. Esel m.
assault, s. Angriff m. tätliche Beleidigung f.; — v. a. angreifen.
assemble, v. a. & n. (sich) versammeln.
assembly, s. Versammlung f.; ~ hall Montagehalle f.; Aula f.; ~ line Fließband n.
assert, v.a. behaupten.
assess, v. a. (ab)schätzen.
assets, s.pl. Aktiva f.
assignment, s. Anweisung f.
assist, v.a. helfen, beistehen.
assistance, s. Hilfe f.; Beistand m.
assistant, s. Gehilfe m.; Assistent m., -in f.
associate, s. Teilhaber m.; — adj. beigeordnet.
association, s. Verbindung f.; Verband m.
assume, v.a. übernehmen; annehmen.
assurance, s. Versicherung f.
assure, v.a. versichern.

astonishment — babble

astonishment, s. Erstaunen n.
astronomy, s. Astronomie f.
at, prep. an; in; bei; auf.
athletics, s. pl. Athletik f.
atmosphere, s. Atmosphäre f.
atom, s. Atom n.
atomic, adj. atomisch; ~ bomb Atombombe f.; ~ energy Atomenergie f.
attach, v.a. anheften; beifügen.
attaché, s. Attaché m.; ~ case Aktentasche f.
attachment, s. Neigung f.
attack, v. a. angreifen; — s. Angriff m.
attain, v.a. erreichen.
attainment, s. Errungenschaft f.
attempt, v.a. versuchen; — s. Versuch m.
attend, v.a. bedienen; behandeln; besuchen.
attendant, s. Begleiter m.; Wärter m.
attention, s. Aufmerksamkeit f.
attitude, s. Stellungnahme f.; Einstellung f.
attorney, s. Anwalt m.
attraction, s. Anziehungskraft f.; Reiz m.
attractive, adj. anziehend; reizend.
attribute, v.a. zuschreiben.
auction, s. Auktion f.
audience, s. Zuhörer(schaft) f., Publikum n.
audio-visual adj. audio--visuell.
auditorium, s. Auditorium n.
August, s. August m.
aunt, s. Tante f.
Australian, adj. australisch; — s. Australier m. -in f.
Austrian, adj. österreichisch; — s. Österreicher m. -in f.
author, s. Verfasser m.; Urheber m.
authority, s. Autorität f.
authorize, v. a. ermächtigen.
automatic, adj. automatisch.
automation, s. Selbstfertigung f.
autonomy, s. Autonomy f.
autumn, s. Herbst m.
avail, v. a. & n. helfen, nützen; ~ oneself of sich einer Sache bedienen.
available, adj. verfügbar; zu haben.
avalanche, s. Lawine f.
average, adj. durchschnittlich; — s. Durchschnitt m.
aversion, s. Widerwille m.; Abneigung f.
avoid, v.a. (ver)meiden.
awake, adj. wach; — v. a. wecken; — v. n. aufwachen.
awaken, v. a. (er)wecken.
award, s. Preis m.; — v. a. verleihen.
aware, adj. be ~ of bewußt sein.
away, adv. weg; fort; abwesend; ~ from entfernt von.
awful, adj. furchtbar; schrecklich.
awkward, adj. ungeschickt; peinlich.
axe, s. Axt f.; Beil n.
axis, s. Achse f.
axle, s. Achse f.

B

babble, v.a. & n. plappern.

baby — **basin**

baby, s. Baby n.
baby-sitter, s. Babysitter m.
bachelor, s. Junggeselle m.
back, s. Rücken m.; Verteidiger m.; — adv. zurück; v.a. wetten auf; v.n. ~ out sich zurückziehen.
background, s. Hintergrund m.
backstairs, s. pl. Hintertreppe f.
backward, adj. zurückgeblieben; — adv. rückwärts; zurück.
backwards, adv. see backward adv.
bacon, s. Speck m.
bad, adj. schlecht; not ~ gar nicht übel.
badge, s. Abzeichen n.
bag, s. Beutel m.; Sack m.; Handtasche f.; Tüte f.
baggage, s. Gepäck n.
bait, s. Köder m.
bake, v.a. & n. backen.
baker, s. Bäcker m.
bakery, s. Bäckerei f.
balance, s. Waage f.; Bilanz f.; — v.a. wägen; ins Gleichgewicht bringen; v. n. balancieren.
balcony, s. Balkon m.
bald, adj. kahl.
ball, s. Ball m.
ball-bearing, s. Kugellager n.
ballet, s. Ballett n.
balloon, s. Ballon m.
ball-(point-)pen, s. Kugelschreiber m.
banana, s. Banane f.
band, s. Band n.; Musikkapelle f.
bandage, s. Verband m.
bang, s. Knall m.
banish, v.a. verbannen.
banister, s Treppengeländer n.
bank[1], s. Bank f.
bank[2], s. Ufer n.
banker, s. Bankier m.
bank-holiday, s. Bankfeiertag m.
bank-note, s. Banknote f.
bankrupt, adj. bankrott.
banner, s. Fahne f.
banquet, s. Bankett n.
baptize, v. a. & n. taufen.
bar, s. Stange f.; Barren m.; Takt(strich) m.; Schenktisch; fig. Gericht n.; Schranke f.; — v.a. verriegeln; (ver)hindern.
barber, s. Barbier m.
bare, adj. bloß; kahl.
bargain, s. Gelegenheitskauf m.; it's a ~ es ist spottbillig; — v. a. & n. handeln; feilschen.
barge, s. Leichter m.
bark, v. n. bellen; — s. Gebell n.
barley, s. Gerste f.
barmaid, s. Schenkmädchen n.
barman, s. Schenkwirt m.; Kellner m.
barn, s. Scheune f.
barometer, s. Barometer n.
baron, s. Baron m.
barrack(s), s. (pl.) Kaserne f.
barrel, s. Faß n.
barren, adj. unfruchtbar.
barrier, s. Schranke f.
barrister, s. Rechtsanwalt m.
bartender, s. see barman.
barter, s. Tausch(handel); — v. a. & n. eintauschen.
base, s. Basis f.
basement, s. Kellergeschoß n.
basic, adj. grundlegend.
basin, s. Becken n.

basis — **berth**

basis, s. Basis f.
basket, s. Korb m.
basket-ball, s. Korbball m.
bass, s. Baß m.
bat¹, s. Fledermaus f.
bat², s. Schläger m.
bath, s. Bad n.; Badeanstalt f.; Badewanne f.; have a ~ baden.
bathe, v. n. baden.
bathing-costume, s. Badeanzug m.
bathroom, s. Badezimmer n.
battery, s. Batterie f.
battle, s. Schlacht f.
bay¹, s. Bai f.; Bucht f.
bay², s. Erker m.
be, v. n. sein; there is, there are es gibt.
beach, s. Strand m.
bead, s. (Glas)Perle f.; Tropfen m.
beak, s. Schnabel m.
beam, s. Balken m.; Strahl m.
bean, s. Bohne f.
bear¹, s. Bär m.
bear², v. a. & n. tragen; gebären; ertragen.
beard, s. Bart m.
bearing, s. Haltung f.; Bezug m.;
beast, s. Vieh n.
beat, v. a. & n. schlagen; (sport) besiegen; — s. Schlag m.; Pulsschlag; m. Revier n.
beautiful, adj. schön.
beauty, s. Schönheit f.
because, conj. weil; denn; ~ of wegen.
beckon, v. a. & n. (zu)winken.
become, v. n. werden.
bed, s. Bett n.; Beet n.
bed-clothes, s. pl. Bettzeug n.
bedroom, s. Schlafzimmer n.

bee, s. Biene f.
beech, s. Buche f.
beef, s. Rindfleisch n.
beef-steak, s. Beefsteak n.
beer, s. Bier n.
beetroot, s. Runkelrübe f., rote Rübe.
before, adv. vorher; früher; — prep. vor; — conj. bevor; ehe.
beforehand, adv. zuvor; vorher.
beg, v. a. & n. bitten. betteln; I ~ your pardon wie bitte?.
beggar, s. Bettler m.
begin, v. a. anfangen.
beginning, s. Anfang m.; Beginn m.
behalf, s. on ~ of im Namen von.
behave, v. n. sich benehmen.
behaviour, s. Benehmen n.
behind, prep. hinter.
Belgian, adj. belgisch; — s. Belgier m.; -in f.
belief, s. Glaube m.
believe, v. a. & n. glauben.
bell, s. Glocke f.; Klingel f.
belly, s. Bauch m.
belong, v. n. gehören.
belongings, s. pl. Habseligkeiten; Zubehör n.
below, adv. unten; — prep. unter.
belt, s. Gürtel m.
bench, s. Bank f.; Arbeitstisch m.
bend, s. Krümmung f., Biegung f.; — v. a. & n. (sich) biegen, (sich) krümmen.
beneath, see below
benefit, s. Wohltat f.; Vorteil m.
bent, s. Biegung f.; Neigung f.
berry, s. Beere f.
berth, s. Koje f.

beside, *prep.* neben; ~ *oneself* außer sich; — *adv. see* **besides**.
besides, *adv.* außerdem; — *prep. fig.* abgesehen von, außer.
best, *adv.* am besten, aufs beste; — *adj.* beste.
bet, *s.* Wette *f.*; — *v. a. & v. n.* wetten.
betray, *v. a.* verraten.
better, *adv. & adj.* besser.
between, *adv.* dazwischen; — *prep.* zwischen.
beyond, *prep.* jenseits.
bias, *s. fig.* Neigung *f.*; Vorurteil *n.*
Bible, *s.* Bibel *f.*
bicycle, *s.* Fahrrad *n.*
big, *adj.* groß, dick.
bill, *s.* Rechnung *f.*; ~ *(of exchange)* Wechsel *m.*;
bin, *s.* Kasten; Behälter *m.*
bind, *v. a. & n.* binden.
biology, *s.* Biologie *f.*
bird, *s.* Vogel *m.*
birthday, *s.* Geburtstag *m.*
biscuit, *s.* Zwieback *m.*
bishop, *s.* Bischof *m.*; *(chess)* Läufer *m.*
bit, *s.* Bißchen *n.*; Stückchen *n.*; *a little* ~ ein wenig.
bite, *v. a. & n.* beißen; — *s.* Biß *m.*
bitter, *adj.* bitter.
black, *adj.* schwarz.
blackbird, *s.* Amsel *f.*
blacksmith, *s.* Schmied *m.*
bladder, *s.* Blase *f.*
blade, *s.* Klinge *f.*
blame, *s.* Tadel *m.*; — *v. a.* tadeln.
blank, *adj.* blank, leer; — *s.* Leere *f.*; Blankformular *n.*
blanket, *s.* Wolldecke *f.*
blast, *s.* Windstoß *m.*; — *v. a.* (in die Luft) sprengen; ~ *it!* verdammt
blaze, *s.* Flamme *f.*; — *v. n.* lodern, flammen.
bleed, *v. n.* bluten.
blend, *v. a. & n.* (sich) (ver)mischen; mengen.
bless, *v. a.* segnen.
blessing, *s.* Segen *m.*
blind[1], *adj.* blind.
blind[2], *s.*; Vorhang *m.*
blindness, *s.* Blindheit *f.*
blink, *v. n. & a.* blinzeln.
bliss, *s.* Wonne *f.*
block, *s.* Block *m.*; Klotz *m.*; *fig.* Stockung *f.*
blond, *s.* Blondine *f.*; *adj.* blond.
blood, *s.* Blut *n.*
bloody, *adj.* blutig; verdammt.
bloom, *s.* Blüte *f.*; — *v. n.* blühen.
blossom, *s.* Blüte *f.*; — *v. n.* blühen.
blot, *s.* Fleck *m.*; Klecks *m.*; — *v. a.* beklecksen, beflecken.
blouse, *s.* Bluse *f.*
blow[1], *s.* Schlag *m.*; Handgemenge *n.*
blow[2], *v. a. & n.* blasen, wehen; ~ *up* explodieren.
blue, *adj.* blau; — *s.* Blau *n.*
blunt, *adj.* stumpf.
blush, *v. n.* erröten.
board, *s.* Brett *n.*; Pension *f.*; Ausschuß *m.*; Behörde *f.*; ~ *and lodging* volle Pension; *on* ~ *ship* an Bord.
boarder, *s.* Pensionär *m.*
boarding-house, *s.* Pension *f.*
boarding-school, *s.* Internat *n.*
boat, *s.* Boot *n.*
boat-train, *s.* Schiffszug *m.*
body, *s.* Körper *m.*;

bog — **break**

Rumpf m.; Leichnam m.; Karosserie f.; Körperschaft f.

bog, s. Sumpf m.

boil[1], v. a. & n. kochen.

boil[2], s. Beule f.; Furunkel m.

boiler, s. Kessel m.

bold, adj. kühn.

bolt, s. Bolzen m.; Blitzstrahl m.; — v. a. verriegeln; — v. n. durchgehen.

bomb, s. Bombe f.; — v. a. bombardieren.

bond, s. Band n.; Schuldschein m.

bone, s. Knochen m.; Gräte f.

bonnet, s. Motorhaube f.

book, s. Buch n.; — v. a. buchen; lösen; bestellen.

bookcase, s. Bücherschrank m.

booking-office, s. Fahrkartenausgabe f.

book-keeper, s. Buchhalter m.

booklet, s. Broschüre f.

bookseller, s. Buchhändler m.

bookshelf, s. Bücherbrett n.

bookshop, s. Buchhandlung f.

book-stall, s. Bücherstand m.

boot, s. Stiefel m.

booth, s. Messestand.

booty, s. Beute f.

border, s. Rand m.; Grenze f.

boring, adj. langweilig.

born, pp. geboren.

borrow, v. a. borgen.

bosom, s. Busen m.

botanical, adj. botanisch.

botany, s. Botanik f.

both, adj., pron. & adv. beid(e); ~ ... and sowohl ... als.

bother, v. a. belästigen.

bottle, s. Flasche f.

bottom, s. Boden m.

bough, s. Zweig m.; Ast m.

bound[1], pp. gebunden, verpflichtet.

bound[2], adj. unterwegs.

boundary, s. Grenze f.

bounty, s. Freigebigkeit f.

bouquet, s. Bukett n.

bow[1], s. Verbeugung f.; — v. n. sich beugen; sich verbeugen; v. a. biegen.

bow[2], s. Bogen m.; Schleife f.

bowels, s. pl. Eingeweide (pl.).

bowl, s. Schale f.

box[1], s. Schachtel f.; Kiste f.; Stallbox f.; Theaterloge f.

box[2], v. a. & n. boxen.

box-office, s. Theaterkasse f.

boy, s. Knabe m.; Bursche m.; Junge m.

boyscout, s. Pfadpfinder m.

bra, s. Büstenhalter m.

brace, s. Gurt m.; Klammer f.; — v. a. fig. kräftigen.

bracelet, s. Armband n.

braces, s. pl. Hosenträger m.

bracket, s. Klammer f.

brain, s. Gehirn n.; fig. Verstand m.

brake, s. Bremse f.; —v. a. bremsen.

branch, s. Zweig m.; Filiale f.; — v. n. abzweigen.

brand, s. (Feuer-)Brand m.; Marke f.; — v. a. brandmarken.

brass, s. Messing n.

brave, adj. tapfer.

bread, s. Brot n.

breadth, s. Breite f.

break, s. Bruch m.; Pause f.; — v. a. bre-

break-down   33.   **butcher**

chen; unterbrechen; v.n. zerbrechen.
break-down, s. Panne f. Betriebsstörung f.; — v. n. niederbrechen.
breakfast, s. Frühstück n.; *have* ~ frühstücken.
breast, s. Brust f.
breath, s. Atem m.
breathe, v. a. & n. atmen.
breeches, s. pl. Kniehosen f. pl.
breed, s. Rasse f.; — v. a. züchten; brüten.
bribe, s. Bestechung f.; — v. a. bestechen.
brick, s. Ziegel(stein) m.;
bride, s. Braut f.
bridegroom, s. Bräutigam m.
bridge, s. Brücke f.
bridle, s. Zaum m.
brief, adj. kurz; bündig.
briefcase, s. Aktentasche f.
bright, adj. hell; glänzend.
brightness, s. Helligkeit f.
brilliant, adj. glänzend.
brim, s. Rand m.; Krempe f.
bring, v. a. & n. bringen; ~ *about* herbeiführen; ~ *up* aufziehen.
brisk, adj. lebhaft.
British, adj. britisch; *the* ~ die Briten pl.
broad, adj. breit.
broadcast, s. Rundfunkübertragung f.; — v. a. & n. funken; senden.
broadcasting, s. Rundfunk m.; ~ *station* Rundfunkstation.
bronze, s. Bronze f.
brooch, s. Brosche f.
brood, s. Brut f.; — v. n. brüten.
brook, s. Bach m.
brother, s. Bruder.
brother-in-law, s. Schwager m.
brow, s. Augenbrand f.

brown, adj. braun.
brush, s. Bürste f.; Pinsel m.; — v. a. & n. bürsten.
brutality, s. Brutalität f.
bubble, s. Blase f.; — v. n. sprudeln.
bucket, s. Eimer m.
bud, s. Knospe f.
budget, s. Voranschlag m.; Budget n.; Haushaltsplan m.
buffet, s. Büfett n.
build, v. a. & n. bauen.
building, s. Gebäude n.
bulb, s. Knolle f.
bulk, s. Umfang m.; Masse f.
bull, s. Stier m.
bullet, s. Kugel f.
bulletin, s. Tagesbericht m.
bump, s. Schlag m.
bumper, s. Puffer m.
bun, s. Milchbrötchen n.
bunch, s. Bündel n.; Bund m.
bundle, s. Bündel n.; Bund m.
bunk, s. Schlafkoje f.
buoy, s. Boje f.
burden, s. Last f.; — v. a. belasten.
burglar, s. Einbrecher m.
burial, s. Begräbnis n.
burn, v. a. & n. (ver)brennen.
burst, s. Bersten n.; *fig.* Ausbruch m.; — v. n. & a. bersten.
bury, v. a. begraben.
bus, s. Omnibus m.
bush, s. Busch m.
business, s. Geschäft n.; Sache f.; ~ *hours* pl. Geschäftszeit f.
businessman, s. Geschäftsmann m.
busy, adj. beschäftigt.
but, conj. aber.
butcher, s. Fleischer m.; Metzger m.

butter — 34. — **carrier**

butter, s. Butter f.
butterfly, s. Schmetterling m.
buttock(s), s. (pl.) Hintere m.
button, s. Knopf m.
buy, v.a. kaufen.
buyer, s. Käufer m.
by, prep. bei; an; neben; entlang; spätestens bis: durch; mit; ~ far bei weitem; ~ Monday bis Montag.

C

cab, s. Taxi n.
cabbage, s. Kohl m.
cabin, m. Kajüte f.; Hütte f.
cabinet, s. Kabinett n.; Schrank m.
cable, s. Kabel n.
cablegram, s. Kabeltelegramm n.
café, s. Café n.
cage, s. Käfig m.
cake, s. Kuchen m.
calculation, s. Kalkulation f.; Schätzung f.
calendar, s. Kalender m.
calf, s. Kalb n.
call, s. Ruf m.; Anruf m.; Aufruf m.; Besuch m.; — v.a. rufen; nennen; besuchen; v.n. rufen.
call-box, s. Fernsprechzelle f.
calm, adj. ruhig.
camel, s. Kamel n.
camera, s. Kamera f.
camp, s. Lager n.; — v.a. lagern.
campaign, s. Feldzug m.; Kampagne f.
can¹, v.n. können.
can², s. Konservendose f.; Kanne f.
canal, s. Kanal m.
canary, s. Kanarienvogel m.

cancel, v.a. widerrufen; absagen.
cancer, s. Krebs m.
candle, s. Kerze f.
cannon, s. Kanone f.
canoe, s. Kanu n.
canteen, s. Kantine f.
canvas, s. Segeltuch n.
cap, s. Mütze f.
capable, adj. fähig.
capacity, s. Inhalt m.; Kapazität f.; Fähigkeit f.
capital, s. Hauptstadt f.; Kapital n.; Großbuchstabe m.
captain, s. Kapitän m.
capture, v.a. erbeuten; gefangennehmen.
car, s. Wagen m.; Auto n.
caravan, s. Wohnwagen m.; Karawane f.
carbon-paper, s. Kohlenpapier n.
carburetter, s. Vergaser m.
card, s. Karte f.
cardinal, s. Kardinal m.
care, s. Sorge f.; Sorgfalt f.; Vorsicht f.; ~ of per Adresse; — v.n. besorgt sein; ~ for sich kümmern um.
career, s. Laufbahn f., Karriere f.
careful, adj. vorsichtig.
cargo, s. Ladung f.; Frachtgut n.
caricature, s. Karikatur f.; — v.a. karikieren.
carnation, s. Nelke f.
car-park, s. Parkplatz m.
carpenter, s. Zimmermann m.
carpet, s. Teppich m.
carriage, s. Eisenbahnwagen m.; Transport m.; Körperhaltung f.
carriage-way, s. Fahrbahn f.
carrier, s. Spediteur m.

carrot, s. Möhre f.
carry, v. a. & n. tragen, halten; ~ **on** fortsetzen; ~ **out** durchführen.
cartridge, s. Patrone f.
carve, v. a. schnitzen; zerlegen.
case[1], s. Kiste f.; Etui n.; Gehäuse n.
case[2], s. Fall m.; Sache f.; Angelegenheit f.
cash, s. Bargeld n.
cash-book, s. Kassabuch n.
cashier, s. Kassierer m. -in f.
cash-register, s. Registrierkasse f.
cask, s. Faß n.
cast, s. Wurf m.; Rollenbesetzung f.; Guß m. — v. a. werfen; gießen.
castle, s. Burg f.; Schloß n.
casual, adj. gelegentlich; beiläufig.
casualty, s. Verlust m.; Unfall m.
cat, s. Katze f.
catalog(ue), s. Katalog m.
catastrophe, s. Katastrophe f.
catch, v. a. fangen; ertappen; ergreifen.
category, s. Kategorie f.
caterpillar, s. Raupe f.
cathedral, s. Kathedrale f.; Dom m.
catholic, adj. katholisch.
cattle, s. (Rind) Vieh n.
cauliflower, s. Blumenkohl m.
cause, s. Ursache f.; Grund m.; — v. a. verursachen.
cautious, adj. vorsichtig.
cave, s. Höhle f.
cavity, s. Höhlung f.; Höhle f.
cease, v. n. & a. aufhören.

ceiling, s. Zimmerdecke f.
celebrate, v. a. & n. feiern.
celebration, s. Feier f.
celery, s. Sellerie m.
cell, s. Zelle f.
cellar, s. Keller m.
cello, s. Cello n.
cellophane, s. Zellophan n.
cement, s. Zement m.; v. a. zementieren.
cemetery, s. Friedhof m.
centenary, s. Hundertjahrfeier f.
central, adj. zentral.
centre, s. Mittelpunkt m.
century, s. Jahrhundert n.
cereal, s. Getreide n.; Getreideflocken pl.
ceremony, s. Zeremonie f.
certain, adj. sicher; gewiß.
certainly, adv. sicher; gewiß, sicherlich.
certificate, s. Zeugnis n.; Attest n.
certify, v. a. bescheinigen.
chain, s. Kette f.
chair, s. Stuhl m.; Lehrstuhl m.; Vorsitz m.
chairman, s. Vorsitzende m.
challenge, s. Herausforderung f.; — v. a. herausfordern.
chamber, s. Kammer f.
champagne, s. Champagner m., Sekt m.
champion, (sport) Meister m.
championship, s. Meisterschaft f.
chance, s. Zufall m.; Gelegenheit f.; by ~ zufällig; — v. a. wagen.
chancellor, s. Kanzler m.
change, s. Veränderung f.; Kleingeld n.; —v.a.&n. (sich) ändern.
channel, s. Kanal m.;

chapel — **cigarette**

the **Channel** der Ärmelkanal.
chapel, *s.* Kapelle *f.*
chaplain, *s.* Kaplan *m.*
chapter, *s.* Kapitel *n.*
character, *s.* Character *m.*; Persönlichkeit *f.*
charge, *s.* Ladung *f.*, Anklage *f.*; Verwaltung *f.*; Kosten *pl.*; *v. a.* laden; anklagen; in Rechnung stellen.
charming, *adj.* charmant.
chart, *s.* Seekarte *f.*; Tabelle *f.*
charter, *s.* Urkunde *f.*; Charterung *f.*
chase, *s.* Jagen *n.*; — *v. a. & n.* jagen.
chassis, *s.* Fahrgestell *n.*
chat, *s.* Gespräch *n.*; — *v. n.* plaudern.
cheap, *adj.* billig.
cheat, *s.* Betrüger *m*, -in *f.*; — *v. a. & n.* betrügen.
check, *s.* Hindernis *n.*; Kontrolle *f.*; Kontrollmarke *f.*, Scheck *m.*; Schach(stellung *f.*) *m.*; — *v. a.* hindern; kontrollieren; nachprüfen; Schach bieten.
checkmate, *s.* Schachmatt *n.*
check-up, *s.* Überprüfung *f.*; Kontrolle *f.*
cheek, *s.* Wange *f.*; Backe *f.*
cheer, *v. a. & n.* erheitern; Beifall spenden; ~ up! sei guten Mutes!
cheese, *s.* Käse *m.*
chemical, *adj.* chemisch; ~s *s.pl.* Chemikalien.
chemist, *s.* Chemiker *m.*; -in *f.*; Apotheker *m.*
chemistry, *s.* Chemie *f.*
cheque, *s.* Scheck *m.*, Zahlungsanweisung *f.*
cheque-book, *s.* Scheckbuch *n.*
cherry, *s.* Kirsche *f.*
chess, *s.* Schach *n.*
chess-board, *s.* Schachbrett *n.*
chest, *s.* Brust *f.*; Kiste *f.*; ~ *of drawers* Kommode *f.*
chestnut, *s.* Kastanie *f.*
chew, *v. a. & n.* kauen.
chicken, *s.* Huhn *n.*
chief, *s.* Chef *m*, Häuptling *m.*; — *adj.* Haupt-.
chiefly, *adv.* hauptsächlich.
child, *s.* Kind *n.*
childhood, *s.* Kindheit *f.*
childish, *adj.* kindisch.
chilly, *adj.* kalt, frostig.
chimney, *s.* Schornstein *m.*
chin, *s.* Kinn *n.*
china, *s.* Porzellan *n.*
Chinese, *adj.* chinesisch; — *s.* Chinese *m.*
chip, *s.* Span *m.*; ~s *pl.* Pommes frites.
chirp, *v. a. & n.* zirpen.
chisel, *s.* Meißel *m.*
chocolate, *s.* Schokolade *f.*
choice, *s.* Wahl *f.*; Auswahl *f.*
choir, *s.* Chor *m.*
choke, *v. a.* (er)wurgen; *v. n.* ersticken.
choose, *v. a.* (aus)wählen; wünschen; — *v. n.* wählen.
chop, *s.* Kotelett *n.*
chorus, *s.* Chor *m.*
Christian, *adj.* christlich; ~ *name* Vorname *m.*; — *s.* Christ *m.* -in *f.*
Christmas, *s.* Weihnachten *f.*
church, *s.* Kirche *f.*
churchyard, *s.* Kirchhof *m.*
cigar, *s.* Zigarre *f.*
cigarette, *s.* Zigarette *f.*

cigarette-case 37. **coal-mine**

cigarette-case, s. Zigarettenetui n.
cigarette-holder, s. Zigarettenspitze f.
cinema, s. Kino n.
cinerama, s. Cinerama n.
circle, s. Kreis m.; — v. a. & n. (um)kreisen.
circuit, s. Kreislauf m.; Stromkreis m.
circular, adj. kreisförmig.
circulate, v. n. zirkulieren; kursieren; v. a. in Umlauf setzen.
circulation, s. Zirkulation f; Kreislauf m.
circumstance, s. Umstand m.; ~s pl. Verhältnisse f.
circus, s. Zirkus m.
citation, s. Vorladung f.; Anführung f.
citizen, s. Bürger m., -in f.
citizenship, s. Staatsangehörigkeit f.
city, s. Stadt f.
civilization, s. Zivilisation f.
civilize, v. a. zivilisieren.
claim, s. Anspruch m.; Forderung f.; — v. a. Anspruch erheben; fordern.
clash, s. Konflikt m.; — v. n. prallen; zusammenstoßen.
clasp, s. Schnalle f.
class, s. Klasse f.
classic, adj. klassisch; s. Klassiker m.
classify, v. a. klassifizieren.
class-room, s. Klassenzimmer n.
clause, s. Nebensatz m.; Klausel f.
clean, adj. rein; sauber; — v. a. reinigen.
cleanse, v. a. reinigen,

clear, adj. klar; hell; rein: — v. a. (auf)klären; verzollen; rechtfertigen.
clergyman, s. Geistliche m.
clerk, s. (Büro-)Schreiber m.; Büroangestellte m., f.
clever, adj. klug.
client, s. Kunde m., Kundin f.; Klient m., -in f.
cliff, s. Felsen m.
climate, s. Klima n.
climb, v. n. & a. (er)steigen; klettern.
clinic, s. Klinik f.; Poliklinik f.
cloak, s. Mantel m.; Cape n.
cloak-room, s. Garderobe f.; Gepäckabgabe f.
clock, s. Uhr f.
close, s. Schluß m.; Ende n.; — v. a. abschließen; v. n. schließen; — adj. verschlossen; eng; ~ by dicht bei.
closet, s. Kabinett n.
cloth, s. Tuch n.; Stoff m.
clothe, v. a. bekleiden.
clothes, s. pl. Kleidung f.
cloud, s. Wolke f.
clover, s. Klee m.
club, s. Klub m. Keule f.; Knüttel m.
clutch, v. a. erfassen, ergreifen; — s. Kuppelung f.
coach, s. (sport) Trainer m.; Privatlehrer m., -in f.; Kutsche f.; — v. a. & n. einpauken; einen auf eine Prüfung vorbereiten; (sport) trainieren.
coal, s. Kohle f.
coalition, s. Koalition f.
coal-mine, s. Kohlengrube f.

coarse   **communicate**

coarse, *adj.* roh, grob.
coast, *s.* Küste *f.*
coat, *s.* Mantel *m.;* Rock *m.;* Schicht *f.*
cock, *s.* Hahn *m.*
cocoa, *s.* Kakao *m.*
code, *s.* Gesetzbuch *n.;* Schlüssel *m.;* — *v. a.* chiffrieren.
coffee, *s.* Kaffee *m.*
coffee-bar, *s.* Espressobar *f.*
coffee-pot, *s.* Kaffeekanne *f.*
coffin, *s.* Sarg *m.*
cogwheel, *s.* Zahnrad *n.*
coil, *s.* Rolle *f.;* Spule *f.;* — *v. a.* aufwickeln.
coin, *s.* Münze *f.*
coincidence, *s.* Zufall *m.*
coke, *s.* Koks *m.*
cold, *adj.* kalt; — *s.* Kälte *f.;* Erkältung *f.;* *catch* ~ Schnupfen *m.;* ~ sich erkälten.
collaborate, *v. n.* mitarbeiten; zusammenarbeiten.
collapse, *s.* Zusammenbruch *m.;* — *v. n.* zusammenbrechen.
collar, *s.* Kragen *m.;* — *v. a.* beim Kragen packen.
colleague, *s.* Kollege *m.*
collect, *v. a.* sammeln; einkassieren.
collection, *s.* Sammlung *f.*
college, *s.* College *n.;* Hochschule *f.*
collide, *v. n.* zusammenstoßen.
colliery, *s.* Kohlengrube *f.*
collision, *s.* Zusammenstoß *m.*
colonel, *s.* Oberst *m.*
colony, *s.* Kolonie *f.*
colour, *s.* Farbe *f.*
colourless, *adj.* farblos.
column, *s.* Säule *f.;* Spalte *f.*
comb, *s.* Kamm *m.;* —
v. a. kämmen.
combat, *s.* Kampf *m.*
combination, *s.* Verbindung *f.;* Kombination *f.*
combine, *v. a. & n.* (sich) verbinden.
come, *v. n.* kommen; ~ *about* sich zutragen; ~ *in!* herein!; ~ *to pass* sich ereignen.
comedy, *s.* Komödie *f.*
comfort, *s.* Trost *m.;* Behaglichkeit *f.;* — *v. a.* trösten.
comfortable, *adj.* bequem, behaglich.
comma, *s.* Komma *n.*
command, *s.* Befehl *m.;* — *v. a. & n.* befehlen.
commander, *s.* Kommandeur *m.*
commander-in-chief *s.* Oberbefehlshaber *m.*
commandment, *s.* Gebot *n.*
commemorate, *v. a.* gedenken, feiern.
commence, *v. a. & n.* beginnen, anfangen.
comment, *s.* Kommentar *m.;* Erläuterung *f.;* — *v. a.* kommentieren; *v. n.* ~ *(up)on* kritische Bemerkungen machen.
commerce, *s.* Handel *m.*
commercial, *adj.* Handels-; kommerziell.
commission, *s.* Kommission *f.;* Auftrag *m.*
commit, *v. a.* anvertrauen; übergeben; begehen.
committee, *s.* Ausschuß *m.,* Komitee *n.*
commodity, *s.* Ware *f.*
common, *adj.* gemein(sam); vereint; üblich.
commonwealth, *s.* Gemeinwesen *n.*
communicate, *v. a.* mit-

communication	conduct
teilen; *v. n.* in Verbindung stehen.	**compliment,** *s.* Kompliment *n.*
communication, *s.* Verbindung *f.*; Mitteilung *f.*; ~ cord (*railway*) Notbremse *f.*	**comply,** *v. n.* erfüllen; sich fügen.
	component, *s.* Bestandteil *m.*
communion, *s.* Gemeinschaft *f.*; Abendmahl *n.*	**compose,** *v. a.* komponieren; verfassen.
communiqué, *s.* Kommuniqué *n.*	**composer,** *s.* Komponist *m.*, -in *f.*
community, *s.* Gemeinde *f.*	**composition,** *s.* Abfassung *f.*; Aufsatz *m.*; Komposition *f.*
companion, *s.* Gefährte *m.*, Gefährtin *f.*	**compound,** *s.* Mischung *f.*; — *adj.* zusammengesetzt.
company, *s.* Gesellschaft *f*,	
compare, *v. a.* vergleichen *v. n.* sich vergleichen (lassen)	**comprehend,** *v. a. & n.* begreifen; verstehen.
	compromise, *s.* Kompromiß *n.*
comparison, *s.* Vergleich *m.*	**compulsory,** *adj.* obligatorisch.
compartment, *s.* Abteil *n.*; Abteilung *f.*	**computer,** *s.* Rechenautomat *m.*
compass, *s.* Umfang *m.*; ~es *pl.* Zirkel *m.*	**comrade,** *s.* Kamerad *m.*
compassion, *s.* Mitleid *n.*	**conceal,** *v. a.* verbergen.
compel, *v. a.* zwingen.	**conceited,** *adj.* eingebildet.
compensate, *v. a. & n.* entschädigen.	**concept,** *s.* Begriff *n.*
compete, *v. n.* konkurrieren.	**concern,** *s.* Angelegenheit *f.*; Geschäft *n.*; — *v. a.* betreffen, sich beziehen auf.
competence, *s.* Fähigkeit *f.*; Kompetenz *f.*	
competition, *s.* Wettbewerb *m.*; Konkurrenz *f.*	**concert,** *s.* Konzert *n.*
	concession, *s.* Konzession *f.*
competitor, *s.* Mitbewerber *m.*	**concise,** *adj.* bündig; kurz.
compilation, *s.* Sammlung *f.*	**conclude,** *v. a.* (be)schließen.
complain, *v. n.* sich beklagen.	**concrete,** *s.* Beton *m.*
complaint, *s.* Klage *f.*; Reklamation *f.*	**condemn,** *v. a.* verdammen.
	condensed, *adj.* verdichtet; abgekürzt.
complement, *s.* Ergänzung *f.*	**condition,** *s.* Zustand *m.*; Bedingung *f.*; Lage *f.*; ~s *pl.* Verhältnisse *n. pl.*; on ~ that unter der Bedingung, daß.
complete, *adj.* vollständig; — *v. a.* vollenden, beendigen.	
complication, *s.* Komplikation. *f.*	**conduct,** *s.* Verhalten *n.*;

| conductor | 40. | contemplate |

Betragen *n.;* — *v. a.* führen; betreiben; dirigieren; *v. n.* dirigieren.
conductor, *s.* Dirigent *m.;* Schaffner *m.*
confectioner, *s.* Konditor *m.*
confederacy, *s.* Bündnis *n.*
confer, *v. a.* erteilen; *v. n.* sich beraten.
conference, *s.* Konferenz *f.*
confess, *v. a.* bekennen.
confession, *s.* Beichte *f.*
confidence, *s.* Vertrauen *n.*
confident, *adj.* zuversichtlich.
confidential, *adj.* vertraulich; vertraut.
confine, *v. a.* begrenzen; einschränken.
confirm, *v. a.* bestätigen; konfirmieren.
conflict, *s.* Konflikt *m.*
confound, *v. a.* verwirren.
confront, *v. a.* gegenüberstellen; *v. n.* gegenüberstehen.
confuse, *v. a.* verwechseln.
congratulate, *v. a.* gratulieren.
congregation, *s.* Gemeinde *f.;* Kongregation *f.*
congress, *s.* Kongreß *m.*
conjunction, *s.* Verbindung *f.;* Bindewort *n.*
connect, *v. a.* verbinden.
connection, *s.* Verbindung *f.;* Zusammenhang *m.*
conquest, *s.* Eroberung *f.*
conscience, *s.* Gewissen *n.*
consciousness, *s.* Bewußtsein *n.*
consent, *s.* Zustimmung *f.;* — *v. n.* zustimmen.
consequence, *s.* Folge *f.*
consequently, *adv.* folglich.
conservative, *adj.* konservativ.
consider, *v. a.* erwägen; betrachten, halten für; *v. n.* überlegen.
considerable, *adj.* beträchtlich.
consideration, *s.* Überlegung *f.* Rücksicht *f.;* Gegenleistung *f.*
consignment, *s.* Zusendung *f.;* Konsignation *f.*
consist, *v. n.* bestehen.
consistent, *adj.* übereinstimmend.
consolation, *s.* Trost *m.*
conspicuous, *adj.* in die Augen fallend; sichtbar.
conspiracy, *s.* Verschwörung *f.*
conspire, *v. n.* sich verschwören.
constable, *s.* Schutzmann *m.*
constant, *adj.* konstant; beständig.
constitute, *v. a.* bilden; ernennen.
constitution, *s.* Konstitution *f.;* Veranlagung *f.;* Verfassung *f.*
constraint, *s.* Zwang *m.*
construct, *v. a.* errichten; konstruieren.
construction, *s.* Bau *m.;* Konstruktion *f.*
consul, *s.* Konsul *m.*
consulate, *s.* Konsulat *n.*
consult, *v. a.* konsultieren; um Rat fragen; nachschlagen; — *v. n.* sich beraten.
consume, *v. a.* verzehren.
consumer, *s.* Konsument *m.;* Abnehmer *m.*
contact, *s.* Kontakt *m.; fig.* Verbindung *f.;* — *v. a. & n.* Kontakt haben.
contain, *v. a.* enthalten; zurückhalten.
contemplate, *v. a.* betrachten; erwägen.

contemporary   **41.**   **corrupt**

contemporary, *adj.* zeitgenössisch; — *s.* Zeitgenosse *m.*
contempt, *s.* Verachtung *f.;* Schmach *f.*
content, *adj.* zufrieden.
contents, *s. pl.* Inhalt *m.*
contest, *s.* Streit *m.;* — *v. a.* anfechten.
continent, *s.* Kontinent *m.*
continental, *adj.* kontinental.
continual, *adj.* ununterbrochen, fortwährend. beständig.
continue, *v. a.* fortsetzen; *v. n.* anhalten.
contract, *s.* Vertrag *m.;* — *v. a.* sich zuziehen; zusammenziehen.
contractor, *s.* Unternehmer *m.*
contradiction, *s.* Widerspruch *m.*
contrary, *adj.* engegengesetzt; *s.* Gegenteil *n.*
contrast, *s.* Kontrast *m.;* Gegensatz *m.;* — *v. a.* konstrastieren.
contribution, *s.* Beitrag *m.*
contributor, *s.* Mitarbeiter *m.*
control, *v. a.* kontrollieren; steuern; — *s.* Kontrolle *f.;* Steuerung *f.;* Regulierung *f.*
controversy, *s.* Streit *m.*
convenience, *s.* Bequemlichkeit *f.;* Komfort *m.;* Wasserklosett *n.*
convenient, *adj.* bequem.
conversation, *s.* Gespräch *n.*
convert, *v. a.* umwandeln; bekehren.
convey, *v. a.* übermitteln; mitteilen.
conveyance, *s.* Transport *m.;* Fuhrwerk *n.*
convict, *s.* Sträfling *m.;* — *v. a.* überführen.
convince, *v. a.* überzeugen.
convoy, *s.* Geleit *n.*
cook, *s.* Koch *m.*, Köchin *f.;* — *v. a. & n.* kochen.
cooking, *s.* Kochen *n.;* Küche *f.*
cool, *adj.* kühl; — *v. a.* (ab)kühlen.
co-op, *s.* Konsum *m.*
co-operate, *v. n.* zusammenarbeiten; mitwirken.
co-operation, *s.* Mitwirkung *f.*
copper, *s.* Kupfer *n.*
copy, *s.* Abschrift *f.;* Exemplar *n.*, Kopie *f.;* — *v. a.* kopieren.
copy-book, *s.* Schreibheft *n.*
copyright, *s.* Copyright *n.*
cord, *s.* Strick *m.*
cordial, *adj.* herzlich.
cork, *s.* Kork *m.*
cork-screw, *s.* Korkzieher *m.*
corn, *s.* Korn *n.*, Getreide *n.*
corner, *s.* Ecke *f.;* Winkel *m.*
corporal[1], *adj.* körperlich.
corporal[2], *s.* Unteroffizier *m.*
corporation, *s.* Gemeindebehörde *f.*
corps, *s.* Korps *n.*
corpse, *s.* Leiche *f.*
correct, *adj.* richtig; — *v. a.* korrigieren.
correction, *s.* Korrektion *f.;* Richtigstellung *f.*
correspond, *v. n.* entsprechen; korrespondieren.
correspondence, *s.* Briefwechsel *m.*, Korrespondenz *f.*
corresponding, *adj.* entsprechend; korrespondierend.
corridor, *s.* Gang *m.*
corrupt, *adj.* verdorben;

korrupt.
cosmetic, *s.* Schönheitsmittel *n.*
cosmic, *adj.* kosmisch.
cost, *s.* Kosten *f. pl.*; Preis *m.*; — *v. n.* kosten.
costume, *s.* Kostüm *n.*
cosy, *adj.* behaglich, gemütlich.
cottage, *s.* Hütte *f.*; Landhäuschen *n.*
cotton, *s.* Baumwolle *f.*
couch, *s.* Couch *f.*, Chaiselongue *f.*
cough, *v. n.* husten; — *s.* Husten *m.*
council, *s.* Rat *m.*
counsel, *s.* Beratung *f.*; Rat *m.*; Anwalt *m.*
count[1]**,** *v. a. & n.* zählen; rechnen.
count[2]**,** *s.* Graf *m.*
countenance, *s.* Miene *f.*
counter, *s.* Ladentisch *m.*; Schalter *m.*
counterfoil, *s.* Kontrollblatt *n.*
countersign, *v. a.* gegenzeichnen.
countless, *adj.* unzählbar.
country, *s.* Land *n.*
countryman, *s.* Landsmann *m.*; Bauer *m.*
countryside, *s.* Gegend *f.*
countrywoman, *s.* Landsmännin *f.*; Bäuerin *f.*
county, *s.* Grafschaft *f.*
couple, *s.* Paar *n.*
courage, *s.* Tapferkeit *f.*; Mut *m.*
course, *s.* Gang *m.*; Kurs *m.*; Wechselkurs *m.*; *of* ~ natürlich.
court, *s.* Hof *m.*; Gerichtshof *m.*; — *v. a.* den Hof machen.
courtesy, *s.* Höflichkeit *f.*
courtyard, *s.* Hof *m.*
cousin, *s.* Vetter *m.*; Kusine *f.*
cover, *s.* Deckel *m.*; Decke *f.*; Kuvert *n.*; Einband *m.*; — *v. a. & n.* (be)decken; schützen; zurücklegen.
cow, *s.* Kuh *f.*
coward, *s.* Feigling *m.*
crab, *s.* Krabbe *f.*
crack, *s.* Knall *m.*; — *v. n. & a.* krachen; brechen.
cradle, *s.* Wiege *f.*
craft, *s.* Handwerk *n.*; List *f.*
craftsman, *s.* Handwerker *m.*
cram, *v. a.* (voll)stopfen; einpauken.
crash, *s.* Krach *m.*; — *v. n.* krachen.
crash-helmet, *s.* Sturzhelm *m.*
crave, sich sehnen.
crawl, *v. a. & n.* (herum)kriechen.
crayon, *s.* Buntstift *m.*
crazy, *adj.* verrückt.
creak, *v. n.* knarren; — *s.* Knarren *n.*
cream, *s.* Sahne *f.*; Creme *f.*
create, *v. a.* (er)schaffen.
creator, *s.* Schöpfer *m.*
creature, *s.* Geschöpf *n.*
credit, *s.* Kredit *m.*
creditor, *s.* Glaubiger *m.*
creek, *s.* Bucht *f.*
creep, *v. n.* kriechen; schleichen.
crew, *s.* Mannschaft *f.*
crib, Krippe *f.*
cricket, *s.* Kricketspiel *n.*
crime, *s.* Verbrechen *n.*
criminal, *s.* Verbrechen *n.* *adj.* kriminell.
cripple, *s.* Krüppel *m.*
crisis, *s.* Krisis *f.*
critic, *s.* Kritiker *m.*
criticize, *v. a.* kritisieren.
critique, *s.* Kritik *f.*
crochet, *s.* Häkeln *n.*
crop, *s.* Ernte *f.*; Ertrag *m.*

cross   **43.**   **dad, daddy**

cross, s. Kreuz n.; — adj. ärgerlich; — v. a. kreuzen; durchqueren.
crossing, s. Übergang m.
crossroad(s), s. Straßenkreuzung f.; fig. Scheideweg m.
cross-word puzzle, s. Kreuzworträtsel n.
crouch, v. n. & a. (sich) ducken.
crow, s. Krähe f.; — v.n. krähen.
crowd, s. Gedränge n.; Menge f.
crowded, adj. überfüllt; zusammengedrängt.
crown, s. Krone f.; Gipfel m.; — v. a. krönen.
crude, adj. roh; Roh-.
cruel, adj. grausam.
cruelty, s. Grausamkeit f.
cruise, s. Seereise f. — v.n. mit Reisegeschwindigkeit fahren.
cruising: ~ speed, Reisegeschwindigkeit f.
crumb, s. Krume f.; — v. a. & n. panieren.
crush, v. a. zerquetschen; fig. zerschmettern; — s. Gedränge n.
crust, s. Kruste f.
crutch, s. Krücke f.
cry, s. Schrei m.; Weinen n.; — v. n. schreien, weinen.
crystal, s. Krystall m.
cub, s. Junge m.
cube, s. Würfel m.
cuckoo, s. Kuckuck m.
cucumber, s. Gurke f.
cue, s. Stichwort n.
cuff, s. Manschette f.
cuff-link, s. Manschettenknopf m.
culminate, v. n. den Höhepunkt erreichen.
culprit, s. Schuldige m.
cultivate, v. a. kultivieren; betreiben.

cultural, adj. kulturell.
culture, s. Kultur f.
cunning, adj. verschlagen; schlau.
cup, s. Tasse f.; sport Pokal m.
cupboard, s. Schrank m.
curdle, v. a. & n. gerinnen (lassen).
cure, s. Kur f.; — v. a. & n. heilen.
curiosity, s. Neugierde f.
curious, adj. neugierig; seltsam.
curl, s. Locke f.
currant, s. Johannisbeere f.
currency, s. Währung f.; Umlauf m.
current, adj. laufend; aktuell; — s. Strömung f.; Strom m.
curse, s. Fluch m.; — v. a. verfluchen.
curtain, s. Vorhang m.; Gardine f.
curve, s. Kurve f.
cushion, s. Kissen m.
custom, s. Gewohnheit f.; Gebrauch m.; Sitte f.; Kundschaft f.; ~s pl. Zoll m.
customer, s. Kunde m.
custom-house, s. Zollamt n.
cut v. a. schneiden; v. n. schneiden; — s. Schnitt m.; Schmiß m.; Schnitte f.
cutlery, s. Eßbesteck n.
cutlet, s. Kotelett n.
cycle, s. Fahrrad n.; — v. n. Radfahren.
cylinder, s. Zylinder m.
Czech, adj. Tschechisch; — s. Tseheche m.

D

dad, daddy, s. Vati m.

dagger — **decline**

dagger, s. Dolch m.
daily, adj. täglich; — s. Tageszeitung f.
dainty, adj. köstlich; zierlich; delikat; — s. Leckerbissen m.
dairy, s. Molkerei f.
daisy, s. Gänseblümchen n.
dam, s. Damm m.
damage, s. Schaden m.; ~s pl. Schadenersatz m.
damn, v. a. verdammen; (curse) verwünschen.
damp, adj. feucht; — s. Feuchtigkeit f.; Dunst m.; — v. a. befeuchten.
dance, s. Tanz m.; — v. a. & n. tanzen.
Dane, s. Däne m.; Dänin f.
danger, s. Gefahr f.
dangerous, adj. gefährlich.
Danish, adj. dänisch.
dare, v. n. wagen; sich unterstehen; v. a. wagen; herausfordern.
dark, adj. dunkel; — s. Dunkelheit f.
darkness, s. Dunkelheit f.
darling, s. Liebling m.
darn, v. a. stopfen.
dart, s. Wurfspeer m.; Abnäher m. (in skirts)
dash, s. Strich m.; Schwung m.; Ansturm m.; Prise f.; Eleganz f.; — v. n. (sich) stürzen; v. a. schleudern;
dash-board, s. Instrumentenbrett n.
data, s. pl. Angaben f.
date[1], s. Datum n.; out of ~ veraltet; up to ~ modern.
date[2], s. Dattel f.
daughter, s. Tochter f.
daughter-in-law, s. Schwiegertochter f.

dawn, s. Dämmerung f.; — v. n. (auf)dämmern.
day, s. Tag m.
daylight, s. Tageslicht n.
daytime, s. Tageszeit f.
daze, v. a. blenden; betäuben.
dead, adj. tot; abgestorben; — s. the ~ der Tote; die Toten.
deaf, adj. taub.
deal, s. Teil m.; Handel m.; Abkommen n.; a great ~ sehr viel; — v. n. ~ with sich befassen mit; handeln von; ~ in Handel treiben mit; v. a. austeilen; (Karten) geben.
dealer, s. Händler m.; Kartengeber m.
dean, s. Dekan m.
dear, adj. teuer; lieb; — s. Teure m., f. n.
death, s. Tod m.
debate, v. a. & n. debatieren; — s. Debatte.
debt, s. Schuld f.
debtor, s. Schuldner m.
decay, s. Verfall m.; v. n. verfallen.
decease, s. Hinscheiden n.; — v. n. hinscheiden.
deceive, v. a. betrügen.
December, s. Dezember m.
decent, adj. anständig.
deception, s. Betrug m.
decide, v. a. entscheiden.
decision, s. Entscheidung f.; Entschluß m.
decisive, adj. entscheidend; endgültig.
deck, s. Deck n.
deck-chair, s. Liegestuhl m.
declaration, s. Erklärung f.; Deklaration f.
declare, v. a. erklären; deklarieren.
decline, v. a. verweigern;

decorate   45.   **deplore**

ablehnen; *v. n.* sich neigen; ablehnen; — *s. fig.* Niedergang *m.*

decorate, *v. a.* zieren; schmücken.

decoration, *s.* Verzierung *f.*

decrease, *s.* Abnahme *f.;* — *v. n.* abnehmen; (sich) vermindern.

decree, *s.* Dekret *n.*

dedicate, *v. a.* widmen.

deduct, *v. a.* abziehen.

deed, *s.* Tat *f.;* Dokument *n.*

deem, *v. a.* halten für.

deep, *adj.* tief.

deer, *s.* Wild *n.;* Hirsch *m.*

defeat, *v.a.* besiegen; — *s.* Niederlage *f.*

defect, *s.* Fehler *m.;* Defekt *m.*

defend, *v. a.* verteidigen.

defer, *v. a.* aufschieben.

defiance, *s.* Trotz *m.*

deficiency, *s.* Unzulänglichkeit *f.;* Mangel *m.;* Defizit *n.*

define, *v. a.* definieren.

definite, *adj.* bestimmt; endgültig.

defroster, *s.* Entfroster *m.*

defy, *v. a.* trotzen; herausfordern.

degrade, *v.a.* degradieren; erniedrigen.

degree, *s.* Grad *m.;* Stufe *f.*

delay, *v.a.* verschieben; aufhalten; *v. n.* zögern; — *s.* Aufschub *m.*

delegate, *s.* Delegierte *m.* Abgeordnete *m.*

delegation, *s.* Delegation *f.,* Abordnung *f.*

deliberate, *adj.* absichtlich; wohlüberlegt; — *v. a. &. n.* überlegen.

delicate, *adj.* zart; fein.

delicious, *adj.* köstlich.

delight, *s.* Vergnügen *n.;* — *v. a.* ergötzen; *v. n.* sich erfreuen.

delinquent, *s.* Verbrecher *m.,* -in *f.*

deliver, *v. a.* (ab)liefern; übergeben; ~ *a speech* eine Rede halten; *v. n.* befreien; ein Urteil fällen.

delivery, *s.* Lieferung *f.*

demand, *v. a. & n.* fordern, verlangen; fragen; — *s.* Forderung *f.;* Nachfrage *f.;* Bedarf *m.*

democracy, *s.* Demokratie *f.*

democratic, *adj.* demokratisch.

demolish, *v. a.* niederreißen.

demonstrate, *v.a. & n.* demonstrieren; beweisen.

demonstration, *s.* Demonstrierung *f.*

denial, *s.* Ablehnung *f.;* Verneinung *f.*

denomination, *s.* Benennung *f.;* Sekte *f.*

denote, *v. a.* bezeichnen; bedeuten.

denounce, *v. a.* denunzieren; anzeigen.

dense, *adj.* dicht.

density, *s.* Dichte *f.*

dentist, *s.* Zahnarzt *m.*

denture, *s.* Zahnprotese *f.*

deny, *v. a.* leugnen; verneinen.

depart, *v. n.* fortgehen; abfahren; hinscheiden.

department, *s.* Abteilung *f.;* Bezirk *m.;* Ministerium *n.*

depend, *v. n.* sich verlassen (auf); ~ *on* abhängen von.

dependence, *s.* Abhängigkeit *f.*

deplore, *v.a.* bedauern, beklagen.

deposit | **diarrhoea**

deposit, *v. a.* ablagern; deponieren; *(money)* einzahlen. — *s.* Ablagerung *f.;* Niederschlag *m.*
depot, *s.* Depot *n.*
deprive, *v. a.* berauben.
depth, *s.* Tiefe *f.*
deputy, *s.* Abgeordnete *m.;* Stellvertreter *m.*
derive, *v.a.* schließen (aus); ableiten (von).
descend, *v. n.* herabsteigen; herstammen (von); *v. a. (steps)* heruntersteigen.
descendant, *s.* Nachkomme *m.;* Abkömmling *m.*
descent, *s.* Abstieg *m.;* Abstammung *f.;* Herkunft *f.*
describe, *v. a.* beschreiben, schildern.
description, *s.* Beschreibung *f.;* Schilderung *f.*
desert[1], *s.* Wüste *f.*
desert[2], *v. a.* verlassen.
deserve, *v. a.* verdienen.
design, *s.* Entwurf *m.*, Plan *m.;* Absicht *f.;* — *v. a.* aufzeichnen; entwerfen; vorhaben.
desirable, *adj.* wünschenswert.
desire, *v. a.* wünschen; — *s.* Wunsch *m.;* Verlangen *n.;* Begierde *f.*
desk, *s.* Schreibtisch *m.*, Pult *n.*
desolation, *s.* Verlassenheit *f.;* Trostlosigkeit *f.*
despair, *v. n.* verzweifeln; — *s.* Verzweiflung *f.*
despatch *see* **dispatch.**
desperate, *adj.* verzweifelt.
despise, *v. a.* verachten.
despite (of), *prep.* trotz.
dessert, *s.* Dessert *n.;* Nachtisch *m.*
destination, *s.* Bestimmungsort *m.;* Bestimmung *f.;* Ziel *n.*
destiny, *s.* Schicksal *n.;* Los *n.*
destroy, *v. a.* zerstören; vernichten.
destruction, *s.* Zerstörung *f.;* Verderben *n.*
detail, *s.* Detail *n.;* ∼s *pl.* Einzelheiten.
detain, *v. a.* festhalten; in Haft behalten.
detect, *v. a.* entdecken.
detective, *s.* Detektiv *m.*
detention, *s.* Vorenthaltung *f.;* Haft *f.*
detergent, *s.* Reinigungsmittel *n.*
deteriorate, *v.n.* (sich) verschlechtern; an Wert verlieren.
determination, *s.* Entschluß *m.;* Absicht *f.*
determine, *v. a.* beschließen; festsetzen.
detrimental, *adj.* schädlich.
develop, *v. a. & n.* (sich) entwickeln.
development, *s.* Entwicklung *f.*
deviation, *s.* Abweichung *f.*
device, *s.* Erfindung *f.;* Einrichtung *f.;* Gerät *n.*
devil, *s.* Teufel *m.*
devise, *v. a.* ersinnen, vermachen.
devote, *v. a.* widmen.
devour, *v. a.* verschlingen.
dew, *s.* Tau *m.*
diagnosis, *s.* Diagnose *f.*
diagram, *s.* Diagramm *n.*
dial, *s.* Zifferblatt *n.;* *(radio)* Skalenscheibe *f.* *(telephone)* Nummernscheibe *f.*
dialogue, *s.* Dialog *m.*
diameter, *s.* Diameter *m.;* Durchmesser *m.*
diamond, *s.* Diamant *m.*
diaper, *s.* Windel *f.*
diarrhoea, *s.* Durchfall *m.*

diary 47. **disguise**

diary, s. Tagebuch n.
dictate, v. a. diktieren.
dictator, s. Diktator m.
dictionary, s. Wörterbuch n.
die¹, v. n. sterben.
die², s. Würfel m.
Diesel engine, s. Dieselmotor m.
diet, s. Diät f.
differ, v. n. sich unterscheiden; anderer Meinung sein.
difference, s. Unterschied m.; Differenz f.
different, adj. verschieden (von); anders (als).
difficult, adj. schwierig.
difficulty, s. Schwierigkeit f.
diffuse, v. a. verbreiten.
dig, v. a. & n. graben.
digest, v. a. verdauen.
dignified, adj. würdevoll.
dignity, s. Würde f.
diligent, adj. fleißig.
dim, adj. trüb; undeutlich.
dimension, s. Dimension f.
diminish, v. a. & n. (ver)mindern; abnehmen.
dine, v. n. speisen.
dining-car, s. Speisewagen m.
dining-room, s. Speisezimmer n.
dinner, s. Essen n. Festessen n.
dinner-jacket, s. Smoking m.
dip, v. a. & n. eintauchen.
diploma, s. Diplom n.
diplomatic, adj. diplomatisch.
direct, adj. gerade; direkt;
— v. a. richten; lenken;
v. n. dirigieren.
directly, adv. direkt; unmittelbar.
director, s. Direktor m.
directory, s. Adressbuch n.; Telephonbuch n.
dirty, adj. schmutzig.
disadvantage, s. Nachteil n.
disagree, v. n. nicht übereinstimmen; nicht bekommen.
disagreeable, adj. unangenehm.
disappear, v. n. verschwinden.
disappointment, s. Enttäuschung f.
disapprove, v. a. mißbilligen.
disaster, s. Unglück n.
disastrous, adj. verhängnisvoll.
disc, s. Scheibe f.; Schallplatte f.
discern, v. a. wahrnehmen, unterscheiden.
discharge, v. a. & n. (sich) entladen; entlasten; — s. Entladung f.
discipline, s. Disziplin f.;
— v. a. ausbilden; disziplinieren.
disclose, v. a. enthüllen.
discontented, adj. unzufrieden.
discourage, v. a. entmutigen; abschrecken.
discover, v. a. entdecken.
discovery, s. Entdeckung f.
discredit, v. a. diskreditieren.
discreet, adj. diskret.
discretion, s. Gutdünken n.; Diskretion f.
discussion, s. Diskussion f.; Besprechung f.
disdain, s. Verachtung f.
disease, s. Krankheit f.
disembark, v. a. & n. (sich) ausschiffen.
disgrace, s. Schande f.; — v. a. schänden.
disgraceful, adj. schändlich.
disguise, v. a. verkleiden;
— s. Verkleidung f.

disgust, v. a. ekeln; — *s.* Ekel *m.*
dish, *s.* Schüssel *f.*; Gericht *n.*
dishonest, *adj.* unehrlich.
dishonour, *s.* Ehrlosigkeit *f.*; Schande *f.*; Ungnade *f.*; — *v. a.* entehren; *(bill)* nicht honorieren.
disinfect, *v.a.* desinfizieren.
disk, *see* **disc.**
dislike, *s.* Abneigung *f.*; — *v.a.* nicht leiden können; nicht mögen.
dismal, *adj.* düster, elend.
dismay, *s.* Bestürzung *f.*; Entsetzen *n.*
dismiss, *v. a.* entlassen.
disobedient, *adj.* ungehorsam.
disorder, *s.* Unordnung *f.*
dispatch, *s.* Absendung *f.*; Versand *m.*; Depesche *f.*; Eilbote *m.*
dispensary, *s.* Apotheke *f.*
dispense, *v. a.* austeilen; spenden; *(medicines)* dispensieren; *v. n.* ∼ *with* verzichten auf; entbehren.
disperse, *v. a. & n.* (sich) zerstreuen; verbreiten.
displacement, *s.* Versetzung *f.*
display, *v. a.* entfalten; *(goods)* ausstellen; — *s.* Entfaltung *f.*; Schaustellung *f.*; Auslage *f.*
disposal, *s.* be at sy's ∼ jm zur Verfügung stehen.
dispose, *v. n.* verfügen (über); ordnen; lenken; wegschaffen.
disposition, *s.* Neigung *f.*; Veranlagung *f.*; Anordnung *f.*
dispute, *s.* Streit *m.*; — *v. a.* bestreiten; streitig machen; *v. n.* streiten.
disqualify, *v. a.* *(sport)* ausschließen; disqualifizieren.
dissatisfy, *v. a.* nicht befriedigen.
dissolve, *v. a.* (auf)lösen; *v. n.* sich auflösen.
distance, *s.* Entfernung *f.*; Abstand *m.*; Strecke *f.*
distant, *adj.* fern; entfernt.
distil, *v. a.* destillieren.
distinction, *s.* Auszeichnung *f.*; Titel *m.*; Rang *m.*; Unterscheidung *f.*
distinguish, *v. a.* unterscheiden; wahrnehmen; auszeichnen.
distraction, *s.* Zerstreutheit *f.*; Verwirrung *f.*
distress, *s.* Elend *n.*; Not *f.*; Gefahr *f.*; — *v. a.* quälen; bedrücken.
distribute, *v. a.* austeilen; verteilen.
district, *s.* Bezirk *m.*; Gegend *f.*; Gebiet *n.*
disturb, *v. a.* stören.
disturbance, *s.* Störung *f.*; Unruhe *f.*
ditch, *s.* Graben *m.*
dive, *v.n.* (unter)tauchen; — *s.* Sturzflug *m.*; *(sport)* Kopfsprung *m.*
divergent, *adj.* verschieden.
divide, *v. a.* (zer)teilen; dividieren; *v. n.* sich teilen.
dividend, *s.* Gewinnanteil *m.*; Dividende *f.*
divine, *adj.* göttlich.
divinity, *s.* Gottheit *f.*; Theologie *f.*
division, *s.* Teilung *f.*; Division *f.*; Abstimmung *f.*
divorce, *s.* Scheidung *f.* — *v. a.* scheiden (von).
dizzy, *adj.* schwindelig.
do, *v. a.* tun, ausführen; handeln; how ∼ you ∼?

dock — **drum**

guten Tag; ~ *with sg* auskommen mit.
dock, *s.* Dock *n.;* — *v. a.* (ein)docken; *v. n.* dokken.
doctor, *s.* Doktor *m.;* Arzt *m.*
doctrine, *s.* Lehre *f.*
document, *s.* Dokument *n.;* Urkunde *f.*
dog, *s.* Hund *m.*
doll, *s.* Puppe *f.*
dollar, *s.* Dollar *m.*
domestic, *adj.* häuslich; inländisch; — *s.* Dienstbote *m.*
domicile, *s.* Wohnsitz *m.*
dominate, *v.a.* beherrschen; *v.n.* dominieren.
dominion, *s.* Dominions *pl.;* Herrschaft *f.*
donkey, *s.* Esel *m.*
doom, *s.* Urteil *n;* Schicksal *n.;* — *v. a.* verurteilen; verdammen.
door, *s.* Tür *f.;* Tor *n.*
dormitory, *s.* Schlafsaal *m.*
dot, *s.* Punkt *m.*
double, *adj.* doppelt; — *s.* Ebenbild *n.*
doubt, *v. n.* & *a.* zweifeln; — *s.* Zweifel *m.*
dough, *s.* Teig *m.*
dove, *s.* Taube *f.*
down, *adv.* herab; unten; abwärts; — *prep.* hinunter; hinab.
downhill, *adv.* bergab.
downstairs, *adv.* unten; die Treppe hinunter.
downward(s), *adv.* abwärts.
dozen, *s.* Dutzend *n.*
draft, *s.* Entwurf *m.,* Abhebung *f.;* Ersatztruppe *f.;* — *v. a.* entwerfen; abkommandieren.
drag, *v. a.* schleppen.
drain, *v. a.* entwässern; *fig.* erschöpfen; — *s.* Abflußgraben *m.*
drama, *s.* Drama *n.*
dramatic, *adj.* dramatisch.
draper, *s.* Textilkaufmann. *m.;* Tuchhändler *m.*
draw, *v.a.* ziehen; beziehen; zeichnen; *v. n.* zeichnen.
drawer, *s.* Schublade *f.*
drawing, *s.* Zeichnung *f.*
drawing-room, *s.* Empfangszimmer *n.;* Salon *m.*
dread, *s.* Furcht *f.;* — *v. a.* & *n.* (sich) fürchten. (vor).
dreadful, *adj.* furchtbar.
dream, *s.* Traum *m.;* — *v. a.* & *n.* träumen.
dress, *s.* Kleid *n.;* — *v. a.* bekleiden; *v. n.* sich ankleiden, sich anziehen.
dress-circle, *s.* erster Rang.
dressing-gown, *s.* Morgenrock *m.*
dressmaker, *s.* Schneiderin *f.*
drift, *s.* Treiben *n.;* Wehe *f.;* — *v. a.* & *n.* treiben.
drill, *s.* Bohrmaschine *f.;* Drill *m.*
drink, *s.* Getränk *n.;* Trinken *n.;* — *v. a.* & *n.* trinken; saufen.
drip, *v. n.* tröpfeln.
drive, *s.* Fahrt *f.;* Fahrweg *m.,* Treiben *n.;* — *v. a.* treiben; *v. n.* (Auto)fahren.
driver, *s.* Fahrer *m.;* Chauffeur *m.*
driving, *s.* Autofahren *n.;* ~ *license* Führerschein *m.*
drop, *s.* Tropfen *m.;* — *v.a.* tropfen (lassen); fallen lassen; *v.n.* tröpfeln; fallen.
drug, *s.* Arzneiware *f.;*
druggist, *s.* Drogist *m.*
drum, *s.* Trommel *f.;* *v. n.*

drunk   50.   **educate**

& *a.* trommeln.
drunk, *adj.* betrunken.
dry, *adj.* trocken; dürr; — *v. a. & n.* trocknen.
dry-clean, *v.a.* trocken reinigen.
dual, *adj.* doppelt.
dub, *v. a. (film)* synchronisieren.
duchess, *s.* Herzogin *f.*
duck¹, *s.* Ente *f.*
duck², *v. n.* untertauchen; — *s.* Ducken *n.*
due, *adj.* fällig; gebührend; ~ *to* zuzuschreiben(d); — *adv.* gerade; — *s.* Gebühren *pl.*; Schuld *f.*
duke, *s.* Herzog *m.*
dull, *adj.* stumpfsinnig; langweilig; matt.
dumb, *adj.* stumm; blöd.
dummy, *s.* Schaufensterpuppe *f.*; Strohmann *m.*; Statist *m.* -in *f.*; Schnuller *m.*
dung, *s.* Dünger *m.*
dupe, *s.* Betrogene *m.*; — *v. a.* übertölpern.
duplicate, *adj.* doppelt; — *s.* Kopie *f.*; Duplikat *n.*; — *v. a.* kopieren; verdoppeln.
during, *prep.* während.
dusk, *s.* Dämmerung *f.*
dust, *s.* Staub *m.*; — *v.a. & n.* abstauben.
dustbin, *s.* Mülleimer *m.*
Dutch, *adj.* holländisch; — *s. the* ~ die Holländer *pl.*
Dutchman, *s.* Holländer *m.*
duty, *s.* Pflicht *f.*; Zoll *m.*; *be on* ~ im Dienst sein.
duty-free, *adj.* zollfrei.
dwarf, *s.* Zwerg *m.*
dwell, *v. n.* wohnen; (ver)weilen.
dwelling, *s.* Wohnung *f.*
dwelling-house, *s.* Wohnhaus *n.*

dye, *s.* Farbstoff *m.*; — *v. a. & n.* (sich) färben.
dynasty *s.* Dynastie *f.*

E

each, *adj. & pron.* jeder, jede, jedes; ~ *other* einander; — *adv.* je, pro Person; pro Stück.
eager, *adj.* (be)gierig; *fig.* eifrig.
eagle, *s.* Adler *m.*
ear, *s.* Ohr *n.*
earl, *s.* Graf *m.*
early, *adj. & adv.* früh.
earn, *v. a.* verdienen.
earnest, *adj.* ernst.
earth, *s.* Erde *f.*
earthenware, *s.* Steingut *n*
earthquake, *s.* Erdbeben *n.*
ease, *s.* Bequemlichkeit *f.*; Leichtigkeit *f.*; Ungezwungenheit *f.*
east, *s.* Osten *m.*; *to the* ~ *of* östlich von; — *adj. & adv.* östlich.
Easter, *s.* Ostern *n./pl.*
eastern, *adj.* östlich.
eastward(s), *adj. & adv.* ostwärts; östlich.
easy, *adj.* leicht.
easy-chair, *s.* Lehnstuhl *m.*
eat, *v. a. & n.* essen.
ebb, *s.* Ebbe *f.*
ecclesiastic, *adj.* kirchlich; — Geistlicher *m.*
economy, *s.* Sparsamkeit *f.*; Wirtschaft *f.*; Wirtschaftslehre *f.*
ecstasy, *s.* Verzückung *f.*
edge, *s.* Schneide *f.*; Ecke *f.*; Kante *f.*; Rand *m.*
edition, *s.* Ausgabe *f.*; Auflage *f.*
editor, *s.* Herausgeber *m.*; Redakteur *m.*
editorial, *s.* Leitartikel *m.*
educate, *v. a.* erziehen;

ausbilden.
education, *s.* Erziehung *f.*; (Aus)Bildung *f.*
effect, *s.* Wirkung *f.*; — *v. a.* bewirken.
effective, *adj.* wirksam; tatsächlich.
efficiency, *s.* Wirksamkeit *f.*; Leistung(sfähigkeit) *f.*
effort, *s.* Anstrengung *f.*; Bemühung *f.*
egg, *s.* Ei *n.*
Egyptian, *adj.* ägyptisch; — *s.* Ägypter *m.*, -in *f.*
eight, *adj.* acht; — *s.* Acht *f.*
eighteen, *adj.* achtzehn; *s.* Achtzehn *f.*
eighth, *adj.* achter, achte, achtes.
eighty, *adj.* achtzig; — *s.* Achtzig *f.*
either, *adj. & pron.* einer von beiden; jeder, jede, jedes; irgendeiner, irgendeine, irgendeines; — *conj.* entweder; ~ ... *or* entweder ... oder; weder ... noch.
elaborate, *adj.* ausgearbeitet; — *v. a.* ausarbeiten.
elastic, *adj.* elastisch; — *s.* Gummiband *n.*
elbow, *s.* Ellbogen *m.*
elderly, *adj.* ältlich.
elect, *v. a.* (er)wählen.
election, *s.* Wahl *f.*
electric(al), *adj.* elektrisch.
electricity, *s.* Elektrizität *f.*
electronic, *adj.* elektronisch.
elegant, *adj.* elegant!
element, *s.* Element *n.*
elementary, *adj.* elementar.
elephant, *s.* Elefant *m.*
eleven, *adj.* elf; — *s.* Elf *f.*
eleventh, *adj.* elfter, elfte,

elftes.
elm, *s.* Ulme *f.*
else, *adv.* sonst; *anything* ~? sonst noch etwas?
elsewhere, *adv.* anderswo; anderswohin.
embankment, *s.* Damm *m.*; Kai *m.*
embark, *v. a.* einschiffen; *v. n.* an Bord gehen; *fig.* ~ *upon* etwas anfangen.
embarrass, *v. a.* in Verlegenheit bringen.
embassy, *s.* Botschaft *f.*
embrace, *v. a.* umarmen.
embroidery, *s.* Stickerei *f.*
emerge, *v. n.* auftauchen; *(fig.)* hervorgehen.
emergency, *s.* Notlage *f.*
emigrant, *s.* Auswanderer *m.*
emigrate, *v. n.* auswandern.
emigration, *s.* Auswanderung *f.*
eminent, *adj.* hervorragend; eminent.
emit, *v. a.* aussenden; von sich geben.
emotion, *s.* Gemütsbewegung *f.*; Rührung *f*
emphasize, *v. a.* betonen.
empire, *s.* Reich *n.*
employ, *v. a.* beschäftigen; verwenden.
employee, *s.* Angestellte *m., f.*
employer, *s.* Arbeitgeber *m.*, -in *f.*
employment, *s.* Beschäftigung *f.*
empty *adj.* leer; — *v. a. & n.* (sich) leeren.
enable, *v. a.* befähigen; ermöglichen.
enclosure, *s.* Umzäunung *f.*; Einlage *f.*
encounter, *v. a. & n.* (sich) begegnen; zusammenstoßen.
encourage, *v. a.* ermuti-

encyclopaedia — **errand**

encyclopaedia, *s.* Enzyklopädie *f.*; Lexikon *n.*
end, *s.* Ende *n.*; Ziel *n.*; — *v. a.* beenden; *v. n.* enden; zu Ende kommen.
endeavour, *v. n.* sich bemühen (um), streben; *v. a.* versuchen; — *s.* Bemühung *f.*
ending, *s.* Ende *n.*; Schluß *m.*
endorse, *v. a.* indossieren, überschreiben.
endorsement, *s.* Indossierung *f.*; Bestätigung *f.*; Aufschrift *f.*
endow, *v. a.* ausstatten; aussteuern.
endure, *v. a.* aushalten; ausstehen; *v. n.* ausharren.
enemy, *s.* Feind *m.*
energetic, *adj.* tätig, energisch.
energy, *s.* Energie *f.*
enforce, *v. a.* geltend machen; vollstrecken; erzwingen.
engage, *v. a.* verpflichten; beschäftigen; verloben.
engagement, *s.* Verpflichtung *f.*; Verlobung *f.*
engine, *s.* Maschine *f.*; Lokomotive *f.*
engine-driver, *s.* Lokomotivführer *m.*
engineer, *s.* Ingenieur *m.*; Maschinist *m.*
English, *adj.* englisch.
Englishman, *s.* Engländer *m.*
Englishwoman, *s.* Engländerin *f.*
enjoy, *v. a.* genießen; ~ *oneself* sich gut unterhalten.
enlarge, *v. a.* erweitern; vergrößern.
enlist, *v. a.* (an)werben.
enormous, *adj.* ungeheuer.
enough, *adv. & adj.* genug.
enquire *see* **inquire**.
enrol, *v. a.* anwerben; einschreiben.
ensign, *s.* Fahne *f.*; Flagge *f.*
ensue, *v. n.* (nach)folgen; sich ergeben aus.
enter, *v. a.* eintreten in; betreten (acc.); *fig.* (etw.) antreten.
enterprise, *s.* Unternehmung *f.*
entertain, *v. a.* unterhalten; bewirten.
entertainment, *s.* Unterhaltung *f.*
enthusiastic, *adj.* begeistert.
entire, *adj.* ganz; vollständig.
entirely, *adv.* völlig; durchaus.
entitle, *v. a.* betiteln; berechtigen.
entrance, *s.* Eingang *m.*; ~ *examination* Aufnahmeprüfung *f.*
entry, *s.* Eintragung *f.*; Eingang *m.*; *(sport)* Nennung *f.*
enumerate, *v. a.* (auf)zählen.
envelope, *s.* Kuvert *n.*, Umschlag *m.*
envious, *adj.* neidisch.
environment, *s.* Umgebung *f.*
envy, *s.* Neid *m.*; — *v. a.* beneiden.
epidemic, *s.* Epidemie *f.*; — *adj.* epidemisch.
equal, *adj.* gleich.
equation, *s.* Gleichung *f.*
equipment, *s.* Ausrüstung *f.*
erect, *v. a.* aufrichten; — *adj.* aufrecht.
err, *v. n.* (sich) irren.
errand, *s.* Auftrag *m.*

error | **excursion**

error, s. Irrtum m.; Fehler m.
escalator, s. Rolltreppe f.
escape, v. n. entkommen; — s. Entkommen n.; Flucht f.
escort, s. Geleit n.; — v. a. geleiten.
essay, s. Aufsatz m. Essay n.; — v. a. & n. versuchen.
essential, adj. wesentlich.
establish, v. a. festsetzen; gründen; etablieren.
establishment, s. Anstalt f.; Institut n.; Festsetzung f.
estate, s. Stand m.; Grundstück n.; Besitztum m.; Nachlaß m.
esteem, v. a. (er)achten; — s. Achtung f.
estimate, v. a. (ab)schätzen, beurteilen; — s. Schätzung f.
eternity, s. Ewigkeit f.
Eucharist, s. Eucharistie f.; Hostie f.
European, adj. europäisch; — s. Europäer m.; -in f.
evacuate, v. a. entleeren; evakuieren.
even, adv. sogar; gerade; not ~ nicht einmal; — adj. eben; gerade.
evening, s. Abend m.
event, s. Ereignis m.
eventually, adv. am Ende; schließlich.
ever, adv. fortwährend; immer; je.
every, adj. jeder, jede, jedes; ~ day jeden Tag.
everybody, pron. jeder(mann).
everyday, adj. Alltags...
everyone, pron. jeder(mann).
everything, alles.
everywhere, adv. überall.
evidence, s. Beweis m.; Zeuge m., -in f.
evident, adj. augenscheinlich; offenbar.
evil, adj. übel; — s. Übel;
evolution, s. Evolution f.; Entwicklung f.
exact, adj. genau; — v. a. fordern.
exactly, adv. genau; (answer) ganz recht.
exaggerate, v. a. & n. übertreiben.
examination, s. Prüfung f.; Untersuchung f.; Examen n.
examine, v.a & n prüfen; untersuchen.
example, s. Beispiel; for ~ zum Beispiel.
excavation, s. Ausgrabung f., Höhle f.
exceedingly, adv. außerordentlich; überaus.
excel, v. a. übertreffen; — v. n. sich auszeichnen.
excellent, adj. vortrefflich.
except, v.a. ausnehmen (von); prep. ausgenommen, außer.
exception, s. Ausnahme f.
excess, s. Übermaß n.; Mehrbetrag m.; — adj. ~ luggage Übergewicht n.
exchange, v. a. umtauschen; vertauschen; eintauschen; umwechseln — s. Tausch m.; Geldumsatz m.; Wechsel m.; Börse f.; Fernsprechamt n.
excitement, s. Aufregung f.; Erregung f.
exclaim, v. n. & a. ausrufen.
exclamation, s. Ausruf m.
exclusive, adj. ausschließlich; exklusiv.
excursion, s. Ausflug m.

excuse   54.   **eyeshade**

excuse, *v. a.* entschuldigen; verzeihen; — *s.* Entschuldigung *f.*; Ausrede *f.*

execute, *v. a.* ausführen; vollziehen; hinrichten.

execution, *s.* Ausführung *f.*; Vollziehung *f.*; Hinrichtung *f.*

executive, *adj.* ausübend, vollziehend; —*s.(power)* Vollziehungsgewalt *f.*

exercise, *s.* Übung *f.*; — *v.a.* üben, drillen; *v. n.* sich üben, *(sport)* trainieren.

exertion, *s.* Anstrengung *f.*

exhaust, *v. a.* erschöpfen.

exhaust(-)pipe, *s.* Auspuffrohr *n.*

exhibit, *v. a.* ausstellen; — *s.* Schaustück *n.*; Exhibitum *n.*

exhibition, *s.* Ausstellung *f.*

exist, *v. n.* existieren, leben.

existence, *s.* Dasein *n.*; Leben.

exit, *s.* Asgang.

expand, *v. a. & n.* (sich) ausbreiten.

expect, *v. a.* erwarten.

expectation, *s.* Erwartung *f.*

expedient, *adj.* ratsam; zweckmäßig.

expedition, *s.* Expedition *f.*

expel, *v. a.* vertreiben; wegjagen.

expense, *s.* Ausgab *f.*; Kosten *f. pl.*

expensive, *adj.* teuer, kostspielig.

experience, *s.* Erfahrung *f.*; Erlebnis *n.*; — *v. a.* erfahren; erleben.

experiment, *s.* Versuch *m.*; Experiment *n.*; *v. n.* experimentieren.

expert, *s.* Fachmann *m.*, Sachkundiger *m.*

expire, *v. n.* sterben; ablaufen.

explain, *v.a.* erklären.

explanation, *s.* Erklärung *f.*

explore, *v. a.* erforschen.

explosion, *s.* Explosion *f.*

export, *v. a.* exportieren, ausführen; — *s.* Export *m.*, Ausfuhr *f.*;

exporter, *s.* Exporteur *m.*

expose, *v. a.* preisgeben; exponieren.

express, *v. a.* ausdrücken; — *s.* Schnellzug *m.*

expression, *s.* Ausdruck *m.*; Gesichtsausdruck *m.*

exquisite, *adj.* köstlich; verfeinert.

extend, *v. a. & n.* (sich) ausdehnen; (sich) strecken.

extensive, *adj.* ausgedehnt.

extent, *s.* Größe *f.*; Ausmaß *n.*; Grad *m.*

extinguish, *v. a.* auslöschen; abschaffen.

extra, *adj.* zusätzlich;.

extract, *v. a.* ausziehen; — *s.* Extrakt *m.*; Auszug *m.*; Exzerpt *n.*

extraordinary, *adj.* außerordentlich.

extravagant, *adj.* verschwenderisch.

extreme, *s.* Extreme *n.*; — *adj.* äußerst; höchst.

extremely, *adv.* äußerst; sehr.

extremity, *s.* (das) Äußerste.

eye, *s.* Auge *n.*; *(needle)* Öhr *n.*; — *v. a.* beäugeln.

eyebrow, *s.* Augenbraue *f.*

eyelid, *s.* Augenlid *n.*

eyepiece, *s.* Okular *n.*

eyeshade *s.* Augenschirm

eyesight — **fearful**

eyesight, s. Augenlicht n., Sehkraft f.
eyewitness, s. Augenzeuge m.

F

fable, s. Fabel f.
fabric, s. Gewebe n.; Stoff m.
face, s. Gesicht n.; Oberfläche f.; Zifferblatt n.; — v. a. gegenüberstehen; gegenüberliegen; fig. entgegenblicken.
facility, s. Leichtigkeit f.; facilities pl. Möglichkeiten f. pl.
fact, s. Tatsache f.
factor, s. Faktor m.
factory, s. Fabrik f.
faculty, s. Fakultät f.; Fähigkeit f.
fade, v. n. (ver)welken; verbleichen.
fail, v. n. fehlen; scheitern; mißlingen.
failure, s. Versagen n.; Mißerfolg m.
faint, adj. schwach; — v. n. in Ohnmacht fallen.
fair, adj. schön, blond; ehrlich; — adv. schön; gerecht, fair; ehrlich.
faith, s. Glaube m.; Vertrauen n.
faithful, adj. treu.
falcon, s. Falke m.
fall, s. Fall m.; — v. n. fallen; (herab)stürzen; ~ down hinunterfallen; ~ through durchfallen.
false, adj. falsch.
falter, v. n. stocken.
fame, s. Ruhm m.
familiar, adj. bekannt; vertraut.
family, s. Familie f.

famous, adj. berühmt.
fan¹, s. Fächer m.; Ventilator m.
fan², s. (sport) Fanatiker m., Liebhaber m.
fancy, s. Phantasie f.; Laune f.
fantastic, adj. phantastisch.
far, adj. fern; — adv. weit-(hin); by ~ bei weitem; so ~ bisher, bis jetzt.
fare, s. Fahrgeld n., Kost f.
farewell, s. Abschied m.; Lebewohl s.
farmer, s. Bauer m.
farming, s. Landbau m.
farmyard, s. Wirtschaftshof m.
farther, adv. weiter.
fashion, s. Mode f.; Art f.; Weise f.
fashionable, adj. modisch.
fast, adj. & adv. schnell.
fasten, v. a. festmachen, befestigen.
fat, adj. fett, dick; — s. Fett n.
fatal, adj. tödlich.
fate, s. Schicksal n.; Los n.
father, s. Vater m.
father-in-law, s. Schwiegervater m.
fatigue, s. Erschöpfung f.
fault, s. Fehler m.; Schuld f.
faultless, adj. tadellos.
faulty, adj. mangelhaft.
favour, s. Gunst f.; Vorliebe f.; — v. a. begünstigen.
favourite, s. Liebling m.; (sport) Favorit m., -in f.
fear, s. Furcht f.; v. a. & n. (sich) fürchten.
fearful, adj. furchtbar, furchtsam.

feast — **fire-engine**

feast, *s.* Fest *n.*; Festessen *n.*
feat, *s.* Heldentat *f.*; Kunststück *n.*
feather, *s.* Feder *f.*
feature, *s.* Gesichtszug *m.*; Merkmal *n.*; Hauptfilm *m.*
February, *s.* Februar *m.*
federal, *adj.* föderativ.
federation, *s.* Bund *m.*
fee, *s.* Gebühr *f.*; Honorar *n.*
feeble, *adj.* schwach.
feed, *v. a.* füttern.
feel, *v. a. & n.* (sich) fühlen; empfinden.
feeling, *s.* Gefühl *n.*
fellow, *s.* Kerl *m.*; Gefährte *m.*; Mitglied *m.*
female, *adj.* weiblich.
feminine, *adj.* weiblich.
fence, *s.* Zaun *m.*; *(sport)* Hindernis *n.*; Fechtkunst *f.*; — *v. a.* einzäunen; *v. n.* fechten
fencing, *s.* Fechten *n.*; Fechtkunst *f.*
fender, *s.* Stoßfänger *m.*
fern, *s.* Farnkraut *n.*
ferry, *s.* Fähre *f.*
ferry-boat, *s.* Fährboot *n.*
fertile, *adj.* fruchtbar.
fertilizer, *s.* Düngmittel *n.*
festival, *s.* Fest *n.*
fetch, *v. a.* holen.
fever, *s.* Fieber *n.*
few, *adj.* wenige; *a* ~ einige; *the* ~ die wenigen.
fiancé, *s.* Verlobter *m.*
fiancée, *s.* Verlobte *f.*
fibre, *s.* Faser *f.*; Fiber *f.*
fiction, *s.* Romanliteratur *f.*
field, *s.* Feld *n.*; Gebiet *n.*
fierce, *adj.* wild.
fifteen, *adj.* fünfzehn; — *s.* Fünfzehn *f.*
fifth, *adj.* fünfter, fünfte, fünftes; — *s.* (der, die, das) Fünfte; Fünftel *n.*; *(music)* Quinte *f.*
fifty, *adj.* fünfzig; — *s.* Fünfzig *f.*
fig, *s.* Feige *f.*
fight, *s.* Kampf *m.*; — *v. a.* kämpfen.
fighter, *s.* Kämpfer *m.*; Jagdflugzeug *n.*
figure, *s.* Zahl *f.*; Ziffer *f.*; Figur *f.*; Gestalt *f.*
file, *s.* Briefordner *m.*; Reihe *f.*; — *v. a.* ablegen *(letters)*; einreihen ordnen.
fill, *s.* Fülle *f.*; — *v. a.* füllen.
film, *s.* Häutchen *n.*; Film *m.*; Kino *n.*
filter, *s.* Filter *m.*; — *v. a.* filtern; filtrieren.
fin, *s.* Flosse *f.*
final, *adj.* endgültig; — *s.* *(sport)* Schlußrunde *f.*
finally, *adv.* endlich, endgültig.
finance, *s.* Finanzwesen *n.*; Finanzen *pl.*
find, *v. a.* finden; (heraus)finden.
fine[1], *adj. & adv.* fein; elegant; spitz.
fine[2], *s.* Geldstrafe *f.*; — *v. a.* mit einer Geldstrafe belegen.
finger, *s.* Finger *m.*
finger-print, *s.* Fingerabdruck *m.*
finish, *v. a.* (be)enden; vollenden.
Finnish, *adj.* finnisch.
fir, *s.* Tanne *f.*; Fichte *f.*
fire, *s.* Feuer *n.*; — *v. a.* entzünden; heizen; abfeuern.
fire-arm, *s.* Feuerwaffe *f.*
fire-brigade, *s.* Feuerwehr *f.*
fire-engine, *s.* Feuerspritze *f.*

firework(s), s. Feuerwerk n.
firm[1], adj. fest; stark.
firm[2], s. Firma f.
firmness, s. Festigkeit f.
first, adj. erster, erste, erstes; — adv. (zu)erst; eher; erstens; — s. (der, die, das) Erste.
first-rate, adj. & adv. ausgezeichnet, erstklassig.
fish, s. Fisch m.; — v. a. & n. Fische fangen.
fisherman, s. Fischer m.
fishmonger, s. Fischhändler m.
fist, s. Faust f.
fit,[1] adj. passend; geeignet; tauglich; — v. n. passen.
fit[2], s. Anfall m.
five, adj. fünf; — s. Fünf f.; Fünfer m.
fix, v. a. befestigen; herrichten.
flag, s. Flagge f.; Fahne f.
flake, s. Flocke f.
flame, s. Flamme f.
flannel, s. Flannel m.
flap, s. Klaps m.
flare, v.a. flackern.
flash, s. Aufblitzen; v. a. aufleuchten.
flashlight, s. Blitzlicht n.
flat[1], s. Fläche f.; — adj. flach, eben.
flat[2], s. Wohnung f.
flatter, v. a. & n. schmeicheln.
flattery, s. Schmeichelei f.
flavour, s. Geschmack m.
flee, v. a. & n. fliehen.
fleece, s. Vlies n.
fleet, s. Flotte f.
flesh, s. Fleisch n.
flexible, adj. biegsam.
flight, Flucht f.; Flug m.
fling, v. a. werfen.
flirt, v. n. kokettieren, flirten; — s. Kokette f.
float, v. a. schwimmen; schwämmen; v.n. schwimmen; schweben.
flock, s. Herde
flood, s. Flut f.; —v. a. überschwemmen.
flood-light, s. Scheinwerfer m.
floor, s. Fußboden m; Stockwerk n.
flour, s. Mehl n.
flourish, v. n. blühen; gedeihen.
flow, v. n. fließen; strömen; — s. Strom m.
flower, s. Blume f.
flower-bed, s. Blumenbeet n.
flu, s. Grippe f.; Influenza f.
flue, s. Rauchfang m.
fluent, adj. fließend; geläufig.
fluid, s. Flüssigkeit f.; — adj. flüssig.
fluorescent, adj. fluoreszierend; ~ lamp Leuchtstofflampe f.
flush[1], v. n. erröten.
flush[2], adj. & adv. eben.
flute, s. Flöte f.
flutter, s. Flatter n.; Erregung f.; — v. n. flattern; v. a. aufregen.
fly[1], v. n. fliegen; fliehen.
fly[2], s. Fliege f.
foam, s. Schaum m.; — v. n. schäumen.
focus, s. Brennpunkt m.
fodder, s. Futter n.
fog, s. Nebel m.
fold, v. a. falten; schließen.
foliage, s. Laubwerk n.
folk, s. Leute f. pl.
follow, v. a & n. (nach)folgen; verfolgen.
following, adj. folgender, folgende, folgendes.
folly, s. Torheit f.
fond, adj. zärtlich; be ~

food   58.   **fracture**

of gern haben.
food, *s.* Speise *f.;* Nährstoff *m.;* Lebensmittel *n. pl.*
fool, *s.* Narr *m.;* Tor *m.*
foolish, *adj.* töricht.
foot, *s.* Fuß *m.*
football, *s.* Fußball *m.*
foot-brake, *s.* Fußbremse *f.*
foot-note, *s.* Fußnote *f.*
footstep, *s.* Schritt *m.*
for, *prep.* von; um; zu; für; *conj.* denn, weil.
forbidden, *adj.* verboten.
force, *s.* Kraft *f.;* Gewalt *f.;* Gültigkeit *f.;* — *v. a.* zwingen.
forearm, *s.* Unterarm *m.*
forecast, *v.a.* vorhersagen; — *s.* Vorhersage *f.*
forefinger, *s.* Zeigefinger *m.*
foreground, *s.* Vordergrund *m.*
forehead, *s.* Stirn *f.*
foreign, *adj.* fremd; ausländisch.
foreigner, *s.* Ausländer *m.;* -in *f.*
foremost, *adj.* vorderster, vorderste, vorderstes; — *adv.* zuerst.
foresee, *v. a.* voraussehen.
forest, *s.* Wald *m.*
foretell, *v. a.* vorhersagen.
foreword, *s.* Vorwort *n.*
forge, *v. a.* schmieden.
forgery, *s.* Fälschung *f.*
forg, *v. a. & n.* vergessen.
forgetful, *adj.* vergeßlich.
forgive, *v. a. & n.* verzeihen.
fork, *s.* Gabel *f.;* *v. a. & n.* (sich) gabeln.
form, *s.* Form *f.;* Gestalt *f.,* Figur *f.;* Formular *n.;* (Schul) Klasse *f.;* — *v. a. & n.* (sich) formen.
formal, *adj.* formal.

formality, *s.* Formalität *f.*
former, *adv.* früher(er), vormaliger.
formerly, *adv.* ehemals; früher.
formula, *s.* Formel *f.*
forsake, *v. a.* verlassen.
fortieth, *s. adj.* vierzigster.
fortification, *s.* Befestigung *f.*
fortnight, *s.* vierzehn Tage.
fortress, *s.* Festung *f.*
fortunate, *adj.* glücklich.
fortune, *s.* Vermögen *n.;* — Glück *n.*
forty, *s.* Vierzig *f.;* — *adj.* vierzig.
forward, *adv.* vorwärts; nach vorn; — *adj.* vorwärts; — *s. (sport)* Stürmer *m.;* — *v. a.* spedieren; nachsenden.
forwarding, *s.* Beförderung *f.*
forwards, *adv. see* forward *adv.*
foul, *adj.* schmutzig; verderbt; *(sport)* foul; unfair.
found, *v. a.* gründen; stiften.
foundation, *s.* Gründung *f.;* Fundament *n.*
founder, *s.* Gründer *m.*
fountain, *s.* Quelle *f.;* Springbrunnen *m.*
fountain-pen, *s.* Füllfeder *f.*
four, *adj.* vier; — *s.* Vier *f.*
fourteen, *s.* Vierzehn *f.;* — *adj.* vierzehn.
fourth, *adj.* vierter, vierte viertes.
fowl, *s.* Geflügel *n.*
fox, *s.* Fuchs *m.*
fraction, *s.* Bruchteil *m.;* Bruch *m.*
fracture, *s.* Knochenbruch *m.*

fragile *adj.* gebrechlich; zerbrechlich.
fragment, *s.* Fragment *n.*; Bruchstück *m.*
fragrant, *adj.* wohlriechend; duftig.
frame, *s.* Rahmen *m.*; Gestell *n.*
framework, *s.* Rahmen *m.*; *fig.* System *n.*
frank, *adj.* offen.
fraud, *s.* Betrug *m.*; Schwindel *m.*
free, *adj.* frei; kostenfrei; — *v. a.* befreien.
freedom, *s.* Freiheit *f.*
freeze, *v. n.* (ge)frieren; *v. a.* gefrieren machen.
freight, *s.* Fracht *f.*
French, *adj.* französich, — *s.* Franzosen *pl.*
French-bean, *s.* grüne Bohnen *pl.*
Frenchman, *s.* Franzose *m.*
Frenchwoman, *s.* Französin *f.*
frequent, *adj.* häufig; — *v. a.* frequentieren.
fresh, *adj.* frisch; neu.
friar, *s.* Mönch *m.*
fricassee, *s.* Frikassee *n.*
friction, *s.* Reibung *f.*; Friktion *f.*
Friday, *s.* Freitag *m.*
fridge, *s.* Kühlschrank *m.*
friend, *s.* Freund *m.*; -in *f.*
friendship *s.* Freundschaft *f.*
fright, *s.* Schreck(en) *m.*
frighten, *v. a.* (er)schrecken.
frock, *s.* Kleid *n.*
frog, *s.* Frosch *m.*
frolic, *s.* Scherz *m.*; — *v. n.* ausgelassen sein.
from, *prep.* von, aus; wegen.
front, *s.* Fasade *f.*; Front *f.* — *adj.* frontal; — *adv.* to the ~ nach vorne, voraus.
front-door, *s.* Haustür *f.*
frontier, *s.* Grenze *f.*
frost, *s.* Frost *m.*
frown, *v. n.* die Stirn in Falten ziehen.
frozen, *adj.* (ein)gefroren.
fruit, *s.* Obst *n.*
fruit-tree, *s.* Obstbaum *m.*
frustrate, *v. a.* vereiteln; enttäuschen.
fry, *v. a. & n.* braten.
frying-pan, *s.* Bratpfanne *f.*
fuel, *s.* Brennstoff *m.*; Treibstoff *m.*;
fulfil, *v. a.* erfüllen; vollbringen.
full, *adj.* voll; ganz; — *s.* (das) Ganze; *in* ~, *to the* ~ vollständig.
fully, *adj.* völlig.
fume, *s.* Dampf *m.*; Dunst *m.*
fun, *s.* Scherz *m.*, Spaß *m.*
function, *s.* Funktion *f.*; Tätigkeit *f.*
fund, *s.* Kapital *n.*; Fonds *m.*; Geldmittel *n. pl.*
fundamental, *adj.* grundlegend, fundamental.
funeral, *s.* Begräbnis *n.*
funnel, *s.* Trichter *m.*; *(ship)* Schornstein *m.*
funny, *adj.* spaßhaft; sonderbar.
fur, *s.* Pelz *m.*; Fell *n.*
furnace, *s.* Schmelzofen *m.*
furnish, *v. a.* versorgen; ausstatten.
furniture, *s.* Möbel *pl.*
furrow, *s.* Ackerfurche *f.*; Rille *f.*
further, *adv. & adj.* ferner, weiter; — *v. a.* fördern, unterstützen.
furthermore, *adv.* ferner; außerdem.
fury, *s.* Zorn *m.*; Wut *f.*

fuss — **giant**

fuss, s. Getue n.
future, s. Zukunft; — adj. zukünftig.

G

gain, s. Gewinn m.; — v. a. gewinnen.
gala, — s. Festlichkeit f.
gale, s. Sturm(wind)
gall, s. Galle f.
gallant, adj. tapfer, galant.
gallery, s. Galerie f.
gallon, s. Gallone f.
gallop, s. Galopp m.; — v. n. galoppieren.
gamble, v. n. um Geld spielen.
game, s. Spaß m.; Spiel n.; Wildbret n.
gamekeeper, s. Wildhüter m.
gang, s. Gruppe f.; Bande f.
gangway, s. Passage f.; Gang m.
gaol see jail
gap, s. Kluft f.; Spalt m.; Lücke f.
gape, v. n. starren, gaffen.
garage, s. Reparaturwerkstatt f.; Garage f.
garden, s. Garten m.
garment, s. Kleidungsstück n.
garnish, v. a. garnieren; — s. Garnierung f.
garter, s. Strumpfband n.
gas, s. Gas n.
gasholder, s. Gasbehälter m.
gasp, v. n. keuchen.
gate, s. Tor n.
gateway, s. Torweg m.
gather, v. a. sammeln; pflücken; (pers.) versammeln; v. n. sich (ver)sammeln.
gathering, s. Versammlung f.
gauge, v. a. abmessen, abschätzen; — s. Eichmaß n.; Kaliber n.; (railway) Spurweite f.
gay, adj. lustig, heiter; lebhaft; bunt.
gear, s. Getriebe n.; Gang m.; Gerät n.
general, adj. allgemein; — s. General m.
generation, s. Generation f.
generator, s. Generator m.
generosity, s. Großmut f.; Freigiebigkeit f.
generous, adj. freigiebig; großzügig.
genial, adj. freundlich, günstig.
genius, s. Genie n.
gentle, adj. sanft; zahm; edel, vornehm.
gentleman, s. Herr m.
genuine, adj. echt.
geographical, adj. geographisch.
geography, s. Geographie f.
geology, s. Geologie f.
geometric, adj. geometrisch.
geometry, s. Geometrie f.
germ, s. Keim m.
German, adj. deutsch.; — s. Deutscher m.; Deutsche f.
gesticulate, v. n. gestikulieren.
get, v. a. bekommen; erhalten; erwerben; v. n. gelangen; sich begeben; werden; ~ back zurückkommen; ~ in einsteigen; ~ off davonkommen; absteigen; ~ on vorwärtskommen; ~ out aussteigen; ~ up aufstehen.
geyser, s. Badeofen m.
ghost, s. Gespenst n.
giant, s. Riese m.

gift   61.   **graduate**

gift, s. Gabe f.; Talent n.;
gill, s. Kieme f.
gin, s. Gin m.
giraffe, s. Giraffe f.
girdle, s. Gürtel m.
girl, s. Mädchen n.
give, v. a. geben; schenken; übergeben; ~ *up* aufgeben; v. n. ~ *(in)* nachgeben.
glacier, s. Gletscher m.
glad, adj. froh.
glance, v. n. blicken; — s. (schneller) Blick.
glare, v. n. strahlen; blenden; v. a. (an)starren; — s. starrer Blick.
glass, s. Glas n.; Trinkglas n.; *(pair of)* ~es pl. Brille f.
gleam, s. Schimmer m.; — v. n. schimmern.
glide, v. n. gleiten.
glider, s. Segelflugzeug n.
glimmer, v. n. glimmern; — s. Glimmen n.; Schimmer m.
glimpse, s. flüchtiger Blick.
glitter, v. n. funkeln.
gloomy, adj. düster;
glorious, adj. herrlich; großartig.
glory, s. Ruhm m., Glorie f.
glove, s. Handschuh m.
glow, v. n. glühen; — s. Glühen n.; Glut f.
glue, s. Leim m.; — v. a. (zusammen-)kleben.
gnaw, v. a. & n. (ab)nagen; *fig.* quälen.
go, v. n. gehen; fahren; abreisen; arbeiten; sich erstrecken; ~ *on* weitergehen; ~ *over* überprüfen; ~ *through* durchsehen; ~ *without* auskommen ohne.

goal, s. Ziel n.; Tor n.
goal-keeper, s. Tormann m.
goat, s. Ziege f.
God, s. Gott m.
god-child, s. Patenkind n.
god-father, s. Pate m.
god-mother, s. Patin f.; Patentante f.
goggles, s. pl. Schutzbrille f.
gold, s. Gold n.
golden, adj. golden; *fig.* kostbar.
golf, s. Golf(spiel) n.
good, adj. gut; recht; — s. (das) Gute; *goods* pl. Waren f. pl.; Güter n.pl.
good-by, s. Lebewohl n.
good-looking, adj. gutaussehend.
goodness, s. Güte f.
goodwill, s. Wohlwollen n.; Firmenwert m.
goose, s. Gans f.
gooseberry, s. Stachelbeere f.
gospel, s. Evangelium n
gossip, s. Klatsch m.; — v. a. & n. klatschen.
Gothic, adj. gotisch; — s. Gotik f.; Fraktur f.; deutsche Schrift.
govern, v. a. & n. regieren; regeln.
government, s. Regierung f.
governor, s. Gouverneur m.; Herrscher m.
gown, s. Talar m.; Frauenkleid n.
grace, s. Anmut f.; Gnade f.; Gunst f.
gracious, adj. gnädig.
grade, s. Grad m.; — v. a. & n. sortieren.
gradual, adj. allmählich.
graduate, v. n. einen akademischen Grad erlangen. — v. a.

abstufen, in Grade einteilen.
grain, s. Getreidekorn n.; Körnchen n.
grammar, s. Grammatik f.
grammar-school, s. Oberschule f., Gymnasium n.
gramme, s. Gramm n.
gramophone, s. Grammophon n.; ~ record Schallplatte f.
grand, adj. großartig; grandios.
grandchild, s. Enkel m.; Enkelin f.
granddaughter, s. Enkelin f.; Enkeltochter f.
grandfather, s. Großvater m.
grandmother, s. Großmutter f.
grandson, s. Enkel m.
grand-stand, s. Haupttribune f.
granite, s. Granit m.
grant, v. a. bewilligen, gewähren; geben; — s. Bewilligung f.; Gewährung f.
grape, s. Traube f.
grape-fruit, s. Pampelmuse f.
graph, s. Diagramm n.
graphic, adj. graphisch; — ~s s.pl. Graphik f.; graphische Kunst.
grasp, v. a. packen; fig. begreifen; — s. fig. Macht f.; Fassungskraft f.
grass, s. Gras n.
grasshopper, s. Heuschrecke f.
grate, v. a. (zer)reiben; s. Gitter n.
grateful, adj. dankbar.
gratitude, s. Dankbarkeit f.

grave[1], s. Grab n.
grave[2], adj. ernst.
gravel, s. Kies m.
gravy, s. Bratensaft n.
gray, adj. grau.
graze, v.n. weiden.
grease, s. Fett n.; Schmiere f.; — v. a. schmieren.
great, adj. groß, beträchtlich; erhaben.
greatly, adv. sehr; höchst; überaus.
greed, s. Gier f.
Greek, s. Grieche m.; Griechin f.; — adj. griechisch.
green, adj. grün; frisch; — s. Dorfplatz m.
greengrocer, s. Obst- und Gemüsehändler m.
greenhouse, s. Treibhaus n.
greet, v. a. (be)grüßen.
greeting, s. Gruß m.
grey, adj. grau.
grief, s. Kummer m.
grievance, s. Beschwerde f.; Groll m.
grill, s. Grill m.; Rostbraten m.; — v a. & n. grillen, rösten.
grim, adj. grimmig.
grin, v. n. & a. grinsen; — s. Grinsen n.
grind, v. a. mahlen.
grip, s. Griff m.; — v. a. ergreifen.
groan, v. n. stöhnen.
grocer, s. Gemischtwarenhändler m.; Kolonialwarenhändler m.
grocery, s. Kolonialwarenhandel m.
groove, s. Rinne f.
gross, adj. brutto, Brutto-; dick; roh; ungeheuerlich; — s. Gros n.
ground, v. a. gründen; — s. Erdboden m.; Grund m.; ~s p.

group — **handy**

Sportplatz *m.*
group, *s.* Gruppe *f.;* — *v. a. & n.* (sich) gruppieren.
grove, *s* Hain *m.*
grow, *v. n.* wachsen; *fig.* zunehmen; werden; *v. a.* pflanzen; kultivieren.
growl, *s.* Knurren *n.;* — *v. n.* knurren;
grown-up, *adj.* erwachsen.
growth, *s.* Wachsen *n.,* Wuchs *m.*
grudge, *v. a.* mißgönnen; — *s.* Widerwille *m.;* Groll *m.*
grumble, *v. n. & a.* brummen; — *s.* Murren *n.;* Brummen *n.*
grunt, *v. n. & a.* grunzen; — *s.* Grunzen *n.*
guarantee, *s.* Bürgschaft *f.;* Garantie *f.;* — *v. a.* bürgen für; garantieren.
guard, *s.* Wache *f.;* Wächter *m.;* Schaffner *m.;* — *v. a.* bewachen; schützen; *v. n.* sich hüten.
guardian, *s.* Vormund *m.*
guess, *v. n.* (herum)raten; *v. a.* (ab)schätzen; (er)raten; — *s.* Vermutung *f.*
guest, *s.* Gast *m.*
guide, *v. a.* führen; lenken; *fig.* anleiten; — *s.* Führer *m.;* Leitfaden *m.*
guide-book, *s.* Reisehandbuch *n.*
guided, *adj.* (fern)gelenkt.
guilt, *s.* Schuld *f.*
guilty, *adj.* schuldig.
guitar, *s.* Gitarre *f.*
gull, *s.* Möwe *f.*
gum¹, *s.* Gummi *n.*
gum², *s.* Zahnfleisch *n.*

gun, *s.* Kanone *f.;* Geschütz *n.;* Flinte *f.*
gush, *v. n.* strömen.
gutter, *s.* Gosse *f.;* Rinne *f.*
gymnasium, *s.* Turnhalle *f.*
gymnastics, *s. pl.* Gymnastik *f.*

H

haberdashery, *s.* Kurzwarengeschäft *n.*
habit, *s.* Gewohnheit *f.*
hail, *s.* Hagel *m.;* — *v. n.* hageln.
hair, *s.* Haar *n.*
hairdresser, *s.* Friseur *m.*
half, *adj.* halb; — *s.* Hälfte *f.; (sport)* Spielhäfte *f.;* Halbzeit *f.*
half-way, *adj. & adv.* auf halbem Wege.
hall, *s.* Halle *f.;* Saal *m.;* Flur *m.*
halt, *s.* Halt *m.;* — *v. n.* anhalten; *v. a.* anhalten lassen.
ham, *s.* Schinken *m.*
hammer, *s.* Hammer *m.*
hand, *s.* Hand *f.;* Handschrift *f.;* Zeiger *m.*
handbag, *s.* Handtasche *f.*
handbook, *s.* Handbuch *n.*
handkerchief, *s.* Taschentuch *n.*
handle, *s.* Griff *m.,* Stiel *m.;* — *v. a.* anfassen; handhaben; behandeln.
hand-made, *adj.* handgemacht.
handsome, *adj.* hübsch.
handwriting, *s.* Handschrift *f.*
handy, *adj.* geschickt; leicht zu handhaben.

hang — **helicopter**

hang, *v. a.* aufhängen.
hanger, *s.* Kleiderbügel *m.;* Aufhänger *m.*
happen, *v. n.* geschehen, sich ereignen, passieren; sich zufällig ergeben.
happiness, *s.* Glück *n.*
happy, *adj.* glücklich.
harbour, *s.* Hafen *m.;* Zufluchtsort *m.;* — *v. a.* beherbergen.
hard, *adj.* hart; schwer; tüchtig; — *adv.* stark; mit Mühe; ∼ up in Not.
hardly, *adv.* kaum.
hardware, *s.* Eisenwaren *f. pl.*
harm, *s.* Schaden *m.;* Leid *n.;* Übel *n.;* — *v.a.* beschädigen; schaden.
harmful, *adj.* schädlich.
harmony, *s.* Harmonie *f.*
harness, *s.* Harnisch *m.*
harp, *s.* Harfe *f.*
harsh, *adj.* herb; grell; schroff.
harvest, *s.* Ernte *f.;* Ertrag *m.*
haste, *s.* Eile *f.;* Hast *f.*
hasten, *v. n.* sich beeilen, eilen.
hat, *s.* Hut *m.*
hatred, *s.* Haß *m.*
haul, *s.* Ziehen *n.;* Schleppen *n.;* — *v.a.* ziehen.
haulage, *s.* Transport *m.;* Transportkosten *pl.*
have, *v.a.* haben; bekommen; *(of meals)* einnehmen; lassen (+ *inf.*)
haversack, *s.* Rucksack *m.*
hawk, *s.* Falke *m.*
hay, *s.* Heu *n.*
hazard, *s.* Zufall *m.;* Risiko *n.;* — *v.a.* riskieren; wagen.
hazy, *adj.* dunstig; nebelhaft.
he, *pron.* er.
head, *v. a.* anführen, leiten; *(sport)* köpfen; — *s.* Kopf *m.;* Haupt *n.;* Leiter *m.;* per ∼ pro Kopf.
headache, *s.* Kopfweh *n.*
heading, *s.* Überschrift *f.*
headlight, *s.* Scheinwerfer *m.*
headline, *s.* Schlagzeile *f.*
headmaster, *s.* Schuldirektor *m.*
headquarters, *s. pl.* Hauptquartier *n.;* Zentrale *f.*
heal, *v. a. & n.* heilen.
health, *s.* Gesundheit *f.*
healthy, *adj.* gesund.
heap, *s.* Haufe(n) *m.;* Menge *f.;* — *v. a.* (auf)häufen.
hear, *v. a. & n.* hören; verhören.
heart, *s.* Herz *n.;* Kern *m.;* by ∼ auswendig.
hearth, *s.* Herd *m.*
hearty, *adj.* herzlich.
heat, *s.* Hitze *f.;* — *v. a.* erhitzen; heiß machen; *v. n.* sich erhitzen.
heating, *s.* Heizung *f.*
heave, *v.a.* hochheben; schwellen; *v.n.* sich heben und senken.
heaven, *s.* Himmel *m.*
heavy, *adj.* schwer; heftig.
hedge, *s.* Hecke *f.*
hedgehog, *s.* Igel *m.*
heed, *s.* Aufmerksamkeit *f.;* Sorgfalt *f.*
heedless, *adj.* unachtsam.
heel, *s.* Ferse *f.;* Absatz *m.*
height, *s.* Höhe *f.;* Gipfel *m.*
heir, *s.* Erbe *m.*
heiress, *s.* Erbin *f.*
helicopter, *s.* Helikopter *m.*

hell, s. Hölle f.
hello, int. hallo!
helm, s. Ruder n.; Steuer n.
helmet, s. Helm m.
help, s. Hilfe f. Dienstpersonal n.; — v. a. & n. helfen.
helpful, adj. behilflich; nützlich.
helping, s. Portion f.
hem, s. Kleidersaum m.
hen, s. Henne f.; Huhn n.
hence, adv. von hier, folglich, daher.
her, pron. sie; ihr; — adj. ihr, ihre.
herb, s. Kraut n.
herd, s. Herde f.
here, adj. & adv. hier; hierher; ~ and there hier und da; hie und da.
heritage, s. Erbschaft f.
hero, s. Held m.
heroic, adj. heldenhaft, heroisch.
heroine, s. Heldin f.
herring, s. Hering m.
hers, pron. ihr, (der, die, das) ihre.
herself, pron. sie selbst; ihr selbst; sich selbst.
hesitate, v.n. zaudern.
hew, v. a. & n. hauen; hacken.
hiccough, hiccup, s. Schlucken m.
hide, v. a. verbergen; v.n. sich verstecken.
hideous, adj. scheußlich; gräßlich.
high, adj. hoch; — adv. high; in die Höhe.
highness, s. Höhe f.
highroad, highway, s. Landstraße f.
hike, v. n. wandern.
hill, s. Hügel m.
him, pron. he; ihn; ihm; sich.

himself, pron. sich; sich selbst.
hinder, v. a. aufhalten; hindern; v. r. hinderlich sein.
hinge, s. Scharnier n.; Gelenk n.; — v. n. ~ upon fig. sich drehen um.
hint, s. Wink m.; Anspielung f.; v. a. andeuten; v. n. eine Andeutung machen.
hip, s. Hüfte f.
hire, v. a. mieten; anstellen; ~ out vermieten; — s. Miete f.
his, adj. sein, seine; — pron. seiner, seine, seines; (der, die, das) seine.
hiss, v.n. zischen; v.a. & n. (aus)pfeifen.
historic, adj. historisch, geschichtlich.
history, s. Geschichte f.
hit, s. Schlag m.; Hieb m.; Treffer m.; Schlager m.; — v. a. einen Schlag versetzen; treffen.
hitch-hike, v.n. per Anhalter fahren.
hive, s. Bienenkorb m.; Bienenschwarm m.
hoard, s. Vorrat m.; — v.a. aufhäufen.
hoarse, adj. heiser.
hobby, s. fig. Steckenpferd. n; Hobby n.; Liebhaberei f.
hockey, s. Hockey n.
hoe, s. Hacke f.
hog, s. Schwein n.
hoist, s. Aufzug m.; — v.a. hochziehen; (flag) hissen.
hold, s. Halt m.; Griff m.; Macht f.; Einfluß m.; — v. a. (fest)halten; v. n. halten.
holder, s. Besitzer m., -in

hole *f.*
hole, *s.* Loch *n.*
holiday, *s.* Feiertag *m.;* ~s *pl.* Ferien *pl.;* Urlaub *m.*
hollow, *adj.* hohl; leer; — *s.* Höhle *f.*
holy, *adj.* heilig.
home, *s.* Heim *n.;* Heimat *f.;* Haus *n.;* Wohnung *f.;* — *adv.* heim; nach Hause; zu Hause; daheim.
homely, *adj.* einfach; reizlos.
homesickness, *s.* Heimweh *n.*
homeward(s), *adv.* heimwärts, nach Hause.
honest, *adj.* ehrlich.
honey, *s.* Honig *m.*
honeycomb, *s.* Honigwabe *f.*
honeymoon, *s.* Flitterwochen *f. pl.*
honour, *s.* Ehre *f.;* Achtung *f.;* Würde *f.;* Auszeichnung *f.;* — *v. a.* verehren, respektieren; beehren.
hood, *s.* Kapuze *f.;* Motorhaube *f.*
hoof, *s.* Huf *m.*
hook, *s.* Haken *m.*
hoop, *s.* Reif(en) *m.*
hoot, *s.* Getute *n.;* — *v.n.* heulen; tuten;
hop, *v. a. & n.* hüpfen.
hope, *s.* Hoffnung *f.;* — *v. a. & n.* hoffen.
hopeful, *adj.* hoffnungsvoll.
horizon, *s.* Horizont *m.*
horizontal, *adj.* waagerecht.
horn, *s.* Horn *n.*
horrible, *adj.* schrecklich; entsetzlich.
horse, *s.* Pferd *n.*
horseback, — *adv.* zu Pferde.
horseman, *s.* Reiter *m.*

horseshoe, *s.* Hufeisen *n.*
hose, *s.* Schlauch *m.;* Strümpfe *pl.*
hospital, *s.* Krankenhaus *n.*
hospitality, *s.* Gastfreundschaft *f.*
host, *s.* Wirt *m.;* Gastgeber *m.*
hostel, *s.* Herberge *f.;* Studentenwohnhaus *n.*
hostess, *s.* Wirtin *f.;* Gastgeberin *f.*
hostile, *adj.* feindlich (gesinnt).
hostility, *s.* Feindseligkeit *f.*
hot, *adj.* heiß, scharf; heftig; eifrig.
hotel, *s.* Hotel *n.*
hour, *s.* Stunde *f.*
house, *s.* Haus *n.*
household, *s.* Haushalt *m.*
housekeeper, *s.* Haushälterin *f.*
housewife, *s.* Hausfrau *f.*
how, *adv.* wie?, wieso?.
however, *adv.* wie auch (immer); wenn auch noch so; jedoch.
howl, *v. n. & a.* heulen; — *s.* Heulen *n.;*
hue[1]**,** *s.* Farbe *f.;* Ton *m.*
hue[2]**,** *s.* Geschrei *n.*
hug *v. a.* umarmen.
huge, *adj.* riesig; ungeheuer; enorm.
hullo, *int.* hallo!
hum, *v. n. & a.* summen.
human, *adj.* menschlich.
humanity, *s.* Menschheit *f.*
humble, *adj.* demütig; bescheiden; — *v. a.* demütigen.
humorous, *adj.* humoristisch; spaßig.
humour, *s.* Laune *f.;* Stimmung *f.;* Humor *m.*

hundred, *adj.* hundert;
— *s.* Hundert *n.*

hundredth, *adj.* hundertster, hundertste, hundertstes.

hundredweight, *s.* Zentner *m.*

Hungarian, *adj.* ungarisch; — *s.* Ungar *m.*, -in *f.*

hunger, *s.* Hunger *m.;* — *v. n.* hungern; Hunger haben.

hungry, *adj.* hungrig.

hunt, *s.* Jagd *f.;* Jagdgebiet *n.;* — *v. a.* & *n.* jagen.

hunter, *s.* Jäger *m.*

hurry, *v. a.* antreiben; *v. n.* eilen; sich beeilen; — *s.* Eile *f.;* Hast *f.*

hurt, *v. a. fig.* verletzen; weh tun; *v. n.* weh tun; schmerzen.

husband, *s.* Ehemann *m.;* Gatte *m.*

hush, *s.* Stille *f.;* — *v. a.* ∼ up *fig.* vertuschen.

husk, *s.* Hülse *f.;* — *v. a.* enthülsen.

hut, *s.* Hütte *f.*

hydrogen, *s.* Wasserstoff *m.*

hygiene, *s.* Hygiene *f.;* Gesundheitspflege *f.*

hymn, *s.* Hymne *f.;* Kirchenlied *n.*

hypnotize, *v. a.* hypnotisieren.

hypocrisy, *s.* Heuchelei *f.*

I

I, *pron.* ich; — *s.* Ich *n.*

ice, *s.* Eis *n.*

ice-cream, *s.* Speiseeis *n.*

idea, *s.* Idee *f.;* Begriff *m.*

ideal, *adj.* ideell; ideal; — *s.* Musterbild *n.*

identical, *adj.* identisch.

identity, *s.* Identität *f.;* ∼ *card* Personalausweis *m.*

idle, *adj.* müßig; — *v.n.* faulenzen.

if, *conj.* wenn, falls, im Falle, daß; ob.

ignition, *s.* Entzündung *f.;* Zündung *f.*

ignorance, *s.* Unwissenheit *f.*

ignorant, *adj.* unwissend.

ignore, *v. a.* ignorieren; nicht beachten.

ill, *adj.* & *adv.* schlecht, übel; krank; unwohl.

illegal, *adj.* ungesetzlich.

illegitimate, *adj.* illegitim; unrecht; unehelich.

illness, *s.* Krankheit *f.*

illusion, *s.* Illusion *f.*

illustrate, *v. a.* illustrieren; erläutern.

illustration, *s.* Illustration *f.;* Erläuterung *f.*

image, *s.* Bild *n.;* Ebenbild *n.*

imagination, *s.* Phantasie *f.;* Einbildungskraft *f.*

imagine, *v. a.* & *n.* sich vorstellen; sich denken.

imitate, *v. a.* nachahmen; imitieren.

immediate, *adj.* unmittelbar; sofort; augenblicklich.

immense, *adj.* unermeßlich; riesig; ungeheuer.

immigrant, *s.* Immigrant *m.*, -in *f.;* Einwanderer *m.*

immigration, *s.* Immigration *f.;* ∼ *officer*, Landungskommissar *m.*

immoral, *adj.* unmoralisch; unsittlich.

immortal, *adj.* unsterblich.

impatient, *adj.* ungedul-

impediment 68. **indiscretion**

dig.
impediment, s. Hindernis n.
impel, v. a. zwingen, bewegen.
imperfect, adj. unvollkommen; mangelhaft.
imperial, adj. kaiserlich.
impertinent, adj. unverschämt.
implement, s. Gerät n.
implication, s. Verwickelung f.
implore, v. a. & n. dringend bitten; anflehen.
imply, v. a. einbegreifen.
import, v. a. importieren, einführen; — s. Import m., Einfuhr f.; Bedeutung f.
important, adj. wichtig.
importer, s. Importeur m.
impose, v. a. auferlegen.
impossible, adj. unmöglich.
impression, s. Eindruck m.; Abdruck m.; Auflage f.
imprison, v. a. einkerkern; verhaften.
improbable, adj. unwahrscheinlich.
improper, adj. ungeeignet; unschicklich.
improve, v. a. verbessern; veredeln; ausnutzen.
improvement, s. Verbesserung f.; Ausnutzung f.; Fortschritt m.
impulse, s. Impuls m.; Antrieb m.
in, prep. in; innerhalb; an; bei; auf; — adv. drin(nen).
inadequate, adj. unzulänglich.
incapable, adj. unfähig.
incense, s. Weihrauch m.
inch, s. Zoll m. (2,54 cm).
incident, s. Zwischenfall m.
incidentally, adv. nebenbei; zufällig.
incline, v. n. sich neigen; — s. Abhang m.
include, v. a. einschließen; enthalten.
inclusive, adj. ~ (of) einschließend; inklusive.
income, s. Einkommen n.
income-tax, s. Einkommensteuer f.
incompatible, adj. unvereinbar.
incompetent, adj. unfähig; unbefugt.
inconsistent, adj. unvereinbar.
inconvenient, adj. ungelegen; unbequem.
increase, v. n. wachsen; zunehmen; — s. Zuwachs m.
incredible, adj. unglaublich.
incurable, adj. unheilbar.
indebted, adj. verschuldet; fig. verpflichtet.
indeed, adv. in der Tat, tatsächlich, wirklich.
independent, adj. unabhängig.
index, s. Zeiger m.; Index m.; Verzeichnis n.; Kennziffer f.; ~ finger Zeigefinger m.
Indian, adj. indisch; (red) indianisch; — s. Inder m., -in f.; (red) Indianer m., -in f.
india-rubber, s. Radiergummi m.
indicate, v. a. anzeigen; andeuten.
indicator, s. Zeiger m.; Indikator m.
indifferent, adj. gleichgültig.
indigestion, s. Verdauungsstörung f.
indignant, adj. entrüstet.
indirect, adj. indirekt.
indiscretion, s. Unbedachtsamkeit; Indis-

indispensable — **inside**

kretion *f.*
indispensable, *adj.* unentbehrlich; *(pers.)* unabkömmlich.
individual, *adj.* persönlich, individuell; — *s.* Individuum *n.*
indoor, *adj.* für das Haus; Zimmer-.; — *adv. see* **indoors.**
indoors, *adv.* im Hause; zu Hause.
induce, *v. a.* veranlassen, bewegen; (künstlich) hervorrufen; induzieren.
indulge, *v. a.* nachsichtig sein; verwöhnen; *v. n.* schwelgen (in); sich hingeben.
industrial, *adj.* industriell, gewerbetreibend.
industry, *s.* Industrie *f.;* Gewerbe *n.;* Fleiß *m.*
inestimable, *adj.* unschätzbar.
inevitable, *adj.* unvermeidlich.
inexpensive, *adj.* billig.
inexplicable, *adj.* unerklärlich.
infallible, *adj.* unfehlbar.
infant, *s.* Säugling *n.;* Kleinkind *n.*
infection, *s.* Infektion *f.;* Ansteckung *f.*
infer, *v. a. & n.* schließen, folgern.
inferior, *adj.* gering, minderwertig; untergeordnet.
infinitive, *s.* Infinitiv *m.*
infirm, *adj.* schwach, schwächlich.
infirmary, *s.* Krankenhaus *n.*
inflame, *v. a. & n.* entflammen.
inflict, *v. a.* zufügen, auferlegen.
influenza, *s.* Grippe *f.;*

Influenza *f.*
inform, *v. a.* benachrichtigen; mitteilen.
information, *s.* Information *f.*
ingenious, *adj.* geistreich; erfinderisch.
inhabit, *v. a.* bewohnen.
inhabitant, *s.* Bewohner *m.*, -in *f.*
inherit, *v. a.* erben.
initial, — *s.* Anfangsbuchstabe *m.*
initiative, *adj.* einleitend; — *s.* Initiative *f.*
injection, *s.* Einspritzung *f.*
injure, *v. a.* verletzen, verwunden.
injury, *s.* Schaden *m.;* Verletzung *f.*
injustice, *s.* Unrecht *n.;* Ungerechtigkeit *f.*
ink, *s.* Tinte *f.*
inland, *s.* Binnenland *n.;* — *adj.* binnenländisch.
inn, *s.* Gasthaus *n.;* Wirtshaus *n.*
inner, *adj.* inner; innerlich;
innocent, *adj.* unschuldig.
innumerable, *adj.* unzählbar.
inoculate, *v. a.* impfen.
inquire, *v. a. & n.* sich erkundigen (nach).
inquiry, *s.* Nachfrage *f.;* Untersuchung *f.*
insane, *adj.* geisteskrank.
inscription, *s.* Aufschrift *f.*
insect, *s.* Insekt *n.*
insensible, *adj.* unempfindlich.
inseparable, *adj.* untrennbar; unzertrennlich.
insert, *v. a.* einfügen; inserieren; — *s.* Einlage *f.*
inside, *s.* Innere *n.; f.;* — *adj.* inner; ~ *left (sport)* Halblinke *m.;* ~ *right (sport)* Halb-

insignificant | **70.** | **into**

rechte *m*.
insignificant, *adj.* unbedeutend.
insist, *v. n.* bestehen (auf); beharren (auf).
inspect, *v. a.* besichtigen; nachsehen; inspizieren.
inspector, *s.* Inspektor *m*.
inspiration, *s.* Inspiration *f.*; Eingebung *f*.
inspire, *v. a.* begeistern.
install, *v. a.* installieren, aufstellen, einsetzen.
instalment, *s.* Teilzahlung *f.*; Rate *f*.
instance, *s.* Beispiel *n.*; *for* ~ zum Beispiel.
instant, *adj.* dringend; ~ *coffee* Pulverkaffee; — *s.* Augenblick *m.*;
instead, *adv.* ~ *of* an (der) Stelle von; (an)statt.
instinct, *s.* Instinkt *m*.
institute, — *s.* (gelehrte) Gesellschaft; Institut *n.*; Akademie *f*.
institution, *s.* Stiftung *f.*; Errichtung *f*.
instruct, *v. a.* belehren; unterrichten.
instruction, *s.* Belehrung *f.*; Unterricht *m*.
instrument, *s.* Instrument *n.*; Werkzeug *n.*; Urkunde *f*.
insufficient, *adj.* unzulänglich, ungenügend.
insult, *s.* Beleidigung *f.*; *v. a.* beleidigen.
insurance, *s.* Versicherung *f*.
insure, *v. a.* versichern.
integral, *adj.* ganz, vollständig; integral.
intellectual, *adj.* intellektuell; — *s.* Intellektuelle *m.*, *f*.
intelligence, *s.* Intelligenz *f.*; Nachricht *f*.
intelligent, *adj.* intelligent, verständig.
intend, *v. a.* beabsichtigen.

intense, *adj.* intensiv, stark; gespannt; heftig.
intensity, *s.* Intensität *f*.
intent, *s.* Absicht *f.*; Ziel *n.*; Plan *m*.
intention, *s.* Absicht *f*.
intercontinental, *adj.* interkontinental; zwischen Kontinenten (bestehend).
interest, *s.* Interesse *n.*; Zins *m.*; Zinsen *m. pl.*; — *v. a.* interessieren, angehen.
interesting, *adj.* interessant; anziehend.
interfere, *v. n.* sich einmengen.
interior, *adj.* inner, inländisch; — *s.* (das) Innere; innere Angelegenheiten *pl*.
intermission, *s.* Unterbrechung *f*.
internal, *adj.* inner(lich); inländisch; ~ *combustion engine* Verbrennungsmotor *m*.
international, *adj.* international.
interpret, *v. a.* verdolmetschen; wiedergeben; übersetzen.
interpretation, *s.* Verdolmetschung *f.*; Auffassung *f.*; Darstellung *f*.
interpreter, *s.* Dolmetscher *m.*, -in *f.*; Übersetzer *m.*, -in *f*.
interrupt, *v. a.* unterbrechen.
interruption, *s.* Unterbrechung *f*.
interval, *s.* Abstand *m.*; Pause *f*.
intervention, *s.* Intervention *f*.
interview, *s.* Interview *n.*; — *v. a.* ein Interview haben mit.
intimate, *adj.* intim.
into, *prep.* in, hinein, zu,

introduce — **jersey**

nach.
introduce, *v. a.* einführen, einleiten; vorstellen.
introduction, *s.* Einführung *f.;* Vorstellung *f.;* Vorwort *n.*
intrude, *v. n.* sich aufdrängen; stören.
invade, *v. a.* überfallen.
invalid¹, *adj.* krank; — *s.* Invalide *m.*
invalid², *adj.* ungültig.
invasion, *s.* Invasion *f.*
invent, *v. a. & n.* erfinden; erdichten.
invention, *s.* Erfindung *f.;* Fiktion *f.*
invest, *v. a.* bekleiden, *(capital)* anlegen.
investigate, *v. a.* untersuchen.
investigation, *s.* Untersuchung *f.*
investment, *s.* Anlage *f.*
invisible, *adj.* unsichtbar.
invitation, *s.* Einladung *f.*
invite, *v. a.* einladen.
invoice, *s.;* Rechnung *f.;* Faktura *f.*
involuntary, *adj.* unfreiwillig; unabsichtlich.
involve, *v. a.* einbegreifen; mit sich bringen.
inward, *adv.* nach innen; — *adj.* innerer, innere, inneres; innerlich.
inwards, *adv.* see **inward** *adv.*
Irish, *s. pl.* Irländer *m.* -in *f.;* Iren *pl.;* — *adj.* irisch, irländisch.
iron, *s.* Eisen *n.;* Bügeleisen *n.* — *adj.* eisern; — *v. a.* bügeln.
ironical, *adj.* ironisch.
ironworks, *s. pl.* Eisenhütte *f.*
irony, *s.* Ironie *f.*
irradiation, *s.* Bestrahlung *f.*
irregular, *adj.* unregelmäßig.
irritate, *v. a.* reizen, irritieren.
island, isle, *s.* Insel *f.*
isolate, *v. a.* isolieren; absondern.
isotope, *s.* Isotop *n.*
issue, *s.* Ausgeben *n.;* Ausgabe *f.;* Nachkommen *m. pl.;* Rechtsfrage *f.;* — *v. a.* ausgeben; in Umlauf setzen; herausgeben; *v. n.* hervorgehen; resultieren.
it, *pron.* es.
Italian, *adj.* italienisch; — *s.* Italiener *m.,* -in *f.*
itch, *s.* Jucken *n.;* — *v. n.* jucken.
item, *s.* Artikel *m.*
its, *pron.* sein, ihr; dessen, deren.
itself, *pron.* sich (selbst).
ivory, *s.* Elfenbein *n.;* — *adj.* Elfenbein-.
ivy, *s.* Efeu *m.*

J

jack, *s.* Hebel *m.* Wagenheber *m.*
jacket *m.* Jacke *f.*
jail, *s.* Gefängnis *n.*
jam, *s.* Marmelade *f.*
January, *s.* Januar *m.*
Japanese, *s.* Japaner *m.,* -in *f.;* — *adj.* japanisch.
jar, *s.* Krug *m.;* (Einmach)Glas *n.*
javelin, *s. (sport)* Speer *m.*
jaw, *s.* Kiefer *m.*
jealous, *adj.* eifersüchtig.
jealousy, *s.* Eifersucht *f.*
jeep, *s.* Jeep *m.;* Geländewagen *m.*
jelly, *s.* Gelee *n.*
jerk, *s.* Ruck *m.;* — *v. a. & n.* stoßen; reißen.
jersey, *s.* Wolljacke *f.*

jet, s. Strahl m.; Düse f.; ~ *plane* Düsenflugzeug n.
Jew, s. Jude m.; Jüdin f.
jewel, s. Juwel n., m.
jeweller, s. Juwelier m.
Jewish, adj. jüdisch.
job, s. Arbeit f.; Beschäftigung f., Stellung f.
join, v. a. verbinden; (pers.) vereinigen; v. n. sich verbinden; sich vereinigen.
joiner, s. Tischler m.
joint, s. Verbindung f.; Gelenk m.; Braten m.; — adj. gemeinsam.
joke, s. Spaß m.; Witz m.
jolly, adj. lustig, fidel, famos.
journal, s. Journal n.; Zeitschrift f.
journalist, s. Journalist m., -in f.
journey, s. Reise f.; Fahrt f.
joy, s. Freude f.
judge, s. Richter m.; Kenner m.; (sport) Schiedsrichter m.; — v. a. & n. urteilen.
judg(e)ment, s. Urteil n.
jug, s. Krug m.
Jugoslav see **Yugoslav**.
juice, s. Saft m.
July, s. Juli m.
jump, s. Sprung m.; — v. a. & n. springen.
jumper, s. Pullover m.
junction, s. Verbindung f.; Knotenpunkt m.
June, s. Juni m.
junior, adj. jünger (als).
jury, s. Geschworenengericht n.; Jury f.
juryman, s. Geschworene m.
just, adj. gerecht; genau; — adv. gerade, soeben, eben nur; ~ *now* eben jetzt.

justice, s. Gerechtigkeit f.; Richter m.
justify, v. a. & n. (sich) rechtfertigen.
juvenile, adj. jung; jugendlich; — s. Jugendliche m., f.

K

keel, s. Kiel m.
keen, adj. scharf; eifrig; scharfsinnig.
keep, v. a. halten; bewahren; v. n. sich halten; ~ *off* sich fernhalten; ~ *on* fortfahren; ~ *up with* Schritt halten mit.
keeper, s. Wächter m.; Aufseher m.; Wärter m.
kernel, s. Kern m.
kettle, s. Kessel m.
key, s. Schlüssel m.; (*music*) Taste f.; Tonart f.
keyboard, s. Klaviatur f.
kick, s. Fußtritt; — v. a. mit dem Fuß stoßen; (*football*) schießen.
kid, s. junge Ziege; Ziegenleder n., Glacéleder n.; Bengel m.
kidney, s. Niere f.
kill, v. a. & n. töten; fig. vernichten.
kilogram(me), s. Kilogramm n.
kilometre, s. Kilometer n.
kin, s. Sippe f.; Verwandschaft.
kind, adj. gütig, freundlich; — s. Art f.; Sorte f.
kindly, adj. freundlich; — adv. freundlich.
kindness, s Freundlichkeit f.; Güte f.
king, s. König m.
kingdom s. Königreich n.

| kiss | 73. | latter |

kiss, s. Kuß m.; — v. a. küssen; v. n. sich küssen.
kit, s. Ausrüstung f.; Werkzeugtasche f.
kitchen, s. Küche f.
knapsack, s. Rucksack m.
knee, s. Knie n.
kneel, v. n. knien.
knife, s. Messer n.
knight, s. Ritter m.
knit, v. a. & n. strikken.
knob, s. Knopf m.; Griff m.
knock, s Stoß m; Klop-; fen n.; — v. a. stoßen; ~ out (boxing) ausschlagen: v. n. klopfen; stoßen.
knot, s. Knoten m.; Schleife f.; — v. a. knoten; verwirren; v. n. knotig werden.
know, v. a. wissen; kennen; erfahren.
knowledge, s. Kenntnis f.; Wissen m.
knuckle, s. Knöchel m.

L

label, s. Etikette f.; Zettel m.; — v. a. etikettieren; bezetteln.
laboratory, s. Laboratorium n.
labour, s. Arbeit f.; Mühe f.
labourer, s. Arbeiter m.
lack, s. Mangel m.; — v. a. ermangeln; v. n. fehlen.
lad, s. Bursche m.
ladder, s. Leiter f.
lading, s. Ladung f.; Fracht f.
lady, s. Dame f.; Lady f.
lag, v. n. ~ (behind) zurückbleiben; — s. Zurückbleiben n.
lake, s. See m.

lamb, s. Lamm n.
lame, adj. lahm.
lamp, s. Lampe f.
lamp-shade, s. Lampenschirm m.
land, s. Festland n.; Land n. —v.a. landen.
landing, s. Landung f.; Treppenabsatz m.
landlady, s. Gutsherrin f.; Hauswirtin f.
landlord, s. Gutsherr m.; Hausherr m.
landscape, s. Landschaft f.
lane, s. Feldweg m.; Gasse f.
language, s. Sprache f.
lap¹, s. Schoß m.
lap², v.a. umschlagen.
lapse, s. Verlauf m. Verfallen n. Versehen n.; — v.n. verfallen.
lard, s. Schmalz n.
large, adj. groß, umfassend.
lark¹, s. Lerche f.
lark², s. Jux m.; Ulk m.; — v.n. Possen treiben; v. a. necken, foppen.
last¹, adj. letzter, letzte letztes; neuester, neueste, neuestes; — adv. zuletzt; als letzter; zum letzten Male; at ~ endlich; zuletzt.
last², v.n. dauern; bestehen.
lasting, adj. dauerhaft; beständig; haltbar.
latch-key, s. Hausschlüssel m.
late, adj. spät; verspätet; verstorben; ehemalig.
lately, adv. neulich; kürzlich.
lathe, s. Drehbank f.
Latin, s. Lateinisch n., — adj. lateinisch.
latter, adj. letzterer, letztere, letzteres; modern.

laugh   **74.**   **let**

laugh, s. Lachen n.; Gelächter n.; — v. n. lachen; v. a. verlachen.

launch, v. a. (ship) vom Stapel lassen; (plane) katapultieren; fig. in Gang setzen.

laundry, s. Wäsche f.; Waschanstalt f.

lavatory, s. Toilette f.

lavish, v. a. verschwenden.

law, s. Gesetz n.; Recht n.

law-court, s. Gerichtshof m.

lawful, adj. gesetzlich, legal; rechtmäßig.

lawn, s. Rasen m.

lawn-mower, s. Rasenmähmaschine f.

lawsuit, s. Klage f.; Prozeß m.

lawyer, s. Rechtsanwalt m.

lay, s. Lage f.; Beschäftigung f.; — v. a. legen; setzen; stellen; — v. n. (eggs) legen; (table) decken.

lay-by s. Parkplatz m.

layer, s. Schicht f.

lazy, adj. träg, faul.

lead[1], s. Blei n.

lead[2], s. Führung f.; Leitung f.; — v. a. führen, leiten; dirigieren; v. n. führen.

leader, s. Führer m., -in f.; Leitartikel m.

leaf, s. Blatt n.

lean, adj. mager.

leap, s. Sprung m.; — v. n. springen; v. a. überspringen.

learn, v. a. & n. lernen; erfahren.

least, adj. kleinster, kleinste, kleinstes; geringster, geringste, geringstes; — adv. am wenigsten.

leather, s. Leder n.

leave[1], v. a. verlassen; abreisen; ~ off aufhören.

leave[2], s. Erlaubnis f.; Urlaub m.

lecture, s. Vortrag m.; Vorlesung f.; — v. n. einen Vortrag halten.

lecturer, s. Dozent m.; Vortragende m., f.

left, adj. linker, linke, linkes; — s. Linke f.; — adv. links.

left-luggage office, s. Gepäckaufbewahrungsstelle f.

leg, s. Bein n.

legal, adj. gesetzlich.

legitimate, adj. legitim; gesetzlich.

leisure, s. Muße f.; — adj. müßig.

lemon, s. Zitrone f.

lemonade, s. Zitronade f.; Limonade f.

lend, v. a. leihen, ausleihen; verleihen.

length, s. Länge f.

lengthen, v. a. verlängern.

lens, s. Linse f.; Objektiv n.

leopard, s. Leopard m.

less, adv. weniger; in geringerem Maße; ~ and ~ immer weniger; — adj. geringer; ~ than weniger als.

lessen, v. n. & a. vermindern.

lesser, adj. kleiner; geringer.

lesson, s. Lektion f.; Hausaufgabe f.; (Unterrichts)Stunde f.; fig. Lehre f.; v. a. & n. belehren.

let, v. a. lassen, erlauben; gestatten; vermieten, verpachten; v. n. vermietet werden; zu ver-

letter — **list**

pachten sein.
letter, s. Buchstabe m.; Type m.; Brief m.
letter-box, s. Briefkasten m.
lettuce, s. Salat m.
level, s. ebene Fläche f.; — adj. eben; horizontal; v. a. ebnen.
lever, s. Hebel m.
levy, s. Erhebung f. (of taxes etc.); Steuer f.; — v. a. auferlegen.
lexicon, s. Lexikon n.
liability, s. Verantwortlichkeit f.; Obligation f.; Haftpflicht f.
liable, adj. verantwortlich; haftbar.
liar, s. Lügner m.
liberal, adj. liberal; freisinnig.
liberty, s. Freiheit f.
library, s. Bibliothek f.; Bücherei f.
licence, s. Genehmigung f.; Erlaubnis f.; Lizenz f.
license, v.a. Genehmigung erteilen; konzessionieren; ermächtigen.
lick, s. Lecken m.; — v. a. lecken; ablecken.
lid, s. Deckel m.; Augenlid m.
lie[1]**,** s. Lüge f.; — v. n. & a. lügen.
lie[2]**,** v.n. liegen; sich legen; ~ down sich niederlegen.
life, s. Leben n.
lift, s. Heben n.; Hub m.; Aufzug m.; Lift m.; Mitfahrgelegenheit f.; Beistand m.; — v. a. aufheben; erheben; v. n. sich heben.
light[1]**,** s. Licht n.; Erleuchtung f.; Helligkeit f.; Tageslicht n.; — adj. hell; licht; — v.a. anzünden; beleuchten; v.n. sich entzünden.
light[2]**,** adj. leicht; locker.
lighten[1]**,** v.n. sich aufhellen; v. a. erhellen; beleuchten.
lighten[2]**,** v. a. entladen.
lighter, s. Leichterschiff.
lighthouse, s. Leuchtturm m.
lighting, s. Beleuchtung f.
lightning, s. Blitz m.
like[1]**,** adj. & adv. gleich; wie; so wie.
like[2]**,** v. a. gern haben; mögen; lieben; I should ~ to ich möchte.
likely, adj. & adv. wahrscheinlich.
likeness, s. Ähnlichkeit f.; Abbild n.
lily, s. Lilie f.
limb, s. Glied n.
limit, s Grenze f.; Schranke f.; — v. a. beschränken, einschränken.
line[1]**,** s. Linie f.; Strich m.; Reihe f.; Zeile f.; Gleis n.; Strecke f.; Leitung f.; Fach n.; Gebiet n.; Schnur f.; — v. n. eine Linie bilden; sich aufstellen.
line[2]**,** v. a. füttern; ausfüttern; anfüllen.
linen, s. Leinwand f.; Leinen n.; Wäsche f.
lining, s. Futter n.; Besatz m.; Saum m.
link[1]**,** s. Kettenglied n.; Bindeglied n.; — v. a. verbinden.
link[2]**,** ~s pl. Golfplatz m.
lion, s. Löwe m.
lip, s. Lippe f.
lipstick, s. Lippenstift m.
liquid, adj. flüssig; — s. Flüssigkeit f.
list, s. Liste f.; — v. a.

listen — verzeichnen, registrieren.

listen, *v. n.* horchen; hören; lauschen.

listener, *s.* Zuhörer *m.* -in *f.*

literature, *s.* Literatur *f.*; Schrifttum *n.*

litter, *s.* Sänfte *f.*; Tragbahre *f.*; Streu *f.*; Wurf *m.*; — *v. a.* mit Stroh bedecken; *v. n.* Junge werfen.

little, *adj.* klein; wenig.

live[1], *v. n.* leben; wohnen.

live[2], *adj.* lebend; lebendig; belebt; lebhaft; *(broadcast)* direkt.

lively, *adj. & adv.* lebhaft, munter, flott.

liver, *s.* Leber *f.*

living-room, *s.* Wohnzimmer *n.*

load, *s.* Last *f.*; Ladung *f.*; — *v. a.* laden.

loaf, *s. (bread)* Laib (Brot) *m.*

loan, *s.* Leihen *n.*; Darlehen *n.*; — *v. a.* verleihen.

loathe, *v. a.* verabscheuen, hassen, nicht leiden können.

lobby, *s.* Vorhalle *f.*; Vestibül *n.*

lobster, *s.* Hummer *m.*

local, *adj.* örtlich.

lock, *s.* Schloß *n.* — *v. a.* einschließen; sperren; *v. n.* sich schließen.

locksmith, *s.* Schlosser *m.*

lodger, *s.* Mieter *m.*; -in *f.*; Zimmergast *m.*

lodging, *s.* Wohnung *f.*; Logis *n.*; Logieren *n.*; Zimmer *n.*; Mietwohnung *f.*

log, *s.* Holzklotz *m.*; Holzblock *m.*; Log *n.*

loin, *s.* Lende *f.*; Lendenstück *n.*

lonely, *adj.* einsam.

long[1], *adj. & adv.* lang; lange.

long[2], *v. n.* sich sehnen (nach).

long-distance, *adj.* Fern-; Weit-; *(sport)* Langstrecken-.

long-playing record, *s.* Langspielplatte *f.*

look, *s.* Blick *m.*; Aussehen *n.*; — *v. n. & p. a.* sehen; schauen; blicken; ∼ *for* suchen; ∼ *on* ansehen; ∼ *upon* betrachten als.

looking-glass, *s.* Spiegel *m.*

loose, *adj.* lose, locker; — *v. a.* lösen; loslassen; freilassen; *v. n.* lösen.

loosen, *v. a. & n.* (sich) lösen; (sich) lockern.

lord, *s.* Herr *m.*; Besitzer *m.*, Gott *m.*

lorry, *s.* Lastwagen *m.*; Lastauto *n.*

lose, *v. a.* verlieren; *v. n.* Verluste erleiden.

loss, *s.* Verlust *m.*; Schaden *m.*

lot, *s.* Los *n.*; Schicksal *n.*

loud, *adj.* laut; grell.

loud-speaker, *s.* Lautsprecher *m.*

lounge, *s.* Halle *f.*; Gesellschaftsraum *m.*; Foyer *n.*; Faulenzen *n.*; — *v. n.* faulenzen.

lounge-suit, *s.* Straßenanzug *m.*

love, *s.* Liebe *f.*; — *v. a.* lieben.

lovely, *adj.* entzückend; reizend; herrlich.

lover, *s.* Liebhaber *m.*; ∼*s* *pl.* Liebespaar *n.*

low, *adj. & adv.* nieder; niedrig; gemein.

lower[1], *adj.* niedriger;

lower² tiefer; unterer, untere, unteres.
lower³, v. a. senken.
loyal, adj. loyal; treu.
lubricate, v. a. & n. schmieren.
luck, s. Glück n.; ill ~ Unglück n.; Pech n.
lucky, adj. glücklich.
luggage, s. Gepäck n.
luggage-van, s. Packwagen m.
lumber, s. Bauholz n.; Gerümpel n.
lump, s. (sugar) Stück n.; Klumpen m.; Beule f.; Menge f.
lunch, luncheon, s. Mittagessen n.
lung, s. Lunge f.
luxurious, adj. luxuriös; üppig.
luxury, s. Luxus m.; Luxusartikel m.
lyric, adj. lyrisch; — s. ~s pl. Lyrik f.

M

machine, s. Maschine f.
machinery, s. Maschinerie f.; Mechanismus m.
mad, adj. wahnsinnig.
madam, s. gnädige Frau.
magazine, s. Munitionslager n.; Zeitschrift f.
magic, s. Magie f.
magistrate s. Polizeirichter m.; Friedensrichter m.
magnet, s. Magnet m.
magnificent, adj. herrlich; großartig.
maid, s. Mädchen n.; Dienstmädchen n.; Jungfrau f.
mail, s. Post f.; Briefpost f.; — v. a. (letter) absenden, aufgeben.
mail-order, s. Bestellung durch die Post.
main, adj. Haupt-; — s. Hauptleitung f.; ~s pl. Stromnetz n.
maintain, v. a. erhalten; unterhalten; unterstützen; behaupten.
maintenance, s. Instandhaltung f.; Unterhalt m.
majesty, s. Majestät f.; königliche Hoheit.
major, s. Major m.; Mündige m., f.; (music) Dur n.; — adj. größerer, größere, größeres.
majority, s. Mehrzahl f.; Mündigkeit f.
make, s. Machart f.; Produkt n.; Marke f.; Typ m.; Herstellung f.; — v. a. machen; verfertigen; schaffen; veranlassen, lassen; ~ over vermachen; ~ out ausstellen; ~ up zusammensetzen, zusammenstellen.
male, adj. männlich; — s. Mann m.
mammal, s. Säugetier n.
man, s. Mann m.; Diener m.
manage, v. a. führen, fertigbringen; verwalten; leiten; v. n. auskommen (mit).
management, s. Verwaltung f.; Direktion f.
manager, s. Leiter m.; Direktor m.
manifest, adj. offenbar; kundig; — v. a. offenbaren; kundtun.
manipulate, v. a. & n. manipulieren; (gesickt) handhaben.
mankind, s. Menschheit f.
manner, s. Weise f.; Art

manoeuvre 78. mature

f.; Sitten *pl.*

manoeuvre, *s.* Manöver *n.*; — *v. a. & n.* manövrieren.

manual, *adj.* Hand-; — *s.* Handbuch *n.*

manufacture, *s.* Verfertigung *f.*; Fabrikation *f.*; — *v. a.* anfertigen; verfertigen; erzeugen.

manufacturer, *s.* Hersteller *m.*; Fabrikant *m.*

manure, *s.* Dünger *m.*; — *v. a.* düngen.

manuscript, *s.* Manuskript *n.*

many, *adj.* viel(e); mancher; manche, manches.

map, *s.* Landkarte *f.*

marble, *s.* Marmor *m.*

march, *v. n. & a.* marschieren; — *s.* Marsch *m.*

March, *s.* März *m.*

margarine, *s.* Margarine *f.*

marine, *adj.* See-; — *s.* Marine *f.*; Matrose *m.*

mariner, *s.* Matrose *m.*, Seemann *m.*

mark, *s.* Markierung *f.*; *fig.* Zeichen *n.*; Merkmal *n.*; Marke *f.*; Schutzmarke *f.*; *(sport)* Ziel *n.*; Schulnote *f.*; — *v. a.* kennzeichnen; bemerken.

market, *s.* Markt *m.*; Absatz *m.*

market-price, *s.* Marktpreis *m.*

marmalade, *s.* Apfelsinenmarmelade *f.*

marriage, *s.* Ehe *f.*; Heirat *f.*

marry, *v. a.* heiraten, vermählen; trauen; *v. n.* sich verheiraten.

marsh, *s.* Sumpf *m.*

marshal, *s.* Marschall *m.*; — *v. a.* arrangieren; *v. n.* sich ordnen.

martyr, *s.* Märtyrer *m.*, -in *f.*

marvellous, *adj.* wunderbar, erstaunlich.

masculine, *adj.* männlich.

mask, *s.* Maske *f.*

mass, *s.* Masse *f.*; Menge *f.*

Mass, *s.* Messe *f.*

mast, *s.* Mast *m.*

master, *s.* Herr *m.*; Meister *m.*; — *v. a.* beherrschen.

masterpiece, *s.* Meisterstück *n.*

mat, *s.* Matte *f.*

match[1], *s.* Streichholz *n.*

match[2], *s.* (der, die, das) Gleiche; Paar *n.*; Partie *f.*; Wettkampf *m.*; Match *m., n.*; — *v. n.* zusammenpassen.

mate, *s.* Maat *m.*; Genosse *m.*, Kamerad *m.*; Ehegefährte *m.*; Gemahl *m.*, -in *f.*; — *v. a. & n.* (sich) paaren.

material, *adj.* materiell; — *s.* Material *m.*

maternal, *adj.* mütterlich; Mutter-.

mathematics, *s.* Mathematik *f.*

matinée, *s.* Nachmittagsvorstellung *f.*

matrimony, *s.* Ehestand *m.*

matron, *s.* Matrone *f.*; Oberin *f.*; Hausmutter *f.*

matter, *s.* Materie *f.*; Material *n.*; Substanz *f.*; Stoff *m.*; Angelegenheit *f.*; Sache *f.* Inhalt *m. (of books)*; *what is the* ~ was ist los?; — *v. n.* von Bedeutung sein; *it does not* ~ es macht nichts.

mattress, *s.* Matratze *f.*

mature, *adj.* reif; — *v. a.*

may   79.   **metropolis**

& *n.* reifen.
may, *v. a.* können; mögen; dürfen; ~ *I?* darf ich?
May, *s.* Mai *m.*
maybe, *adv.* vielleicht.
mayor, *s.* Bürgermeister *m.*
me, *pron.* mich; mir.
meadow, *s.* Wiese *f.*
meal, *s.* Mahl *n.;* Mahlzeit *f.*
mean[1], *v. a.* beabsichtigen; meinen; wollen.
mean[2], *adj.* gemein; niedrig; schäbig.
mean[3], *s.* Mitte *f.;* (das) Mittlere; Durchschnitt *m.;* Mittelweg *m.;* ~s *pl.* Geldmittel *n. pl.*
meaning, *s.* Bedeutung *f.;* Sinn *m.*
meantime, meanwhile, *adv.* mittlerweile; inzwischen.
measure, *s.* Maß *n.;* Takt *m.;* Maßnahme *f.;* — *v. a.* messen.
meat, *s.* Fleisch *n.*
mechanic, *s.* Mechaniker *m.;* ~s *pl.* Mechanik *f.;* — *adj.* mechanisch.
mechanism, *s.* Mechanismus *m.*
mechanize, *v. a.* mechanisieren; motorisieren.
medal, *s.* Medalie *f.*
mediaeval, *adj.* mittelalterlich.
medical, *adj.* medizinisch; ärztlich.
medicine, *s.* Medizin *f.*
meditate, *v. n.* grübeln; meditieren.
medium, *s.* Mittelweg *m.;* Durchschnitt *m.;* Medium *m.;* — *adj.* mittelmäßig.
meet, *adj.* passend; schicklich; angemessen; — *v. a.* begegnen; treffen; empfangen; abholen; erfüllen; *v. n.* sich treffen; sich versammeln.
meeting, *s.* Begegnung *f.;* Konferenz *f.;* Zweikampf *m.; (sport)* Wettkampf *m.*
mellow, *adj.* reif; sanft.
melody, *s.* Melodie *f.*
melon, *s.* Melone *f.*
melt, *v. a. & n.* (zer)schmelzen.
member, *s.* Glied *n.;* Mitglied *n.*
memorial, *s.* Denkmal *n.*
memory, *s.* Gedächtnis *n.;* Andenken *n.*
mend, *v. a.* (aus)bessern; flicken; stopfen.
mental, *adj.* geistig; Kopf-
mention, *v. a.* erwähnen; don't ~ it! bitte!
menu, *s.* Speisekarte *f.*
merchandise, *s.* Ware *f.*
merchant, *s.* Kaufmann *m.*
merciful, *adj.* barmherzig; gnädig.
mercy, *s.* Barmherzigkeit *f.;* Gnade *f.*
mere, *adj.* bloß; lauter.
merit, *s.* Verdienst *m.;* — *v. a.* verdienen.
merry, *adj.* lustig, heiter; fröhlich.
mess, *s.* Verwirrung *f.;* Unordnung *f.;* Patsche *f.;* — *v. a.* speisen; beschmieren.
message, *s.* Botschaft *f.;* Mitteilung *f.*
metal, *s.* Metall *n.*
meteorology, *s.* Meteorologie *f.;* Wetterkunde *f.*
meter, *s.* Messer *m.;* Meßinstrument *n.*
method, *s.* Methode *f.;* Verfahren *n.*
metre, *s.* Meter *n.*
metropolis, *s.* Haupt-

microfilm 80. misunderstand

stadt *f.;* Metropole *f.*
microfilm, *s.* Mikrofilm *m.*
microscope, *s.* Mikroskop *n.*
middle, *s.* Mitte *f.;* — *adj.* mittlerer, mittlere, mittleres.
middle-class, *adj.* zum Mittlestand gehörig.
midnight, *s.* Mitternacht *f.;* — *adj.* mitternächtlich.
might, *s.* Macht *f.;* Gewalt *f.*
mighty, *adj.* mächtig, gewaltig; —*adv.* höchst; kolossal.
migrate, *v. n.* fortziehen.
mild, *adj.* mild; gelind.
mile, *s.* Meile *f.*
mileage, *s.* Meilenlänge *f.;* Kilometergeld *n.*
military, *adj.* militärisch; — *s.* Militär *n.*
milk, *s.* Milch *f.*
milkman, *s.* Milchmann *m.*
mill, *s.* Mühle *f.;* Fabrik *f.;* Werk *n.;* — *v. a.* mahlen.
milliner, *s.* Modistin *f.;* Putzmacherin *f.*
millionaire, *s.* Millionär *m.;* -in *f.*
mince, *v. a.* zerhacken.
mind, *s.* Sinn *m.;* Gemüt *n.;* Geist *m.;* Absicht *f.;* Lust *f.;* Gesinnung *f.;* — *v.a.* merken, beachten; sich in acht nehmen; sorgen für; *v. n.* aufpassen, bedenken.
mine¹, *pron.* der, die, das meinige.
mine², *v. a.* verminen; — *s.* Mine *f.*
mineral, *s.* Mineral *n.;* ∼s *pl.* Mineralwasser *n.;* — *adj.* mineralisch.

mingle, *v. a. & n.* (sich) mengen.
minister, *s.* Priester *m.;* Minister *m.*
ministry, *s.* Ministerium *n*
minor, *adj.* kleiner, minderjährig; — *s.* Minderjährige *m., f.;* Moll *n.*
minstrel, *s.* Spielmann *m.;* Minnesänger *m.*
mint¹, *s.* Minze *f.*
mint², *s.* Münze *f.*
minute¹, *s.* Minute *f.;* Konzept *n.;* Verhandlungsprotokoll *n.;* Sitzungsbericht *m.*
minute², *adj.* sehr klein, winzig.
miracle, *s.* Wunder *n.*
mirror, *s.* Spiegel *m.;* — *v.a.* (wider)spiegeln.
misadventure, *s.* Mißgeschick *n.*
miscellaneous, *adj.* gemischt; verschiedenartig.
mischief, *s.* Unheil *n.;* Schaden *m.*
miserable, *adj.* elend.
misery, *s.* Elend *n.;* Not *f.*
misfortune, *s.* Unglück *n.;* Mißgeschick *n.*
miss, *v. a.* verpassen; versäumen; *v. n.* fehlen; mißglücken.
Miss, *s.* Fräulein *n.*
missile, *s.* Wurfgeschoß *n.*
mission, *s.* Mission *f.*
missionary, *s.* Missionär *m.*
mist, *s.* Nebel *m.*
mistake, *v. a.* sich irren in; — *s.* Irrtum *m.*
Mister, *s.* Herr.
mistress, *s.* Herrin *f.;* Lehrerin *f.*
mistrust, *s.* Mißtrauen *n.;* — *v. a.* mißtrauen.
misunderstand, *v. a.* miß-

mitten   81.   **mother-in-law**

verstehen.
mitten, s. Fausthandschuh m.
mix, v. a. (ver)mischen, verwechseln; — s. Mischung f.
mixture, s. Mischung f.; Gemisch n.
moan, v. n. stöhnen, ächzen.
mob, s. Mob m.; Pöbel m.
mobilization, s. Mobilisierung f.
mobilize, v. a. mobilisieren.
mock, v. a. verspotten, verhöhnen; — s. Spott m.; Hohn m.
mockery, s. Spott m.; Nachäffung f.
model, s. Modell n.
moderate, adj. mäßig; — v. a. & n. (sich mäßigen.
moderation, s. Mäßigung f.; Mäßigkeit f.
modern, adj. modern.
modest, adj. bescheiden.
modify, v. a. abändern.
moisten, v. a. befeuchten; v. n. feucht werden.
moisture, s. Feuchtigkeit f.
moment, s. Augenblick m.; Bedeutung f.
momentary, adj. augenblicklich; vorübergehend.
monarchy, s. Monarchie f.
Monday, s. Montag m.
money, s. Geld n.
money-order, s. Postanweisung f.
monitor, s. Monitor m.
monk, s. Mönch m.
monkey, s. Affe m.
monopolize, v. a. monopolisieren.
monopoly, s. Monopol n.

monotonous, adj. monoton; eintönig.
monstrous, adj. ungeheuer; gräßlich; enorm.
month, s. Monat m.
monthly, adj. monatlich; — s. Monatsschrift f.
monument, s. Denkmal n.; Monument n.
mood, s. Stimmung f.; Laune f.
moon, s. Mond m.; Monat m.
moonlight, s. Mondschein m.
moor, s. Moor n.
Moor, s. Maure m., Mohr m.
mop, s. Scheuerlappen m.; Mop m.; — v. a. aufwischen; abwischen.
moral, adj. moralisch; sittlich; — s. Moral f.
more, adj. mehr; — adv. mehr; noch; once ~ noch einmal.
moreover, adv. außerdem; überdies, noch dazu.
morning, s. Morgen m.; Vormittag m.
mortal, adj. sterblich; tödlich.
mortgage, s. Verpfändung f.; Pfandgut n.; Hypothek f.; — v. a. verpfänden.
mosquito, s. Moskito m.; Mücke f.
moss, s. Moos n.
most, adj. meister, meiste, meistes; die meisten; — adv. am meisten; überaus.
mostly, adv. größtenteils; hauptsächlich.
motel, s. Motel n. Raststätte f.
moth, s. Motte f.
mother, s. Mutter f.
mother-in-law, s. Schwie-

germutter *f.*
mother-tongue, *s.* Muttersprache *f.*
motion, *s.* Bewegung *f.*; — *v. a.* zuwinken.
motive, *s.* Motiv *n.*
motor, *s.* Motor *m.*; Kraftmaschine *f.*; Kraftwagen *m*; Motorfahrzeug *n.*
motor-bicycle, motor-bike, *s.* Motorrad *n.*
motor-boat, *s.* Motorboot *n.*
motor-car, *s.* Auto(mobil) *n.*; Kraftwagen *m.*
motor-coach, *s.* Autobus *m.*
motor-cycle, *s.* Motorrad *n.*; Kraftrad *n.*; — *v. n.* motorradfahren.
motorway, *s.* Autobahn *f.*; Autostraße *f.*
mould, *s.* Gußform *f.*; *v. a.* formgießen.
mount[1], *s.* Berg *m.*; Hügel *m.*
mount[2], *v.a.* besteigen; montieren; — *v.n.* emporsteigen.
mountain, *s.* Berg *m.*; ~s *pl.* Gebirge *n.*
mountain-range, *s.* Gebirgszug *m.*
mourn, *v. n. & a.* trauern.
mouse, *s.* Maus *f.*
moustache, *s.* Schnurrbart *m.*
mouth, *s.* Mund *m.*; Öffnung *f.*
move, *v. a.* bewegen; fortbringen; veranlassen; *v.n.* sich bewegen; ~ *for* beantragen.
movement, *s.* Bewegung
movie, *s.* ~s *pl.* Kinovorstellung *f.*; Film *m.*
mow, *v. a. & n.* (ab)mähen.
mower, *s.* Mäher *m.*, -in *f.*; Mähmaschine *f.*

much, *adj.* viel; — *adv.* sehr; *as* ~ *as* so viel wie; *not so* ~ *as* nicht einmal.
mud, *s.* Schlamm *m.*; Kot *m.*
muddle, *s.* Verwirrung *f.*
multiply, *v. a. & n.* multiplizieren.
multitude, *s.* Menge *f.*
municipal, *adj.* städtisch.
murder, *s.* Mord *m.*; *v. a.* ermorden.
murmur, *s.* Gemurmel *n.*
muscle, *s.* Muskel *n.*
museum, *s.* Museum *n.*
mushroom, *s.* Pilz *m.*
music, *s.* Musik *f.*; Musikstück *n.*
musical, *adj.* musikalisch; ~ *comedy* Operette *f.*; ~ *instrument* Musikinstrument.
music-hall, *s.* Konzerthalle *f.*
musician, *s.* Musiker *m.*, -in *f.*
must, *v. aux.* muß, müssen; *you* ~ *not* du darfst nicht.
mustard, *s.* Senf *m.*
muster, *s.* Musterung *f.*
mute, *adj.* stumm
mutter, *s.* Gemurmel *n.*; — *v. n. & a.* murren.
mutton, *s.* Hammelfleisch *n.*
mutual, *adj.* gegenseitig; gemeinsam.
my, *pron.* mein, meine, mein.
myself, *pron.* (ich) selbst; mich; mir selbst; mich selbst.
mysterious, *adj.* geheimnisvoll; mysteriös.
myth, *s.* Sage *f.*

N

nail, *s.* Nagel *m.*; — *v.a.*

| nail-brush | 83. | ninety |

(an)nageln.
nail-brush, s. Nagelbürste f.
name, s. Name m.; Ruf m.; — v.a. (be)nennen.
namely, adv. nämlich.
nap, s. Schläfchen n.; — v. n. schlummern.
napkin, s. Serviette f.; Windel f.
narrate, v.a. & n. erzählen.
narrow, adj. eng; schmal.
nation, s. Nation f.; Volk n.
national, adj. national.
nationality, s. Nationalität f., Staatsangehörigkeit f.
native, adj. einheimisch; — s. Eingeborener m.
natural, adj. natürlich.
naturalization, s. Naturalisierung f.
nature, s. Natur f.
naughty, adj. unartig.
navel, adj. Marine-
navy, s. Flotte f.; Kriegsmarine f.
near, adv. nahe, beinahe; — adj. nahe(liegend); — v. a. & n. sich nähern.
neat, adj. ordentlich; nett.
necessary adj. notwendig; nötig; — s. Bedürfnis n.
necessity, s. Notwendigkeit f.; Bedürfnis n.
neck, s. Hals m.
necktie, s. Kravatte f.
need, s. Not f.; Bedürfnis n.; — v.a. brauchen; — v. n. nötig sein.
needle, s. Nadel f.
needless, adj. unnötig; ~ to say selbstverständlich.

negative, adj. negativ; ablehnend; verneinend; — s. Verneinung f.
neglect, v a. vernachlässigen; — f.; Nachlässigkeit f.; Übergehen n.
negligence, s. Nachlässigkeit
negotiation: s. Verhandlung f.
negro, s. Neger m.
neighbour, s. Nachbar m.
neighbourhood, s. Nachbarschaft f.
neither, adj. & pron. keiner, keine, keines (von beiden).
nephew, s. Neffe m.
nervous, adj. nervös.
nest, s. Nest n.
net, s. Netz n.
network, s. Netz n.
neutral, adj. neutral.
never, adv. nie, niemals.
nevertheless, adv. nichtsdestoweniger; dennoch.
new, adj. neu; — adv. neulich; soeben.
news, s. pl. (das) Neue, Nachrichten f. pl.
newspaper, s. Zeitung f.
New Year, s. Neujahr n.
next, adj. nächster, nächste, nächstes; — adv. & prep. zunächst.
nice, adj. fein; zart; schön.
niece, s. Nichte f.
night, s. Nacht; by ~, at ~ bei Nacht, nachts; last ~ gestern abend.
night-porter, s. Nachtportier m.
nine, adj. neun; — s. Neun f.; Neuner m.
nineteen, adj. neunzehn; — s. Neunzehn f.
ninety, s. Neunzig f.;

ninth — *adj.* neunzig.
ninth, *adj.* neunter, neunte, neuntes.
nitrogen, *s.* Nitrogen *n.*
no, *adv.* nein; *adj.* kein(e).
noble, *adj.* adlig; edel; — *s.* Edelmann *m.*
nobleman, *s.* Edelmann *m.*
nobody, *pron.* niemand; keiner.
nod, *s.* Nicken *n.*; Wink *m.*; — *v. a. & n.* nikke
noise, *s.* Lärm *m.*
noisy, *adj.* geräuschvoll; laut.
none, *pron.* keiner, keine, keines; niemand; *adv.* keineswegs.
nonsense, *s.* Unsinn *m.*
non-smoker, *s.* Nichtraucher *m.*
noon, *s.* Mittag *m.*
nor, *conj.* noch; *neither...* ~ weder... noch; auch nicht.
normal, *adj.* normal.
north, *adj.* nördlich, Nord-; — *adv.* nördlich; — *s. in the North* im Norden; *to the North of* nördlich von.
northeast, *s.* Nordost(en) *m.*; — *adj.* nordöstlich, — *adv.* nordöstlich; nach Nordosten.
northwest, *s.* Nordwesten *m.*; — *adj.* nordwestlich; — *adv.* nordwestlich; nach Nordwesten.
nose, *s.* Nase *f.*
nostril, *s.* Nasenloch *n.*
not, *adv.* nicht; ~ *a* kein(e); ~ *that* nicht daß; nicht als ob.
notable, *adj.* bemerkenswert; beträchtlich.
notch, *s.* Kerbe *f.*
note, *s.* (Kenn)zeichen *n.*; Ruf *m.*; Notiz *f.*;
— *v.a.* bemerken.
note-book, *s.* Notizbuch *n.*
noted, *adj.* berühmt.
nothing, *pron.* nichts.
notice, *s.* Notiz *f.*; Nachricht *f.*; — *v.a.* bemerken; beachten; kündigen.
notify, *v. a.* bekanntgeben; benachrichtigen.
notion, *s.* Begriff *m.*
nought, *s. & pron.* nichts; Null *f.*
noun, *s.* Hauptwort *n.*; Substantivum *n.*
nourish, *v. a.* (er)nähren; erhalten; *v. n.* nähren.
novel, *adj.* neu; — *s.* Roman *m.*
novelty, *s.* Neuheit *f.*; (etwas) Neues.
November, *s.* November *m.*
now, *adv.* nun; jetzt; (so)eben; — *conj.* nun aber.
nowadays, *adv.* heutzutage, jetzt.
nowhere, *adv.* nirgends, nirgendwo.
nuclear, *adj.* nukleär; Kern-.
nuclear bomb, *s.* Atombombe *f.*
nucleus, *s.* Kern *m.*
nuisance, *s.* Plage *f.*; Unfug *m.*
number, *s.* Zahl *f.*; Nummer *f.*
number-plate, *s.* Nummerschild *n.*
numerous, *adj.* zahlreich.
nurse, *s.* Krankenschwester *f.*; — *v. a.* nähren; stillen.
nursery, *s.* Kinderzimmer *n.*; Kindertagesstätte *f.*
nut, *s.* Nuß *f.*
nylon, Nylon *n.*; Nylonstrümpfe *pl.*

O

oak, s. Eiche f.; Eichenholz n.
oar, v. a. & n. rudern; — s. Ruder n.
oath, s. Schwur m.; Eid m.
obedient, adj. gehorsam.
obey, v. a. & n. gehorchen, folgen.
object, v. a. fig. einwenden; v. n. protestieren; — s. Objekt n.; Zweck m.; Gegenstand m.; Ziel n.
objection, s. Einwand m.
obligation, s. Verpflichtung f.
oblique, adj. schief, schräg.
obscure, adj. dunkel; unklar.
observation, s. Beobachtung f.; Bemerkung f.
observe, v. a. beobachten; bemerken.
observer, s. Beobachter m.
obstacle, s. Hindernis n.
obstinate, adj. hartnäckig; eigensinnig.
obtain, v. a. erlangen; erhalten.
obvious, adj. klar; offensichtlich.
occasion, s. Gelegenheit f.
occasional, adj. gelegentlich.
occupation, s. Beschäftigung f.; Beruf m.
occupy, v. a. in Besitz nehmen; (pers.) beschäftigen.
occur, v. n. sich ereignen; vorkommen.
ocean, s. Ozean m.
o'clock, Uhr (Zeit).
October, s. Oktober m.
odd, adj. sonderbar; ungerade.
odious, adj. verhaßt.
of, prep. von; aus; an; bei; über.

off, adv. fort; weg; davon; ab; — prep. weg von; fort von; — adj. weiter entfernt.
offence, s. Vergehen n.
offend, v. a. & n. verletzen, kränken;
offensive, s. Offensive f.
offer, v. a. anbieten; — s. Angebot n.
office, s. Büro n., Amt n.
officer, s. Offizier m.
official, adj. offiziell, amtlich; — s. Beamte m., Beamtin f.
often, adv. oft.
oil, s. Öl n.
old, adj. alt.
old-fashioned, adj. altmodisch.
omelet(te), s. Omelett n.
omit, v. a. weglassen.
on, prep. auf, an, in; über; — adv. an, auf, über.
once, adv. einmal. at ~ auf einmal; sofort.
one, adj. ein, eine, ein; — s. Eins f.; (das) einzelne; — pron. einer, eine, eines; man.
onion, s. Zwiebel m.
onlooker, s. Zuschauer m.
only, adj. einziger, einzige, einziges; — adv. nur; — conj. jedoch; nur.
onward, adv. vorwärts; weiter vorn; adj. nach vorn.
open, v. a. öffnen; eröffnen; v. n. sich öffnen; — adj. offen.
opening, s. Öffnung f.
opera, s. Oper f.
operate, v. n. arbeiten; funktionieren (pers.) be ~d (up)on operiert werden; v. a. operieren.
operation, s. Wirken n.; Betrieb m.; Gang m.; Operation f.

opinion, s. Meinung *f.*
opponent, s. Gegner *m.;* -in *f.*
opportunity, s. Gelegenheit *f.*
oppose, v. a. entgegensetzen.
opposite, adj. gegenüberliegend; entgegengesetzt; — *s.* Gegenteil *n.*
opposition, s. Widerstand *m.;* Opposition *f.*
or, conj. oder; entweder.. oder.
oral, adj. mündlich.
orange, s. Apfelsine *f.;* Orange *f.*
oratory, s. Oratorium *n.*
orchard, s. Obstgarten *m.*
orchestra, s. Orchester *n.*
order, s. Ordnung *f.;* Befehl *m.;* Bestellung *f.;* — *v. a.* befehlen; bestellen.
order-form, s. Bestellschein *m.*
ordinary, adj. üblich; gewöhnlich.
ore, s. Erz *n.*
organ, s. Organ *n.;* Orgel *f.*
organization, s. Organisation *f.*
organize, v. a. organisieren.
Orient, s. Osten *m.;* Orient *m.*
origin, s. Ursprung *m.;* Herkunft *f.*
original, adj. ursprünglich; original; originell.
ornament, s. Verzierung *f.;* Ornament *n.*
orphan, s. Waisenkind *n.*
other, adj. & pron. anderer, andere, anderes; anders (als); *each* ~ einander; — *adv.* anders (als).
otherwise, adv. sonst; anders; — *adj.* sonstig.

ought, v. aux. sollte, sollten.
ounce, s. Unze *f.* (30 gr.)
our, adj. unser.
ours, pron. (der, die, das) unsere.
ourself, ourselves, pron. uns (selbst).
oust, v. a. vertreiben; berauben.
out, adv. & adj. hinaus, heraus; außen, draußen.
outboard-motor, s. Außenbordmotor *m.*
outbreak, s. Ausbruch *m.*
outdoors, adv. im Freien.
outfit, s. Ausrüstung *f.*
outing, s. Ausflug *m.*
outline, s. Umriß *m.;* — *v. a. fig.* einen Überblick geben über; entwerfen.
outlive, v. a. überleben.
outlook, s. Aussicht *f.*
outnumber, v. a. an Zahl übertreffen.
outpost, s. Außenposten *m.; fig.* Vorposten *m.*
output, s. Produktion *f.;* Arbeitsertrag *m.*
outset, s. Anfang *m.*
adj. äußerer, äußere, äußeres; äußerst; — *adv.* draußen; außerhalb; heraus; hinaus; *prep.* außerhalb.
outskirts, s. Umgebung *f.;* Randgebiet *n.*
outward, adj. äußerer, äußere, äußeres; äußerlich; oberflächlich.
outwards, adv. nach außen.
oven, s. Backofen *m.*
over, prep. über; — *adv.* (hin)über; darüber; drüben; vorbei; übermäßig; allzu; — *adj.* oberer, obere, oberes.
overcoat, s. Mantel *m.*
overcome, v. a. besiegen, überwältigen.
overdo, v. a. übertreiben.

overexpose, *v. a.* überbelichten.
overflow, *v. n.* überlaufen. überfließen; *v. a.* überfluten.
overleaf, *adj.* umseitig.
overlook, *v. a.* übersehen; überblicken.
overtake, *v. a.* einholen; nachholen.
overthrow, *v. a.* umstürzen; — *s.* Sturz *m.*
overtime, *s.* Überstunden *pl.*
overturn, *v. a. & n.* umstürzen.
owe, *v. a.* schuldig sein; verdanken; *v. n.* Schulden haben.
owing, *adj.* ~ *to* infolge; wegen.
own, *v. a.* besitzen; zugeben; *v. n.* sich bekennen; — *adj.* eigen.
owner, *s.* Eigentümer *m.*, -in *f.*
ox, *s.* Ochse *m.*
oxygen, *s.* Sauerstoff *m.*

P

pace, *s.* Schritt *m.*; Tempo *n.*; — *v. a.* durchschreiten; *v. n.* schreiten.
pack, *s.* Pack *m.*; Packung *f.*; Paket *n.*; Meute *f.*; Rudel *n.*; — *adj.* Pack-; — *v. a.* einpacken; *v. n.* packen.
package, *s.* Paket *n.*; Packung *f.*
pact, *s.* Pakt *m.*;
pad, *s.* Polster *n.*; Schreibblock *m.*; *v. a.* (aus)polstern.
paddle, *s.* Ruder *n.*; — *v. a. & n.* rudern, paddeln.
page, *s.* (Buch)Seite *f.*
pail, *s.* Eimer *m.*
pain, *s.* Schmerz *m.*; Mühe *f.*; — *v. n.* weh tun.
painful, *adj.* schmerzhaft; peinlich.
paint, *s.* Farbe *f.*; — *v. a.* (be)malen; *v. n.* malen.
painter, *s.* Maler *m.*, -in *f.*
painting, *s.* Gemälde *m.*; Malerei *f.*
pair, *s.* Paar *n.*
palace, *s.* Palast *m.*
palate, *s.* Gaumen *m.*
pale, *adj.* blaß; bleich.
palm[1], *s.* Palme *f.*
palm[2], *v. a.* (innere) Handfläche *f.*
pan, *s.* Pfanne *f.*
pane, *s.* Fensterscheibe *f.*
panel, *s.* Holztafel *f.*; Geschworenenliste *f.*;
panorama, *s.* Panorama *n.*
pant, *v. n.* keuchen.
pantry, *s.* Vorratskammer *f.*, Speisekammer *f.*
pants, *s. pl.* Hose *f.*, Unterhose *f.*; Schlüpfer *m.*
paper, *s.* Papier *n.*; Zeitung *f.*; Aufsatz *m.*; Abhandlung *f.*; — *v. a.* tapezieren.
parachute, *s.* Fallschirm *m.*
paradise, *s.* Paradies *n.*
paraffin, *s.* Paraffin *n.*
paragraph, *s.* Absatz *m.*; Paragraph *m.*
parallel, *adj.* parallel; — *s.* Parallele *f.*
parcel, *s.* Paket *n.*
pardon, *s.* Verzeihung *f.*; Ablaß *m.*; — *v. a.* verzeihen.
parents *s. pl.* Eltern *pl.*
parish, *s.* Gemeinde *f.*; Pfarrei *f.*
park, *s.* Park *m.*; Parkplatz *m.*; — *v. a. & n.* parken.
parliament, *s.* Parlament *n.*
parlour, *s.* Wohnzimmer *n.*; Salon *m.*

parrot 88 **pearl**

parrot, *s.* Papagei *m.*
part, *s.* Teil *m.*; Stück *n.*; Rolle *f.*; Anteil *n.*; Amt *n.*; *(music)* Stimme *f.*; take ~ teilnehmen; — *v. a.* teilen; zerteilen; *v. n.* auseinandergehen; sich trennen; — *adv.* teilweise.
partial, *adj.* partiell, parteiisch.
participant, *s.* Teilnehmer *m.*, -in *f.*; — *adj.* teilnehmend.
participation, *s.* Teilnahme *f.*;
participle, *s.* Partizip(ium) *n.*
particle, *s.* Teilchen *n.*; Partikel *f.*
particular, *adj.* sonderbar; speziell; eigentümlich; seltsam; — *s.* Einzelheit *f.*; Personalien *pl.*
partly, *adv.* teilweise; zum Teil.
partner, *s.* Teilnehmer *m.*; Tänzer *m.*; -in *f.*
party, *s.* Partei *f.*; Partie *f.*; Abteilung *f.*; Gesellschaft *f.*
pass¹, *s.* Zugang *m.*; Paß *m.*
pass², *v. a.* vorbeigehen; vorbeifahren; zubringen; verbringen; billigen; *v. n.* sich fortbewegen; geraten; — *s.* Reisepaß *m.*
passenger, *s.* Passagier *m.*
passer-by, *s.* Vorübergehende *m.*, *f.*
passion, *s.* Leidenschaft *f.*; Zorn *m.*
passive, *adj.* untätig; geduldig; passiv.
passport, *s.* Reisepass *m.*
past, *adj.* vergangen; ehemalig; — *s.* Vergangenheit *f.*; — *adv.* vorbei, vorüber; über.

pastime, *s.* Zeitvertreib *m.*; Kurzweil *f.*
pastor, *s.* Pfarrer *m.*; Pastor *m.*
pastry, *s.* feines Gebäck; Torten *f. pl.*; Pasteten *f. pl.*
patch, *s.* Fleck *m.*; Stück *n.* Land *n. v. a.* flicken.
patent, *s.* Patent *n.*; *(shoe)* Lackschuh *m.*
path, *s.* Pfad *m.*; Weg *m.*; *(sport)* Bahn *f.*
patience, *s.* Geduld *f.*
patient, *adj.* geduldig; — *s.* Patient *m.*, -in *f.*
patriot, *s.* Patriot *m.*, -in *f.*
patrol, *s.* Patrouille *f.*; — *v. a. & n.* (ab)patrouillieren.
patron, *s.* Patron *m.*
pattern, *s.* Muster *n.*; Schablone *f.*; Schnittmuster *n.*
pause, *s.* Pause *f.*; Unterbrechung *f.*; — *v. n.* pausieren.
pave, *v. a.* pflastern, *fig.* bahnen.
pavement, *s.* Pflaster *n.*
pavilion, *s.* Pavillon *m.*
paw, *s.* Pfote *f.*; Tatze *f.*
pay, *s.* Bezahlung *f.*; Lohn *m.*; Sold *m.*; — *v. a.* bezahlen; belohnen; *v. n.* zahlen.
payable, *adj.* zahlbar; fällig.
payment, *s.* Bezahlung *f.*; Lohn *m.*; Sold *m.*
pea, *s.* Erbse *f.*
peace, *s.* Friede *m.*; Ruhe *f.*
peaceful, *adj.* friedlich.
peach, *s.* Pfirsich *m.*
peacock, *s.* Pfauhahn *m.*
peak, *s.* Spitze *f.*; Gipfel *m.*; *(sport)* Spitzenleistung *f.*
pear, *s.* Birne *f.*
pearl, *s.* Perle *f.*

peasant — **picture**

peasant, s. Bauer m.
peck, v. a. picken, hacken.
peculiar, adj. eigen(tümlich); eigen(artig), seltsam.
pedestrian, s. Fußgänger m.
peel, s. Schale f.; Rinde f. — v. a. (ab)schälen.
peer, s. Ebenbürtige n., f.
peg, s. Pflock m.; Haken m.; Propf m.; Dübel m.
pen, s. Feder f.
penalty, s. Strafe f.
pencil, s. Bleistift m.; Stift m.
penicillin, s. Penicillin n.
peninsula, s. Halbinsel f.
penny, s. Penny.
pension, s. Pension f.; — pensionieren.
people, s. Volk n.; Leute pl.
pepper, s. Pfeffer m.; Paprika m.
per, prep. per; laut; pro; ~ cent Prozent n.
perceive, v. a. & n. wahrnehmen; bemerken.
perch, s. Stange f.
perfect, adj. vollkommen; perfekt; — v. a. vollenden.
perform, v. a. machen, ausführen; vollziehen; aufführen; v. n. funktionieren; eine Vorstellung geben; auftreten.
performance, s. Aufführung f.; Vortrag m.; Leistung f.
parfume, s. Parfüm n.
perhaps, adv. vielleicht, möglicherweise.
peril, s. Gefahr f.
period, s. Periode f.; Zeitabschnitt m.
periodical, adj. periodisch; — s. Zeitschrift f.
periscope, s. Periskop n.
perish, v. n. umkommen.

perishable, adj. verderblich.
permanent, adj. dauern, bleibend; ständig.
permission, s. Erlaubnis f.; Genehmigung f.
permit, v. a. & n. erlauben; — s. Erlaubnis f.
persecution, s Verfolgung f.; Hetzjagd f.
Persian, adj. persisch; — s. Perser m.; -in f.
persist, v. n. ausharren; verharren.
person, s. Person f.
personal, adj. persönlich.
personality, s. Persönlichkeit f.
perspiration, s. Schweiß m.; Schwitzen n.
persuade, v. a. überreden; bewegen; überzeugen.
pertain, v. n. angehören.
pet, s. Haustier n.; Liebling m.
petrol, s. Benzin n.
petroleum, s. Petroleum n.; Erdöl n.
pheasant, s. Fasan m.
philosopher, s. Philosoph m.
philosophy, s. Philosophie f.
phone, s. Telephon n.; Fernsprecher m.; — v. a. anrufen; v. n. telephonieren.
photograph, s. Photographie f.; — v. a. & n. photographieren.
phrase, s. Phrase f.;
physical, adj. physisch.
physician, s. Arzt m.
physics, s. pl. Physik f.
pianist, s. Klavierspieler m., -in f.
piano, s. Klavier n.
pick, v. a. auswählen; (aus)suchen; pflücken; v. n. hacken; ernten.
picnic, s. Picknick n.
picture, s. Bild n.; Ge-

pie — **plight¹**

mälde n.; the ~s pl. Kino.
pie, s. Fleischpastete f.; Obsttorte f.
piece, s. Stück n.; — v. a. ergänzen; flicken.
pier, s. Pfeiler m.; Landungssteg m.
pierce, v. a. durchbohren; v. n. eindringen.
pig, s. Ferkel n.; Schwein n.; Roheisen n.
pigeon, s. Taube f.
pile, s. Haufen m.; Masse f.; — v. a. ~ up aufstapeln; aufschichten.
pill, s. Pille f.
pillar, s. Pfeiler m.
pillar-box, s. Briefkastensäule f.
pillow, s. Kopfkissen n.
pilot, s. Pilot m.
pin, s. Stecknadel f.; — v. a. anheften; befestigen.
pinch, s. Kniff m.; Prise f.
pine, s. Kiefer f.
pineapple, s. Ananas f.
pink, adj. rosa(farben); — s. Nelke f.
pint, s. Pinte f. (0,57 Liter)
pioneer, s. Pionier m.
pious, adj. fromm.
pipe, s. Pfeife f.; Röhre f.; Rohr n.
pipe-line, s. Röhrenleitung f.
pistol, s. Pistole f.
pit, s. Grube f. (theatre); Parterre n.; (scar) Narbe f.
pitch¹, s. Pech n.
pitch², v.a. (tent) aufschlagen, aufstellen; — s. Werfen n.; Wurf m.; (music) Tonhöhe f.
pitcher, s. Krug m.
pity, s. Mitleid n.; — v. a. bemitleiden.
place, s. Platz m.; Ort m.; Dienst m.; Amt n.; — v. a. stellen, setzen; legen; anstellen; (sport) placieren.
plain, adj. einfach, — adv. klar, deutlich; — s. Ebene f.
plan, s. Plan m. — v. a. & n. planen.
plane¹, adj. flach, eben; — s. Ebene f.
plane², s. Hobel m.
plane³, s. Flugzeug n.
planet, s. Planet m.
plank, s. Planke f.
plant, s. Pflanze f.; Betriebsanlage f.; Werk n.; — v. a. anpflanzen; aufstellen.
plantation, s. Plantage f.
plaster, s. Pflaster n.; — v. a. bepflastern.
plastic, adj. plastisch; Plastik-; — s. Kunststoff m.; Plastikstoff m.
plastics, s. pl. Kunststoffe.
plate, s. Platte f.
platform, s. Plattform f.; Podium n.; Bahnsteig m.
platinum, s. Platin n.
play, s. Spiel n.; Schauspiel n.; — v. a. & n. spielen.
playground, s. Spielplatz.
plaything, s. Spielzeug n.
plea, s. Rechtseinwand m.
plead, v. n. plädieren.
pleasant, adj. angenehm.
please, v. a. gefallen, angenehm sein; v. n. if you ~ bitte.
pleasure, s. Vergnügen n.
pledge, s. Pfand n.; Gelübde n.; Versprechen n.; — v. a. versprechen.
plenty, s. Fülle f.; Überfluß m.
plight¹, s. (schlechter)

plight — **possess**

Zustand *m.*
plight², *v. a.* (Wort, Ehre) verpfänden; versprechen.
plot, *s.* Grundstück *n.*; Handlung *f.*; Komplott *n.*
plough, *s.* Pflug *m.*; — *v. a. & n.* pflügen.
plug, *s.* Stecker *m.*; Dübel *m.*; — *v. a.* ~ *in* einstöpseln.
plum, *s.* Pflaume *f.*
plump, *adj.* rundlich, dick; beleibt.
plunder, *s.* Raub *m.*; Diebstahl *m.*; Beute *f.*; — *v. a. & n.* plündern.
plunge, *s.* Tauchen *n.*
plus, *prep.* plus.
pocket, *s.* Tasche *f.*
pocket-book, *s.* Notizbuch *n.*
poem, *s.* Gedicht *n.*
poet, *s.* Dichter *m.*
poetry, *s.* Dichtkunst *f.*; Poesie *f.*
point, *s.* Spitze *f.*; Punkt *m.*; (kritischer) Punkt; Gesichtspunkt *m.*; — *v. a.* spitzen; zeigen.
poison, *s.* Gift *n.*; — *v. a.* vergiften.
poke, *v. a.* stoßen.
poker, *s.* Feuerhaken *m.*
polar, *adj.* polar.
pole¹, *s.* Stange *f.*; Pfosten *m.*; Springstab *m.*
pole², *s.* (Erd)Pol *m.*
Pole, *s.* Pole *m.*; Polin *f.*
police, *s.* Polizei *f.*
policeman, *s.* Polizist *m.*
police-station, *s.* Polizeiwache *f.*
policy¹, *s.* Politik *f.*; Taktik *f.*; Verfahren *n.*
policy², Versicherungsschein *m.*; Police *f.*
polish, *v. a.* polieren; — *s.* Politur *f.*; Glanz *m.*; *fig.* Schliff *m.*
Polish, *adj.* polnisch; — *s.* Polnisch *n.*
polite, *adj.* höflich.
political, *adj.* politisch.
politician, *s.* Politiker *m.*
poll, *v. n.* wählen; — *s.* Wahl *f.*; Wählen *n.*
pond, *s.* Teich *m.*
ponder, *v. a.* erwägen; *v. n.* nachdenken; grübeln.
pony, *s.* Pony *m.*
pool¹, *s.* Teich *m.*; Pfuhl *m.*
pool², *s.* Spieleinsatz *m.*
poor, *adj.* arm; armselig.
pope, *s.* Papst *m.*
poplar, *s.* Pappel *f.*
popular, *adj.* populär; volkstümlich.
popularity, *s.* Popularität *f.*; Beliebtheit *f.*
population, *s.* Bevölkerung *f.*,
porch, *s.* Portal *n.*; Vorhalle *f.*
pore, *s.* Pore *f.*
pork, *s.* Schweinefleisch *n.*
port, *s.* Hafen *m.*
portable, *adj.* tragbar; — *s.* (*grammophone*) Reisegrammophon *n.*; (*wireless*) Kofferempfänger *m.*
portal, *s.* Portal *n.*; *fig.* Pforte *f.*
porter¹, *s.* Pförtner *m.*
porter², *s.* Gepäckträger *m.*
portfolio, *s.* Mappe *f.*
portion, *s.* Teil *m., n.*; —*v. a.* einteilen; zuteilen.
portrait, *s.* Porträt *n.*; Bildnis *n.*
Portuguese, *s.* Portugiese *m.*; Portugiesin *f.*; — *adj.* portugiesisch.
position, *s.* Lage *f.*;
positive, *adj.* bestimmt; positiv.
possess, *v. a.* besitzen;

possibility — **prescription**

beherrschen.
possibility, s. Möglichkeit f.
possible, adj. möglich.
post¹, s. Pfahl m.; Posten.
post², s. Posten m.; Platz m.; Stelle f.; Stellung f. Amt n.; — v. a. aufstellen; postieren; stationieren.
post³, s. Post f.; Postamt n.; — v. n. Post aufgeben; v.a. zur Post geben, aufgeben.
postage, s. Porto n.; Postgebühr f.; ~ stamp Briefmarke f.
postal-order, s. Postanweisung f.
postcard, s. Postkarte f.
poster, s. Plakat n.; Anschlag m.
post-free, adj. franko.
postman, s. Briefträger m.
post-office, s. Postamt n.
postpone, v. a. verschieben.
postscript, s. Nachschrift f.
pot, s. Topf m.
potato, s. Kartoffel f.
pottery, s. Töpferware f.; Töpferei f.
poultry, s. Geflügel n.
pound, s. Pfund n.
pour, v. a. gießen.
poverty, s. Armut f.
powder, s. Pulver n.; Puder n.
power, s. Kraft f.; Macht f. (mechanische) Energie.
powerful, adj. kräftig.
power-plant, s. Kraftanlage f.
power-station, s. Kraftwerk n.
practicable, adj. ausführbar.
practice, s. Praxis f.; Übung f.; Brauch m.
practise, v.a. ausüben; betreiben; einüben; v.n. üben; praktizieren.
praise, s. Lob n.; — v. a. loben, preisen.
pray, v. a. beten; bitten; anflehen; v. n. beten.
preach, v. a. & n. predigen.
precede, v. a. & n. vorangehen; vorgehen; führen; einleiten.
precious, adj. kostbar.
precise, adj. genau.
precocious, adj. frühreif, altklug.
predecessor, s. Vorgänger m.
predict, v. a. vorhersagen; prophezeien.
prefabricated, adj. vorfabriziert.
preface, s. Vorrede f.; Vorwort n.
prefer, v. a. (es) vorziehen.
preference, s. Vorliebe f.
pregnant, adj. schwanger; trächtig.
prejudice, s. Voreingenommenheit f.
preliminary, adj. einleitend; — s. preliminaries pl. Einleitung f.
premature, adj. vorzeitig; verfrüht.
premier, s. Premierminister m.
premises, s. pl. Grundstück n.
premium, s. Prämie f.
preparation, s. Vorbereitung f.
prepare, v.a. vorbereiten; zurechtmachen; v. n. sich vorbereiten.
prepay, v. a. vorausbezahlen; frankieren.
preposition, s. Präposition f.
prescribe, v. a. vorschreiben, verordnen.
prescription, s. Rezept

presence *n.;* Vorschrift *f.*
presence, *s.* Gegenwart *f.;* Anwesenheit *f.*
present¹, *adj.* gegenwärtig. — *s.* Gegenwart *f.*
present², *s.* Geschenk *n.;* — *v. a.* beschenken; *(pers.)* vorstellen.
presently, *adv.* sogleich, augenblicklich.
preserve, *v. a.* (auf)bewahren; — *s. pl.* Eingemachte *n.;* Wildreservat *n.*
president, *s.* President *m.;* Vorsitzende *m.*
press, *v. a.* auspressen; ausbügeln; — *s.* Presse *f.*
pressure, *s.* Druck *m.*
prestige, *s.* Prestige *n.*
presume, *v. a. & n.* annehmen; vermuten.
pretend, *v. a.* vorgeben; *v. n.* sich verstellen.
pretty, *adj.* hübsch.
prevail, *v. n.* vorherrschen.
prevent, *v. a.* verhüten.
previous, *adj.* vorhergehend.
prey, *s.* Raub *m.;* Opfer *n.*
price, *s.* Preis *m.;* Kosten *pl.*
price-list, *s.* Preisliste *f.*
prick, *s.* Stich *m.;* Stachel *m.; v. a. & n.* stechen.
pride, *s.* Stolz *m.;* Hochmut *m.*
priest, *s.* Priester *m.*
primary, *adj.* erster, erste, erstes; primär.
prime, *adj.* erster, erste, erstes; Haupt-; *Prime Minister* Ministerpräsident *m.*
primitive, *adj.* primitiv.
prince, *s.* Fürst *m.;* Prinz *m.*
principal, *adj.* rster, erste, erstes; — *s.* Prinzipal *m.*
principle, *s.* Prinzip *n.*

print, *s.* Abdruck *m.;* Auflage *f.;* Druck *m.;* — *v. a.* drucken (lassen).
printed matter, *s.* Drucksache *f.*
printing office, *s.* Druckerei *f.*
prison, *s.* Gefängnis *n.*
prisoner, *s.* Gefangene *m.*
private, *adj.* privat; persönlich; — *s. (soldier)* Gemeine *m.*
privilege, *s.* Privileg *n.;* Vorrecht *n.*
prize¹, *s.* Preis *m.;* Beute *f.;* Lotteriegewinn *m.*
prize², *v. a.* hochschätzen.
probability, *s.* Wahrscheinlichkeit *f.*
probable, *adj.* wahrscheinlich.
probably, *adv.* wahrscheinlich.
problem, *s.* Problem *n.;* Aufgabe *f.*
procedure, *s.* Verfahren *n.*
proceed, *v. n.* weitergehen; — *s.* ~s *pl.* Ertrag *m.*
proceedings, *s. pl.* Verfahren *n.;* Protokolle *n. pl.*
process, *s.* Verfahren *n.;* Prozeß *m.;* — *v. a.* verarbeiten.
procession, *s.* Prozession *f.*
proclaim, *v. a.* proklamieren; erklären.
produce, *v. a.* erzeugen; herstellen.
producer, *s.* Hersteller *m.;* Fabrikant *m.;* Regisseur *m.*
product, *s.* Produkt *n.*
production, *s.* Produktion *f.;* Herstellung *f.*
productive, *adj.* produktiv.
profess, *v. a.* bekennen.
profession, *s.* Beruf *m.;*

professor 94. **pull**

Gewerbe *n.*; Glaubensbekenntnis *n.*
professor, *s.* Professor *m.*, -in *f.*
profit, *s.* Profit *m.*; Gewinn *m.*; — *v. n.* von Nutzen sein; ~ *by* Nutzen ziehen aus.
profitable, *adj.* nützlich; vorteilhaft.
programme, *s.* Programm *n.*
progress, *s.* Fortschritt *m.*; — *v. n.* fortschreiten; weitergehen.
prohibition, *s.* Verbot *n.*
project, *s.* Plan *m.*; Projekt *n.*
projector, *s.* Projektionsapparat *m.*
prolong, *v. a.* verlängern.
prominent, *adj.* hervorragend.
promise, *s.* Versprechen *n.*; — *v.a.* versprechen.
promote, *v. a.* (be)fördern.
prompt, *adj.* unverzüglich; — *adv.* pünktlich; — *v. a.* zuflüstern.
prone, *adj.* geneigt.
pronoun, *s.* Fürwort *n.*
pronounce, *v. a.* aussprechen.
pronunciation, *s.* Aussprache *f.*
proof, *s.* Beweis *m.*; Probe *f.*
propeller, *s.* Propeller *m.*; Luftschraube *f.*; Schiffsschraube *f.*
proper, *adj.* richtig; passend.
property, *s.* Eigentum *n.*
proportion, *s.* Verhältnis *n.*; Proportion *f.*
proposal, *s.* Vorschlag *m*; Heiratsantrag *m.*
propose, *v. a.* vorschlagen; beantragen; beabsichtigen; — *v. n.* planen.
proposition, *s.* Vorschlag *m.*; Antrag *m.*
prosecute, *v. a.* (gerichtlich) verfolgen.
prospect, *s.* Aussicht *f.*
prosper, *v. n.* gedeihen.
prosperity, *s.* Wohlstand *m.*
prosperous, *adj. fig.* blühend; günstig.
protect, *v. a.* schützen.
protest, *s.* Protest *m.*; —*v.a. & n.* protestieren.
Protestant, *adj.* protestantisch; — *s.* Protestant *m.*, -in *f.*
proud, *adj.* stolz.
prove, *v. a.* beweisen.
proverb, *s.* Sprichwort *n.*
provide, *v. a.* versorgen; ~*ed that* vorausgesetzt, daß.
providence, *s.* Vorsehung *f.*; Fügung *f.*
province, *s.* Provinz *f.*; *fig.* Gebiet *n.*; Fach *n.*
provincial, *adj.* provinziell; kleinstädtisch.
provision, *s.* Vorräte *f.*; Lebensmittel *n. pl.*
provoke, *v. a.* herausfordern.
prudent, *adj.* klug; vorsichtig.
psalm, *s.* Psalm *m.*
psychology, *s.* Psychologie *f.*
public, *adj.* öffentlich; — *s.* Öffentlichkeit *f.*;
publication, *s.* Bekanntmachung *f.*
publicity, *s.* Öffentlichkeit *f.*
publish, *v. a.* herausgeben, verlegen.
publisher, *s.* Herausgeber *m.*; Verleger *m.*
pudding, *s.* Pudding *m.*
pull, *s.* Zug *m.*; Ruck *m.*; — *v. a. & n.* ziehen; ~ *back* zurückziehen; ~ *up* hochziehen.

pulpit — **rabbi**

pulpit, s. Kanzel f.
pulse, s. Puls(schlag) m.; — v. n. pochen.
pump[1], s. Pumpe f.; — v.a. & n. pumpen.
pump[2], s. Tanzschuh m.
pumpkin, s. Kürbis m.
punch[1], s. Locheisen n.; v. a. durchlöchern.
punch[2], s. Schlag m.; — v. a. schlagen; boxen.
punctual, adj. pünktlich.
puncture, s. Reifenpanne f.; — v. a. stechen; v. n. platzen.
punishment, s. Strafe f.
pupil, s. Schüler m.
purchase, v.a. kaufen; — s. Kauf m.;
pure, adj. rein; echt.
purify, v. a. reinigen; v. n. sich läutern.
purpose, s. Absicht f.; Zweck m.; Vorsatz m.
purse, s. Geldbeutel m.
pursue, v. a. verfolgen, fortsetzen; v. n. fortfahren;
pursuit, s. Verfolgung f.; Streben n.; ~s pl. Beschäftigung f.
push, s. Stoß m.; —v. a. & n. stoßen, schieben.
put, v. a. & n. legen, stellen; setzen; stecken; ~ by beiseite legen; ~ down niederlegen, notieren; ~ on (clothes) anlegen; (weight) zunehmen; ~ out (light) auslöschen; ~ up (umbrella) aufmachen; ~ up with sg sich etwas gefallen lassen.
puzzle, s. Rätsel n.
pyjamas, s. pl. Schlafanzug m.
pyramid, s. Pryamide f.

Q

quadrangle, s. Viereck n.; Schulhof m.
qualification, s. Qualifikation f.
qualify, v. a. befähigen; näher bestimmen.
quality, s. Eigenschaft f.
quantity, s. Quantität f.
quarrel, s. Zank m.; Streit m.; — v. n. sich zanken.
quarry, s. Steinbruch m.
quart[1], s. Quart n. (1,15 liter)
quart[2], s. (fencing) Quart f.
quarter, s. Viertel n.
quarters, s. pl. Quartier n.
quay, s. Kai m.
queen, s. Königin f.
queer, adj. sonderbar; seltsam.
quench, v. a. fig. löschen, unterdrücken.
quest, s. Nachforschen n.; Suchen n.
question, s. Frage f.; — v.a. Frage stellen; v. n. sich erkundigen.
questionnaire, s. Fragebogen m.
queue, s. Schlange f.; v. n. ~ (up) Schlange stehen.
quick, adj. schnell.
quiet, adj. ruhig; still; — s. Ruhe f.
quilt, s. Steppdecke f.
quit, v. a. verlassen v. n. aufhören.
quite, adj. ganz; durchaus.
quiz, v. a. prüfen; — s. Ausfragen n.; Quiz n.
quotation, s. Anführung f.; Preisangabe f.; Valutennotierung f.
quote, v. a. & n. zitieren.

R

rabbi, s. Rabbiner m.

rabbit — **ready**

rabbit, s. Kaninchen n.
race¹ s. (sport) Wettrennen n.
race², s. Rasse f.; Geschlecht n.; Stamm m.
race-course, s. Rennbahn f.
rack, s. Gerüst n.; Gestell n.
racket¹, s. Tennisschläger m.
racket², s. Lärm m.; v. n. lärmen.
radar, s. Radar n.
radiate, v. a. & n. (aus)strahlen; rundfunken.
radiator, s. Heizkörper m.; Kühler m.
radical, adj. radical; (pers.) Radikale m., f.; Wurzel f.
radio, s. Radio n.; Funk m.
radioactive, adj. radioaktiv.
radiogram, s. Radiogramm n.
radish, s. Rettich m.
rage, s. Wut f. Mode f.; — v. n. toben; rasen.
raid, s. Überfall m.
rail, s. Querstange f.; Eisenbahn f.
railroad, railway, s. Eisenbahn f.
rain, s. Regen m.; — v. n. regnen.
rainy, adj. regnerisch.
raise, v. a. erheben; züchten; (children) erziehen; — s. (salary) Gehaltserhöhung f.
rake, s. Rechen m.
rally, s. Tagung f.; Massenversammlung f.
ramification, s. Verzweigung f.
ranch, s. Viehfarm f.
random, adj. ziellos; — s. at ~ aufs Geratewohl; zufällig.
range, s. Reihe f.; Bergkette f.; Kollektion f.; Küchenherd m.
rank, s. Rang m.; Klasse f.; — v. a. einreihen; v.n. sich reihen.
ransom, s. Lösegeld n.
rap, s. Klaps m.
rape, s. Raub m.; Entführung f.; Notzucht f.
rapid, adj. schnell; rasch; — s. ~s pl. Stromschnelle f.
rare, adj. selten.
rash¹, adj. hastig; vorschnell; unbesonnen.
rash², s. Hautausschlag m.
rate, s. Tarif m.; Kurs m.; — v. a. bewerten; rechnen.
rather, adv. ziemlich, fast; lieber, eher.
ratify, v. a. ratifizieren; genehmigen.
ratio, s. Verhältnis n.
ration, s. Ration f. — v. a. rationieren.
rattle, s Gerassel n.; v. n. & a. rasseln.
raven, s. Rabe f.
raw, adj. roh.
ray, s. Strahl m.
razor, s. Rasiermesser n.
razor-blade, s. Rasierklinge f.
reach, v. a. erreichen; v. n. reichen, sich erstrecken (bis); — s. Reichweite f., Bereich m.
react, v. n. reagieren.
reaction, s. Reaktion f.; Rückwirkung f.
reactor, s. Reaktor m.; Umwandlungsanlage f.
read, v. a. & n. lesen.
reader, s. Leser m.; -in; (university) Dozent m.; Lesebuch n.
reading, s. Lesen n.; Vorlesung f.; Lektüre f.
ready, adj. bereit, fertig.

real 97. **reference**

real, *adj.* wirklich, echt.
reality, *adj.* Wirklichkeit *f.*
realize, *v. a.* verwirklichen; realisieren.
realm, *s.* Königreich *n.*; Reich *n.*
reap, *v. a. & n.* (corn) schneiden; mähen; ernten.
reaper, *s.* Mähmaschine *f.*
rear[1], *v. a.* aufziehen; züchten.
rear[2], *s.* Hinterseite *f.*; — *adj.* hinterer, hintere, hinteres.
reason, *s.* Grund *m.*; Anlaß *m.*; Vernunft *f.*;
reasonable, *adj.* vernünftig; billig.
rebate, *s.* Rabatt *m.*
rebellion, *s.* Rebellion *f.*; Aufruhr *m.*
rebuke, *v. a.* tadeln, zurechtweisen.
receipt, *s.* Empfang *m.*; Quittung *f.*; Kochrezept *n.*
receive, *v. a. & n.* empfangen; erhalten.
receiver, *s.* Empfänger *m.*
recent, *adj.* neu; frisch.
recently, *adv.* neulich.
reception, *s.* Aufnahme *f.*, (Radio)Empfang *m.*
receptionist, *s.* Empfangsdame *f.*
reciprocal, *adj.* gegenseitig.
recital, *s.* (Solo)Vortrag *m.*
recite, *v.a. & n.* vortragen; aufsagen.
reckless, *adj.* rücksichtslos; leichtsinnig.
reckon, *v. a. & n.* rechnen; vermuten.
recognize, *v. a.* anerkennen; erkennen; zugeben.
recollect, *v.a.* sich erinnern.
recommend, *v. a.* empfehlen.
reconcile, *v. a.* versöhnen; Streit schlichten.
reconstruction, *s.* Wiederherstellung *f.*
record, *s.* Aufzeichnung *f.*; Protokoll *n.*; Schallplatte *f.*; (sport) Rekord *m.*; — *v. a.* aufzeichnen; eintragen.
recorder, *s.* Registrierapparat *m.*; Tonwiedergabegerät *n.*
records, *s. pl.* Papiere *f. pl.*; Akten *f. pl.*
recount, *v.a.* erzählen.
recover, *v. a.* wiedererlangen; *v. n.* sich erholen.
recruit, *s.* Rekrut *m.*
rectangle, *s.* Rechteck *n.*
rector, *s.* Pfarrer *m.*
recur, *v. n.* zurückkehren.
red, *adj.* rot.
redeem, *v. a.* erlösen; wiedergutmachen.
redress, *s.* Abhilfe *f.*; — *v. a.* abhelfen; entschädigen.
reduce, *v. a.* herabsetzen; ermäßigen; *v. n.* sich vermindern.
reduction, *s.* Reduktion *f.*; Ermäßigung *f.*; Rabatt *m.*
reed, *s.* Rohr *n.*
reef[1], *s.* Riff *n.*; Untiefe *f.*
reef[2], *s.* Reff *n.*
reel[1], *s.* Haspel *f.*
reel[2], *v. n.* wirbeln, drehen.
refer, *v. a.* verweisen; *v. n.* ~ *to* verweisen, betreffen; sich wenden (an)
referee, *s.* Schiedsrichter *m.*; Referent *m.*
reference, *s.* Referenz *f.*;

reflect — **remit**

Verweisung *f. with* ~ *to* hinsichtlich; in betreff; *work of* ~ Nachschlagewerk *n.*
reflect, *v.a.* zurückwerfen; wiederspiegeln.
reflection, *s.* Reflexion *f.*
reform, *s.* Verbesserung *f.*; Reform *f.*; — *v. a.* reformieren.
refrain, *v. n.* (sich) enthalten; *v. a.* zurückhalten.
refresh, *v. a.* erfrischen; *v. n.* sich erholen.
refreshment, *s.* Erfrischung *f.*
refrigerator, *s.* Kühlschrank *m.*
refuge, *s.* Zuflucht *f.*
refugee, *s.* Flüchtling *m.*
refusal, *s.* Ablehnung *f.*
refuse¹, *v.a.* verweigern.
refuse², *s.* Abfall *m.*; Kehricht *m.*; Müll *m.*
refute, *v. a.* widerlegen, zurückweisen.
regain, *v. a.* wiedererlangen; wiedergewinnen.
regard, *v. a.* betrachten; beachten; in Betracht ziehen; — *s.* Blick *m.*; Rücksicht(nahme) *f.*; *with* ~ *to* in Hinsicht auf.
regarding, *prep.* hinsichtlich, betreffs.
regent, *s.* Regent *m.*
regiment, *s.* Regiment *n.*
region, *s.* Gegend *f.*
register, *s.* Register *n.*; Verzeichnis *n.*; — *v. a.* aufzeichnen; registrieren; *v.n.* sich melden.
regret, *s.* Bedauern *n.*
regular, *adj.* regelmäßig; richtig; regulär.
regulate, *v. a.* regeln; regulieren.
rehearsal, *s.* Probe *f.*
reign, *s.* Herrschaft *f.*; Regierung *f.*; *v. n.* herrschen.
rein, *s.* Zügel *m.*
reject, *v. a.* ablehnen; verwerfen; verweigern.
relate, *v. a.* erzählen; *v. n.* sich beziehen (auf).
relation, *s.* Verwandte *m., f.*; Erzählung *f.*; Verhältnis *n.*
relative, *adj.* relativ; — *s.* Verwandte *m., f.*
relax, *v. a.* entspannen.
relay, *s.* Ablösung *f.*; Übertragung *f.*; — *v.a. & n.* ablösen; (durch Zwischenstationen) übertragen.
release, *v. a.* freilassen, erlösen; — *s.* Freilassung *f.*; Befreiung *f.*; *(film)* Uraufführung *f.*
reliable, *adj.* zuverlässig.
relic, *s.* Reliquie *f.*
relief¹, *s.* Erleichterung *f.*; Trost *m.*
relief², *s.* Relief *n.*
relieve, *v. a.* lindern; entlasten; erleichtern.
religion, *s.* Religion *f.*
reluctant, *adj.* widerstrebend; zögernd.
rely, *v. n.* sich verlassen (auf).
remain, *v. n.* bleiben; übrigbleiben; — *s.* ~*s pl.* Reste *m. pl.*
remark, *v. a.* bemerken. *v. n.* eine Bemerkung machen; — *s.* Bemerkung *f.*
remarkable, *adj.* bemerkenswert; merkwürdig.
remedy, *s.* Heilmittel *n.*; Abhilfe *f.*; — *v.a.* heilen; abhelfen.
remember, *v. a. & n.* sich erinnern.
remind, *v. a.* erinnern; mahnen (an).
remit, *v. a.* vergeben; *(money)* überweisen;

remorse — **resistance**

v.n. nachlassen.
remorse, *s.* Gewissensbisse *m. pl.*
remote, *adj.* entfernt.
removal, *s.* Beseitigung *f.;* Wegräumen *n.;* Entfernung *f.;* Umzug *m.*
remove, *v. a.* entfernen; *v. n.* umziehen.
render, *v. a.* vortragen; ausdrücken; übersetzen.
renew, *v. a.* erneuern.
renounce, *v. a.* entsagen; verzichten (auf).
rent, *s.* Miete *f.;* Pacht *f.;* — *v. a.* vermieten; verpachten.
reorganization, *s.* Neugestaltung *f.;* Reorganisation *f.*
repair, *v. a.* reparieren; ausbessern; — *s.* Reparatur *f.*
repay, *v. a.* zurückzahlen; *v.n.* vergelten.
repeat, *v. a.* wiederholen; *v.n.* sich wiederholen.
repetition, *s.* Wiederholung *f.*
replace, *v. a.* ersetzen.
reply, *s.* Antwort *f.;* Erwiderung *f.;* — *v. a. & n.* antworten; erwidern.
report, *s.* Bericht *m.;* Gerücht *n.;* Knall *m.;* — *v. a. & n.* berichten.
reporter, *s.* Reporter *m.;* Berichterstatter *m.*
represent, *v. a.* verkörpern; vertreten.
representation, *s.* Darstellung *f.* Vertretung *f.*
representative, *s.* Vertreter *m.*
reprint, *s.* Neudruck *m.*
reproach, *s.* Vorwurf *m.;* — *v. a. & n.* (sich) Vorwürfe machen.

reproduce, *v. a.* wiedererzeugen; fortpflanzen; *v. n.* sich fortpflanzen.
reproduction, *s.* Wiedererzeugung *f.;* Fortpflanzung *f.* Reproduktion *f.*
reprove, *v. a.* tadeln.
republic, *s.* Republik *f.*
republican, *adj.* republikanisch; — *s.* Republikaner *m.,* -in *f.*
repulsive, *adj.* abstoßend.
reputation, *s.* Ruf *m.;* Ansehen *s.*
request, *s.* Gesuch *n.;* — *v. a.* bitten (um); ersuchen (um).
require, *v. a.* erfordern; *v. n.* verlangen.
requirement, *s.* Erfordernis *n.*
rescue, *s.* Befreiung *f.;* — *v. a.* befreien, retten.
research, *s.* Nachforschung *f.;* Forschung *f.;* — *v. n.* forschen.
resemble, *v. a.* ähnlich sein; *v. n.* sich ähnlich sein.
resent, *v. a. & n.* übelnehmen.
reserve, *s.* Vorrat *m.;* Reserve *f.*
reshuffle, *v. a.* umgruppieren; — *s.* Umgruppierung *f.*
reside, *v. n.* wohnen, ansässig sein.
residence, *s.* Wohnsitz *m.*
resident, *adj.* ortsansässig, — *s.* Einwohner *m.,* -in *f.*
resign, *v. n.* resignieren; zurücktreten; abdanken; verzichten.
resignation, *s.* Abdankung *f.;* Rücktritt *m.*
resist, *v. a. & n.* widerstehen.
resistance, *s.* Widerstand

resolution 100. **rig**

m.
resolution, s. Resolution f., Entschlossenheit f.
resolve, v. a. auflösen; beschließen; v. n. sich auflösen; sich entschließen; — s. Vorsatz m.; Entschluß m.
resort, v. n. Zuflucht nehmen; sich begeben (zu); — s. Erholungsort m.
resource, s. Hilfsquelle f.; ~s pl. Mittel n. pl.
respect, s. Hinsicht f.; Beziehung f.; Achtung f.; with ~ to mit rücksicht auf; in ~ of in Anbetracht; — v. a. Rücksicht nehmen auf.
respectful, adj. ehrerbietig, höflich.
respite, s. Frist f.
respond, v. n. & a. antworten; reagieren.
response, s. Antwort f.; Reaktion f.
responsibility, s. Verantwortlichkeit f.; Verantwortung f.
rest¹, s. Ruhe f.; Rast f.; v. n. ruhen.
rest², s. Rest m.
restaurant, s. Restaurant n.; Gaststätte f.
restless, adj. ruhelos.
restore, v. a. wiederherstellen; ersetzen.
restrain, v. a. zurückhalten (von).
restrict, v. a. einschränken, beschränken.
result, s. Ergebnis n.; Resultat n.; — v. n. sich ergeben.
resume, v. a. & n. wiederaufnehmen.
retain, v. a. behalten.
retire, v. n. sich zurückziehen; in Pension gehen.
retreat, s. Rückzug m. — v. n. (sich) zurückziehen; zurücktreten.
return, v. n. zurückkehren; v. a. erwidern; — s. Rückkehr f.; ~s pl. Gewinn m.; Ertrag m.; Vergeltung f.
reveal, v. a. & n. offenbaren; verraten; offenbar werden.
revenge, s. Rache f.; Revanche f.; — v. a. & n. rächen; sich rächen.
revenue, s. Einkommen n.; ~s pl. Einkünfte pl.
reverend, adj. ehrwürdig; — s. Geistlicher m.
reverse, adj. umgekehrt; — s. Gegenteil n.
review, s. Kritik f.; v. a. überprüfen; revidieren.
revision, s. Revision f.
revival, s. Wiederbelebung f.; Erneuerung f.
revolt, s. Revolte f.
revolution, s. Revolution f.; Kreislauf m.
revolve, v. n. & n. (sich) drehen.
reward, s. Entgelt m., n.; Lohn m.; — v. a. vergelten.
rheumatism, s. Rheumatismus m.
rhyme, s. Reim m.
rhythm, s. Rhythmus m.; Takt m.
rib, s. Rippe f.
ribbon, s. Band n.
rice, s. Reis m.
rich, adj. reich.
rid, v. a. befreien. get ~ of loswerden.
riddle, s. Rätsel n.
ride, v. n. & a. reiten; fahren.
ridge, s. Rücken m.; Gebirgskamm m.
ridiculous, adj. lächerlich.
rifle, s. Gewehr n.
rig, s. Takelung f.; — v. a.

right   101.   **ruby**

~ *out*, ~ *up* ausrüsten.
right, *adj.* recht, richtig; *be* ~ recht haben; *all* ~*l* alles in Ordnung!; — *adv.* recht, richtig;
rim, *s.* Felge *f.*; Rand *m.*
ring¹, *s.* Ring *m.*
ring², *v.n.* läuten; ~ *sy up* anklingeln, anrufen.
rink, *s.* (künstliche) Eisbahn *f.*
rinse, *v.a.* (aus)spülen.
riot, *s.* Aufruhr *m.*; — *v.n.* an einem Aufruhr teilnehmen; schwelgen.
rip, *v.n.* reißen; — *s.* Riß *m.*
ripe, *adj.* reif.
rise, *s.* Gehaltserhöhung *f.*; *fig.* Aufstieg *m.*; Erhöhung *f.*; Zuwachs *m.*; — *v.n.* aufstehen, sich erheben; revoltieren.
risk, *s.* Gefahr *f.*; Risiko *n.*; — *v.a.* wagen, riskieren.
rival, *s.* Nebenbuhler *m.*, -in *f.*; Konkurrent *m.*, -in *f.*; — *v.a. & n.* rivalisieren; konkurrieren (mit).
river, *s.* Fluß *m.*; Strom *m.*
road, *s.* Landstraße *f.*; *fig.* Weg *m.*
roar, *v.n.* brüllen; — *s.* Brüllen *n.*; Gebrüll *n.*
roast, *v.a. & n.* braten; rösten; — *s.* Braten *m.*
rob, *v.a.* (be)rauben.
robber, *s.* Räuber *m.*, -in *f.*
robbery, *s.* Raub *m.*; Diebstahl *m.*
robe, *s.* Talar *m.*
robin, *s.* Rotkehlchen *n.*
rock¹, *s.* Fels(en) *m.*

rock², *v.a.* wiegen, *v.n.* sich schaukeln.
rocket, *s.* Rakete *f.*
rocket-range, *s.* Raketenversuchsgelände *n.*
rocky, *adj.* felsig.
rod, *s.* Rute *f.*; Stab *m.*
roll, *s.* Rolle *f.*; Walze *f.*; Semmel *f.*; Verzeichnis *n.*; — *v.a. & n.* rollen; wälzen.
roller-towel, endloses Handtuch.
Roman, *adj.* Römisch; — *s.* Römer *m.*; -in *f.*
romance, *s.* Romanze *f.*; Romantik *f.*; — *adj.* abenteuerlich.
romantic, *adj.* romantisch.
roof, *s.* Dach *m.*
room, *s.* Zimmer *n.*
root, *s.* Wurzel *f.*
rope, *s.* Seil *n.*; Tau *n.*
rose, *s.* Rose *f.*
rot, *v.a. & n.* faulen; — *s.* Fäulnis *f.*
rotate, *v.n.* rotieren; kreisen; sich drehen;.
rotten, *adj.* verfault; modrig.
rough, *adj.* rauh; herb.
roughly, *adv.* rauh, im allgemeinen.
round, *adj.* rund; dick; — *s.* Kreis *m.*; Ring *m.*; Runde *f.*; — *adv.* rund herum, ringsum; — *prep.* (rund) um.
route, *s.* Reiseroute *f.*
routine, *s.* Routine *f.*
row¹, *s.* Reihe *f.*
row², *s.* Krach *m.*
royal, *adj.* königlich.
rub, *s.* Reiben *n.*; — *v.a. & n.* reiben.
rubber¹, *s.* Gummi *n.*
rubber², *s.* (*cards*) Robber *m.*
rubbish, *s.* Schutt *m.*; Unsinn *m.*
ruby, *s.* Rubin *m.*

| rudder | 102. | sandwich |

rudder, s. (Steuer) Ruder.
rude, adj. grob, unhöflich.
rue, v. a. bereuen.
rug, s. Teppich m.; Bettvorleger m.
ruin, s. Ruin m.; ~s pl. Ruine(n pl.) f.; — v. a. ruinieren; v. n. zerfallen; zugrunde gehen.
rule, s. Regel f., Vorschrift f.; Reglerung f., Lineal n.; — v. a. beherrschen.
ruler, s. Herrscher m.; -in f.; Lineal m.
rumour, s. Gerücht n.; — v. a. als Gerücht verbreiten.
run, s. Rennen n.; Verlauf m.; Gang m.; — laufen; umlaufen; arbeiten; triefen; zerlaufen; v. a. laufen (durch); fahren; segeln; entfliehen; laufen lassen; in Gang halten, bedienen.
runner, s. Renner m.; Läufer m.
runner-up, s. (sport) Zweitbeste m., f.
rupture, s. Bruch m.; — v. a. & n. brechen.
rural, adj. ländlich.
rush, s. Andrang m.; Hauptgeschäftsstunden pl.; — v. n. stürzen, jagen, hetzen.
Russian, s. Russe m.; Russin f.; russisch n. — adj. russisch
rust, s. Rost m.; — v. n. & a. verrosten; einrosten (lassen).
rustic, adj. ländlich; bäurisch.
rustle, v. n. & a. rascheln, knistern.
rye, s. Roggen m.

S

sabre, s. Säbel m.
sack, s. Sack m.; — v. a. rausschmeißen.
sacrament, s. Sakrament n.
sacrifice, s. Opfer n.; — v. a. & n. opfern.
sad, adj. traurig; kläglich.
saddle, s. Sattel m.; — v. a. satteln.
safe, adj. sicher; — s. Geldschrank.
safety, s. Sicherheit f.
sail, s. Segel n.; Segelfahrt f.; — v. n. (ab)segeln; abfahren.
sailor, s. Matrose m.; Seemann m.
saint, s. Heilige m., f.; — adj. heilig.
sake: for the ~ of um ... willen; zuliebe.
salad, s. Salat m.
salary, s. Gehalt n.
sale, s. Verkauf m.; Ausverkauf m.
sale-room, s. Auktionsraum m.
salesman, s. Verkäufer m.
salmon, s. Lachs m.
saloon, s. Salon m.
salt, s. Salz n.; — v. a. salzen.
salvation, s. Erlösung f.; Heil n.; fig. Rettung f.
same, adj. selber, selbe, selbes; — pron. (der-, die-, das-)selbe.
sample, s. Muster n.
sanatorium, s. Heilanstalt f.; Sanatorium n.
sanction, s. Genehmigung f.; Sanktion f.
sanctity, s. Heiligkeit f.
sand, s. Sand m.; ~s pl. Sandbank f.
sandal, s. Sandale f.
sandwich, s. belegtes

Brot.
sane, *adj.* geistig gesund; vernünftig.
sanitary, *adj.* Gesundheits-; Sanitär-.
sanity, *s.* gesunder Verstand *m.*
sap, *s.* Saft *m.*
sarcastic, *adj.* beißend; sarkastisch.
sardine, *s.* Sardine *f.*
Satan, *s.* Satan *m.*; Teufel *m.*
satellite, *s.* Satellit *m.*
satire, *s.* Satire *f.*
satisfaction, *s.* Befriedigung *f.*
satisfactory, *adj.* befriedigend.
satisfy, *v. a.* befriedigen.
Saturday, *s.* Samstag *m.*; Sonnabend *m.*
sauce, *s.* Soße *f.*; Tunke *f.*
saucepan, *s.* Kasserolle *f.*
saucer, *s.* Untertasse *f.*
sausage, *s.* Wurst *f.*
save[1], *v. a. & n.* retten; — erlösen; sparen.
save[2], *prep. & conj.* außer.
savings, *s. pl.* Ersparnisse *n. pl.*; ~ **bank** Sparkasse *f.*
saviour, *s.* Retter *m.*; Erlöser *m.*
saw, *s.* Säge *f.*; —*v. a. & n.* sägen.
say, *v. a.* sagen; reden; aufsagen; *v. n.* sagen, meinen; — *s.* Rede *f.*
scale[1], *s.* Schuppe *f.*
scale[2], *s.* Waagschale *f.*; ~*s pl.* Waage *f.*
scandal, *s.* Skandal *m.*; Klatsch. *m.*
scanty, *adj.* spärlich; dürftig.
scar, *s.* Narbe *f.*
scarce. *adj.* knapp; selten.
scarcely, *adv.* kaum.
scare, *s.* Schrecken *m.*; Panik *f.*; — *v. a.* erschrecken.

scarf, *s.* Schal *m.*
scarlet, *s.* Scharlachrot *n.*; — *adj.* scharlachrot.
scatter, *v. a. & n.* (sich) zerstreuen.
scene, *s.* Szene *f.*; Auftritt *m.*; Schauplatz *m.*
scenery, *s.* Szenerie *f.*;
scent, *s.* Wohlgeruch *m.*; — *v. a.*
schedule, *s.* Fahrplan *m.*; Lehrplan *m.*; — *v. a.* zusammenstellen; festsetzen.
scheme, *n.* Schema *n.*; Entwurf *m.*; — *v. a.* planen; *v. n.* Pläne machen.
scholar, *s.* Schüler *m.*, -in *f.*; Gelehrte *m.*
school, *s.* Schule *f.*
schoolmaster, *s.* Schulmeister *m.* Lehrer *m.*
schoolroom, *s.* Schulzimmer *n.*; Klassenzimmer *n.*
science, *s.* Wissenschaft *f.*; Naturwissenschaften *f. pl.*
scientific, *adj.* naturwissenschaftlich.
scientist, *s.* Gelehrte *m.*
scissors, *s. pl.* Schere *f.*
scold, *v. a.* schelten.
scooter, *s.* Kinderroller *m.*; Motorroller *m.*
scope, *s.* Bereich *m.*
scorch, *v. a.* versengen.
score, *s. (sport)* Punktzahl *f.*; Rechnung *f.*; *(music)* Partitur *f.*; — *v. a. (football)* ein Tor schießen; *v. n.* gewinnen.
scorn, *s.* Verachtung *f.*; — *v. a.* verachten; *v. n.* spotten.
Scot, *s.* Schotte *m.*, Schottin *f.*
Scotch, *adj.* schottisch; — *s. the* ~ die Schotten.

scour	send
scour, v. a. & n. scheuern.	kunde f.; fig. Augenblick m.; Moment m.
scout, s. Späher m.; Pfadfinder m.	**secondary,** adj. sekundär; untergeordnet.
scramble, v. n. klettern; ~d eggs pl. Rührei n.	**second-hand,** adj. gebraucht; antiquarisch.
scrape, s. Kratzen n.; fig. Not f.; Klemme f.	**secret,** adj. geheim; — s. Geheimnis n.
scratch, s. Ritz m.; — v.a. zerkratzen; v. n. kratzen.	**secretary,** s. Sekretär m.; ~ (of State) Minister m.
scream, s. Geschrei n.; Schrei m.; — v. a. & n. schreien.	**section,** s. Sektion f.; Abschnitt m.; Paragraph m.
screen, s. Schutzschirm m.; Projektionswand f. Filmleinwand f.; Röntgenschirm m.; Schutz m. — v. a. durchleuchten.	**secure,** adj. sicher. — v. a. sichern; sich etwas sichern.
	security, s. Sicherheit f.; Garantie f.; securities pl. Wertpapiere f.
screw, s. Schraube f.; — v. a. festschrauben.	**sedative,** — s. Beruhigungsmittel n.
script, s. Manuscript n.	**see¹,** v. a. sehen; besuchen; ersehen; v. n. sehen; einsehen, verstehen; ~ off fortbegleiten; ~ out hinausbegleiten.
Scripture, s. Heilige Schrift f.	
scrub¹, s. Gestrüpp n., Busch m.	
scrub², v. a. & n. scheuern.	
scrupulous, adj. gewissenhaft; genau.	**see²,** s. Bischofssitz m.
sculptor, s. Bildhauer m.	**seed,** s. Samen m.
sculpture, s. Skulptur f.	**seek,** v. a. & n. suchen; trachten nach; forschen.
sea, s. See f.; Meer n.	
seal, s. Siegel n.	
seam, s. Saum m.; Naht f.	**seem,** v. n. scheinen, erscheinen.
seaport, s. Seehafen m.	**seize,** v.a. ergreifen; pakken; v. n. ~ upon etwas ergreifen.
search, s. Suche f. — v. a. erforschen; v. n. suchen, forschen.	
	seldom, adv. selten.
search-light, s. Scheinwerfer m.	**select,** v. a. auswählen; — adj. auserwählt.
season, s. Jahreszeit f.; Saison f.; — v. a. würzen.	**self,** pron. selbst; — adj. einfarbig; — s. Selbst n.; Persönlichkeit f.
seat, s. Sitz m. Wohnsitz m.; — v. a. sich setzen.	**selfish,** adj. selbstsüchtig.
	self-service, s. Selbstbedienung f.
second¹, adj. zweiter, zweite, zweites; — s. Sekundant m.; zweiter Gang; (music) Sekunde f.; — adv. zweitens.	**sell,** v. a. verkaufen; v. n. handeln.
	seller, s. Verkäufer m.
	senate, s. Senat m.
	senator, s. Senator m.
second², s. (time unit) Se-	**send,** v. a. senden, schik-

sender   105.   **shatter**

ken. *v. n.* ~ *for* kommen lassen.

sender, *s.* Absender *m.;* — in *f.*

sense, *s.* Sinn *m.;* Gefühl *n.;* Bedeutung *f.;* — *v.a.* empfinden, fühlen; spüren.

sensible, *adj.* vernünftig, klug; fühlbar.

sensitive, *adj.* empfindlich.

sentence, *s.* Satz *m.;* Urteil *n.;* — *v. a.* verurteilen.

separate, *adj.* getrennt; —*v.a.* & *n.* (sich) scheiden.

September, *s.* September *m.*

serenade, *s.* Serenade *f.,* Ständchen *n.*

sergeant, *s.* Feldwebel *m.;* Wachtmeister *m.*

serial, *s.* Fortsetzungsroman *m.;* Serie *f.*

series, *s. sing.* & *pl.* Reihe *f.;* Serie *f.*

serious, *adj.* ernst.

sermon, *s.* Predigt *f.*

servant, *s.* Diener *m.* Magd *f.*

serve, *v. a.* dienen, bedienen.

service, *s.* Dienst *m.;* Bedienung *f.;* Gottesdienst *m.*

session, *s.* Sitzung *f.*

set, *s.* Garnitur *f.;* Service *n.;* Rundfunkgerät *n.;* Fernsehempfänger *m.;* — *v. a.* setzen, stellen; *v. n.* sitzen, passen; fest werden; ~ *forth* darlegen.

settle, *v.a.* festsetzen; etablieren; erledigen; *v. n.* ~ *(down)* sich niederlassen.

settlement, *s.* Regelung *f.;* Erledigung *f.;* Schlichtung *f.;* Ansiedlung *f.*

seven, *adj.* sieben.

seventeen, *adj.* siebzehn.

seventh, *adj.* siebenter, siebente, siebentes.

seventy, *adj.* siebzig.

several, *adj.* mehrere; verschiedene.

severe, *adj.* streng, schwer; heftig.

sew, *v. a.* & *n.* nähen.

sewing-machine, *s.* Nähmaschine *f.*

sex, *s.* Geschlecht *n.;* Sex *m.;* — *adj.* sexuell.

sexual, *adj.* sexuell.

shabby, *adj.* schäbig.

shade, *s.* Schatten *m.;* Schirm *m.*

shadow, *s.* Schatten *m.;* Schattenbild *n.*

shaft, *s.* Schaft *m.;* Welle *f.;* Achse *f.*

shake, *s.* Schütteln *n.;* Beben *n.;* Triller *f.;* — *v. n.* sich schütteln; zittern; *v. a.* erregen.

shall, *v. aux.* werden; sollen.

shallow, *adj.* seicht.

shame, *s.* Scham *f.* — *v. a.* beschämen.

shampoo, *s.* Haarwäsche *f.;* Haarwaschmittel *n.;* Schampun *m.;* — *v.a.* schampunieren.

shape, *s.* Gestalt *f.;* Form *f.;* —. *v. a.* gestalten, formen.

share, *s.* Teil *m.;* Anteil *m.;* — *v. a.* verteilen *v. n.* teilnehmen, sich beteiligen (an).

shareholder, *s.* Aktionär *m.*

sharp, *adj.* scharf; gerissen; *(music)* erhöht; — *v. a.* erhöhen; — *s. (music)* Kreuz *n.;* Erhöhung *f.*

sharpen, *v.a.* verschärfen; *(music)* erhöhen.

shatter, *v. a.* zerschmet-

shave — **sigh**

tern; *v. n.* zerbrechen.
shave, *v. a.* rasieren; *v. n.* sich rasieren; — *s.* Rasur *f.*; Rasieren *n.*
shawl, *s.* Schal *m.*
she, *pron.* sie.
shear, *s.* Schere *f.*; Blechschere *f*
sheath, *s.* Scheide *f.*
shed¹, *s.* Hütte *f.*
shed², *v. a.* vergießen; abwerfen; *v. n.* sich mausern; sich häuten.
sheep, *s. sing. & pl.* Schaf *n.*; Schafleder *n.*
sheet, *s.* Platte *f.* Blatt *n.*; Bettuch *n.*; Druckbogen *m.*
shelf, *s.* Brett *n.*; Fach *n.*
shell, *s.* Schale *f.*; Hülse *f.*; Muschel *f.*; — *v. a.* schälen; bombardieren.
shelter, *s.* Obdach *n.*; *fig.* Schutz *m.*; — *v. a.* beschützen.
shepherd, *s.* Schäfer *m.*
shield, *s.* Schild *m.*
shine, *s.* Schein *m.*; Glanz *m.*; — *v. n.* scheinen.
ship, *s.* Schiff *n.*; — *v. a.* verladen; *v. n.* sich einschiffen.
shipment, *s.* Versand *m.*; Schiffsladung *f.*
shipwreck, *s.* Schiffbruch *m.*
shipyard, *s.* Schiffswerft *f.*
shirt, *s.* Hemd *n.*
shiver, *s.* Schauer *m.*; — *v. n.* schaudern.
shock, *s.* Stoß *m.*, Erschütterung *f.*; — *v. a.* empören; Anstoß erregen.
shoe, *s.* Schuh *m.*
shoemaker, *s.* Schuhmacher *m.*
shoot, *s.* Schießen *n.*; Sproß *m.*; *v. a. & n.* (er)schießen.
shop, *s.* Laden *m.*; Geschäft *n.*; Werkstatt *f.*

shop assistant, *s.* Verkäufer *m.*, -in *f.*
shopkeeper, *s.* Ladenbesitzer *m.*, -in *f.*
shore, *s.* Ufer *n.*; Strand *m.*
short, *adj.* kurz; klein; — *s.* Kürze *f.*
shorten, *v. a.* kürzer machen *v. n.* kürzer werden.
shorthand, *s.* Kurzschrift *f.*
shortly, *adv.* bald.
shot, *s.* Schuß *m.*; Filmaufnahme *f.*; Spritze *f.*
shoulder, *s.* Schulter *f.*
shout, *s.* Schrei *m.*, *v. n.* laut schreien.
shovel, *s.* Schaufel *f.*
show, *v. a.* zeigen, ausstellen; *v. n.* sich zeigen erscheinen; — *s.* Schau *f.*; Ausstellung *f.*
shower, *s.* Schauer *m.*; Dusche *f.*
shrill, *adj.* schrill, gellend.
shrink, *v. n.* schrumpfen; einlaufen.
shroud, *s.* Leichentuch *n.*
shrub, *s.* Strauch *m.*; Busch *m.*
shudder, *v. n.* schaudern; erbeben; — *s.* Schauder *m.*
shut, *v. a.* (ver)schließen, zumachen; *v. n.* zugehen.
shutter, *s.* Fensterladen *m.*; *(photo)* Verschluß *m.*
shy, *adj.* scheu.
sick, *adj.* krank; unwohl.
sickness, *s.* Krankheit *f.*
side, *s.* Seite *f.*; *(sport)* Mannschaft *f.*
siege, *s.* Belagerung *f.*
sieve, *s.* Sieb *n.*
sift, *v. a.* sieben.
sigh, *s.* Seufzer *m.*; —

sight | **slap**

v.n. aufseufzen; seufzen.
sight, *s.* Sehvermögen *n.;* Visier *n.;* ~s *pl.* Sehenswürdigkeiten *f. pl.*
sightseeing, *s.* Besichtigung *f.* von Sehenswürdigkeiten.
sign, *s.* Zeichen *n.;* Wink *m.;* — *v. n.* winken; *v.a.* unterzeichnen.
signal, *s.* Signal *n.;* . — *v.a. & n.* Signale geben; winken.
signature, *s.* Unterschrift *f.*
signify, *v. a.* bezeichnen, bedeuten.
silence, *s.* Ruhe *f.;* Stille *f.*
silent, *adj.* still; stumm.
silk, *s.* Seide *f.*
silly, *adj.* albern, töricht.
silver, *s.* Silber *n.*
similar, *adj.* ähnlich, gleich.
simple, *adj.* einfach, schlicht.
simultaneous, *adj.* gleichzeitig.
sin, *s.* Sünde *f.*
since, *adv.* seit; *long* ~ schon lange; — *conj.* seit(dem); weil; —*prep.* seit; ~ *when?* seit wann?
sincere, *adj.* aufrichtig.
sinew, *s.* Sehne *f.*
sing, *v.n. & a.* singen; — *s.* Singen *n.;* Gesang *m.*
singer, *s.* Sänger *m.;* -in *f.*
single, *adj.* einzeln; einsam; unverheiratet.
singular, *adj.* einzigartig, sonderbar; — *s.* Singular *m.;* Einzahl *f.*
sink, *v. n.* sinken, sich senken; — *s.* Ausguß *m.*
sinner, *s.* Sünder *m.,* -in *f.*
sir, *s.* Herr *m.*
sister, *s.* Schwester *f.;* Ordensschwester *f.;* Oberschwester *f.*
sister-in-law, *s.* Schwägerin *f.*
sit, *v. n.* sitzen; tagen; brüten; passen; *v. a.* setzen; ~ *down* sich setzen; ~ *up* sich aufsetzen.
site, *s.* Bauplatz *m.*
sitting-room, *s.* Wohnzimmer *n.*
situation, *s.* Lage *f.;* Stellung *f.;* Zustand *m.*
six, *adj.* sechs.
sixteen, *adj.* sechzehn *f.*
sixth, *adj.* sechster, sechste, sechstes.
sixty, *adj.* sechzig.
size, *s.* Größe *f.;* Maß *n.;* (Schuh-)Nummer *f.*
skate, *s.* Schlittschuh *m.;* — *v. n.* eislaufen; Schlittschuh laufen.
sketch, *s.* Skizze *f.;* — *v. a.* skizzieren.
ski, *s.* Schi *m.;* Ski *m.;* — *v. n.* Ski laufen.
skill, *s.* Geschicklichkeit *f.;* Fertigkeit *f.*
skim, *v. a.* abschöpfen.
skin, *s.* Haut *f.;* Fell *n.*
skip, *v. n.* hüpfen; springen; *v. a.* überspringen.
skipper, *s.* Schiffer *m.;* Kapitän *m.*
skirt, *s.* Rock *m.;* Schoß *m.*
skull, *s.* Schädel *m.*
sky, *s.* Himmel *m.*
slack, *adj.* schlaff; lose.
slacken, *v. a.* lockern, entspannen; *v. n.* nachlassen.
slander, *s.* Verleumdung *f.;*—*v. a. & n.* verleumden, schmähen.
slanting, *adj.* schräge.
slap, *s.* Klaps *m.;* — *v. a. & n.* klopfen.

slate — **soldier**

slate, s. Schiefer m.
slaughter, s. Schlachten n.; — v. a. schlachten.
slave, s. Sklave m.
sledge, s. Schlitten m.; — v. n. Schlitten fahren.
sleep, v. n. schlafen; v. a. ausschlafen; — s. Schlaf m.
sleeping-car, s. Schlafwagen m.
sleepy, adj. schläfrig.
sleeve, s. Ärmel m.
slender, adj. schlank.
slice, s. Schnitte f.; Scheibe f.; — v. a. aufschneiden.
slide, v. n. gleiten.
slight, adj. schmächtig; schwach; — s. Verachtung f.; — v. a. geringschätzig behandeln.
slim, adj. schlank.
sling, s. Schleuder f.; — v. a. schleudern.
slip, v. n. schüpfen; v. a. entgehen; entfallen; — s. Fehltritt m.; Unterrock m.; Kissenbezug m.
slipper, s. Pantoffel m.
slope, s. Abhang m.; — v. a. abschrägen; v. n. sich neigen.
slot, s. Schlitz m.
slow, adj. & adv. langsam; — v. n. & a. ~ down verlangsamen.
slumber, v. n. schlummern; — s. Schlummer m.
slump, v. n. fallen, stürzen; — s. Sturz m.
sly, adj. schlau.
small, adj. klein.
smart, adj. klug, nett; — s. Schmerz m.; — v. n. schmerzen.
smell, s. Geruch m.; — v. a. & n. riechen.
smile, s. Lächeln n.; — v. n. lächeln.
smoke, s. Rauch m.; — v. a. & n. rauchen.
smooth, adj. glatt; — v. a. glätten; fig. ebnen.
smuggle, v. a. & n. schmuggeln.
snake, s. Schlange f.
snap, s. Knallen n.; Krachen n.; Krach m.; — v. n. schnappen.
snatch, v. a. erschnappen; — s. Zugreifen n.
sneeze, v. n. niesen; — s. Niesen n.
snore, v. n. schnarchen — s. Schnarchen n.
snow, s. Schnee m.; — v. n. schneien.
so, adv. so, dermaßen; — conj. daher; int. so!
soak, v. a. einweichen.
soap, s. Seife f.; — v. a. einseifen.
soar, v. n. sich aufschwingen, sich erheben.
sob, s. Schluchzen n.; — v. a. & n. schluchzen.
sober, adj. nüchtern; — v. a. ernüchtern; v. n. nüchtern werden.
social, adj. gesellschaftlich; sozial.
socialism, s. Sozialismus m.
society, s. Gesellschaft f.; Verein m.
sock, s. Socke f.
socket, s. Hülse f.; Steckdose f.
soda-water, s. Sodawasser n.
sofa, s. Sofa n.
soft, adj. & adv. weich; leise, sanft.
soil[1], s. Boden m.; Erde f.
soil[2], v. a. beschmutzen; beflecken; — s. Fleck m.; Schmutz m.
soldier, s. Soldat m.

| solicit | 109. | specialist |

solicit, *v. a.* bitten; sich bemühen um; *v. n.* nachsuchen.
solicitor, *s.* Anwalt *m.*; Vertreter *m.*
solidarity, *s.* Solidarität *f.*
solution, *s.* Auflösung *f.*, Lösung *f.*
solve, *v. a.* lösen.
some, *adj.* irgendein; einige; manche; etwas, ein wenig; etwa; — *pron.* einer, eine, eines, etwas.
somebody, *pron.* jemand, irgendeiner.
someone, *pron. sing.* jemand, irgendeiner.
something, *s.* irgend etwas; — *adv.* ~ *like* so etwas wie.
sometime, *adv.* einmal; — *adj.* früherer, ehemaliger.
somewhat, *adv.* etwas.
somewhere, *adv.* irgendwo; irgendwohin.
son, *s.* Sohn *m.*
song, *s.* Lied *n.*; Gesang *m.*
son-in-law, *s.* Schwiegersohn *m.*
soon, *adv.* bald, eher.
soprano, *s.* Sopran *m.*
sore, *adj.* wund; empfindlich; — *s.* wunde Stelle *f.*
sorrow, *s.* Sorge *f.*; — *v.n.* sich grämen.
sorry, *adj.* bekümmert; *I am* ~! es tut mir leid; Verzeihung!
sort, *s.* Sorte *f.*; Weise *f.*;
soul, *s.* Seele *f.*
sound¹, *adj.* gesund; vernünftig.
sound², *s.* Ton *m.*; Laut *m.*; Klang *m.*; — *v. n.* tönen, ertönen; *v. a.* ertönen.
soup, *s.* Suppe *f.*
sour, *adj.* sauer; —*v.a.* säuern; *v. n.* sauer werden.
source, *s.* Quelle *f.*; Ursprung *m.*
south, Süden *m.*; — *adj.* südlich; — *adv.* nach Süden; südwärts.
southern, *adj.* südlich; Süd-.
southwest, *s.* Südwest(en) *m.*; — *adj.* südwest.
sovereign, *adj.* höchst; —*s.* Herrscher *m.*,- in *f.*
Soviet, *s.* Sowjet *m.*; — *adj.* sowjetisch.
sow¹, *s.* Sau *f.*
sow², *v. a.* säen.
space, *s.* Raum *m.*
space-flight, *s.* Weltraumflug *m.*
spaceman, *s.* Weltraumfahrer *m.*
space-ship, *s.* Raumschiff *n.*
space-suit, *s.* Raumanzug *m.*
spade¹, *s.* Spaten *m.*; — *v. n.* graben; *v. a.* umgraben.
spade², *s. (cards)* Pik *n.*
span, *s.* Zeitspanne *f.*; Spannweite *f.*
Spaniard, *s.* Spanier *m.*
Spanish, *adj.* spanisch; — *s.* (die) Spanier *pl.*
spanner, *s.* Schraubenschlüssel *m.*
spare, *adj.* spärlich; — *s.* Ersatzteil *m.*; — *v.a.* ersparen; *v. n.* sparen; sparsam sein.
spark, *s.* Funken *m.*; — *v. n.* Funken sprühen.
sparkle, *v. n.* funkeln.
sparrow, *s.* Sperling *m.*
speak, *v. n.* sprechen; sich unterhalten.
speaker, *s.* Sprecher *m.*
spear, *s.* Speer *m.*
special, *adj.* besonder.
specialist, *s.* Specialist

| specific | 110. | squirrel |

m.; Fachmann m.; Facharzt m.
specific, adj. bestimmt.
specify, v. a. spezifizieren.
specimen, s. Probe f.; Muster n.; Exemplar n.
speck, s. Fleck m.
spectacle, s. Schauspiel n.; Anblick m. ~s pl. Brille f.
spectator, s. Zuschauer m.
speculate, v. n. spekulieren.
speech, s. Sprache f.
speed, s. Geschwindigkeit f.; Eile f.
speedway, s. Schnellstraße f.; Autobahn f.
spell[1], v. a. & n. buchstabieren; richtig schreiben.
spell[2], s. Zauber m.
spelling, s. Rechtschreibung f.
spend, v.a. ausgeben; verbrauchen; verbringen.
sphere, s. Kugel f.; Sphäre f., Gebiet n.
spice, s. Gewürz n.
spill, v. a. verschütten; vergießen.
spin, v. a. spinnen; v. n. wirbeln.
spinach, s. Spinat m.
spine, s. Rückgrat n.
spiral, adj. spiral; — s. Spirale f.
spire, s. Turmspitze f.
spirit, s. Geist m.; Spiritus m.; ~s pl. Stimmung f.
spite, s. Bosheit f.
splash, s. Spritzen n.; Plätschern n.
splendid, adj. glänzend; prächtig; herrlich.
splinter, s. Splitter m.; — v. n. zersplittern.
split, s. Spalt m.; Riß m.; fig Spaltung f.; — v. n. sich aufspalten.
spoil, s. Beute f.; Raub m.; — v. a. & n. verderben
sponge, s. Schwamm m.
spontaneous, adj. freiwillig.
spoon, s. Löffel m.; — v. a. löffeln.
sport, s. Sport m.; Spiel n. — v. n. Sport treiben.
spot, s. Fleck m.; Tupf m.
spotless, adj. unbefleckt.
spout, s. Schnauze f.; Wasserspeier m.
spray, s. Sprühregen m.; — v.a. verstäuben; v. n. sprühen.
spread, v. a. ausbreiten; bestreichen; v. n. sich ausbreiten, sich verbreiten.
spring, s. Sprung m.; Quelle f.; Frühling m.; — v. a. zersprengen; v. n. springen, entspringen.
sprinkle, v. a. sprenkeln; v. n. sprühen.
sprout, v. n. sprossen; — s. Sproß m.; ~s pl. Kohlsprossen f. pl.; *Brussels* ~s Rosenkohl m.
spy, s. Späher m.; -in f.; Spion m.
squander, v. a. & n. verschwenden.
square, adj. viereckig; ehrlich; offen; — s. Quadrat n.; Viereck n.
squeeze, v. a. & n. (sich) drücken, (sich) pressen.
squire, s. Gutsbesitzer m.
squirrel, s. Eichhörnchen n.

stability, s. Beständigkeit f.
stable[1], adj. stabil; beständig.
stable[2], s. Stall m.
stack, s. Schober m.; — v. a. aufschobern; aufstapeln.
stadium, s. Stadion n.
staff, s. Stab m.; Stock m.; Notensystem n.; Personal n.; Lehrkörper m.; Beamtenstab m.; Oberkommando n.
stag, s. Hirsch m.
stage, s. Bühne f.
stagger, v. n. taumeln; v. a. ins Wanken bringen; — s. Schwanken n.
stain, s. Flecken m.; — v. a. beflecken.
stair, s. Stufe f.; ∼s pl. Treppe f.; Stiege f.
staircase, s. Treppenhaus n.
stake[1], s. Pfahl m.
stake[2], s. Wetteinsatz m.; Anteil n.; Einsatz m.; Risiko n.; — v. a. einsetzen, wagen.
stall, s. Stand m.; Box f.; Sperrsitz m.; — v. a. festfahren; blockieren; v. n. steckenbleiben.
stammer, v. n. stottern; — s. Stottern n.
stamp, s. Stempel m.; Briefmarke f.; — v. a. stempeln, prägen; frankieren.
stand, s. Stehen n.; Tribüne f.; — v. n. stehen; ∼ back zurücktreten; ∼ up sich erheben; v. a. hinstellen.
standard, s. Standarte f.; Fahne f.; — adj. maßgebend.

star, s. Stern m.; Star m.
stare, v. n. starren; v. a. anstarren; — s. Blick m.
start, s. Auffahren n.; (sport) Ablauf m.; — v. n. auffahren; (sport) ablaufen, starten.
starve, v. a. verhungern lassen; v. n. verhungern.
state, s. Staat m.; Zustand m.; Lage f.; Rang m.; — v. a. feststellen; erklären; behaupten.
statement, s. Erklärung f.; Bericht m.
statesman, s. Staatsmann m.
station, s. Station f.; — v. a. postieren.
stationer, s. Schreibwarenhändler m.
station-wagon, s. Kombiwagen m.
statistical, adj. statistisch.
statistics, s. pl. Statistik f.
status, s. Zustand m.; Stand m.
stay, v. n. bleiben; sich aufhalten, wohnen; weilen; v. a. aufhalten; stillen; — s. Aufenthalt m.; Halt m.; Stockung f.; Strebe f.
steady, adj. stetig; fest; — v. a. sicher machen.
steak, s. Steak m.
steal, v. a. stehlen, entwenden; v. n. sich davonstehlen.
steam, s. Dampf m.; — v. n. dampfen.
steamboat, s. Dampfschiff n.
steam-engine, s. Dampfmaschine f.
steamer, s. Dampfer m.
steamship, s. Dampfschiff

steel — **strain**

n.
steel, s. Stahl m.; v. a. verstählen; fig. stärken.
steep, adj. steil; jäh.
steeple, s. Kirchturm m.
steeple-chase, s. Hindernisrennen n.
steer¹, s. Ochse m.
steer², v. a. & n. steuern, lenken.
steering-wheel, s. Steuerrad n.
stem¹, s. Stamm m.
stem², v. a. aufhalten, hemmen.
step, s. Schritt m.; Stufe f.; — v. n. schreiten, treten; v. a. abschreiten; ~ up fig. erhöhen, steigern.
stepmother, s. Stiefmutter f.
stereo, adj. dreidimensional, Stereo-.
stern, adj. ernst, streng.
stew, v. a. & n. schmoren, dämpfen; — s. Schmorgericht n.
steward, s. Verwalter m.
stewardess, s. Stewardeß f.; Flugbegleiterin f.
stick¹, s. Stock m.; Stab m.; Kleinholz n.
stick², v. n. stecken; kleben; v. a. ankleben.
stiff, adj. steif; starr.
still¹, adj. still, ruhig.
still², adv. (immer) noch; noch immer; — conj. dennoch.
stimulate, v. a. anregen; v. n. stimulieren.
sting, s. Stachel m.
stink, s. Gestank m.; — v.n. stinken.
stipulate, v. a. bedingen.
stir, v. a. rühren; v. n. sich rühren; — s. Aufregung f.
stitch, s. Stich m.; — v. n. & n. nähen; heften.
stock, s. Lager n.; Bestand m.; Vorrat m.; — adj. auf Lager; vorrätig; — v. a. ausstatten, beliefern; v. n. vorrätig haben.
stock-exchange, s. Börse f.; Effektenbörse f.
stockholder, s. Effektenbesitzer m.; -in f. Aktionär m. -in f.
stocking, s. Strumpf m.
stomach, s. Magen m.
stone, s. Stein m.; Kern m.
stool, s. Schemel m.; Hokker m.; Stuhlgang m.
stoop, v. n. sich beugen, sich bücken; v. a. neigen; — s. Beugung f., Erniedrigung f.
stop, v. a. anhalten; unterbrechen, plombieren; v. n. stehenbleiben; innehalten; — s. Ende n.; Aufenthalt m.; (music) Griff m.; Ventil n.; Register n.; Punkt m.
storage, s. Lagerung f.; Lagergeld n.
store, s. Lager n.; Bestand m.; ~s pl. Vorräte pl.; Warenhaus n. — v. a. versorgen; aufspeichern; lagern.
stork, s. Storch m.
storm, s. Sturm m.
story¹, s. Geschichte f.; Erzählung f.
story², s. Stockwerk n.
stout, adj. stark, dick; — s. Starkbier n.
stove, s. Ofen m.
straight, adj. gerade; ehrlich; — adv. geradeaus; sofort; — s. Gerade f.
strain, s. Druck m.; Zug m.; Spannung f.; — v. a. anspannen, anstrengen; vn. sich span-

nen; sich anstrengen.
strait, s. Meerenge f.; Not f.
strand[1], s. Strand m.
strand[2], s. Strang m.
strange, adj. fremd; seltsam; sonderbar.
stranger, s. Fremde m.
strategy, s. Kriegskunst f.; Strategie f.
straw, s. Stroh n.; Strohhalm m.
strawberry, s. Erdbeere f.
stray, v. n. irregehen; abirren.
stream, s. Bach m.; Strom m.; Strömung f.; — v. n. strömen; v. a. überströmen.
street, s. Straße f.
strength, s. Stärke f.; Kraft f.
strengthen, v. a. stärken; v.n. erstarken.
stress. s. Druck m.; Betonung f.; Spannung f.; — v. a. betonen; beanspruchen; überlasten.
stretch, v.a. strecken; ausdehnen; v.n. sich erstrecken; sich dehnen; sich anstrengen.
stretcher, s. Tragbahre f.
strew, v. a. & n. (be)streuen.
strict, adj. streng, genau.
strife, s. Streit m.
strike, s. Streik m.; — v. a. schlagen; v. n. treffen, schlagen, streiken.
string, s. Schnur f.; Bindfaden m.
strip, v. a. entkleiden, entblößen; v. n. sich ausziehen; — s. Streifen m.
stripe, s. Streifen m.; v. a. streifen.
strip-lighting, s. Neonbeleuchtung f.
strip-tease, s. Striptease n.
strive, v. n. sich mühen; bestreben.
stroke, s. Schlag m.; Schlaganfall m.; — v.n. streicheln.
stroll, s. Spaziergang m.; m.; — v. n. herumspazieren.
strong, adj. stark; kräftig; fest.
structure, s. Bau m.; Struktur f.; Gefüge n.
struggle, s. Kampf m.; — v. kämpfen.
stubborn, adj. eigensinnig; stur.
student, s. Student m., -in f.; Gelehrte m.
study, s. Studium n.; Arbeitszimmer n.; Studie f.; — v. n. studieren; v. a. einstudieren.
stuff, s. Stoff m.; Zeug n. — v. a. stopfen; v.n. sich vollstopfen.
stumble, v. n. stolpern.
stupid, adj. dumm.
sturdy, adj. kräftig.
subdue, v.a. unterwerfen; bezwingen.
subject, s. Untertan m.; Staatsangehörige m., f.; Subjekt n.; Gegenstand m.; Thema n.; Lehrfach n.; — v. a. unterwerfen; — adj. abhängig, ausgesetzt.
sublime, adj. erhaben.
submarine, s. Unterseeboot n.
submit, v. a. vorlegen; unterwerfen; v. n. sich unterwerfen.
subordinate, s. Unterordnung f.
subscribe, v. a. unterschreiben; v. n. zeichnen (für); abonnieren.

subscriber 114. **supposition**

subscriber, s. Unterschreiber m., -in f.
subsequent, adj. folgend; später.
subsidy, s. Geldbeihilfe f.; Zuschuß m.
subsist, v. n. bestehen; v. a. erhalten.
substance, s. Substanz f.
substantial, adj. wesentlich; nahrhaft; kräftig.
substitute, s. Stellvertreter m.; Ersatzmittel n.; — v. a. ersetzen; v. n. vertreten.
substract, v. a. abziehen; subtrahieren.
subtle, adj. fein, zart.
suburb, s. Vorstadt f.
subway, s. Untergrundbahn f.
succeed, v. n. gelingen; v. a. nachfolgen.
success, s. Erfolg m.
succession, s. Nachfolge f.; Reihenfolge f.
successor, s. Nachfolger m.; -in f.
such, adj. & pron. solcher, solche, solches; — adv. so, derart; — pron. and ~ (like) und dergleichen.
suck, v. a. saugen.
sudden, adj. plötzlich.
suffer, v. n. leiden; v. a. erleiden.
suffering, s. Leiden n.
sufficient, adj. genügend.
sugar, s. Zucker m.; — v. a. & n. (ver)zuckern.
suggest, v. a. eingeben; vorschlagen; andeuten.
suggestion, s. Anregung f.; Vorschlag m.
suicide, s. Selbstmord m.
suit, s. Anzug m.; Kostüm n.; Prozeß m.; (cards) Farbe f.; Gesuch n.; — v. a. kleiden; jm. bekommen; gefallen; v. n. passen; übereinstimmen; angenehm sein.
suitable, adj. passend, geeignet.
suitcase, s. Handkoffer m.
suitor, s. Freier m.
sulk, v. n. schmollen.
sum, s. Summe f.; Betrag m.; — v. a. ~ up zusammenrechnen; v. n. sich belaufen (auf).
summary, s. Zusammenfassung f.; Übersicht f.; Abriß m.
summer, s. Sommer m.
summit, s. Gipfel m.
summon, v. a. auffordern, vorladen.
summons, s. pl. gerichtliche Vorladung f.
sun, s. Sonne f.
Sunday, s. Sonntag m.
sunny, adj. sonnig.
sunrise, s. Sonnenaufgang m.
sunset, s. Sonnenuntergang m.
sunshine, s. Sonnenschein m.
sunstroke, s. Sonnenstich m.
superb, adj. prächtig.
superfluous, adj. überflüssig.
superior, adj. überlegen; — s. Vorgesetzte m., f.
supermarket, s. Supermarket m.
supersonic-, adj. Ultraschall-.
supper, s. Abendessen n.
supplement, s. Beilage f.
supply, v. a. liefern, versorgen; — s. Vorrat m.; Lieferung f.
support, s. Stütze f.; Unterstützung f. —v. a. unterstützen.
suppose, v. a. annehmen; vermuten.
supposition, s. Voraus-

suppress — **table-cloth**

setzug *f.*; Vermutung *f.*
suppress, *adj.* unterdrükken.
supreme, *adj.* höchst;
sure, *adj.* sicher; gewiß.
surely, *adv.* sicherlich.
surface, *s.* Oberfläche *f.*
surgeon, *s.* Chirurg *m.*
surgery, *s.* Chirurgie *f.*
surname, *s.* Familienname *m.*
surpass, *v. a.* übertreffen.
surprise, *s.* Überraschung *f.*
surrender, *s.* Ergebung *f.*; — *v. a.* übergeben *v. n.* sich ergeben.
surroundings, *s. pl.* Umgebung *f.*
survey, *s.* Überblick *m.*; Vermessung *f.*; — *v. a.* überblicken; vermessen.
survive, *v. a.* überleben.
survivor, *s.* Überlebende *m., f.*
suspect, *s.* Verdächtige *m., f.*; — *adj.* verdächtig; — *v. a.* verdächtigen.
suspenders, *s. pl.* Strumpfhalter *m.*
suspense, *s.* Spannung *f.*
suspicion, *s.* Verdacht *m.*; Argwohn *m.*
suspicious, *adj.* verdächtig.
sustain, *v. a.* ertragen; erleiden.
swallow¹, *s.* Schwalbe *f.*
swallow², *s.* Schluck *m.*; — *v. a.* hinunterschlucken; *v.n.* schlucken.
swamp, *s.* Sumpf *m. v. a.* überschwemmen.
swan, *s.* Schwan *m.*
swarm, *s.* Schwarm *m.*
swear, *v. n. & a.* schwören; fluchen.
sweat, *s.* Schweiß *m.*;— *v. n.* schwitzen.
sweater, *s.* Pullover *m.*; Strickjacke *f.*
Swedish, *adj.* schwedisch.
sweep, *v. a.* fegen, kehren; — *s.* Fegen *n.*; Schornsteinfeger *m.*
sweet, *adj.* süß; — *s.* ~s *pl.* Süßigkeiten *f. pl.*
sweetheart, *s.* Liebchen *n.*
swell, *v. n. & a.* aufschwellen; — *adj.* flott.
swift, *adj.* geschwind.
swim, *v. n.* schwimmen. — *s.* Schwimmen *n.*
swine, *s.* Schwein *n.*
swing, *v. n. & a.* schwingen.
Swiss, *s.* Schweizer *m.*, -in *f.*; — *adj.* schweizerisch.
switch, *s.* Schalter *m.*; Weiche *f.*; — *v. a. & n.* schalten.
sword, *s.* Schwert *n.*; Degen *m.*
symbol, *s.* Symbol *n.*; Sinnbild *n.*
symmetrical, *adj.* symmetrisch.
sympathy, *s.* Sympathie *f.*; Mitgefühl *n.*
symphony, *s.* Symphonie *f.*
symptom, *s.* Symptom *n.*; Zeichen *n.*
synagogue, *s.* Synagoge *f.*
syndicate, *s.* Syndikat *n.*
synthetic, *adj.* synthetisch.
syringe, *s.* Spritze *f.*
syrup, *s* Sirup *m.*
system, *s.* System *n.*
systematic(al), *adj.* systematisch; planmäßig.

T

table, *s.* Tisch *m.*
table-cloth, *s.* Tischtuch *n.*

tack, s. Nagel m.; Reißnagel m.; Zwecke f.
tackle, s. Gerät n.; Werkzeug n.; Takel n.; Flaschenzug m.; — v. a. in Angriff nehmen; anpacken; lösen, fertig werden mit; v. n. (sport) angreifen.
tactical, adj. taktisch.
tag, s. Zettel m.; Etikette f.; — v. a. etikettieren.
tail, s. Schwanz m. Schweif m.; Haarzopf m.; Schleppe f.; ~s pl. Frack m.; (of coin) Rückseite f.
tailor, s. Herrenschneider m.; — v. n. schneidern.
taint, s. Fleck m.; — v. a, & n. beflecken.
take, v. a. (weg)nehmen; ergreifen; hinbringen; übernehmen; vornehmen; v.n. nehmen, fassen; ~ about herumführen; ~ after nach jm. arten; ~ down aufschreiben; ~ off ausziehen, ablegen, starten; ~ out entnehmen; ausführen; ~ over übernehmen; ~ up aufnehmen.
tale, s. Erzählung f.
talent, s. Talent n.
talk, s. Gespräch n.; — v.n. & a. reden, sprechen.
talkative, adj. gesprächig, redselig.
tall, adj. lang, hoch.
tame, adj. zahm; — v.a. bezähmen; bändigen.
tan, s. Lohe f.; — adj. lohfarben; — v. a. gerben.
tangible, adj. fühlbar, greifbar.
tank, s. Wasserbehälter m.; Tank m.; — v. a. & n. tanken.
tap¹, s. Pochen n.; Klaps m.; v. a. & n. klopfen, pochen.
tap², s. Zapfen m.; Hahn m.;
tape, s. Band n.; (sport) Zielband n.; Tonband n.; — v.a. umbinden; mit einer Maßschnur messen; auf Tonband aufnehmen.
tape measure, s. Bandmaß n.; Zentimetermaß n.
tape-recorder, s. Tonband(aufnahme)gerät n.
tapestry, s. Wandteppich m.
target, s. Schießscheibe f.; fig. Ziel n.; Soll n.
tariff, s. Tarif m.
tart, s. Fruchttorte f.
task, s. Aufgabe f.; — v. a. beschäftigen.
taste, s. Geschmack m.; Neigung f.; — v. a. kosten; schmecken; v. n. kosten (von); schmecken (nach).
tasty, adj. schmackhaft.
tavern, s. Schenke f.
tax, s. Steuer f.; Abgabe f.; — v. a. besteuern; fig. in Anspruch nehmen.
taxi, s. Taxi n.; Mietauto n.
tea, s. Tee m.
teach, v. a. & n. lehren, unterrichten.
teacher, s. Lehrer m.; -in f.
team, s. Gespann n.; (sport) Mannschaft f.
tea-pot, s. Teekanne f.
tear¹, v. a. (zer)reißen; v. n. zerreißen; rasen, stürmen; — s. Riß m.
tear², s. Träne f.
tease, v. a. necken, fop-

pen; ärgern.
teaspoon, s. Teelöffel m.
technical, adj. technisch.
technique, s. Technik f.; mechanische Fertigkeit; Methode f.
tedious, adj. langwierig, ermüdend; umständlich.
teem, v. n. wimmeln.
teenager, s. Teenager m.
telecast, s. Fernsehsendung f.; — v. a. im Fernsehen übertragen.
telecommunication, s. Fernverbindung f.; ~s pl. Fernmeldetechnik f.
telegram, s. Telegramm n.
telegraph, s. Telegraph m.; Fernschreiber m.; — v. a. & n. telegraphieren, drahten.
telephone, s. Telephon n.; Fernsprecher; — v. a. jm. anrufen; telephonieren; v. n. telephonieren.
telephone-exchange, s. Fernsprechamt n.; Telephonzentrale f.
teleprinter, telex, s. Fernschreiber m.
telescope, s. Teleskop n.; Fernrohr n.
televise, v. a. durch Fernsehsender übertragen.
television, s. Fernsehen n.
television-set, s. Fernsehempfänger m.; Fernseh(empfangs)gerät n.
tell, v. a. sagen; erzählen; berichten; mitteilen; melden; — v. n. berichten, erzählen.
temper, s. Temperament n.; Veranlagung f.; — v. a. mildern; mä-
ßigen; lindern; tempern, temperieren.
temperature, s. Temperatur f.
tempest, s. Sturm m.; Gewitter n.
temple¹, s. Tempel m.
temple², s. Schläfe f.
temporary, adj. zeitweilig, vorläufig.
tempt, v. a. versuchen, verleiten, verlocken.
ten, adj. zehn.
tenant, s. Pächter m.; Mieter m.; Bewohner m.
tend¹, v. n. dazu neigen; eine Neigung haben.
tend², v. a. bedienen; in Gang halten; pflegen.
tendency, s. Neigung f.; Tendenz f.
tender,¹ s. Angebot n.; Kostenanschlag m.; — v. a. anbieten; v. n. ein Angebot machen.
tender,² adj. zart; empfindlich.
tender,³ s. Wärter m., -in f.; Pfleger m., -in f.
tennis, s. Tennis(spiel) n.
tense¹, adj. gespannt.
tense², s. Zeitform f.
tension, s. Spannung f.
tent, s. Zelt n.
tenth, adj. zehnter, zehnte, zehntes.
term, s. Fachausdruck m.; Termin m.; Zeit f.; Dauer f.; Frist f.; Semester n.; ~s pl. Bedingungen f. pl.; Beziehungen f. pl.
terminate, v. a. begrenzen; beendigen; v. n. endigen.
terminus, s. Endpunkt m.; Endstation f.
terrace, s. Terrasse f.; Häuserreihe f.
terrible, adj. schrecklich.

territory, s. Gebiet n.
terror, s. Entsetzen n.; Schrecken n.; Terror m.
test, s. Probe f.; Versuch m.; Prüfung f.; Test m.; — v. n. prüfen, erproben; testen.
testament, s. Testament n.
testify, v. a. bezeugen; als Zeuge aussagen.
testimony, s. Zeugnis n.
text, s. Text m.
text-book, s. Lehrbuch n.
than, conj. als.
thank, v. a. danken; — ~s pl. Dank m.
thankful, adj. dankbar.
that[1], pron. & adj. das; jener, jene, jenes; — adv. so, dermaßen.
that[2], conj. daß; damit; weil, als.
thaw, s. Tauwetter n.; — v. n. auftauen.
the[1], der, die, das.
the[2], adv. desto, um so.
theatre, s. Theater n.; fig. Schauplatz m.
their, pron. ihr, ihre.
theirs, pron. der, die, das ihrige.
them, pron. sie; ihnen.
theme, s. Thema n.; Aufgabe f.; Aufsatz m.
themselves, pron. (sie) selbst; sich (selbst).
then, adv. damals; dann; ferner; außerdem; also; *every now and* ~ von Zeit zu Zeit; — adj. damalig.
theology, s. Theologie f.
theoretical, adj. theoretisch.
theory, s. Theorie f.
there, adv. da, dort; dorthin; darin; ~ *is,* ~ *are* es gibt; es sind; — int. da!, schau her!
thereby, adv. dadurch, damit; demzufolge; deswegen; davon.
therefore, adv. & conj. deshalb, deswegen, darum, daher; folglich, also.
thermometer, s. Thermometer n.
thermo-nuclear, adj. thermonuklear.
thermos, s. Thermosflasche f.
these, pron. diese.
they, pron. sie (pl.); es; ~ *who* die (jenigen) welche.
thick, adj. dick; dicht; trüb; — adv. dick; dicht; — s. Dickung f.
thicket, s. Dickicht n.
thief, s. Räuber m.
thigh, s. Schenkel m.
thimble, s. Fingerhut m.
thin, adj. dünn; leicht.
thing, s. Ding n.; Sache f.; Geschöpf n.; ~s pl. Sachen f. pl.; *the* ~ das Richtige.
think, v. n. denken; meinen, glauben; *I* ~ *so* ich glaube ja; v. a. denken; halten für; ~ *over* sich etwas überlegen.
third, adj. dritter, dritte, drittes.
thirst, s. Durst m.; — v. n. dursten (nach).
thirteen, adj. dreizehn; —s. Dreizehn f.
thirty, adj. dreißig.
this, pron. & adj. dieser, diese, dieses; dies, die, das; *like* ~ *so; after* ~ danach; — adv. so; ~ *much* so viel.
thorn, s. Dorn m.
thorough, adj. vollkommen; vollständig; vollendet.

thoroughfare, *s.* Durchgang *m.;* Hauptverkehrsstraße *f.*
those, *pron.* jene, die, diejenigen.
though, *conj.* obwohl, obgleich, wenn auch; — *adv.* aber, trotzdem.
thought, *s.* Gedanke *m.*
thousand, *adj.* tausend; *fig.* viele; — *s.* Tausend *n.;* ~s Tausende.
thrash, *v. a.* dreschen, verprügeln.
thread, *s.* Faden *m.* Schraubengewinde *n.;* — *v. a.* einfädeln.
threat, *s.* Drohung *f.*
threaten, *v. a.* bedrohen, androhen; *v. n.* drohen.
three, *adj.* drei;
threshold, *s.* Schwelle *f.*
thrifty, *adj.* sparsam.
thrill, *s.* Schauer *m.;* Erregung *f.;* — *v. a. & n.* erregen.
thrive, *v. n.* gedeihen; blühen.
throat, *s.* Kehle *f.;* Gurgel *f.;* Hals *m.;* Schlund *m.*
throne, *s.* Thron *m.*
throng, *s.* Gedränge *n.;* Menge *f.;* Schar *f.;* — *v. n. & a.* (sich) drängen.
through, *prep.* durch; mittels; aus, vor, zufolge; — *adv.* durch; ~ and ~ durch und durch.
throughout, *prep.* hindurch; während; — *adv.* durch und durch; ganz und gar; überall; die ganze Zeit.
throw, *v. a.* werfen; schleudern; abwerfen; abstreifen; *v. n.* werfen; — *s.* Werfen *n.;* Schleudern *n.;* Wurf *m.*
thrust, *s.* Stoß *m.;* Hieb *m.;* — *v. a. & n.* stoßen.
thumb, *s.* Daumen *m.*
thunder, *s.* Donner *m.;* — *v.n.* donnern.
Thursday, *s.* Donnerstag *m.*
thus, *adv.* so, folgendermaßen; somit.
tick, *s.* Ticken *n.;* Moment *m.;* Haken *m.;* — *v. n. & a.* ticken.
ticket, *s.* Eintrittskarte *f.;* Fahrkarte *f.;* Schein *m.;* Etikett *n.;* Zettel *m.*
tickle, *v. a. & n.* kitzeln; jucken.
tide, *s.* Gezeiten *f. pl.;* Ebbe *f.* und Flut *f.*
tie, *s.* Band *n.;* Schleife *f.;* Halstuch *n.;* Kravatte *f.;* Bindung *f.;* — *v. a.* binden; verbinden; *v.n.* *(sport)* punktgleich sein.
tiger, *s.* Tiger *m.*
tight, *adj.* dicht; eng; knapp; straff; prall.
tile, *s.* Dachziegel *m.;* Kachel *f.;* Fliese *f.;* — *v. a.* mit Ziegeln decken.
till[1], *prep. & conj.* bis.
till[2]: *v. a.* bebauen, beackern; *v. n.* ackern, pflügen.
till[3], *s.* Schalterkasse *f.*
tilt[1], *s.* Neigung *f.;* Stoß *m.;* Lanzenbrechen *n.;* — *v. a.* kippen.
tilt[2], *s.* Verdeck *n.*
timber, *s.* Bauholz *n.*
time, *s.* Zeit *f.,* Takt *m.;* Zeitmaß *n.;* Tempo *n.*
timetable, *s.* Zeittabelle *f.;* Stundenplan *m.*
timid, *adj.* furchtsam, ängstlich.
tin, *s.* Zinn *m.;* Weißblech *n.;* Konservenbüchse *f.;* — *v. a.*

tin-opener — **torpedo**

verzinnen; eindosen.
tin-opener, s. Dosenöffner m.
tint, s. Farbe f.; Farbton m.; Schattierung f.
tiny, adv. winzig.
tip¹, s. Spitze f.; Mundstück n.
tip², s. Umkippen n.; Kippvorrichtung f.; — v. n. sich neigen.
tip³, s. Trinkgeld n.; Tip m.; Wink m.; — v. a. ein Trinkgeld geben; einen Tip geben; warnen; — v. n. Trinkgeld geben.
tiptoe, s. Zehenspitze f.
tire¹, s. Radreifen m.; ~s. pl. Bereifung f.
tire², v. a. & n. müde machen; müde werden.
tiresome, adj. ermüdend; lästig.
tissue, s. Gewebe n.; (paper) Seidenpapier n.
titbit, s. Leckerbissen m.
title, s. Ehrentitel m.; Überschrift f.; Rechtsanspruch m.; — v. a. betiteln, benennen.
to, prep. zu, nach, an, in, auf; gegen; um zu; für; — adv. zu, in geschlossenem Zustand; ~ and fro hin und her; auf und ab.
toad, s. Kröte f.
toast¹, s. Toast m., geröstetes Brot n.; — v. a. & n. toasten, rösten.
toast², s. Trinkspruch m.; Toast m.; — v. a. & n. trinken auf; toasten.
tobacco, s. Tabak m.
tobacconist, s. Tabakhandler m.
today, to-day, adv. heute.
toe, s. Zehe f.; Spitze f.
together, adv. zusammen; zugleich; miteinander.

toil, v. n. (mühsame) Arbeit f.; Mühe f.; Plage f.; — v. n. sich abmühen.
toilet, s. Toilette f.
toll¹, v. a. & n. läuten; — s. feierliches Geläut n.
toll², s. Zoll m.; Marktgeld n.; Brückengeld n.; Tribut n.; Opfer n.
tomato, s. Tomate f.
tomb, s. Grab(mal) n.
tomorrow, to-morrow, adv. morgen.
ton, s. Tonne f.
tone, s. Ton m.; Klang m. — v. a. einen Ton geben; stimmen; v. n. stimmen.
tongs, s. pl. (eine) Zange f.
tongue, s. Zunge f.; fig. Sprache f.
tonight, to-night, adv. heute abend.
tonnage, s. Tonnengehalt n.; Tonnengeld n.
tonsil, s. Mandel f.
too, adv. zu, allzu, auch, noch dazu.
tool, s. Werkzeug n.; Gerät n.
tooth, s. Zahn m.
toothache, s. Zahnweh n.
toothpaste, s. Zahnpaste f.
toothpick, s. Zahnstocher m.
top¹, s. Spitze f.; Gipfel m.; höchster Punkt; Krone f.; — adj. oberster, oberste, oberstes.
top², s. Kreisel m.
topic, s. Gegenstand m.; Thema n.
torch, s. Fackel f.
torment, s. Qual f.; Folter f.; Pein m.; Marter f.; — v. a. peinigen, foltern, martern; quälen.
torpedo, s. Torpedo m.

torrent, s. Gießbach m.; Strom m.
tortoise s. Schildkröte f.
toss, s. Werfen n.; Wurf m.; Hochwerfen n.; — v. a. & n. (sich) hin und her werfen.
total, adj. total; ganz; gänzlich; — s. Gesamtbetrag m.; — v. a. sich belaufen auf; ausmachen.
touch, v. a. berühren, anrühren; — s. Gefühl n.; Berührung f.; Tastsinn m.
tough, adj. zäh; schwer, hart.
tour, s. Rundreise f.; Tour(nee) f.; — v.a. bereisen.
tourist, s. Tourist m., -in f.
tournament, s. Turnier n.
tow, s. Schlepptau n.; — v. a. schleppen.
toward(s), prep. gegen, auf; nach ... zu; auf ...; in der Richtung von; zwecks.
towel, s. Handtuch n.; Badetuch n.
tower, s. Turm m.; — v. n. sich türmen; sich erheben.
town, s. Stadt f.
town hall, s. Rathaus n.
toy, s. Spielzeug n.; ~s pl. Spielwaren f. pl.
trace, s. Spur f.; Grundriß m.; — v. a. nachspüren, verfolgen; v. n. ~ back zurückgehen.
track, s. Spur f.; (sport) Bahn f.; Pfad m.; Geleise n.; Fährte f.; — v.a. nachprüfen; verfolgen; v. n. Spur halten.
tractor, s. Trecker m.; Traktor m.; Zugmaschine f.
trade, s. Handel m.; Geschäft n., Gewerbe n.; Handwerk n.; — v. n. Handel treiben; handeln.
trade-mark, s. Fabrikzeichen n.; Warenzeichen n.
tradesman, s. Handelsmann m.
trade(s)-union, s. Gewerkschaft f.
trade-wind, s. Passatwind m.
tradition, s. Tradition f.
traffic, s. (öffentlicher) Verkehr m.; Straßenverkehr m.; Handel m.
tragedy, s. Tragödie f.
trail, s. Schleppe f.; Schweif m.; Schwanz Spur f.; Pfad m.; — v. a. nachschleppen; v.n. (sich) schleppen.
trailer, s. Kriechpflanze f.; Anhängewagen m.; Anhänger n.; Filmvorschau f.
train, s. Zug m.; Reihe f.; Kette f.; Gefolge n.; Schleppe f.; — v. a. erziehen; abrichten; ausbilden; (sport) trainieren; v. n. (sich) üben; trainieren.
traitor, s. Verräter m.
tram, s. Straßenbahn-(wagen) m.
tramp, s. Landstreicher m. Wanderbursche m.; — v. n. trampeln, treten; v. a. durchwandern.
transaction, s. Geschäft n.; Abwicklung f.
transatlantic, adj. transatlantisch.
transfer, v. a. übertragen, versetzen; — s. Übertragung f.; Überweisung f.; Verlegung f.
transform, v. a. umformen; verwandeln.
transfusion, s. Blutüber-

| transgress | 122. | trick |

transgress ... **tragung** f., Transfusion f.
transgress, v. a. überschreiten, übertreten; verletzen; v. n. sich vergehen.
transistor, s. Transistor m.
transit, s. Durchgang m.; Transit m.; Durchfuhr f.
translate, v. a. übersetzen, übertragen.
translation, s. Übersetzung f.
translator, s. Übersetzer m., -in f.
transmission, s. Übermittlung f.; Übertragung f. (radio) Sendung f.
transmit, v. a. übermitteln, übersenden; übertragen; fortpflanzen.
transmitter, s. Übermittler m., -in f.; (radio) Sender m.
transparent, adj. durchsichtig.
transport, v. a. fortschaffen, befördern; transportieren; — s. Beförderung f.; Transport m.; Versand m.; Spedition f.
trap, s. Falle f.; — v. a. fangen; fig. ertappen.
travel, v. n. reisen, eine Reise machen; v. a. bereisen; durchwandern; — s. Reise f.
traverse, v. a. überqueren, durchqueren; fig. durchkreuzen.
tray, s. Servierbrett n.; Tablett n.; Auslegekästchen n.
treacherous, adj. verräterisch; treulos; heimtückisch.
tread, v. n. treten; schreiten; v. a. treten; betreten; — s. Tritt m.; Schritt m.; Lauffläche f.
treason, s. Verrat m.
treasure, s. Schatz m.; Reichtum m.; — v. a. ansammeln; hegen.
treasury, s. Schatzkammer f.
treat, v. a. behandeln; umgehen mit; bewirten; spendieren; v. n. ~ of handeln (von); unterhandeln; — s. Festlichkeit f.; Schulfest n.
treatment, s. Behandlung f.
treaty, s. Staatsvertrag m.
tree, s. Baum m.; Leisten m.
tremble, v. n. zittern.
tremendous, adj. schrecklich; außerordentlich; enorm.
trench, s. Graben m.; Schützengraben m.; v. a. umgraben; v. n. sich eingraben.
trend, s Richtung f.; fig. Lauf m.; Strömung f.; Tendenz f.
trespass, s. Vergehen n.; Übertretung f.; Eingriff m.; — v. n. widerrechtlich betreten; sich vergehen.
trial, s. Versuch m.; Probe f.; Prüfung f.; Verhör n.; Prozeß m.; Gerichtsverfahren n.
triangle, s. Dreieck n.
tribe, s. Stamm m.; Geschlecht n.; Zunft f.; Sippe f.
tribute, s. Tribut m., Zins m.; fig. Huldigung f.
trick, s. Kniff m.; List f.; Kunstgriff m.; Streich m.; ~ film Trickfilm

trifle 123. **tune**

m.; — v.a. betrügen.
trifle, s. Kleinigkeit f.; Lappalie f.; — v. n. spielen; tändeln; v. a. ~ *away* vertändeln.
trigger, s. Auslöshebel m.; Abzug m.; Drücker m.
trim, adj. nett; — v. a. zurecht machen; garnieren; trimmen; v. n. trimmen.
trip, v. n. trippeln, tänzeln; stolpern; fig. straucheln; v. a. ~ *up* ein Bein stellen; ertappen; — s. (kurze) Reise f.; Ausflug m.; Fehltritt m.
triple, adj. dreifach; dreimalig.
triumph, s. Triumph m.; Sieg m.; — v. n. triumphieren, siegen.
triumphant, adj. siegreich.
trivial, adj. trivial, banal; unbedeutend.
trolley, s. Karren m.; Teewagen m.; Förderwagen m.
trolley-bus, s. Oberleitungsbus m.; Trolleybus m.
troop, s. Trupp m.; Haufe(n) m.; Schar f.
trophy, s. Trophäe f.; Siegeszeichen n.; Andenken n.
tropic(al), adj. tropisch.
tropics, s. pl. Tropen pl.
trot, v. n. traben, trotten, im Trab gehen; v. a. ~ *out* fig. vorführen.
trough, s. Trog m.
trousers, s. pl. Hosen f. pl.
trout, s. Forelle f.
truce, s. Waffenstillstand m.
truck, s. Güterwagen m.; Lorre f.; Förderwagen m.; Lastwagen m.
true, adj. wahr; echt; treu; genau; — adv.

wahrhaftig, richtig.
trumpet, s. Trompete f.; Schalltrichter m.; Hupe f.
trunk, s. Baumstamm m.; Rumpf m.; Rüssel m.; Schrankkoffer m.
trunk-call, s. Ferngespräch n.
trust, s. Vertrauen n.; Obhut f.; Treuhand f.; Trust m.; — v. n. & a. Vertrauen haben; sich verlassen auf; hoffen.
trustee, s. Bevollmächtigte m., f.; Treuhänder m.
truth, s. Wahrheit f.
try, v. a. versuchen; probieren; prüfen; verhandeln; verhören; anprobieren; v. n. *(at)* versuchen; sich bemühen; — s. Versuch m.; Probe f.; Experiment n.
tub, s. Faß n.; Kübel m.; Badewanne f.
tube, s. Rohr n.; *(radio)* Röhre f.; Tube f.; Tunnel m.; Untergrundbahn f.
tuck, s. Falte f.; Abnäher m.; — v. a. (weg)stecken, ~ *in* einhüllen.
Tuesday, s. Dienstag m.
tuft, s. Buschel n.; Busch m.
tug, v. a. & n. ziehen, zerren; — s. Ruck m.; Zerren n.; Schlepper m.
tug-boat, s. Schlepper m.
tuition, s. Unterricht m.
umble, v. n. fallen, purzeln; sich wälzen; v. a. werfen; (um)stürzen, — s. Sturz m., Fall m.
tumour, s. Geschwulst f.
tune, s. Melodie f.; Lied n.; — v. a. & n. stimmen; ~ *in (radio)* ein-

tunnel 124. **uncertainty**

stellen.
tunnel, s. Tunnel m.; Stollen m.
turbine, s. Turbine f.
turbo-jet (engine), s. Strahlturbine f.; Turbostrahltriebwerk n.
turbo-prop (engine), s. Turbo-Propellertriebwerk n.
turf, s. Rasen m.; Torf m.; Rennbahn f.
turkey, s. Truthahn m.; Pute f.
Turkish, adj. türkisch.
turn, v. a & n. (sich) drehen; (sich) wenden; ~ out sich herausstellen; ~ up auftauchen; — s. Drehung f.; Wendung f.
turning, s. Drechseln n.; Wendung f.; Biegung f.
turnip, s. Rübe f.
turnover, s. Umsatz m.; Umschlag m.
tusk, s. Fangzahn m.
tutor, s. Hauslehrer m.; Privatlehrer m.; — v. a. unterrichten.
twelfth, adj. zwölfter, zwölfte, zwölftes.
twelve, adj. zwölf.
twenty, adj. zwanzig.
twice, adv. zweimal.
twig, s. (dünner) Zweig m.; Rute f.
twilight, s. Dämmerung f.
twin, adj. Zwillings-; doppelt; — s. Zwilling m.
twine, s. Bindfaden m.
twinkle, v. n. & a. glitzern, funkeln; blinzeln; — s. Funkeln n.
twitter, v. n. & a. zwitschern; piepsen; — s. Gezwitscher n.
two, adj. zwei; beide; — s. Zwei f.
two-seater, s. Zweisitzer m.

type, s. Typ(us) m.; Urbild n.; Vorbild n.; Type f. — v. a. & n. auf der Maschine schreiben.
type-script, s. Schreibmaschinenschrift f.
typewriter, s. Schreibmaschine f.
typist, s. Maschinenschreiber m.; -in f.
tyranny, s. Tyrannei f.
tyre, s. Radreifen m.

U

U-boat, s. Unterseeboot n.
ugly, adj. häßlich, garstig.
ultimate, adj. letzt; endlich.
ultraviolet, adj. ultraviolett.
umbrella, s. Regenschirm m.
umpire, s. Schiedsrichter m.
unable, adj. unfähig.
unaccustomed, adj. ungewöhnlich, ungewohnt.
unaided, adj. nicht unterstützt, ohne Hilfe, hilflos.
unanimous, adj. einmütig, einig; einstimmig.
unarmed, adj. unbewaffnet, ungerüstet.
unassisted, adj. ohne Hilfe.
unauthorized, adj. nicht autorisiert, unbefugt.
unaware, adj. nicht gewahr, in Unkenntnis.
unawares, adj. unversehens, unabsichtlich.
unbearable, adj. unerträglich.
uncertain, adj. unsicher, ungewiß, unbestimmt.
uncertainty, s. Unsicherheit f.; Ungewißheit f.

unchangeable, *adj.* unveränderlich.
uncle, *s.* Onkel *m.*
uncomfortable, *adj.* unangenehm; unbequem.
uncommon, *adj.* ungewöhnlich, — *adv.* sehr.
unconditional, *adj.* unbedingt; vorbehaltlos.
unconscious, *adj.* unbewußt; bewußtlos, ohnmächtig.
uncontrollable, *adj.* unkontrollierbar.
uncover, *v. a.* aufdecken, *fig.* enthüllen.
undamaged, *adj.* unbeschädigt.
undecided, *adj.* unentschieden.
undefined, *adv.* unbegrenzt, unbestimmt.
undeniable, *adj.* unleugbar.
under, *prep.* unter; unterhalb von; in; bei; — *adv.* darunter, unter; — *adj.* unterer, untere, unteres.
undercarriage, *s.* Untergestell *n.*
underclothes, *s. pl.* Unterkleidung *f.*; Unterwäsche *f.*
underdeveloped country, *s.* unterentwickeltes Land *n.*
underdone, *adj.* ungar; (halb) roh.
undergo, *v. a.* erfahren, erleben; durchmachen.
undergraduate, *s.* Student *m.*, -in *f.*; — *adj.* Studenten-.
underground, *adv.* unter der Erde; heimlich; — *adj.* unterirdisch; Untergrund-.
underline, *v. a.* unterstreichen, betonen; — *s.* Unterstreichung *f.*

underneath, *prep.* unterhalb; — *adv.* unten, darunter; — *adj.* unterer, untere, unteres.
undersigned, *adj.* unterzeichnet; unterschrieben; — *s. the* ~ der (die) Unterzeichnete(n)
understand, *v. a.* verstehen, begreifen.
undertake, *v. a.* übernehmen, sich befassen mit; — *v. n.* eine Verpflichtung übernehmen.
undertaking, *s.* Übernahme *f.*; Übernehmen *n.*; Unternehmen *n.*
underwear, *see* underclothes.
undesirable, *adj.* unerwünscht.
undisturbed, *adj.* ungestört; unberührt.
undo, *v. a.* wegschaffen; zunichte machen; aufknüpfen; auflösen.
undress, *v. a.* entkleiden, ausziehen; — *v. n.* sich entkleiden; — *s.* Alltagskleid *n.*; Hauskleid *n.*; Negligé *n.*
undue, *adj.* nicht fällig; unpassend.
uneasy, *adj.* unruhig.
uneducated, *adj.* unerzogen, ungebildet.
unemployed, *adj.* arbeitslos; — *s.* Arbeitslose *m., f.*
unemployment, *s.* Arbeitslosigkeit *f.*
unequal, *adj.* ungleich; nicht gewachsen; unregelmäßig.
uneven, *adj.* uneben, holperig; ungerade *(of number).*
unexpected, *adj.* unerwartet, plötzlich.
unfair, *adj.* unfair; unsportlich; nicht anstän-

unfavourable | **unsuccessful**

dig; ungerecht.
unfavourable, *adj.* ungünstig, unvorteilhaft.
unfinished, *adj.* unbeendet; unvollendet.
unfortunate, *adj.* unglücklich.
ungrateful, *adj.* undankbar.
unhappy, *adj.* unglücklich, traurig.
unhealthy, *adj.* ungesund.
uniform, *adj.* gleichförmig; — *s.* Uniform *f.*
union, *s.* Vereinigung *f.;* Eintracht *f.;* Verein *m.*
unique, *adj.* einzig — *s.* Einzige *n.*
unit, *s.* Einheit *f.;* Anlage *f.*
unite, *v. a.* vereinigen; verheiraten; *v. n.* sich vereinigen; sich anschließen.
unity, *s.* Eintracht *f.;* Solidarität *f.*
universal, *adj.* universal, ganz; — *s.* (das) Allgemeine.
universe, *s.* Universum *n.;* Welt *f.*
unjust, *adj.* ungerecht; unbillig.
unkind, *adj.* unfreundlich.
unknown, *adj.* unbekannt; fremd; — *s.* (der, die, das) Unbekannte.
unless, *conj.* wenn ... nicht; ausgenommen (wenn); *prep.* außer.
unlike, *adj.* ungleich; — *prep.* verschieden von, anders als; nicht wie.
unload, *v. a.* ausladen, entladen, abladen; *v. n.* ausgeladen werden.
unlock, *v. a.* aufschließen; öffnen; *v. n.* sich öffnen.
unmarried, *adj.* unverheiratet, ledig.

unnecessary, *adj.* unnötig; sinnlos.
unnoticed, *adj.* unbemerkt; unbeachtet.
unoccupied, *adj.* leer; nicht belegt, unbewohnt; unbeschäftigt.
unpack, *v. a.* auspacken.
unpaid, *adj.* unbezahlt.
unparalleled, *adj.* unvergleichlich; beispiellos.
unpleasant, *adj.* unfreundlich.
unpopular, *adj.* unpopulär
unprecedented, *adj.* beispiellos, unerhört, noch nie dagewesen.
unprejudiced, *adj.* unparteiisch; unbeeinträchtigt.
unprepared, *adj.* unvorbereitet.
unprofitable, *adj.* unrentabel; nutzlos.
unpromising, *adj.* nicht vielversprechend.
unqualified, *adj.* unqualifiziert; unbefähigt.
unquestionable, *adj.* unbestreitbar.
unreasonable, *adj.* vernunftlos; unvernünftig.
unsatisfactory, *adj.* unbefriedigend, unzulänglich.
unseen, *adj.* ungesehen; unbemerkt.
unselfish, *adj.* selbstlos; uneigennützig.
unsettled, *adj.* nicht festgesetzt; unbeständig; unerledigt.
unskilled, *adj.* unerfahren.
unsolved, *adj.* ungelöst.
unspeakable, *adj.* unbeschreiblich, unsäglich.
unsteady, *adj.* unbeständig; unregelmäßig.
unsuccesful, *adj.* erfolglos,

unsuitable, *adj.* unpassend; unangemessen.
unthinkable, *adj.* undenkbar.
untidy, *adj.* unordentlich.
until, *prep. & conj.* bis; not ~ nicht eher als.
unusual, *adj.* außergewöhnlich.
unwell, *adj.* unwohl.
up, *adv.* nach oben, hoch; hinauf; in die Höhe; oben; ~ *and* ~ höher und höher; — *prep.* auf; hinauf; empor; entlang; oben an; oben auf; — *int.* ~*!* auf!; hoch!
uphill, *adv.* bergauf.
uphold, *v. a.* aufrechterhalten.
upper, *adj.* oberer, obere, oberes; höherer, höhere, höheres.
upright, *adj. & adv.* aufrecht, gerade, nach oben gerichtet.
uproar, *s.* Aufruhr *m.*; Lärm *m.*
upset, *v. a.* umwerfen; *fig.* umstürzen; vereiteln; aus der Fassung bringen; *v. n.* umfallen, umkippen; — *s.* Umwerfen *n.*; Umsturz *m.*
upside-down, *adj.* umgekehrt.
upstairs, *adv.* die Treppe hinauf; nach oben; — *adj.* im oberen Stockwerk.
up-to-date, *adj.* zeitgemäß, modern; modisch.
upward, *adv.* aufwärts; nach oben; bergauf; stromaufwärts; — *adj.* nach oben gerichtet; ansteigend.

upwards, *adv. see* upward *adv.*
urge, *v. a.* drängen; — *s.* Drang *m.*
urgent, *adj.* dringend.
urn, *s.* Urne *f.*
us, *pron.* uns.
use, *s.* Gebrauch *m.*; Benutzung *f.*; Verwendung *f.*; Nutzen *m.*;
— *v. a.* gebrauchen; benutzen; anwenden; ~ *up* verbrauchen; *v. n.* ~*d to do* zu tun pflegen; gewohnt sein.
useful, *adj.* brauchbar, nützlich.
useless, *adj.* unnütz; unbrauchbar.
usher, *s.* Platzanweiser *m.*; Türhüter *m.*; Pförtner *m.*; Gerichtsdiener *m.*; — *v. a.* hineinführen, hineingeleiten; ankündigen.
usual, *adj.* gewöhnlich; üblich.
utensil, *s.* Gerät *n.*; Geschirr *n.*; ~*s pl.* Utensilien *pl.*
utility, *s.* Nützlichkeit *f.*; Nutzen *m.*
utilize, *v. a.* ausnutzen; sich zunutze machen; verwenden.
utmost, *adj.* äußerster, äußerste, äußerstes; *fig.* höchster, höchste, höchstes; — *s.* (das) Äußerste; (das) Möglichste.
utter, *adj.* äußerster, äußerste, äußerstes; — *v. a.* äußern, ausdrücken; ausstoßen.
utterance, *s.* Äußerung *f.*
utterly, *adv.* äußerst, völlig, ganz.

V

vacancy, s. Leere f.; freier Platz m. freie Stelle f.
vacant, adj. leer; frei, unbesetzt.
vaccination, s. Impfung f.
vacuum-cleaner, s. Staubsauger m.
vague, adj. wag; unbestimmt; unklar.
vain, adj. eitel; fig. leer; vergeblich; in ~ vergebens.
valid, adj. gültig.
validity, s. Gültigkeit f.
valley, s. Tal n.
valuable, adj. wertvoll; — s. ~s pl. Wertsachen f. pl.
value, s. Wert m.; Nutzlichkeit f.; — v. a. schätzen; achten.
valve, s. Klappe f.; (radio) Röhre f.
van, s. Möbelwagen m.; Frachtwagen m.; Lieferwagen m.
vanish, v. n. (ver)schwinden.
vanity, s. Eitelkeit f.; Anmaßung f.; Nichtigkeit f.
vapour, s. Dunst m.; Dampf m.
various, adj. mannigfaltig; wechselvoll.
varnish. s. Lack m.; Politur f. — v. a. lackieren; polieren
vary, v. a. (ver)ändern; wechseln; v. n. sich (ver)ändern; abweichen.
vase, s. Vase f.
vast, adj. ungeheuer, gewaltig.
vault, s. Gewölbe n.; Wölbung f.; Gruft f.; — v. a. (über)wölben; v. n. sich wölben.
veal, s. Kalbfleisch n.
vegetable, s. Pflanze f.; Gemüse n.
vehement, adj. heftig; ungestüm.
vehicle, s. Fuhrwerk n.; Fahrzeug n.
veil, s. Schleier m.; Dunstschleier m.; — v. a. & n. verschleiern, verhüllen.
vein, s. Ader f.; Vene f.; Blutgefäß n.
velvet, s. Samt m.
venerable, adj. ehrwürdig.
vengeance, s. Rache f.
venison, s. Wildbret n.
vent, s. Öffnung f.; Loch n.; fig. Ausbruch m.; freier Lauf; — v. a. freien Lauf lassen.
ventilation, s. Ventilation f.
ventilator, s. Ventilator m.
venture, s. Wagnis n.; Spekulation f.; — v. a. wagen; riskieren; v. n. sich wagen.
verb, s. Zeitwort n.
verdict, s. Wahrspruch m.; fig. Urteil n.
verge, s. Rand m.; — v. n. sich nähern; grenzen an.
verify, v. a. nachprüfen; beweisen; bestätigen.
vermicelli, s. Fadennudeln f. pl.
verse, s. Vers m.; Strophe f.
version, s. Übersetzug f.; Darstellung f.; Auffassung f.
vertical, adj. vertikal, senkrecht.
very, adv. sehr; — adj. wahrhaftig; wirklich; schon; bloß.
vessel, s. Gefäß n.; Schiff

vest — **volunteer**

n.
vest, s. Unterjacke f.; Weste f.; — v. a. bekleiden.
vestry, s. Sakristei f.
veteran, s. Veteran m.; — adj. kampferprobt; fig. erfahren.
veto, s. Veto n.; — v. a. Veto einlegen.
vex, v. a. ärgern, belästigen, aufregen.
via, prep. via, über.
vibration, s. Schwingung f.; Vibrieren n.
vice¹, s. Schraubstock m.
vice², s. Laster n.; Verderbtheit f.; Zuchtlosigkeit f.
vice-president, s. Vizepräsident m.
vicinity, s. Nachbarschaft f.
victim, s. Opfer n.
victorious, adj. siegreich.
victory, s. Sieg m.
victual, s. ∼s pl. Proviant m.; Nahrungsmittel pl.
view, s. Aussicht f. Sicht f.; Blick m.; Anblick m.; fig. Ansicht f. Anschauung f.; — v. a besichtigen, betrachten.
viewer, s. Zuschauer m., -in f.
viewfinder, s. Bildsucher m.
vigour, s. Kraft f.; Energie f.; Lebenskraft f
vile, adj. abscheulich, gemein; schlecht.
village, s. Dorf n.
villain, s. Schurke m.; Schuft m.
vine, s. Weinstock m. Rebe f.
vinegar, s. Weinessig m.
vineyard, s. Weinberg m.
vintage, s. Weinlese f; Jahrgang m.
violation, s. Verletzung f.; Vergewaltigung f.; Schändung f.
violence, s. Gewalttätigkeit f.; Gewalttat f.; Heftigkeit f.; Gewalt f.
violet, s. Veilchen n.
violin, s. Violine f.; Geige f.
violinist, s. Violinist m., -in f.
virgin, s. Jungfrau f.
virtue, s. Tugend f.
visa, s. Sichtvermerk n., Visum n.
visibility, s. Sicht f.; Sichtbarkeit f.
visible, adj. sichtbar.
vision, s. Sehvermögen n.; fig. Einsicht f.; Vision f.; Erscheinung f.
visit, v. a. besuchen; v. n. Besuche machen; — s. Besuch m.
visitor, s. Besucher m.
vital, adj. lebenswichtig; wesentlich.
vitamin, s. Vitamin n.
vivid, adj. lebhaft, lebendig.
vocabulary, s. Wörterverzeichnis n.; Wortschatz m.
vocation, s. Berufung f.
voice, s. Stimme f.; — v. a. äußern.
void, adj. leer, nichtig, ungültig.
volcano, s. Vulkan m.
voltage, s. Spannung f.
volume, s. Band m.; Umfang m.; Kubikinhalt m.; Volumen n.
voluntary, adj. freiwillig; willkürlich.
volunteer, s. Freiwillige m. — adj. freiwillig; — v. n. sich freiwillig

vomit melden; *v. a.* freiwillig anbieten.
vomit, *v. a. & n.* (sich) erbrechen; — *s.* Ausgebrochene *n.*
vote, *s.* Wahlstimme *f.;* Abstimmung *f.;* Stimmrecht *n.;* — *v. a.* stimmen für; *v. n.* abstimmen, wählen.
voter, *s.* Stimmberechtigte *m., f.;* Wähler *m.,* -in *f.*
voucher, *s.* Beleg *m.,* Gutschein *m.;* Unterlage *f.*
vouchsafe, *v. a.* gewähren; verstatten; *v. n.* geruhen.
vow, *s.* Gelübde *n.;* — *v.a.* geloben.
voyage, *s.* Seereise *f.;* — *v. n.* reisen, fahren.
vulture, *s.* Geier *m.*

W

wade, *v. n.* waten; *v. a.* durchwaten.
wafer, *s.* Waffel *f.;* Oblate *f.;* Hostie *f.*
wag, *v. a. & n.* wackeln; wedeln.
wage¹, *s.* ~s *pl.* Lohn *m.;* Entgelt *n.*
wage², *v. a.* ~ *war* Krieg führen.
wage earner, *s.* Lohnempfänger *m.*
wage freeze, *s.* Lohnstopp *m.*
wag(g)on, *s.* Lastwagen *m.;* Güterwagon *m.*
wail, *s.* Klagen *n.;* Jammer *m.;* — *v.a.* beklagen; beweinen; *v. n.* klagen, jammern.
waist, *s.* Taille *f.*
waistcoat, *s.* Weste *f.*
wait, *v. n.* warten; abwarten; *v. a.* warten; abwarten; aufwarten bei; bedienen.
waiter, *s.* Kellner *m.*
waiting-room, *s.* Wartezimmer *n.*
wake¹, *s.* Kielwasser *n.;* Luftsog *m.; fig.* Spur *f.*
wake², *v. n.* erwachen; wachen; *v. a.* ~ *(up)* erwecken, aufwecken; — *s.* Wache *f.*
waken, *v. n.* aufwachen; *v. a.* aufwecken.
walk, *s.* Gehen *n.;* Spaziergang *m.;* — *v. n.* (zu Fuß) gehen; spazierengehen; Schritt gehen; ~ *off* davongehen; ~ *up to sy* zu jm hingehen.
walkie-talkie, *s.* tragbares Funksprechgerät.
walking-tour, *s.* Fußtour *f.*
wall, *s.* Wand *f.;* Mauer *f.*
wallet, *s.* Brieftasche *f.*
wall-socket, *s.* Steckdose *f.*
walnut, *s.* Walnuß *m.*
waltz, *s.* Walzer *m.;* — *v. n.* walzen.
wand, *s.* Stab *m.;* Stock *m.;* Zauberstab *m.;* Taktstock *m.*
wander, *v. n.* wandern, ziehen; abschweifen; ~ *about* umherwandern; — *v. a.* durchwandern; — *s.* Wandern *n.*
want, *s.* Mangel *m.;* Bedürfnis *n.;* Not *f.;* — *v. n.* ermangeln; *be* ~*ing in* es fehlen lassen an; *v. a.* bedürfen, nötig haben, brauchen; verlangen; ~*ed* gesucht.
war, *s.* Krieg *m.;* — *v. n.* Krieg führen.

ward, s. Bezirk *m.*; Krankensaal *m.*; Gefängniszelle *f.*; Haft *f.*; Schutz *m.*; — *v. a.* ~ off parieren, abwehren.

warden, s. Aufseher *m.*; Vorsteher *m.*; Gefängnisdirektor *m.*

warder, s. Gefangenenwärter *m.*; Wächter *m.*

wardrobe, s. Kleiderschrank *m.*

ware, s. Ware *f.*; Geschirr *n.*

warehouse, s. Warenlager *n.*; Lagerhaus *n.*; — *v. a.* einlagern.

warfare, s. Kriegsführung *f.*

warm, adj. warm; — *v. a.* ~ (up) warm machen, wärmen; *v. n.* warm werden, sich erwärmen.

warmth, s. Wärme *f.*

warn, v. a. warnen; ermahnen.

warning, s. Warnung *f.* Mahnung *f.*; Kündigung *f.*

warp, s. Kette *f.*; Aufzug *m.*; Verkrümmung *f.*; Biegung *f.*; — *v. n.* sich werfen; warpen; anscheren; *v. a.* verziehen, werfen, krümmen.

warrant, s. Vollmacht *f.*; *fig.* Berechtigung *f.*; Bürgschaft *f.*; — *v. a.* bevollmächtigen; garantieren.

warrior, s. Krieger *m.*

wash, v. a. waschen, (be-)spülen; *v. n.* sich waschen; — *s.* Waschen *n.*; Wäsche *f.*

wash-basin, s. Waschbecken *n.*

washing-machine, s. Waschmaschine *f.*

washing-up, s. Aufwaschen *n.*

wash-stand, s. Waschtisch *m.*

wasp, s. Wespe *f.*

waste, s. Verschwendung *f.*; Verfall *m.*; Verschleiß *m.*; Abfall *m.*; Ausschuß *m.*; — *v. a.* verschwenden, verschleißen; *v. n.* brachliegen; verfallen.

watch, s. Wache *f.*; Wachsamkeit *f.*, Hut *f.*; Taschenuhr *f.*; Armbanduhr *f.*; — *v. n.* beobachten, wachen; *v. a.* beobachten, wahrnehmen.

watch-maker, s. Uhrmacher *m.*

watchman, s. Wächter *m.*

water, s. Wasser *n.*

watercolour, s. Wasserfarbe *f.*; Aquarellmalerei *f.*

waterfall, s. Wasserfall *m.*

watering-place, s. Badeort *m.*

waterproof, adj. wasserdicht.

wave, s. Welle *f.*; Woge *f.*; — *v. n.* wogen; *v. a.* schwenken; in Wellen legen; winken mit; jm. zuwinken.

wave-length, s. *(radio)* Wellenlänge *f.*

waver, v. n. wanken, schwanken; — *s.* Wanken *n.*; Zaudern *n.*

wax¹, s. Wachs *n.*; Siegellack *m.*; — *v. a.* wachsen; bohnern.

wax², v. n. wachsen; zunehmen.

way, s. Weg *m.*; Pfad *m.*; Bahn *f.*; Art *f.*

we — **whatever**

und Weise *f.;* by the ~ beiläufig.
we, *pron.* wir.
weak, *adj.* schwach.
weaken, *v.a.* schwächen; *v. n.* schwach werden.
wealth, *s.* Wohlstand *m.;* Reichtum *m.; fig.* Fülle *f.*
wealthy, *adj.* reich, wohlhabend.
weapon, *s.* Waffe *f.;* Wehr *f.*
wear, *v.a. & n.* tragen; ~ away abtragen, abnutzen; ~ out erschöpfen; — *s.* Tragen *n.;* Bekleidung *f.;* Mode *f.;* Verschleiß *m.;* Haltbarkeit *f.*
weary, *adj.* müde; *fig.* überdrüssig; — *v. a.* ermüden; langweilen; *v. n.* müde werden.
weather, *s.* Wetter *n.;* Witterung *f.;* — *v.a.* überstehen, *v. n.* verwittern.
weather-forecast, *s.* Wetterbericht *m.;* Wettervorhersage *f.*
weave, *v. n. & a.* weben, wirken; — *s.* Gewebe *n.*
web, *s.* Gewebe *n.;* Gespinst *n.;* Netz *n.*
wedding, *s.* Hochzeit *f.*
wedding-ring, *s.* Trauring *m.*
wedge, *s.* Keil *m.;* — *v. a.* einkeilen; eindrängen.
Wednesday, *s.* Mittwoch *m.*
weed, *s.* Unkraut *n.;* — *v. a.* jäten; ausrotten.
week, *s.* Woche *f.*
week-day, *s.* Wochentag *m.*
week-end *s.* Wochenende *n.*

weekly, *adv.* wöchentlich; — Wochenblatt *n.*
weep, *v. n.* weinen.
weigh, *v. a.* wägen; wiegen; *fig.* abwägen; *v. n.* wiegen; ausschlaggebend sein.
weight, *s.* Gewicht *n.;* — *v. a.* mit einem Gewicht belasten; *fig.* beschweren.
welcome, *int.* willkommen!; — *s.* Willkommen *n.;* — *v. a.* bewillkommen; — *adj.* willkommen, gern gesehen.
welfare, *s.* Wohlfahrt *f.;* Fürsorgetätigkeit *f.*
well[1], *adv.* gut, wohl; genau; gründlich; ganz; — *adj.* wohl; gesund; *int.* Na!, ja!
well[2], *s.* Brunnen *m.;* *fig.* Quelle *f.*
wellbred, *adj.* wohlerzogen.
well-informed, *adj.* gut unterrichtet; informiert.
well-to-do, *adj.* wohlhabend.
west, *s.* Westen *m.;* — *adj.* westlich; — *adv.* westwärts; nach Westen.
western, *adj.* westlich; westwärts.
westward, *adj.* westlich; — *adv.* in westlicher Richtung.
westwards, *adv. see* westward *adv.*
wet, *adj.* naß, feucht.
wharf, *s.* Kai *m.*
what, *pron.* was?, wie?, was für ein(e)?; welcher, welche, welches?; — *adj.* was; was für ein(e).
whatever, *pron.* was auch immer; alles was; —

adj. welcher, welche, welches; überhaupt.

wheat, *s.* Weizen *m.*

wheel, *s.* Rad *n.;* — *v. a. & n.* drehen, radeln.

when, *adv. & conj.* wann; wenn; als; während.

whence, *adv.* woher; woraus, wodurch, wie?, von wo.

whenever, *conj.* wann auch immer.

where, *adv.* wo; worin; — *conj.* wo, (da) wo; — *pron.* da wo, dort wo.

wherefore, *adv. & conj.* wofür, weshalb, wozu; warum.

wherever, *adv. & conj.* wo(hin) denn (nur); wohin auch immer.

whether, *conj.* ob.

which, *pron. & adj.* welcher, welche, welches.

whichever, *pron. & adj.* welcher, welche, welches (auch) immer.

while, *s.* Weile *f.;* Zeit *f.;* — *v. a.* verbringen; — *conj.* während.

whip, *s.* Peitsche *f.;* Geißel *f.;* — *v. a.* peitschen.

whirlwind, *s.* Wirbelwind *m.*

whisk, *s.* Eierschläger *m.* Wisch *m.;* — *v. a.* wegwischen, fegen; *v. n.* wischen.

whisper, *v. a. & n.* flüstern; — *s.* Geflüster *n.*

whistle, *s.* Pfeife *f.;* Pfiff *m.;* — *v. n. & a.* pfeifen.

white, *adj.* weiß.

Whitsuntide, *s.* Pfingsten *n.*

who, *pron.* wer; wen; wem; welcher, welche, welches.

whoever, *pron.* wer (auch) immer, jedermann der.

whole, *adj.* ganz; gesamt; heil, unversehrt; — *s.* (das) Ganze; Gesamtheit *f.*

wholesale, *s.* Großhandel *m.;* — *adv.* im Großen.

wholesome, *adj.* gesund, heilsam; bekömmlich.

whom, *pron.* wen; welchen, welche, welches, denjenigen welchen, dem, welchem, welcher, welchen.

whose, *pron.* wem, dessen, deren.

why, *adv. & pron.* warum, weshalb; wozu; — *s.* Warum *n.;* — *int.* ja, doch!, je nun!

wicked, *adj.* böse, schlimm.

wide, *adj. & adv.* weit, weitverbreitet; weitgehend.

widow, *s.* Witwe *f.*

widower, *s.* Witwer *m.*

width, *s.* Weite *f.;* Breite *f.*

wife, *s.* Ehefrau *f.;* Gattin *f.;* Frau *f.*

wild, *adj.* wild; toll.

will[1], *v. aux.* werden; wollen; geneigt sein; gewohnt sein, pflegen zu; *v. a. & n.* wollen, wünschen.

will[2], *s.* Wille *m.;* Testament *n.;* — *v. a.* wollen, verfügen, vermachen; — *v. n.* wollen, begehren.

willing, *adj.* gewillt, geneigt, bereit.

willow, *s.* Weide *f.*

win, *v. a.* gewinnen; erringen; *v. n.* gewinnen, siegen; — *s.* (sport) Sieg *m.*

winch, *s.* Haspel *m., f.;* Winde *f.*

wind¹, s. Wind m.; Luft f.; Atem m.; Blähung f.; Blasinstrumente n. pl.; — v. a. lüften; wittern; außer Atem bringen.

wind², s. Windung f.; Biegung f.; — v. n. sich winden, sich schlängeln; sich verziehen; v. a. aufwickeln; aufziehen.

windmill, s. Windmühle f.

window, s. Fenster n.

windscreen, s. Windschutzscheibe f.

wine, s. Wein m.

wing, s. Flügel m.

wink, s. Blinzeln n.; Wink m.; — v. n. blinzeln, zwinkern, winken.

winner, s. Sieger m., -in f.; Gewinner m., -in f.

winter, s. Winter m.; ~ sports Wintersport m.; — v. n. & a. überwintern.

wipe, v. a. abwischen, aufwischen; abtrocknen.

wire, s. Draht m.; Leitungsdraht m.; Telegramm n.; by ~ telegraphisch; — v. a. verdrahten; drahten, telegraphieren; v. n. drahten, telegraphieren.

wireless, s. Radioapparat m.; Radio n.

wisdom, s. Weisheit f.; Klugheit f.

wise¹, adj. weise, klug.

wise², s. Weise f.; Art f.

wish, v. a. wünschen wollen, ersehnen; — s. Wunsch m., Verlangen n.

wit, s. Witz m.; Verstand m.

with, prep. mit, für; mittels, durch; bei, von, für.

withdraw, v. a. entziehen; zurückziehen; v. n. sich zurückziehen; abtreten.

withhold, v. a. zurückhalten; vorenthalten; v. n. sich enthalten.

within, prep. innerhalb, binnen; — adv. innen, drinnen, darin.

without, prep. ohne; außerhalb; jenseits; — adv. außen, außerhalb, draußen.

withstand, v. a. widerstehen.

witness, s. Zeuge m.; Zeugin f.; — v. a. bezeugen; v. n. zeugen (für, gegen).

witness-box, s. Zeugenstand m.

witty, adj. witzig; geistreich.

woe, s. Weh n.; Leid m.

wolf, s. Wolf m.; — v. a. verschlingen.

woman, s. Frau f.; Weib n.; — adj. weiblich.

womb, s. Gebärmutter f.; Mutterleib m.; fig. Schoß m.

wonder, s. Wunder n.; Verwunderung f.; — v. n. sich verwundern; wissen mögen, neugierig sein (ob).

wonderful, adj. wunderbar, erstaunlich.

wood, s. Wald m.; Gehölz n.; Holzblasinstrumente n. pl.; — adj. hölzern.

wooden, adj. hölzern.

woodman, s. Förster m., Holzfäller m.

wool, s. Wolle f.

woollen, *adj.* wollen; — *s.* ~s *pl.* Wollsachen *f. pl.*
word, *s.* Wort *n.;* Nachricht *f.;* Text *m.;* — *v. a.* in Worten ausdrücken; abfassen.
work, *s.* Arbeit *f.;* Werk *n.;* ~s *pl.* Werk *n.;* — *v.n.* arbeiten, funktionieren, wirken; *v.a.* bearbeiten, verarbeiten.
worker, *s.* Arbeiter *m.*, -in *f.*
workman, *s.* Arbeitsmann *m.;* Arbeiter *m.;* Handwerker *m.*
workshop, *s.* Werkstätte *f.*
world, *s.* Welt *f.*
worldly, *adj.* weltlich.
world-power, *s.* Weltmacht *f.*
World-War, *s.* Weltkrieg *m.*
world-wide, *adj.* über die ganze Welt verbreitet.
worm, *s.* Wurm *m.;* Raupe *f.;* — *v. n.* kriechen.
worn, *adj.* benutzt, abgetragen; *fig.* müde.
worry, *v. n.* (sich) beunruhigen; (sich) quälen.
worse, *adj. & adv.* schlechter, schlimmer.
worship, *s.* Verehrung *f.;* Anbetung *f.;* Gottesdienst *m.;* — *v. a.* verehren; anbeten.
worst, *adj.* schlechtest; schlimmst.
worth, *adj.* wert; würdig; *to be* ~ wert sein; kosten.
worthy, *adj.* würdig.
would, *see* will[1]
wound, *s.* Wunde *f.;* — *v. a.* verwunden, verletzen.
wounded, *adj.* verwundet; — *s.* Verwundete *m., f.*
wrap, *v. a.* wickeln; — *s.*

X

X-ray, *s.* X-Strahl *m.;* Röntgenstrahl *m.;* — *v.a.* durchleuchten; mit Röntgenstrahlen behandeln.

Y

yacht, *s.* Yacht *f.*
yachting, *v. n.* auf einer Yacht fahren; segeln.
yard[1], *s.* Yard *n.;* Elle *f.* (0,91 Meter).
yard[2], *s.* Hof *m.;* Arbeitsstätte *f.;* Werkplatz *m.;* Rangierbahnhof *m.*
yarn, *s.* Garn *n.;* — *v. a.* Geschichten erzählen.
yawn, *v. n.* gähnen; — *s.* Gähnen *n.*
year, *s.* Jahr *n.*
yearly, *adj. & adv.* jährlich.
yeast, *s.* Hefe *f.*
yell, *v. a. & n.* schreien, aufschreien; — *s.* Schrei *m.*
yellow, *adj.* gelb; — *s.* Gelb *n.*
yes, *adv.* ja.
yesterday, *adv.* gestern; — *adj.* gestrig.
yet, *adv.* (immer) noch, noch immer; schon (jetzt); bis jetzt; selbst, sogar; *as* ~ bis jetzt; *not* ~ noch nicht; — *conj.* jedoch; gleichwohl.
yield, *v. a.* ergeben, erbringen, eintragen,

liefern; — *s.* Ertrag *m.;* Ausbeute *f.*
Hülle *f.;* Decke *f.;* Schal *m.;* Mantel *m.*
wrapper, *s.* Hülle *f.;* Umschlag *m.;* Morgenrock *m.;* Buchumschlag *m.*
wrath, *s.* Zorn *m.*
wreath, *s.* Kranz *m.;* Girlande *f.*
wreck, *s.* Wrack *n.;* Schiffbruch *m.;* — *v. a. fig.* zum Scheitern bringen; vernichten; *v. n.* Schiffbruch erleiden; *fig.* scheitern.
wrench, *v. a.* winden, drehen; verrenken; — *s.* Verdrehung *f.;* Verrenkung *f.;* Schraubenschlüssel *n.*
wrestle, *v. n. & a.* ringen — *s.* Ringen *n.;* Ringkampf *m.*
wrestler, *s.* Ringkämpfer *m.*
wretched, *adj.* elend; erbärmlich.
wring, *v. a.* ausdrücken, auspressen; — *s.* Wringen *n.;* Auswinden *n.*
wrinkle, *s.* Runzel *f.;* Falte *f.;* — *v. n. & a.* (sich) runzeln, (sich) falten.
wrist, *s.* Handgelenk *n.*
writ, *s.* Schrift *f.,* gerichtlicher Befehl *m.;* Verhaftungsbefehl *m.*
write, *v. a. & n.* schreiben.
writer, *s.* Schreiber *m.;* Schriftsteller *m.*
writing,-desk *s.* Schreibtisch *m.*
wrong, *adj.* falsch, unrecht; verkehrt; — *s.* Unrecht *n.;* — *v. a.* ungerecht sein gegen.

yolk, *s.* Eidotter *m.,* Eigelb *n.*
you, *pron.* du, ihr, Sie; dir, euch, Ihnen; dich, euch, Sie; dir, euch, sich; dich euch sich.
young, *adj.* jung; — *s.* Junge(n) *pl.*
youngster, *s.* Junge *m.*
your, *pron. & adj. sing.* dein(e); *pl.* euer, eure; *sing.* or *pl.* Ihr(e).
yours, *pron. sing.* deiner, deine, deines; der, die, das deinige, die deinigen; *pl.* euer, eures; der, die, das eurige, die eurigen; die Deinigen, die Euren, die Ihren.
yourself, -ves, *pron. sing.* du, Sie selbst, *pl.* ihr Sie selbst; *sing.* dir, dich, sich; *pl.* euch, sich; *by* ~ selbst; selbständig; allein.
youth, *s.* Jugend *f.*
youth-hostel, *s.* Jugendherberge *f.*
Yugoslav, *s.* Jugoslawe *m.,* Jugoslawin *f.;* — *adj.* jugoslawisch.

Z

zeal, *s.* Eifer *m.*
zebra, *s.* Zebra *n.;* ~ *crossing* Zebrastreifen *m. pl.*
zero, *s.* Null *f.;* Nullpunkt *m.*
zinc, *s.* Zink *n.*
zipper, *s.* Reißverschluß *m.*
zone, *s.* Zone *f.*
zoo, *s.* Zoo *m.*
zoology, *s.* Zoologie *f.*

GERMAN-ENGLISH

DICTIONARY

Wörterbuch 138

A

ab, *adv.* off; ~ *und zu* now and then; — *prep.* from; ex; ~ *Hafen* ex harbour.

abändern, *v.a.* alter; modify.

Abbau, *m.* (~e) working (of a mine).

Abbildung, *f.* (~en) representation; picture.

abblenden, *v. a. & n.* dim; dip.

ábbrechen*, break off;— *v. a. & n.* leave off; pull down.

Abc, Abece, *n.* (—) ABC, alphabet.

abdanken, *v. n.* resign.

Abdruck, *m.* (~e) copy.

Abend, *m.* (~e) evening; *guten* ~ good evening.

Abendblatt, *n.* evening newspaper.

Abendessen, *n.* supper; dinner.

Abendmahl, *n.* supper.

Abenteurer, *m.* (~) adventurer.

Abenteuer, *n.* (~) adventure.

aber, *conj.* but, however; — *adv.* again.

abermals, *adv.* again.

Abfahrt, *f.* (~en) departure, start(ing).

Abfall, *m.* fall(ing) off; waste, slope; defection.

abfertigen, *v. a.* dispatch.

abfliegen*, *v. n.* fly off; take off.

Abfluß, *m.* outlet; discharge; sink.

Abfuhr, *f.* (~en) transport.

Abführmittel, *n.* purgative, laxative.

Abgabe, *f.* (~n) delivery, tax.

abgelegen, *adj.* remote.

abgemacht, *adj.* all right.

Abgeordnete, *m., f.* (~n) deputy; representative, Member of Parliament.

Abgesandte *m., f.* (~n) delegate.

abgesehen, ~ *von* apart from; irrespective of.

Abgott, *m.* idol.

Abgrund, *m.* abyss, precipice.

Abhandlung, *f.* (~en) discussion; treatise.

Abhang, *m.* (~e) slope.

abhängen, *v. n.* depend on.

Abhängigkeit, *f.* (~en) dependence.

Abhilfe, *f.* remedy.

abholen, *v. a.* fetch; call for.

Abhörer, *m.* monitor.

Abkomme, *m.* (~n) descendant.

Abkommen, *n.* (~) agreement.

Abkunft, *f.* (~e) descent; birth.

abladen*, *v. a.* unload.

Ablauf, *m.* outlet; expiration.

ablegen, *v. a.* take off; put down; discard.

ablehnen, *v. a.* refuse.

ableiten, *v. a.* divert; derive.

ablenken, *v. a. & n.* divert; *sich* ~ relax.

abliefern, *v. a.* deliver.

ablösen, *v. a.* relieve.

Abmachung, *f.* (~en) agreement; settlement.

abmessen*, *v. a.* measure; weigh.

abnehmen*, *v. a.* take

Abnehmer 139. **Abt**

away; take off; amputate; buy; *v. n.* decline.

Abnehmer, *m.* (~) buyer.

Abneigung, *f.* (~en) disinclination; dislike.

abnutzen, abnützen, *v. a.* use up; wear out.

Abonnement, *n.* (~s) subscription.

Abonnent, *m.* (~en) subscriber.

Abordnung, *f.* (~en) delegation.

Abort, *m.* (~e) lavatory, water-closet.

abrechnen, *v. a.* deduct; *v. n.* settle accounts.

Abrechnungshaus, *n.* clearing-house.

Abrede, *f.* (~n) agreement; *in ~ stellen* deny.

Abreise, *f.* (~n) departure.

abreisen, *v. n.* start, depart, leave.

abreißen*, *v. a.* tear off; pull down; *v. n.* come off.

Abriß, *m.* (-isse) sketch; summary.

Abrüstung, *f.* demobilization, disarmament.

absagen, *v. a.* refuse; call off; cancel; decline.

Absatz, *m.* stop; paragraph; heel; market; sale; outlet; landing.

abschaffen, *v. a.* abolish; do away with.

abscheulich, *adj.* abominable.

abschicken, *v. a.* send off; dispatch.

Abschied, *m.* (~e) departure; *~ nehmen* take leave.

Abschlag, *m.* (⁓e) discount.

Abschlagszahlung *f.* instalment.

abschließen*, *v. a.* lock up; shut up; close; conclude.

Abschluß, *m.* (-üsse) conclusion; settlement.

abschneiden*, *v. a.* cut off; *v. n.* come off (well, badly).

Abschnitt, *m.* paragraph; section; coupon.

abschreiben*, *v. a.* copy.

Abschrift, *f.* copy; transcript.

Abschußbasis, *f.* launching site.

abschweifen, *v. n.* deviate.

abschwören*, *v. a.* abjure.

absenden*, *v. a.* dispatch; send; mail.

Absender, *m.* (~) sender.

Absicht, *f.* (~en) intention; *mit ~* on purpose.

absolut, *adj.* absolute; — *adv.* absolutely.

absondern, *v. a.* separate; detach.

absperren, *v. a.* shut up; shut off; block.

abspielen, *v. a.* play; *sich ~* take place.

Abstammung, *f.* (~en) descent.

Abstand, *m.* (⁓e) distance; interval.

abstatten, *v. a.* make; render.

Abstecher, *m.* (~) trip; *fig.* digression.

absteigen*, *v. n.* descend; put up (at).

abstellen, *v. a.* stop; turn off; redress.

Abstimmung, *f.* (~en) vote; ballot.

abstoßen*, *v. a. fig.* repel.

abstreiten*, *v. a.* dispute, contest.

abstumpfen, *v. a.* blunt; dull.

Absturz, *m.* (⁓e) fall; crash.

absurd, *adj.* absurd.

Abt, *m.* (⁓e) abbot.

Abtei — ähnlich

Abtei, *f.* (~en) abbey.
Abteil, *n.* (~e) compartment.
Abteilung, *f.* (~en) division; department; section, compartment.
abtreten*, *v. n.* retire; cede; *v. a.* wear off.
Abtritt, *m.* (~e) exit; retreat.
abtrocknen, *v. a.* dry; wipe; *v. n.* dry (up).
abwarten, *v. a. & n.* wait (for).
abwärts, *adv.* downward(s).
abwaschen, *v. a.* wash off.
Abwasser, *n.* (~) waste water.
abwechseln, *v. a. & n.* vary; *sich* ~ alternate.
Abwechselung, *f.* (~en) change; *zur* ~ for a change.
abweichen*, *v. n.* deviate.
Abweichung, *f.* (~en) deviation.
abweisen*, *v. a.* reject; refuse.
abwenden*, *v. a.* turn away; avert.
abwerfen*, *v. a.* throw off; drop; cast off.
abwesend, *adj.* absent.
abwischen, *v. a.* wipe off.
abzahlen, *v. a.* pay off.
Abzahlungssystem, *n.* hire-purchase system.
Abzeichen, *n.* (~) badge.
abziehen*, *v. a.* draw off; divert; bottle; subtract; *v. n.* depart.
Abzug, *m.* (~e) departure; retreat; deduction; proof-sheet; print.
Abzweigung, *f.* (~en) branch-line.
Achse, *f.* (~n) axis; axle.
Achsel, *f.* (~n) shoulder.
acht, *adj.* eight.
Acht: *nimm dich in* ~! take care!
achte, *adj. der, die, das* ~ the eighth.
achten, *v. a.* observe; respect; esteem; *v. n.* ~ *auf* attend to; take care of.
achtgeben*, *v. n.* pay attention; look out.
Achtung, *f.* esteem; regard; ~! look out! attention!.
achtzehn, *adj.* eighteen.
achtzig, *adj.* eighty.
Acker, *m.* (~) field.
Ackerbau, *m.* agriculture.
ackern, *v. a. & n.* plough; till.
addieren, *v. a. & n.* add.
Adel, *m.* nobility.
Ader, *f.* (~n) vein, blood-vessel.
Adjutant, *m.* (~en, ~en) aid-de-camp.
Adler, *m.* (~) eagle.
Admiral, *m.* (~e) admiral.
Admiralität, *f.* Admiralty.
adoptieren, *v. a.* adopt.
Adressbuch, *n.* directory.
Adresse, *f.* (~n) address.
Advent, *m.* (~e) advent.
Adverb, *n.* (~ien) adverb.
Advokat, *m.* (~en, ~en) lawyer, barrister, counsel.
Affe, *m.* (~n, ~n) monkey.
affektiert, *adj.* affected.
Afrikaner, *m.* (~); -in *f.* (~nen) African.
afrikanisch, *adj.* African.
Agent, *m.* (~en, ~en) agent.
Agentur, *f.* (~en) agency.
Ägypter, *m.* (~); -in *f.* (~nen) Egyptian.
ägyptisch, *adj.* Egyptian.
Ahne, *m.* (~n, ~n) ancestor.
ahnen, *v. a.* anticipate.
ähnlich, *adj.* like; similar, resembling; ~ *sein*

Ähnlichkeit   141.   **Altertum**

look like.
Ähnlichkeit, *f.* (~en) likeness, resemblance.
Ahnung, *f.* (~en) presentiment; foreboding.
Akademie, *f.* (~n) academy.
akklimatisieren, *v. a.* acclimatize.
Akkord, *m.* (~e) chord; agreement; contract.
Akkordarbeit, *f.* piecework.
Akkreditiv, *n.* (~e) letter of credit.
Akkumulator, *m.* (~en) accumulator.
Akkusativ, *m.* (~e) accusative.
Akt, *m.* (~e) act; nude.
Akte, *f.* (~n) document; ~n *pl.* deeds.
Aktentasche, *f.* attaché-case, briefcase.
Aktie, *f.* (~n) shares *pl.*, stocks *pl.*
Aktiengesellschaft, *f.* joint-stock company.
Aktieninhaber, *m.* shareholder.
Aktion, *f.* (~en) action; encounter.
Aktionär, *m.* (~e) shareholder.
aktuell, *adj.* topical, current.
Akustik, *f.* (~en) acoustics.
Akzent, *m.* (~e) accent, stress.
Akzept, *m.* (~e) acceptance.
Akzeptant, *m.* (~en) acceptor.
akzeptieren, *v. a.* accept; honour.
Alarm, *m.* (~e), alarm.
Album, *n.* (Alben) album.
alkoholisch, *adj.* alcoholic.
all, *adj.* all; *sie* ~e all of them; ~es in ~em all in all; *trotz* ~em after all; — *adv.* ~e all spent; —*s. das All* the universe.
Allee, *f.* (~n) alley, 'avenue.
allein, *adj.* alone, — *adv.* only; — *conj.* but.
allemal, *adv.* always; *ein für* ~ once for all.
allenfalls, *adv.* perhaps; if necessary.
allerdings, *adv.* indeed; of course.
allerhand, allerlei, *adj.* of all kinds.
allerliebst, *adj.* most charming.
allgemein, *adj.* general, universal; common; *im* ~en in general; — *adv.* generally; commonly.
alliiert, *adj.* allied.
alljährlich, *adj.* annual.
allmächtig, *adj.* almighty.
alltäglich, *adj.* daily, everyday; common.
allzu, *adv.* too.
Almosen, *n.* (~) alms; charity.
Alphabet, *n.* (~e) alphabet.
als, *adv.* as, — *conj.* but; both ... and; as if; as; while; when.
alsbald, *adv.* at once, immediately.
alsdann, *adv.* then.
also, *adv.* so, thus; *conj.* therefore; — *int. na* ~! well then!
alt, *adj.* old; ancient; antique; *3 Jahre* ~ three years old.
Alt, *m.* (~e) contralto, alto.
Altar, *m.* (~e) altar.
Alter, *n.* (~) age; *hohes* ~ old age.
älter, *adj. (pers)* elder; older (than).
Altertum, *s.* (~er) antiq-

ältest — **Anfang**

uity.
ältest, *adj.* oldest; eldest; senior.
altmodisch, *adj.* old-fashioned.
Aluminium, *n.* aluminium.
am, *prep.* (= an dem) at, in, on; ~ *Main* on the Main; ~ *Montag* on Monday; ~ *Morgen* in the morning.
Amateur, *m.* (~e) amateur; *(sport)* non-professional.
Ameise, *f.* (~n) ant.
Amerikaner, *m.* (~); ~in *f.* (~nen) American.
amerikanisch, *adj.* American.
Amsel, *f.* (~n) blackbird.
Amt, *n.* (⸚er) office; employment; authorities *pl.* board; administration; *(telephone)* exchange; *von* ~s *wegen* officially.
amtieren, *v.n.* be in office; hold office; officiate.
amtlich, *adj.* official; — *adv.* officially.
Amtmann, *m.* magistrate.
an, *adv.* on; from; ever since; *von nun* ~ from now; — *prep.* at, on; upon; by; to.
analysieren, *v. a.* analyze.
Ananas *f.* (~se) pineapple.
Anarchie, *f.* (~n) anarchy.
Anatomie, *f.* (~n) anatomy.
anbauen, *v. a.* cultivate, grow; annex; *sich* ~ settle.
anbei, *adv.* herewith; enclosed.
anbelangen, *v. a.*; *was mich anbelangt* for my part; as for me.
anbeten, *v.a.* worship; adore.

Anbetreff, *m.*; *in* ~ concerning; regarding.
anbetreffs, *prep.* see *in Anbetreff*.
anbieten*, *v. a. & n.* offer.
Anblick, *m.* sight; look; view.
anblicken, *v. a.* look at.
Andacht, *f.* (~en) devotion.
Andenken, *s.* (~) remembrance; memory; souvenir.
andere, andre, *adj. & pron. der, die, das* ~ the other; other (than).
anderenfalls, anderenteils, *adv.* otherwise.
ändern, *v. a.* alter; change.
anders, *adv.* otherwise; ~ *als* different from; — *pron.* jemand ~ somebody else.
anderseits, *adv.* on the other hand.
anderswo(hin) *adv.* elsewhere.
anderthalb, *adj.* one and a half.
Änderung, *f.* (~en) change; alteration.
Andeutung, *f.* (~en) indication, suggestion; hint.
andrehen, *v. a.* turn on.
aneignen, *v. n.* (sich) appropriate; adopt; take possession of.
aneinander, *adv.* together.
Anekdote, *f.* (~n) anecdote.
anerkennen*, *v.a.* acknowledge, recognize.
Anerkennung, *f.* (~en) recognition; acknowledg(e)ment.
Anfall, *m.* (⸚e) attack; assault; fit.
Anfang, *m.* (⸚e) beginning; outset; *am* ~ at first, at the beginning.

anfangen*, *v. a. & n.* begin, start, commence.

Anfänger, *m.* (~) beginner.

anfangs, *adv.* at first, at the beginning.

anfassen, *v. a. & n.* take hold of; seize; touch.

Anfechtung, *f.* (~en) contestation; challenge; temptation.

anfertigen, *v.a.* make, manufacture; produce.

anfeuern, *v. a.* inflame; incite, kindle.

anflehen, *v.a.* implore, beseech.

Anforderung, *f.* (~en) demand; requirement.

Anfrage, *f.* (~n) inquiry;

anführen, *v. a.* lead; quote, cite; advance; take in.

Anführung, *f.* (~en) quotation, citation; reference.

anfüllen, *v. a.* fill (up); stock (with); stuff.

Angabe, *f.* (~n) statement; declaration; data *pl.*

angeben*, *v. a.* declare, state.

angeblich, *adj.* alleged; reputed; — *adv.* supposedly; allegedly.

angeboren, *adj.* born, congenital.

Angebot, *s.* (~e) offer, supply; offering; ~ *und Nachfrage f.* supply and demand.

angehen*, *v. n.* be admissible; *v.a.* concern; apply to.

angehören, *v. n.* belong (to).

Angehörige, *f., m.* (~n) relation, relative.

Angeklagte, *f., m.* (~n) accused.

Angelegenheit, *f.* (~en) matter.

angeln, *v. n. & a.* fish.

Angelsachse, *m.* Anglo-Saxon.

angelsächsisch, *adj.* Anglo-Saxon.

angemessen, *adj.* adequate; suitable; proper.

angenehm, *adj.* agreeable, pleasant.

angesichts, *adv.* in view of; considering.

Angestellte, *f., m.* (~n) employee.

Angewohnheit, *f.* (~en) habit.

angreifen, *v.a.* attack undertake; fatigue.

Angriff, *m.* (~e) attack.

Angst, *f.* (~̈e) fear anxiety.

ängstlich, *adv.* anxious; uneasy; nervous.

anhalten, *v. a.* stop; *v. n.* continue; last; stop; halt; propose.

Anhalter, *m.* (~) hitchhiker; *per ~ fahren* hitch-hike.

Anhang, *m.* (~̈e) appendix; appendage; party.

Anhänger, *m.* (~) follower; adherent; trinket; see **Anhängewagen**.

Anhängewagen, *m.* trailer.

anhäufen, *v. a.* accumulate; hoard.

anhören, *v. a.* listen (to).

Ankauf, *m.* (~̈e) purchase.

ankaufen, *v. a.* buy, purchase.

Anker, *m.* (~) anchor.

ankern, *v. n. & a.* anchor.

Anklage, *f.* (~n) accusation.

anklagen, *v. a.* accuse.

Ankläger, *m.* (~) accuser.

Anklang, *m.* (~̈e) appeal; interest; concern.

ankleiden, *v. a. & n.* (sich)

anklopfen — **ansehnlich**

dress.
anklopfen, *v. n.* knock (at).
ankommen*, *v. a. & n.* reach; arrive; *es kommt darauf an* it depends on.
Ankündigung, *f.* (~en) announcement; notice.
Ankunft, *f.* (≈e) arrival.
Anlage, *f.* (~n) lay-out; plan, arrangement; park; investment; enclosure.
Anlaß, *m.* (-lässe) cause; occasion.
Anlasser, *m.* (~) *(motor)* starter.
anläßlich, *prep.* on the occasion of.
Anlauf, *m.* (≈e) start; run; attempt.
anlegen, *v. a.* put on; build; install; invest; *v. n.* land; aim (at).
Anleihe, *f.* (~n) loan; ~ *aufnehmen* borrow (from).
Anleitung, *f.* (~en) instruction; guidance; introduction.
anliegend, *adj.* adjacent; enclosed; tight.
anlocken, *v. a.* allure; attract.
anmachen, *v. a.* fasten; fix; prepare; *(of lamp)* light, switch on.
anmelden, *v. a. & n.* announce; notify; *sich* ~ register.
Anmerkung, *f.* (~en) note; comment, remark.
Anmut, *f.* grace, charm.
annähen, *v a.* sew on.
annähernd, *adj.* approximate; — *adv.* approximately.
Annahme, *f.* (~n) acceptance; supposition.
annehmen*, *v. a.* accept; get, receive; suppose.

Annehmlichkeit, *f.* (~en) convenience; amenities *pl.*
Annonce, *f.* (~n) advertisement.
annoncieren, *v. a.* advertise.
anordnen, *v. a.* arrange; put in order.
Anordnung, *f.* (~en) rule; order, arrangement.
anpassen, *v. a.* fit, adapt; adjust; *v. n. sich* ~ accommodate oneself.
anprobieren, *v. a.* try on.
Anrecht, *s.* (~e) right, claim, title.
Anrede, *f.* (~n) address.
anregen, *v. a.* stimulate.
anrichten, *v. a.* prepare; serve (up); cause.
anrufen*, *v. a.* telephone; ring up; call (up).
ansammeln, *v. a.* accumulate; gather, collect.
ansässig, *adj.* resident.
Anschauung, *f.* (~en) view; opinion; idea.
Anschein, *m.* (~e) appearance.
Anschlag, *m.* (≈e) stroke; estimate; plot; touch; placard; poster.
anschlagen, *v. a.* strike; affix, post up; estimate; tax; touch; — *v. n.* take root, aim.
anschließend, *adv.* subsequently.
Anschluß, *m.* (-lüsse) connexion, addition.
Anschrift, *f.* (~en) address.
Ansehen, *s.* look; appearance; prestige; reputation.
ansehen*, *v. a.* look at; regard.
ansehnlich, *adj.* consid-

erable.
Ansicht, *f.* (~en) view; opinion; sight; view
Ansichtskarte, *f.* picture postcard.
Ansiedler, *m.* (~) settler.
anspielen, *v. n.* ~ *auf* hint at; allude to.
Anspielung, *f.* (~en) allusion, hint.
Ansprache, *f.* (~en) address, speech.
Anspruch, *m.* (≈e) claim; pretension.
anspruchsvoll, *adj.* pretentious, exacting.
Anstalt, *f.* (~en) establishment, institution.
Anstand, *m.* (≈e) grace, decency; objection.
anstatt, *prep. & conj.* instead of.
anstecken, *v. a.* infect; set on fire; light.
ansteckend, *adj.* catching, contagious.
ansteigend, *adj.* uphill; rising.
anstellen, *v. a.* place; appoint; employ; *sich* ~ behave; pretend.
Anstellung, *f.* (~en) place; position; appointment.
Anstoß, *m.* (≈e) impulse; shock; offence.
anstreben, *v.a. & n.* aspire (to).
anstreichen*, *v. a.* paint.
anstrengen, *v. a. sich* ~ try hard; exert oneself.
Anstrengung, *f.* (~en) effort; exertion.
Anteil, *m.* (~e) share; interest.
Antenne, *f.* (~n) aerial; antenna.
antik, *adj.* ancient, antique.
antiseptisch, *adj.* antiseptic.

Antrag, *m.* (≈e) offer; proposal; motion.
antreffen*, *v.a.* meet; find.
antreiben, *v. a. & n.* carry along; urge on; incite; drift ashore.
antreten*, *v. a. fig.* begin, enter upon; *v. n.* take one's place; line up.
Antrieb, *m.* (~e) impulse; propulsion.
Antwort, *f.* (~en) answer.
antworten, *v. a. & n.* answer.
anvertrauen, *v. a.* confide; entrust.
Anwalt, *m.* (≈e) solicitor, lawyer; attorney.
Anweisung, *f.* (~en) advice, intruction; assignation; cheque.
anwenden*, *v. a.* use; employ.
Anwendung, *f.* (~en) use; application.
anwesend, *adj.* present.
Anwesenheit, *f.* presence.
Anzahl, *f.* amount, number, quantity.
Anzeige, *f.* (~n) notice; advertisement, announcement.
anzeigen, announce, notify; advertise; denounce.
anziehen*, *v. a.* put on; attract; *sich* ~ dress.
Anzug, *m.* (≈e) suit, dress; approach.
Apfel, *m.* (≈) apple.
Apfelbaum, *m.* apple tree.
Apfelsine, *f.* (~n) orange.
Apostel, *m.* (~) apostle.
Apotheke, *f.* (~n) chemist's shop; drug-store; dispensary.
Apparat, *m.* (~e) apparatus; equipment.
appellieren, *v. n.* appeal (to).

Appetit, m. appetite.
Applaus, m. applause.
Aprikose, f. (~n) apricot.
April, m. (~e) April.
Aquarell, n. (~e) watercolour.
Araber, m. (~); -in f. (~innen) Arab.
arabisch, adj. Arabian, Arab.
Arbeit, f. (~en) work, labour; piece of work.
arbeiten, v. a. & n. work, labour.
Arbeiter, m. (~) worker; workman.
Arbeitgeber, m. employer.
Arbeitseinstellung, f. (~en) strike.
Arbeitslohn, m. wages *pl.*
arbeitslos, adj. unemployed.
Arbeitslosigkeit, f. (~en) unemployment.
Arbeitstag, m. working day, workday.
Arbeitsvermittlung, f. labour exchange.
Arbeitszimmer, n. study.
Architekt, m. (~en; ~en) architect.
Architektur, f. architecture.
arg, adj. bad; wicked.
Argentinier, m. (~); -in f. (~innen) Argentine.
argentinisch, adj. Argentine; Argentinian.
Ärger, m. anger; vexation.
ärgern, v. a. make angry; anger; vex; *sich ~* get angry; be annoyed.
Argument, n. (~e) argument.
Argwohn, m. suspicion.
Arie, f. (~n) tune, air, aria.
Aristokrat, m. (~en) aristocrat.
Arm, m. (~e) *(part of body)* arm.

arm, adj. poor.
Armband, m. bracelet.
Armbanduhr, f. wrist watch.
Armee, f. (~n) army.
Ärmel, m. (~) sleeve.
Ärmelkanal, m. the English Channel.
Armut, f. poverty.
Arrest, m. (~e) arrest.
Art, f. (~en) kind; sort; species; way, manner.
Arterie, f. (~n) artery.
artig, adj. good; wellbred.
Artikel, m. (~) article.
Artillerie, f. (~n) artillery.
Artischocke, f. (~n) artichoke.
Arznei, f. (~n) medicine.
Arzt, m. (~̈e) physician, doctor.
ärztlich, adj. medical.
As^1, n. (~se) *(cards)* ace.
As^2, n. *(music)* A flat.
Asbest, m. asbestos.
Asche, f. ashes *pl.*
Aschenbecher, m. ashtray.
Asiat, m. (~en) Asiatic.
asiatisch, adj. Asiatic.
Assistent, m. (~en; ~en) assistant.
Ast, m. (~̈e) branch.
ästhetisch, adj. artistic, aesthetic.
Astronom, m. (~en; ~en) astronomer.
Astronomie, f. astronomy.
Atem, m. breath; breathing; respiration.
Athlet, m. (~en; ~en) athlete.
Athletik, f. athletics *pl.*
atlantisch, adj. Atlantic.
atmen, v. n. & a. breathe.
Atmen, n. breathing, respiration.
Atmosphäre, f. (~n) at-

mosphere.
Atom, *n.* (~e) atom.
Atombombe, *f.* atomic bomb; nuclear bomb.
Atomenergie, *f.* atomic energy.
Atomforschung, *f.* nuclear research.
atomisch, *adj.* atomic.
Atomkraft, *f.* atomic power.
Atomkraftwerk, *n.* nuclear power station.
attestieren, *v. a.* certify.
auch, *conj.* also; too; likewise; *sowohl als* ~ both ... and; as well as; *wenn* ~ even if, although.
audio-visuell, *adj.* audio-visual.
auf, *prep.* on, upon; in: at; of; by; ~ *der Straße* in the street; ~ *dem Tisch* on the table; — *adv.* up, upwards; ~ *und ab* up and down; to and fro.
Aufbau, *m.* (~ten) building; construction, erection.
aufbauen, *v. a.* build (up); erect; construct.
aufbewahren, *v. a.* keep, preserve; take care of.
aufdringen* *v. a.* press upon, urge on.
Aufenthalt, *m.* stay, stop.
auffallen*, *v. n.* be conspicuous.
auffangen*, *v. a.* catch; snatch.
Auffassung, *f.* (~en) conception; opinion, interpretation.
auffordern, *v. a.* summon, invite, challenge.
Aufforderung, *f.* (~en) invitation; summons *pl.*; challenge.
Aufführung, *f.* (~en) performance; conduct.

Aufgabe, *f.* (~n) task; work; lesson.
aufgeben*, *v. a.* give up; leave; desert; post; book.
aufgehen*, *v. n.* open, rise.
aufgelegt, *adj.* disposed (to); inclined (to).
aufhalten,* *v. a.* stop, detain; obstruct; keep from; *sich* ~ stay.
aufhängen*, *v. a.* hang up.
aufheben*, *v. a.* lift up; pick up.
aufhören, *v. n.* cease; stop.
aufkaufen, *v. a.* buy up.
Aufklärung, *f.* (~en) explanation.
aufladen*, *v. a.* load.
Auflage, *f.* (~n) edition.
auflegen, *v. a.* impose; apply.
auflösen, *v. a.* solve, dissolve.
aufmachen, *v. a.* open; undo; untie; *sich* ~ start; set out.
aufmerksam, *adj.* observing, attentive.
Aufmerksamkeit, *f.* (~en) attention.
Aufnahme, *f.* (~n) reception; admission; survey; photo(graph).
aufnehmen*, *v. a.* receive, take up; survey; raise; *(photo)* take.
aufpassen, *v. n.* pay attention.
Aufregung, *f.* (~en) excitement, agitation.
aufrichten, *v. a.* set up; build, erect.
aufrichtig, *adj.* open; sincere.
Aufruf, *m.* outcry; call; proclamation.
Aufruhr, *m.* (~e) revolt; riot.

Aufsatz, m. theme, essay, composition.
aufschieben*, v. a. postpone, delay, defer.
Aufschlag, m. increase, rise; raising; reverse, lapel.
aufschlagen*, v. a. open, raise; set up; **v. n.** serve.
Aufschluß, m. information.
aufschreiben*, v. a. note, write down.
Aufschrift, f. (~en) inscription; *(of letter)* address.
Aufschwung, m. (~̈e) development; boom.
Aufsehen, n. excitement, sensation.
Aufseher, m. (~) overseer; inspector.
aufsetzen, v. a. & n. put on; serve up; draw up.
Aufsicht, f. inspection, supervision.
Aufstand, m. riot, insurrection.
aufstehen*, v. n. stand up; rise, get up.
aufsteigen*, v. n. mount, climb; rise, take off.
aufstellen, v. a. build, erect; set (up); establish.
Aufstieg, m. (~e) ascent; *fig.* rise.
aufsuchen, v. a. look for.
Auftrag, m. (~̈e) order, errand; commission.
auftreten*, v. n. appear, enter.
Auftritt, m. (~e) performance; scene.
aufwachen, v. n. & a. awake; wake up.
aufwachsen*, v. n. grow up.
Aufwand, m. (~̈e) expense; expenditure.
aufwärmen, v. a. warm (up).
aufwärts, adv. upwards.
aufzählen, v. a. count up, enumerate.
Aufzeichnung f. (~en) note.
aufziehen*, v. a. lift, hoist; raise; wind.
Aufzug, m. (~̈e) procession; parade; act; hoist; lift.
Augapfel, m. eyeball.
Auge, n. (~n) eye.
Augenarzt, m. oculist.
Augenblick, m. moment.
augenblicklich, adj. momentary; immediate; — **adv.** at the moment; at present.
Augenbraue, f. eyebrow.
Augenglas, n. eye-glass.
Augenlicht, n. eyesight.
Augenlid, n. (~er) eyelid.
augenscheinlich, adv. evidently; apparently.
Augenzeuge, m. eye-witness.
August, m. (~e) August.
Auktion, f. (~en) auction.
aus, prep. out of; from; of; by; on; in; — **adv.** out; over.
ausarbeiten, v. a. work out; elaborate.
ausbessern, v. a. repair; mend.
ausbeuten, v. a. exploit.
ausbilden, v. a. form; instruct, educate.
Ausblick, m. outlook, prospect.
ausbrechen*, v. n. break out; burst out.
Ausbruch, m. (~̈e) outbreak.
Ausdauer, f. perseverance, endurance.
ausdehnen, v. a. extend; prolong.

Ausdruck, *m.* (⁓e) expression.
ausdrücken, *v. a.* express; manifest; squeeze.
auseinander, *adv.* apart; asunder.
Auseinandersetzung, *f.* discussion; dispute.
auserwählen, *v. a.* select.
Ausfall, *m.* (⁓e) sortie; loss; falling out, falling off.
ausfallen,* *v. n.* fall out; sally out; turn out.
ausfertigen, *v. a.* write out; make out.
Ausflug, *m.* (⁓e) excursion, outing, trip.
Ausflügler, *m.* (⁓) tripper; excursionist.
Ausfuhr, *f.* (⁓en) export(ation).
ausführen, *v. a.* carry out, execute; export.
ausführlich, *adj.* detailed.
Ausführung, *f.* (⁓en) execution.
Ausgabe, *f.* (⁓n) edition, delivery; expense.
Ausgang, *m.* (⁓e) way out, exit.
ausgeben*, *v. a. & n.* spend, publish; *sich* ⁓ *für* set up for.., pretend to be somebody.
ausgenommen, *adj.* except.
ausgezeichnet, *adj. & adv.* first-rate, excellent.
ausgießen*, *v. a.* pour out.
Ausguß *m.* (-üsse) sink.
aushalten*, *v. a.* bear, endure.
aushändigen, *v. a.* deliver; hand over.
aushelfen*, *v. n.* help out.
auskleiden, *v. a. & n.* undress.
Auskunft, *f.* (⁓e) information.
auslachen, *v. a.* laugh at.
ausladen*, *v. a.* unload.
Auslage, *f.* (⁓n) shopwindow; expenditure.
Ausland, *n.* foreign country.
Ausländer, *m.* (⁓), -in *f.* (⁓nen) foreigner.
auslegen, *v. a.* lay out; display; explain.
Auslese, *f.* (⁓n) selection.
auslöschen, *v. a.* put out.
Auslösehebel, *m.* release lever; trigger.
auslösen, *v. a.* redeem.
Auslöser, *m.* (⁓) release, trigger.
Ausnahme, *f.* (⁓n) exception.
ausnutzen, *v. a.* utilize.
auspacken, *v. a.* unpack.
ausprobieren, *v. a.* try (out).
Auspuffrohr, *n.* exhaust-pipe.
Ausrede, *s.* (⁓n) excuse.
ausreichen, *v. n.* suffice.
ausreißen*, *v. a.* pluck, *v. n.* run away; bolt.
Ausruf, *m.* exclamation.
Ausrufungszeichen, *n.* exclamation mark.
ausrüsten, *v. a.* equip.
Aussage, *f.* declaration; statement; deposition.
Ausschlag, *m.* (⁓e) eruption.
ausschließlich, *adj.* exclusive.
Ausschluß *m.* (-schlüsse) exclusion; *(sport)* disqualification.
ausschneiden,* *v. a.* cut out.
Ausschuß, *m.* rubbish; *pl.* committee; board.
aussehen*, *v. n.* appear, look; *gut* ⁓ look well.
außen, *adv.* outside, out of doors.
Außenbordmotor, *m.* out-

aussenden — **Auto**

board motor.
aussenden*, *v. a.* send out, emit.
Außenhandel, *m.* foreign trade.
außer, *prep.* out (of); besides; except; ~ *sich* beside oneself; — *conj.* except, but; ~ *wenn* unless.
außerdem, *adv.* in addition; besides; moreover.
äußere, *adj.* exterior, outer; external.
Äußere, *n.* appearance; exterior.
außergewöhnlich, *adj.* unsual, exceptional.
außerhalb, *prep.* outside, beyond; — *adv.* on the outside.
äußerlich, *adj.* external; outward; — *adv.* externally; outwards.
äußern, *v. a.* express, utter.
außerordentlich, *adj.* extraordinary.
äußerst, *adj.* extreme; utmost.
Äußerste, *n.* ich werde mein ~s tun I will do my best.
Äußerung, *f.* (~en) expression; utterance.
aussetzen, *v. a.* set out; expose.
Aussicht, *f.* (~en) sight; *fig.* prospect, view.
Aussichtswagen, *m.* observation-car.
Aussprache, *f.* (~n) pronunciation.
aussprechen*, *v. a.* pronounce.
Ausspruch, *m.* (⁓e) statement; sentence.
ausstatten, *v. a.* fit up; furnish; endow; equip.
Ausstattung, *f.* (~en) equipment; outfit; dowry.

ausstehen*, *v. a.* bear, suffer, endure.
aussteigen*, *v. n.* get out; alight.
ausstellen, *v. a.* exhibit; display, draw.
Ausstellung, *f.* (~en) exhibition; display.
ausstoßen*, *v. a. & n.* expel; *(cry)* utter.
ausstrahlen, *v. a. & n.* radiate; emit.
aussuchen, *v. a.* choose, select.
Austausch, *m.* exchange.
austeilen, *v. a.* distribute.
Auster, *f.* (~n) oyster.
austrinken*, *v. a.* drink up, empty.
ausüben, *v. a.* exercise, practise.
Ausverkauf, *m.* (⁓e) (clearance) sale.
Auswahl, *f.* choice, selection; assortment.
auswählen, *v. a.* choose, select.
Auswanderer, *m.* emigrant.
auswandern, *v. n.* emigrate.
auswärts, *adv.* outward(s), out of doors.
Ausweg, *m.* (⁓e) way out.
ausweichen, **v. n.* make way; *fig.* avoid, evade.
Ausweis, *m.* (~e) identification; statement.
ausweisen*, *v. a.* expel; banish; prove; *sich* ~ prove one's identity.
auswendig, *adv.* by heart.
auszahlen, *v. a.* pay (for).
Auszeichnung, *f.* (~en) distinction.
ausziehen*, *v. a.* draw out; remove; take off; *sich* ~ undress.
Auszug, *m.* (⁓e) departure; extract; summary.
Auto, *n.* (~s) motor-

Autobahn   151.   **barock**

car.
Autobahn, *f.* motorway.
Autobus, *m.* motor-coach.
Autofahrer, *m.* motorist.
Autogramm, *n.* (~e) autograph.
Automat, *m.* (~en; ~en) slot-machine.
automatisch, *adj.* automatic.
Automobil, *n.* (~e) motor-car.
Autoparkplatz, *m.* (⁀e) parking place.
Autor, *m.* (~en) author.
Autorität, *f.* (~en; ~en) authority.
Autostraße, *f.* motor-road, motorway.
Autovermietung, *f.* car-hire.
Axt, *f.* (⁀e) axe.

B

Baby, *n.* baby.
Bach, *m.* (⁀e) brook.
Backe, *f.* (~n) cheek.
backen*, *v. a. & n.* bake.
Bäcker, *m.* (~) baker.
Bäckerei, *f.* bakery.
Bad, *n.* (⁀er) bath; watering-place.
Badeanstalt *f.,* baths *pl.;* swimming-pool; bathing establishment.
Badeanzug, *m.* bathing-suit, bathing-costume.
baden, *v.n.&a.* (in the open) bathe; have a bath.
Badeofen, *m.* geyser
Badeort, *m.* watering-place; spa.
Badewanne, *f.* (bath-)tub.
Badezimmer, *n.* bathroom.
Bahn, *f.* (~en) path; road;
Bahnhof, *m.* station.

Bahnsteig, *m.* platform.
Bahnsteigkarte, *f.* platform ticket.
Bahnübergang, *m.* level-crossing.
Bahre, *f.* (~n) stretcher.
Bakterie, *f.* (~n) bacterium.
balancieren, *v. a. & n.* balance.
bald, *adv.* soon; nearly; almost.
baldig, *adj.* early, speedy.
Balkon, *m.* (~e) balcony.
Ball¹, *m.* (⁀e) ball.
Ball², *m.* (⁀e) ball; dance.
Ballade, *f.* (~n) ballad.
Ballen, *m.* (~) bundle; bale.
Ballett, *n.* (~e) ballet.
baltisch, *adj.* Baltic.
Banane, *f.* (~n) banana.
Band¹, *m.* (⁀e) volume.
Band², *n.* (⁀er) band, ribbon. tie; tape.
Bande, *f.* (~n) gang.
bändigen, *v. a.* tame.
Bank¹, *f.* (⁀e) bench, seat.
Bank², *f.* (~en) bank.
Bankier, *m.* (~s) banker.
Bankkonto, *n.* (-konten) bank-account.
Banknote, *f.* bank-note.
bankrott, *adj.* bankrupt.
Bann, *m.* (⁀e) ban; spell; excommunication.
bannen, *v. a.* banish.
Bantamgewicht, *n.* *(sport)* bantam-weight.
bar, *adj.* bare; naked.
Bar, *f.* (~s) bar.
Bär, *m.* (~en) bear.
Barbier, *m.* (~e) barber.
barfuß, *adj. & adv.* bare-foot(ed).
Bariton, *m.* (~e) *(voice)* baritone.
barmherzig, *adj.* merciful; charitable.
barock, *adj.* baroque.

Barometer | **Beförderungsmittel**

Barometer, *m.* (~) barometer.
Baron, *m.* (~e) baron.
Bart, *m.* (~e) beard.
Barzahlung, *f.* cash payment.
Basis, *f.* (Basen) base.
Baß, *m.* (Bässe) bass.
Bassist, *m.* (~en; ~en) bass (singer).
Batterie, *f.* (~en) battery.
Bau, *m.* (~ten) building, construction.
Bauch, *m.* (~e) belly.
bauen, *v. a.* build, construct; *v. n.* rely on.
Bauer,[1] *m.* (~n) farmer; countryman; peasant.
Bauer[2], *n., m.* (~) (bird-) cage.
Baukunst, *f.* architecture.
Baum, *m.* (~e) tree.
Baumeister, *m.* master-builder.
Baumwolle, *f.* cotton.
Bauwerk, *n.* building.
Bazillus, *m.* (-llen) bacillus.
beabsichtigen, *v.a.* intend.
beachten, *v. a.* pay attention (to); consider.
Beachtung, *f.* (~en) attention, notice; regard.
Beamte, *m.* (~n; ~n) official; civil servant.
beanspruchen, *v. a.* demand, claim; call for.
beanstanden, *v. a.* object (to); reject.
bearbeiten, *v. a.* work; cultivate; treat.
Bearbeitung, *f.* arrangement; adaptation; treatment.
beauftragen, *v. a.* charge, commission.
Becher, *m.* (~) goblet, cup.
Becken, *n.* (~) basin.
bedanken, *v. a. sich ~ für* thank for.
Bedarf, *m.* need, want; demand.
bedauern, *v. a.* pity, regret.
bedecken, *v.a.* cover.
Bedenken, *n.* doubt.
bedeuten, *v.a.* mean, signify.
bedeutend, *adj.* important; considerable.
bedienen, *v. a. & n.* serve on, wait on; *sich ~* help oneself to.
Bediente, *m., f.* (~n) servant.
Bedienung, *f.* service.
Bedingung, *f.* (~en) condition; stipulation.
bedrücken, *v. a.* oppress.
Bedürfnis, *n.* (~se) need; want; necessity; requirement.
Beefsteak, *n.* (~e) (beef-) -steak.
beeinflussen, *v. a.* influence.
beendigen, beenden, *v. a.* complete; finish; end.
Beerdigung, *f.* (~en) burial; funeral.
Beere, *f.* (~n) berry.
Beet, *n.* (~e) (flower-)bed.
Befähigung, *f.* (~en) qualification.
befangen, *adj.* embarrassed; shy.
befassen, *v. a. sich ~ mit etw.* be engaged in sg.
Befehl, *m.* (~e) command, order.
befehlen*, *v. a.* command, order.
befestigen, *v. a.* fasten; fix; fortify.
Befestigung, *f.* (~en) fortification.
befinden*, *v. a. & n.* find; *sich ~* be; feel.
befördern, *v. a.* forward; promote.
Beförderungsmittel, *s.*

befreien 153. **Bekenntnis**

(means of) conveyance.
befreien, *v.a.* deliver; free; liberate.
befreunden, *v. n. sich ~* make friends with.
befriedigen, *v. a.* satisfy.
begabt, *adj.* gifted.
begegnen, *v. n.* meet; come across.
begehen*, *v. a.* commit.
Begeisterung, *f.* (~en) enthusiasm.
Begierde, *f.* (~n) desire, lust.
begierig, *adj.* eager.
Beginn, *m.* beginning.
beginnen*, *v. a.&n.* begin, commence.
beglaubigen, *v. a.* attest; certify.
begleiten, *v.a.* accompany, escort.
Begleitung, *f.* (~en) company; *(music)* accompaniment.
beglückwünschen, *v. a.* congratulate.
Begräbnis, *n.* (~se) burial; funeral.
begreifen*, *v. a. fig.* understand; grasp.
begrenzen, *v. a.* limit; border.
Begriff, *m.* (~e) idea, concept(ion); term; *im ~ sein* be about to.
begründen, *v. a.* found; establish; prove.
begrüßen, *v. a.* greet; *fig.* welcome.
begünstigen, *v. a.* favour.
behalten*, *v.a.* keep.
Behälter, *m.* (~) container; bin; tank.
behandeln, *v. a.* handle, treat; attend.
Behauptung, *f.* (~en) statement; assertion.
beherrschen, *v. a.* rule, control; master.
behilflich, *adj.* helpful, serviceable, useful.

Behörde, *f.* (~n) authorities *pl.*
bei, *prep.* by, near, at; on; with; about; *~ Tisch* at table; *~ Tage* by day.
beide, *adj.* both, either.
beiderseitig, *adj.* mutual, bilateral.
Beifall, *m.* applause.
Beil, *n.* (~e) hatchet, axe.
Beilage, *f.* (~n) addition supplement.
beiläufig, *adv.* by the way.
Beileid, *n.* condolence.
beiliegend, *adv.* enclosed.
Bein, (~e) leg.
beinah(e), *adv.* almost, nearly.
Beiname, *m.* (~n) surname; nickname.
beisammen, *adv.* together.
beiseite, *adv.* aside, apart.
Beispiel, *s.* (~e) example; *zum ~* for example.
beißen*, *v. a.* bite; sting.
Beistand, *m.* (~e) help, aid; assistance.
Beistimmung, *f.* (~en) approval, assent.
Beitrag, *m.* (~e) contribution.
beitreten*, *v. n.* agree, assent; join.
Beiwagen, *m.* side-car; trailer.
beiwohnen, *v. n.* be present, attend.
bejahen, *v. a.* affirm.
bekannt, *adj.* known.
Bekannte, *m., f.* acquaintance.
bekanntlich, *adv.* as is well-known.
Bekanntschaft, *f.* acquaintance.
bekennen*, *v. a. & n.* admit; confess.
Bekenntnis, *n.* (~se) con-

beklagen — **154.** — **berücksichtigen**

fession.
beklagen, *v. a.* deplore; bewail.
bekommen*, *v. a.* get; receive; obtain.
bekümmern, *v. a. & n.* grieve, trouble.
Belagerung, *f.* (~en) siege.
belästigen, *v. a.* molest; annoy.
belaufen*, *v. a.* amount (to).
Beleg, *m.* (~e) voucher; receipt.
belehren, *v. a.* advise, instruct.
Beleidigung, *f.* (~en) offence; insult.
beleuchten, *v. a.* light (up), illuminate.
Beleuchtung, *f.* (~en) lighting; illumination.
Belgier, *m.* (~); -in *f.* (~nen) Belgian.
belgisch, *adj.* Belgian.
belichten, *v. a.* expose.
Belichtung, *f.* (~en) exposure.
beliebig, *adj.* any; whatever.
Beliebtheit, *f.* popularity.
bellen, *v. n.* bark, bay.
belohnen, *v. a.* reward.
Belohnung, *f.* (~en) reward.
bemächtigen, *v. n.* sich ~ take possession of.
bemerkbar, *adj.* perceptible.
bemerken, *v. a.* perceive, notice.
Bemerkung, *f.* (~en) remark, observation.
bemitleiden, *v. a.* pity.
Bemühung, *f.* (~en) trouble, pains; effort.
benachbart, *adj.* adjoining; neighbouring.
benachrichtigen, *v. a.* inform.
benehmen, *v. n.* sich ~ behave.
Benehmen, *n.* conduct, behaviour.
beneiden, *v. a.* envy.
benutzen, *v. a.* use, make use of.
Benzin, *n.* petrol.
beobachten, *v. a.* watch; observe.
Beobachter, *m.* (~) observer.
Beobachtung, *f.* (~en) observation.
bequem, *adj.* comfortable, convenient.
beraten, *v. a. & n.* sich mit jm ~ consult with sy.
Beratung, *f.* (~en) consutation, conference.
berauben, *v. a.* rob; deprive.
berauschen, *v. a.* intoxicate.
berechtigen, *v. a.* authorize; entitle.
Bereich, *m.* (~e) scope; compass; sphere; reach.
bereifen, *v. a.* tyre.
bereit, *adj.* ready, willing.
bereiten, *v. a.* prepare.
bereits, *adv.* already.
bereitwillig, *adj.* willing; ready.
bereuen, *v. a.* repent, regret.
Berg, *m.* (~e) mountain.
bergab, *adv.* downhill.
bergauf, *adv.* uphill.
Bergbau, *m.* mining.
bergen*, *v. a.* hide, conceal; save, salve, recover.
Bergmann, *m.* (-leute) miner.
Bergwerk, *s.* mine.
Bericht, *m.* (~e) report.
berichten, *v. a. & n.* report, give account.
Berichterstatter, *m.* reporter.
berücksichtigen, *v. a.* consider.

Beruf, *m.* (~e) occupation; profession; trade; vocation.
berufen, *v. a. & n.* call together, convoke; appoint; *sich ~ auf* appeal to; refer to.
Berufung, *f.* (~en) appeal, call; reference.
beruhen, *v. n.* rest on; be based upon.
beruhigen, calm; pacify.
berühmt, *adj.* famous.
berühren, *v. a.* touch.
Besatzung, *f.* (~en) crew; garrison.
beschädigen, *v. a.* hurt, damage.
Beschaffenheit, *f.* nature, character; condition.
beschäftigen, *v. a.* occupy; employ.
Beschäftigung, *f.* (~en) occupation; business.
Bescheid, *m.* (~e) information; answer.
bescheiden, *adj.* modest.
Bescheinigung, *f.* (~en) certificate; receipt, voucher.
Bescherung, *f.* (~en) distribution of presents; *eine schöne ~!* a pretty business!
beschimpfen, *v. a.* insult; call names.
beschlagen*, *v. a. (horse)* shoe; mount; — *adj.* expert.
beschleunigen, *v. a.* hurry, accelerate.
beschließen*, *v. a.* resolve, decide; conclude.
Beschluß, *m.* conclusion; resolution.
beschmutzen, *v. a.* soil.
Beschränkung, *f.* (~en) limitation, restriction.
beschreiben*, *v. a.* describe.
beschuldigen, *v. a.* accuse of; charge with.

beschützen, *v. a.* protect.
Beschwerde, *f.* (~n) complaint; trouble.
beschwören, *v. a.* conjure; entreat.
Besen, *m.* (~) broom.
besetzen, *v. a.* occupy; garrison.
besiegen, *v. a.* conquer.
besinnen*, *v. n.* remember, reflect; recollect.
Besitz, *m.* (~e) property; possession.
besitzen*, *v. a.* possess; own.
Besitzer, *m.* (~) owner; proprietor.
Besoldung, *f.* (~en) pay; salary.
besonders, *adv.* especially, particularly.
besorgen, *v. a.* take care; procure; provide; effect.
Besprechung, *f.* (~en) talks *pl.;* conference.
besser, *adj. & n.* better.
Besserung, *f.* (~en) improvement; amelioration, recovery.
best, *adv. & a.* best.
beständig, *adj.* stable, constant; settled.
bestätigen, *v. a.* confirm; ratify.
beste, *adj.* der, die, das ~ the best.
Beste, *n.., f., n.* best part.
bestechen, *v. a.* bribe, corrupt.
Besteck, *n.* (~e) knife and fork; cutlery.
bestehen*, *v. a. & n.* exist; pass; *~ aus* consist of; *~ auf etw.* insist on sg.
besteigen*, *v. a.* climb; mount.
bestellen, *v. a.* order, deliver; summon.
Bestellschein, *m.* order-

-form.
Bestellung, *f.* (~en) order; delivery.
bestens, *adv.* best.
bestimmen, *v. a.* determine, decide; destine.
bestimmt, *adj.* certain.
Bestimmung, *f.* (~en) destination
bestrafen, *v. a.* punish.
Bestrahlung, *f.* irradiation; radiotherapy, ray-treatment.
bestreben, *v.n.* *sich* ~ endeavour.
bestürzt, *adj.* alarmed, dismayed.
Besuch, *m.* (~e) visit; *einen ~ abstatten* pay a visit.
besuchen, *v. a.* go to see; visit; call on sy; attend.
Besucher, *m.* visitor.
betagt, *adj.* aged.
beteiligen, *v.a.* share; *sich ~ an* take part in, participate (in).
Beteiligung, *f.* (~en) share; participation.
beten, *v. n.* pray.
beteuern, *v.a.* assert, protest.
Beton, *m.* (~s) concrete.
betonen, *v. a.* stress, accent.
Betracht, *m.* consideration; regard.
betrachten, *v. a.* look at; watch; observe.
beträchtlich, *adj.* considerable.
Betrag, *m.* (~e) amount.
betragen*, *v. a.* amount (to); *sich* ~ behave.
Betragen, *n.* conduct, behaviour.
Betreff, *m. in* ~ with reference to; as for.
betreffen*, *v. a.* concern; befall.
betreffs, *adv.* concerning, with reference to.

betreiben*, *v. a.* carry on; be engaged in; pursue.
betreten*[1], *v.a.* enter.
betreten[2], *adj.* embarrassed, perplexed.
Betrieb, *m.* (~e) management; workshop; works *(sing. & pl.)*; *in ~ setzen* put in operation.
Betriebskapital *n*, working capital.
Betriebskosten, *pl.* working costs.
betroffen, *adj.* surprised; astounded.
betrüben, *v. a.* grieve; afflict.
Betrug, *m.* deceit, cheat.
betrügen*, *v. a.* deceive, cheat.
betrunken, *adj.* drunk, intoxicated.
Bett, *n.* (~en) bed; *zu ~ gehen* go to bed.
Bettdecke, *f.* blanket; quilt; bedspread.
Bettler, *m.* (~) beggar.
Bettuch, *n.* sheet.
Bettzeug, *n.* bed-clothes *pl.*; bed-linen.
beugen, *v. a.* bend; inflect; *v. n. sich* ~ bow; *fig.* submit.
beunruhigen, *v. a.* worry.
beurteilen, *v. a.* judge.
Beute, *f.* (~n) booty; prey.
Beutel, *m.* (~) bag; purse.
Bevölkerung, *f.* (~en) population.
bevollmächtigen, *v. a.* authorize.
Bevollmächtigte, *m., f.*, deputy; proxy.
bevor, *conj.* before.
bevorstehen*, *v. n.* impend.
bevorzugen, *v. a.* prefer, favour.
bewachen, *v. a.* guard, watch.

bewaffnen, *v.a.* arm.
bewahren, *v.a.* protect, guard; preserve.
bewähren, *v.n.* verify; *sich* ~ prove true.
bewältigen, *v.a.* overcome; master.
bewandert, *adj.* versed; skilled (in).
Bewässerung, *f.* irrigation.
bewegen*, *v. a.* move, induce.
Beweggrund, *m.* motive.
beweglich, *adj.* movable.
Bewegung, *f.* (~en) movement; emotion.
Beweis, *m.* (~e) proof; evidence.
beweisen*, *v.a.* prove; demonstrate.
bewerben*, *v. a. & n.* *sich* ~ *um* apply for; tender for; court.
bewerkstelligen, *v. a.* perform, effect, contrive.
bewilligen, *v.a.* grant; allow.
bewirken, *v.a.* cause; effect.
bewirten, *v. a.* entertain; treat.
bewohnen, *v. a.* inhabit live in.
Bewohner, *m.* (~) inhabitant.
bewölkt, *adj.* cloudy.
Bewunderer, *m.* (~) admirer.
bewundern, *v. a.* admire.
bewundernswert, *adj.* admirable; wonderful.
Bewunderung, *f.* (~en) admiration.
bewußt, *adj.* known; conscious; *sich* ~ *sein* be aware (of).
bewußtlos, *adj.* unconscious; senseless.
Bezahlung, *f.* (~en) payment; pay.
bezeichnen, *v.a.* mark, designate, devote.
bezeugen, *v.a.* testify, attest.
beziehen*, *v. a.* cover; move into; procure; *sich* ~ *auf* refer to.
Beziehung, *f.* (~en) relation; connection.
beziehungs eise, *adv.* respectively.
Bezirk, *m.* (~e) district.
Bezug, *m.* (~e) covering; relation; reference; *in* ~ *auf* in relation to; as for; as to; ~ *nehmen auf* refer to.
bezüglich, *adj.* as for; referring to; relative to.
bezwecken, *v. a.* aim at.
bezweifeln, *v. a.* doubt.
Bibel, *f.* (~n) Bible.
Bibliothek, *f.* (~en) library.
biblisch, *adj.* biblical.
biegen*, *v. n. & a.* bend, bow; inflect.
Biene, *f.* (~n) bee.
Bienenstock, Bienenkorb, *m.* bee-hive.
Bier, *n.* beer.
bieten*, *v. a.*, offer, bid.
Bilanz, *f.* (~en) balance.
Bild, *n.* (~er) painting, picture; image; photo.
bilden, *v. a.* form, constitute; cultivate.
bildend, *adj.* plastic; educational.
Bilderbuch, *n.* picture--book.
Bildergalerie, *f.* picture--gallery.
Bildfunk, *m.* picture transmission; television.
Bildhauer, *m.* sculptor.
Bildnis, *n.* (~se) portrait, likeness.
Bildsäule, *f.* statue.
Bildsucher, *m.* *(photo)* viewfinder.
Bildtelegraphie, *f.* picture

telegraphy, photo-telegraphy.
Bildübertragung, f. picture transmission.
Bildung, f. (~en) formation; education.
Billard, n. billiards pl.
billig, adj. cheap; just.
billigen, v. a. approve.
Binde, f. (~n) band; sling.
binden*, v. a. bind; tie.
binnen, prep. within.
Binnenhandel, m. home trade.
Biographie, f. (~n) biography.
Biologie, f. biology.
Birmane, Burmese m., (~n); -in f. (~innen) Burmese.
birmanisch, burmesisch, adj. Burmese.
Birnbaum, m. pear-tree.
Birne, f. (~n) pear; bulb.
bis, adv. to; ~ an up to; ~ damals till then; — conj. till, until.
Bischof, m. (~e) bishop.
bisher, adv. till now, hitherto; as yet.
Biß, m. (Bisse) bite.
bißchen, adj. & adv. ein ~ a little, a bit.
Bissen, m. (~) morsel, bite.
Bitte, f. (~n) request, petition.
bitten*, v. a. ask (for); request; v. n. bitte please!; not at all!; wie bitte? I beg your pardon?
bitter, adj. bitter.
Bittschreiben, n. petition.
blamieren, v. a. ridicule.
blank, adj. bright; blank.
Blase, f. (~n) bubble.
blasen*, v. a. & n. blow.
Blasinstrument, n. wind-instrument.

blaß, adj. pale.
Blässe, f. paleness.
Blatt, n. (~er) leaf; blade; sheet; (news)paper.
blau, adj. blue.
Blaubeere, f. (~n) bilberry.
Blechinstrument, n. brass instrument.
Blei, n. lead.
bleiben*, v. n. remain; stay; ~ lassen leave, let alone.
bleich, adj. pale.
Bleistift, m. (~e) pencil.
Blende, f. (~n) blind, screen; diaphragm.
blenden, v. a. blind, screen; fig. dazzle.
Blick, m. (~e) look, glance; auf den ersten ~ at first sight.
blicken, v. n. look at, glance.
blind, adj. blind; blank.
Blinddarmentzündung, f. appendicitis.
Blindheit, f. blindness.
blinzeln, v. n. blink, twinkle.
Blitz, m. (~e) flash; lighting.
Blitzableiter, m. lighting-conductor.
blitzen, v. n. lighten, flash; shine.
Blitzlicht, n. flash-light.
Blockade, f. (~n) blockade.
blockieren, v. a. blockade.
blöd(e), adj. stupid.
blond, adj. fair, blond(e).
bloß, adj. bare; naked; mere; pure; — adv. barely, merely; only.
blühen, v. a. bloom, blossom; fig. flourish.
Blume, f. (~n) flower.
Blumenhändler, m. florist.
Blumenkohl, m. cauliflower.
Blumenstrauß, m. bunch

blumig   **159.**   **brennbar**

of flowers, bouquet.
blumig, *adj.* flowery.
Bluse, *f.* (~n) blouse.
Blut, *n.* blood.
Blutdruck, *m.* blood pressure.
Blüte, *f.* (~n) blossom.
bluten, *v. n.* bleed.
Blutgeschwür, *n.* boil.
blutig, *adj.* bloody.
Blutprobe, *f.* blood test.
Blutspender, *m.* (blood) donor.
Blutübertragung, *f.* blood-transfusion.
Blutvergiftung, *f.* blood-poisoning.
Blutzirkulation, *f.* circulation of the blood.
Bock, *m.* (≈e) buck.
Boden, *m.* (≈) bottom; soil; ground; floor; loft.
Bogen *m.* (≈) sheet; bow; arch; arc; bend; curve; sheet.
Bogengang, *m.* arcade.
Böhme, *m.* (~n); -in *f.* (-innen) Bohemian.
böhmisch, *adj.* Bohemian.
Bohne, *f.* (~n) bean; *grüne* ~n French beans *pl.*
bohren, *v. a.* bore, drill.
Bohrer, *m.* drill; gimlet.
Boje, *f.* (~n) buoy.
Bolzen, *m.* (~) latch, bolt.
Bombe, *f.* (~n) bomb.
Boot, *n.* (~e) boat.
Bord, *m.* (≈e) board; edge; rim; *an* ~ on board.
borgen, *v. a.* borrow; lend.
Börse, *f.* (~n) purse; (stock-)exchange.
Börsenkurs, *m.* rate of exchange.
böse, *adj.* bad; evil; wicked; cross.
boshaft, *adj.* spiteful; malicious.
Bosheit, *f.* malice.

Botanik, *f.* botany.
Bote, *m.* (~n) messenger.
Botschaft, *f.* (~n) message; embassy.
Botschafter, *m.* (~) ambassador.
boxen, *v. n.* box.
Boxer, *m.* (~) boxer.
Boxkampf, *m.* boxing-match.
Brand, *m.* (≈e) fire; burning; fire-brand.
Brandbombe, *f.* incendiary bomb.
Brandmal, *n.* stigma, scar from burning.
Brandwunde, *f.* burn; scald.
Brandzeichen, *n.* brand mark.
Branntwein, *m.* brandy.
Brasilianer, *m.* (~); ~in *f.* (~nen) Brazilian.
brasilianisch, *adj.* Brazilian.
braten*, *v. a. & n.* roast; grill; fry; bake.
Braten, *m.* (~) roast (meat).
Bratkartoffeln, *pl.* fried potatoes.
Bratpfanne, *f.* frying-pan.
Brauch, *m.* (≈e) custom; usage.
brauchbar, *adj.* useful; serviceable.
brauchen, *v. a.* need; require, want.
Braue, *f.* (~n) eyebrow.
braun, *adj.* brown.
Braut, *f.* (≈e) fiancée.
Bräutigam, *m.* (~e) fiancé, bridegroom.
Brautpaar, *n.* engaged couple.
brav, *adj.* brave; honest; good.
brechen*, *v. n.* break, burst; *v. a.* break.
breit, *adj.* broad.
Bremse, *f.* (~n) brake.
brennbar, *adj.* combus-

brennen*   **160.**   **Bündnis**

tible.
brennen*, *v. a.* burn; *v. n.* burn; catch fire.
Brennmaterial, *n.* fuel.
Brennpunkt, *m.* focus.
Brennstoff, *m.* fuel.
Brett, *n.* (~er) board; shelf.
Brief, *m.* (~e) letter.
Brücke, *f.* (~n) bridge.
Bruder, *m.* (~) brother.
Bruderschaft, *f.* fraternity.
Brühe, *f.* (~n) broth.
brüllen, *v. n.* roar.
brummen, *v. n. & a.* growl; grumble.
Brunnen, *m.* (~) well fountain.
Brust, *f.* (~e) breast bosom; chest.
Brustschwimmen, *n.* breaststroke.
brutal, *adj.* brutal.
brüten, *v. n. & a.* brood, hatch.
brutto, *adv.* in gross.
Bube, *m.* (~n) boy, lad.
Buch, *n.* (~er) book.
Buchdruckerei, *f.* printing-office.
Buche, *f.* (~n) beech(-tree).
Briefkasten, *m.* letter-box.
Briefmarke, *f.* stamp.
Briefpapier, *n.* note-paper.
Brieftasche, *f.* wallet.
Briefträger, *m.* postman.
Briefwechsel, *m.* correspondence.
Brille, *f.* (~n) glasses, (pair of) spectacles.
bringen*, *v. a.* bring, fetch; carry.
britisch, *adj.* British.
Brombeere, *f.* blackberry.
Bronze, *f.* bronze.
Brosche, *f.* (~n) brooch.
Brot, *n.* (~e) bread; loaf; *belegtes* ~ sandwich.
Brötchen, *n.* (~) roll.

Bruch, *m.* (~e) break; fracture; rupture; fraction.
Bücherbrett, *n.* bookshelf.
Bücherschrank, *m.* bookcase.
Bücherstand, *m.* bookstall.
Buchführung, *f.* bookkeeping.
Buchhalter, *m.* bookkeeper.
Buchhändler, *m.* bookseller.
Buchhandlung, *f.* bookshop.
Buchmacher, *m.* (*sport*) book-maker.
Büchse, *f.* (~n) tin; rifle; box.
Buchstabe, *m.* (~n) letter.
buchstäblich, *adj.* literal, verbal.
Buckel, *m.* (~) hump.
bücken, *v. n. sich* ~ stoop.
Bude, *f.* (~n) stall; booth; shed.
Bügeleisen, *n.* (flat-)iron.
bügeln, *v. a.* iron, press.
Bühne, *f.* (~n) stage; platform.
Bühnenleiter, *m.* stage-manager.
Bukett, *n.* (~e) bouquet; posy.
Bulgare, *m.* (~n); ~in *f.* (~nen) Bulgarian.
bulgarisch, *adj.* Bulgarian.
Bulle, *m.* (~n) bull.
Bund, *m.* (~e) confederation; union; league.
Bundesgenosse, *m.* confederate, ally.
Bundesstaat, *m.* federal state.
Bündnis, *n.* (~se) confed-

bunt   161.   **daher**

eracy, alliance.
bunt, *adj.* coloured.
Burg, *f.* (~en) castle.
Bürge, *n.* (~n) bail, surety.
Bürger, *m.* (~); ~in *f.* (~nen) citizen.
Bürgerkrieg, *m.* civil war.
bürgerlich, *adj.* civil, civic.
Bürgermeister, *m.* (~) mayor, Lord Mayor.
Bürgerrecht, *n.* citizenship.
Bürgerschaft, *f.* citizens *pl.*
Bürgersteig, *m.* pavement.
Bürgschaft, *f.* surety, bail.
Büro, *n.* (~s) office.
Bursche, *m.* (~n) lad, youth, fellow.
Bürste, *f.* (~n) brush.
bürsten, *v. a.* brush.
Busch, *m.* (≈e) bush; shrub.
buschig, *adj.* bushy; shaggy.
Busen, *m.* (~) bosom, breast(s).
Buße, *f.* (~n) penance; penalty; fine.
büßen, *v.a.* expiate.
Büste, *f.* (~n) bust.
Büstenhalter, *m.* bra.
Butter, *f.* butter.
Butterbrot, *n.* bread and butter.

C

Café, *n.* (~s) café, coffee-house.
Camping, *n.* camping.
Campingplatz, *m.* camping place.
Cellist, *m.* (~en) violoncellist.
Cello, *n.* (~s) violoncello.
Champagner, *m.* (~) champagne.
Chaos, *n.* chaos.
Charakter, *m.* (~e) character.
Chauffeur, *m.* (~e) chauffeur.
Chef, *m.* (~s) chief. boss.
Chemie, *f.* chemistry.
Chemiker, *m.* (~) chemist.
chemisch, *adj.* chemical.
Chinese, *m.* (~n) Chinese, Chinaman.
Chinesin, *f.* (~nen) Chinese.
chinesisch, *adj.* Chinese.
Chor, *m.* (≈e) chorus.
Christ, *m.* (~en; ~en) Christian.
Christus, *m.* Christ.
Chrom, *m.* chromium.
Chronik, *f.* (~en) chronicle.
chronologisch, *adj.* chronological.
Cinerama, *n.* cinerama.
Cis, *n.* (~) C sharp.
Cocktail, *m.* (~s) cocktail.
Couch, *f.* (~es) couch.
Courtage, *f.* (~n) brokerage.
Creme, *f.* (~s) cream.

D

da, *adv.* there; then; — *conj.* as, since; because; — *int.* there!
dabei, *adv.* there, besides, moreover.
Dach, *n.* (≈er) roof.
dadurch, *adv.* thereby.
dafür, *adv.* for that; in return.
dagegen, *adv.* against (that); in exchange; in return; — *conj.* on the contrary.
daheim, *adv.* at home.
daher, *adv.* thence;

dahin hence; — *conj.* therefore.

dahin, *adv.* there; along; on, away.

dahinter, *adv.* behind that.

damals, *adv.* then, at that time.

Dame, *f.* (~n) lady; *(notice)* Damen Ladies.

damit, *adv.* therewith; with; — *conj.* in order to; ~ *nicht* lest.

Damm, *m.* (~̈e) dike; embankment.

Dämmerung, *f.* (~en) dawn; twilight.

Dampf, *m.* (~̈e) steam.

dämpfen, *v. a.* damp; suppress; quench.

Dampfer, *m.* (~) steamer.

Dämpfer, *m.* (~) mute; damper.

Dampfmaschine, *f.* steam-engine.

Dampfschiff, *n.* steam-boat.

danach, *adv.* after that; afterwards.

Däne, *m.* (~n); -in *f.* (-innen) Dane.

dänisch, *adj.* Danish.

Dank, *m.* thanks *pl.*; *schönen* ~many thanks.

Dankbarkeit, *f.* gratitude.

danken, *v.a.* thank.

dann, *adv.* then; ~ *und wann* now and then.

daran, *adv.* at it; on it; thereon.

darauf, *adv.* thereupon; after that.

daraus, *adv.* from this; out of it.

darin, *adv.* in it; therein.

darlegen*, *v. a.* state, explain.

Darlehen, *n.* (~) loan.

Darm, *m.* (~̈e) gut; intestines *pl.*; bowels *pl.*

Darstellung, *f.* (~en) representation; performance; statement; exposition.

darüber, *adv.* over that; beyond that; above.

darum, *adv.* therefore; around it, after it.

darunter, *adv.* under that; less; among them.

Dasein, *s.* being; existence;

daß, *conj.* that; *vorausgesetzt* ~provided that.

Dattel, *f.* (~n) date.

Datum, *n.* (-ten) date.

Dauer, *f.* duration, term.

dauern, *v. n.* last; *v. a. er dauert mich* I pity him, I am sorry for him.

Dauerwellen, *pl.* permanent waves, perm.

Daumen, *m.* (~) thumb.

Daune, *f.* (~n) down.

davon, *adv.* of, thereof, by. it; hence.

davonlaufen*, *v. n.* run away.

davontragen*, *v. a.* carry off.

davor, *adv.* before it.

dazu, *adv.* to it; besides.

dazwischen, *adv.* among; between.

dazwischenreden, *v. n.* interrupt.

Deck, *n.* (~e) deck.

Decke, *f.* (~n) ceiling; cover; blanket.

Deckel, *m.* (~) cover; lid.

decken, *v. a.* cover; protect; pay off; *den Tisch* ~ lay the table.

Defizit, *n.* deficiency, deficit.

Degen, *m.* (~) sword.

dehnen, *v. a. & n.* extend; stretch.

Deich, *m.* (~e) dike.

dein, deine, dein, *pron.* your.

deinethalben, deinetwegen, *adv.* for your sake

Dekan, *m.* (~e) dean.
Dekoration, *f.* decoration, scenery.
Dekret, *n.* (~e) decree.
Delegierte, *m., f.* (~n) deputy, delegate.
Delikatesse, *f.* (~n) delicacy.
demnächst, *adv.* soon; shortly.
Demokratie, *f.* (~n) democracy.
demokratisch, *adj.* democrat(ic).
Demut, *f.* humility.
demütig, *adj.* humble.
denken*, *v. a. & n.* think; imagine; fancy; ~ *sie sich!* just fancy!
Denken, *n.* thinking; thought; reasoning.
Denker, *m.* (~) philosopher; thinker.
Denkmal, *n.* (~er) monument.
Denkschrift, *f.* (~en) memoir; memorandum; report, inscription.
denn, *conj.* for; — *adv.* then.
dennoch, *conj.* however, nevertheless, yet.
Depesche, *f.* (~n) dispatch; telegram, wire.
Depot, *n.* (~s) store-house.
Deputierte, *m., f.* (~n) deputy.
der, die, das, *pron.* that, who, which; the.
derb, *adj.* compact; firm; *fig.* rough.
dergleichen *adj.* the like, such.
derjenige, diejenige, dasjenige, *pron.* he (who), she (who), that (which).
derlei, *adj.* of that kind.
derselbe, dieselbe, dasselbe *pron.* the same.
Des *n.* (~) d flat.
deshalb, *adv.* therefore; that is why.
desinfizieren, *v. a.* disinfect.
Dessert, *n.* (~s) dessert.
desto, *adv.* the more; ~ *besser* (so much) the better.
deswegen, *adv.* therefore.
Detail, *n.* details *pl.*; particulars.
Detektiv, *m.* (~e) detective.
deuten, *v. a. & n.* explain, interpret; point out.
deutlich, *adj.* clear, distinct.
deutsch, *adj.* German.
Deutsche, *m., f.* (~n) German.
Devise, *f.* (~n) device, motto; ~n *pl.* foreign currency.
Dezember, *m.* (~) December.
Diagnose, *f.* (~n) diagnosis.
Dialekt, *m.* (~e) dialekt.
Dialog, *m.* (~e) dialog(ue).
Diamant, *m.* (~en) diamond.
Diapositiv, *n.* (~e) diapositive.
Diät, *f.* (~en) diet.
dich, *pron.* you.
dicht, *adj.* thick; dense.
dichten, *v. a. & n.* compose, invent.
Dichter, *m.* (~) poet.
dick, *adj.* thick; fat; stout.
Dieb, *m.* (~e) thief.
Diebstahl, *m.* (~e) theft.
dienen, *v. a.* serve; attend.
Diener, *m.* (~) servant.
Dienst, *m.* (~e) service; duty; post.
Dienstag, *m.* Tuesday.
Dienstmädchen, *n.* maid (-servant).
Dienstreise, *f.* official

Dieselmotor 164. **Drehbleistift**

trip.
Dieselmotor, *m.* Diesel engine.
dieser, diese, dieses, *pron.* this; *pl.* these.
diesmal, *adv.* this time.
diesseits, *adv.* on this side (of).
Differenz, *f.* (~en) difference.
Diktat, *n.* (~e) dictation.
Diktator, *n.* (~en) dictator.
diktieren, *v. a.* dictate.
Dilettant, *m.* (~en) amateur; dilettante.
Dimension, *f.* (~en) dimension.
Ding, *n.* (~e) thing.
Diplom, *n.* (~e) diploma; charter.
Diplomatie, *f.* (~n) diplomacy.
direkt, *adj.* direct.
Direktor, *m.* (~en) director; manager.
Dirigent, *m.* (~en) conductor, leader.
dirigieren, *v. a.* direct; lead; conduct.
Dis, *n.* (~) d sharp.
Diskont, *m.* (~e) discount.
diskontieren, *v. a.* discount.
diskret, *adj.* discreet.
Diskus, *m.* (~se) discus.
Diskussion, *f.* (~en) discussion.
disponieren, *v. n.* dispose (of).
disqualifizieren, *v.a.(sport)* disqualify.
Disziplin, *f.* (~en) discipline.
Dividende, *f.* (~n) dividend.
Division, *f.* (~en) division.
doch, *adv. & conj.* yet; however; but.
Dock, *m.* (~s) dock.

Doktor, *m.* (~en) doctor.
Dokument, *n.* (~e) document.
Dolch, *m.* (~e) dagger.
Dolmetscher, *m.* (~) interpreter.
Dom, *m.* (~e) cathedral.
Donner, *m.* (~) thunder.
Donnerstag, *m.* Thursday.
Doppelbett, *n.* double bed.
Doppeldecker, *m.* biplane, double-decker.
Doppelpunkt, *m.* colon.
doppelt, *adj.* double; twofold; — *adv.* twice.
Doppelzimmer, *n.* double (bed)room.
Dorf, *n.* (~er) village.
Dorn, *m.* (~en) thorn.
dort, *adv.* there, yonder.
dorthin, *adv.* there, that way.
Dose, *f.* (~n) tin.
Dosis, *f.* (-sen) dose.
Dotter, *m.* (~) yolk.
Dozent, *m.* (~en, ~en) lecturer, reader.
Drache, *m.* (~n) dragon; kite.
Draht, *m.* (~e) wire.
drahten, *v. a. & n.* wire, cable, telegraph.
drahtlos, *adj.* wireless.
Drahtseilbahn, *f.* funicular-railway, cable-railway.
Drama, *n.* (Dramen) drama.
dramatisch, *adj.* dramatic.
Drang, *m.* pressure; impulse.
draußen, *adv.* outside; out of doors; abroad.
Dreck, *m.* (~e) dirt, filth, muck.
Drehbank, *f.* turning-lathe.
Drehbleistift, *m.* propelling pencil.

Drehbuch, *n.* scenario, script.
drehen, *v. a. & n.* turn; twist, revolve; rotate.
Drehkreuz, *n.* turnstile.
Drehstuhl, *m.* swivel-chair.
drei, *adj.* three.
dreidimensional, *adj.* three-dimensional.
Dreieck, *n.* triangle.
Dreieinigkeit, *f.* Trinity.
dreifach, *adj.* threefold, triple, treble.
dreifarbig, *adj.* three-coloured.
dreihundert, *adj.* three hundred.
Dreikönigsfest, *n.* Twelfth Night.
dreimal, *adv.* three times.
dreißig, *adj.* thirty.
dreißigste, *adj.* thirtieth.
dreizehn, *adj.* thirteen.
dreschen*, *v.a.* thrash.
Drescher, *m.* (~) thresher.
Dreschmaschine, *f.* threshing-machine.
dressieren, *v. a.* train; break in.
drillen, *v. a.* drill.
dringen*, *v. n. & a.* press; penetrate; urge.
dringend, *adj.* urgent.
drinnen, *adv.* inside, within.
Drittel, *n.* (~) third.
dritter, dritte, drittes, *adj.* third.
Droge, *f.* (~n) drug.
Drogerie, *f.* (~n) druggist's (shop); pharmacy.
drohen, *v. n.* threaten.
drüben, *adv.* over there, yonder.
Druck, *m.* pressure, burden; printing, print.
drucken, *v.a.* print.
drücken, *v. a. & n.* press; oppress; pinch.
Drücker, *m.* (~) push-button; trigger.
Druckerei, *f.* (~n) printing office.
Druckfehler, *m.* misprint.
Drucksache, *f.* printed matter.
Drüse, *f.* (~n) gland.
du, *pron.* you.
Duell, *n.* (~e) duel.
Duett, *n.* (~e) duet.
Duft, *m.* (~e) perfume; fragrance.
duften, düften, *v. a. & n.* smell sweetly.
dulden, *v. a.* bear, suffer; endure.
dumm, *adj.* dull, stupid.
Dummheit, *f.* (~en) nonsense; stupidity.
Düne, *f.* (~n) dune.
düngen, *v.a.* dung; fertilize.
Dünger, *m.* dung, manure.
dunkel, *adj.* dark.
Dunkelkammer, *f.* dark room.
dünken*, *v. n.* seem, appear, look.
dünn, *adj.* thin.
Dunst, *m.* steam; haze.
dunstig, *adj.* damp; hazy.
Dur, *n.* (music) major.
durch, *prep.* through; by (means of).
durchaus, *adv.* by all means; quite; ~ **nicht** by no means; not at all.
durchbohren, *v. a.* pierce, perforate.
durchbrechen*, *v. a. & n.* pierce; break through.
durchdringen*, *v. n.* penetrate.
Durcheinander, *n.* confusion, mess.
Durchfahrt, *f.* passage; thoroughfare.
Durchfahrtszoll, *m.* transit duty.
durchfallen*, *v. n.* fall through; fail.
Durchfuhr, *f.* passage;

| durchfuhren | 166. | Ehre |

transit.
durchführen, *v.a.* lead through; carry out.
Durchgang, *m.* thoroughfare, passage; transit.
Durchgangsverkehr, *m.* through traffic.
Durchgangszug, *m.* corridor-train.
durchgehen*, *v. n.* go through; bolt.
durchkommen*, *v. n.* get through; pass; succeed; recover.
durchkreuzen, *v. a.* cross.
Durchlaucht, *f.* Highness.
durchleuchten, *v. a.* fill with light; X-ray.
durchlöchern, *v. a.* perforate.
durchmachen*, *v. a.* experience; suffer.
Durchmesser, *m.* diameter.
durchqueren, *v. a.* traverse, cross.
Durchschnitt, *m.* cutting through; *im ~* on the average.
durchsehen*, *v. n.* see through; *v. a.* look over; inspect; revise.
durchsetzen, *v. a.* carry through; enforce.
durchsichtig, *adj.* transparent.
Durchweg, *m.* thoroughfare.
dürfen*, *v. n.* be allowed to; be permitted to; *ich darf* I may; *ich darf nicht* I must not.
dürr, *adj.* dry.
Durst, *m.* thirst; *~ haben* be thirsty.
durstig, *adj.* thirsty.
Dusche, *f.* (~n) shower (-bath); douche.
Düse, *f.* (~n) jet.
Düsenflugzeug, *n.* jet plane.
düster, *adj.* dark; dismal.
Dutzend, *n.* (~e) dozen.
duzen, *v.a.* use thou--form.
Dynamo, *m.* (~s) dynamo.
Dynastie, *f.* (~n) dynasty.
D-Zug, *m.* (~e) corridor--train; fast train.

E

Ebbe, *f.* (~n) ebb.
eben, *adj.* flat; level; — *adv.* evenly; just; precisely.
Ebene, *f.* (~n) plain; plane.
ebenfalls, *adv.* likewise, also.
Ebenholz, *n.* ebony.
ebenso, *adv.* just so, likewise; *~ ... wie* as ... as.
ebnen, *v. a.* level; even off.
Echo, *n.* (~s) echo.
echt, *adj.* real, genuine.
Ecke, *f.* (~n) corner.
Eckplatz, *m.* corner-seat.
edel, *adj.* noble.
Edelmann, *m.* nobleman.
Edelstein, *m.* precious stone; gem.
E-dur, *n.* E major.
Effekt, *m.* (~e) effect; *~en pl.* personal effects *pl.*
ehe, *conj.* before; — *adv.* rather; sooner.
Ehe, *f.* (~n) marriage; matrimony.
Ehebruch, *m.* adultery.
Ehefrau, *f.* wife.
ehemalig, *adj.* former; late.
ehemals, *adv.* formerly, once.
Ehemann, *m.* husband.
Ehepaar, *n.* married couple.
Ehescheidung, *f.* divorce.
Ehre, *f.* (~n) honour.

ehren, *v.a.* honour.
Ehrenmann, *m.* man of honour.
Ehrenwort, *n.* word of honour.
Ehrfurcht, *f.* reverence; respect.
Ehrgeiz, *m.* ambition.
ehrlich, *adj.* fair; honest.
ehrwürdig, *adj.* reverend, venerable.
Ei, *n.* (~er) egg.
Eiche, *f.* (~n) oak(-tree).
Eichel, *f.* (~n) acorn; *(cards)* club.
eichen, *v. a.* gauge.
Eichhörnchen, *n.* (~) squirrel.
Eid, *m.* (~e) oath.
Eidbruch, *m.* perjury.
Eidotter, *m.*; **Eigelb**, *n.* yolk.
Eierbecher, *m.* egg-cup.
Eifer, *m.* zeal.
Eifersucht, *f.* jealousy.
eifrig, *adj.* eager, keen.
eigen, *adj.* own.
Eigenart, *f.* peculiarity.
Eigenschaft, *f.* (~en) property; quality.
eigensinnig, *adj.* obstinate.
eigentlich, *adj.* proper; real; — *adv.* properly.
Eigentum, *n.* (~̈er) property.
Eigentümer, *m.* (~) owner.
eigentümlich, *adj.* peculiar; odd.
eignen, *v. n.* own; *sich* ~ suit, be suitable for.
Eilbote, *m.* courier.
Eilbrief, *m.* express letter.
Eile, *f.* haste, speed, hurry.
eilen, *v. n.* hasten, make haste; hurry.
Eilgut, *n.* express goods *pl.*
eilig(st), *adj. & adv.* poste-haste.
Eilzug, *m.* fast train; express.
Elmer, *m.* (~) bucket.
ein[1], *art.* a, an; — *adj. & pron. eine f.; ein n.; einer, eine, eines* one; the same.
ein[2], *adv.* in; within; into.
einander, *adv.* each other, one another.
einatmen, *v. a.* inhale; breathe.
Einbahnstraße, *f.* one--way street.
Einband, *m.* binding.
einbegriffen, *adj.* included.
Einbildungskraft *f.* imagination.
einbrechen*, *v. n.* break in.
Einbrecher, *m.* (~) burglar.
einbürgern, *v. a.* naturalize.
Eindecker, *m.* (~) monoplane.
Eindringling, *m.* (~e) intruder.
Eindruck, *m.* impression; ~ *machen* make an impression.
einerseits, *adv.* on the one hand.
einfach, *adj.* simple.
Einfahrt, *f.* (~en) entrance, gateway.
Einfall, *m.* idea; brain--wave.
einfallen*, *v.n.* fall in; invade (a country); occur (to sy).
einfassen, *v. a.* border; trim; frame.
einflößen, *v. a.* inspire.
Einfluß, *m.* influence.
einfügen, *v. a.* insert.
Einfuhr, *f.* (~en) imports; importation.
einführen, *v. a.* import; *(pers)* introduce.

Eingang | **einst**

Eingang, *m.* entrance.
Eingangszoll, *m.* import-duty.
eingeben*, *v. a.* give; inspire.
eingebildet, *adj.* conceited.
eingeboren, *adj.* native; innate.
Eingebung, *f.* (~en) intuition.
eingießen*, *v. a.* pour (in, out).
eingreifen*, *v.a.* intervene.
einhändigen, *v. a.* hand over; deliver.
einheimisch, *adj.* native.
Einheit, *f.* (~en) unity; unit.
einheitlich, *adj.* uniform.
einholen, *v. a.* overtake.
einig, *adj.* united, one; — *adv.* in concord.
einige, *pron. pl.* any; some; a few; several.
einigen, *v. a. & n.* unite; *sich* ~ agree.
Einkauf, *m.* (~e) purchase.
inkaufen, *v. a.* buy; purchase; *v. n.* go shopping.
einladen*, *v. a.* invite.
Einladung, *f.* (~en) invitation.
Einlage, *f.* enclosure.
einlassen*, *v.a.* admit.
einlegen*, *v. a.* insert, interpose.
Einleitung, *f.* (~en) introduction.
einliegend, *adj.* enclosed.
einlösen, *v.a.* redeem; honour.
einmal, *adv.* once; some time; *auf* ~ suddenly; all at once.
einmalig, *adj.* unique.
einmischen, *v. a. & n.* intermix.
Einnahme, *f.* (~n) receipt; takings *pl.*

einnehmen*, take; receive; occupy
Einöde, *f.* (~n) desert.
einordnen, *v. a.* classify.
einpacken, *v. a.* pack.
einreichen, *v. a.* hand in; present.
Einrichtung, *f.* (~en) arrangement; furniture; fittings *pl.*
einrücken, *v. a.* insert; advertise.
Eins, *f.* (number) one.
einsam, *adj.* lonely.
Einsatz, *m.* (~e) stake.
einschalten, *v.a.* switch on; turn on.
einschätzen, *v.a.* estimate; assess.
einschiffen, *v.a. & n.* embark; go on board.
einschlafen*, *v. n.* go to sleep; fall asleep.
einschließen*, *v. a.* lock in; enclose; include.
einschränken, *v. n.* limit; restrain.
Einschreibebrief, *m.* registered letter.
einsegnen, *v. a.* consecrate; confirm.
einsehen*, *v. a.* see; understand, realize.
einseitig, *adj.* one-sided; unilateral.
einsenden*, send in; remit; transmit.
einsetzen, *v. a.* put in; deposit; install; *sich* ~ use one's influence; *v. n.* begin.
Einsicht, *f.* insight; judgement; discretion.
einsperren, *v. a.* shut up; imprison.
Einsprache, *f.* objection, protest.
Einspritzung, *f.* injection.
einspurig, *adj.* single-track.
einst, *adv.* one, one day; some day.

einstecken, einsteigen*

einstecken, *v. a.* pocket.
einsteigen*, *v. n.* get in.
einstellen, *v. a.* put in; stop; strike; adjust; tune in; *sich ~ auf* adjust oneself.
einstimmig, *adj.* unanimous.
einstweilen, *adv.* meanwhile; for the present.
Einteilung, *f.* (~en) distribution; classification.
eintönig, *adj.* monotonous.
Eintracht, *f.* concord.
Eintrag, *m.* entry.
eintragen*, *v.a.* enter; book; register.
eintreffen*, *v. n.* arrive; happen; come true.
eintreten*, *v. n.* enter.
Eintritt, *m.* entrance.
Einverständnis, *n.* agreement; understanding.
Einwand, *m.* (⩳e) objection.
Einwanderer *m.* immigrant.
Einwendung, *f.* (~en) objection; protest.
Einwilligung *f.* (~en) consent.
Einwirkung, *f.* (~en) influence.
Einwohner, *m.* (~); -in *f.* (~nen) inhabitant.
Einzahl, *f.* singular.
Einzelheit, *f.* (~en) detail.
einzeln, *adv.* one by one; *adj.* single, one; separate.
Einzelzimmer, *n.* single room.
einziehen*, *v. a.* call up; draw in, pull in; *v. n.* enter, march in.
einzig, *adj.* only, one; unique.
Eis, *n.* ice.

Eisbahn, *f.* (skating-)rink.
Eisberg, *m.* iceberg.
Eisen, *n.* iron.
Eisenbahn, *f.* railway; railroad.
Eisenbahnabteil, *n.* compartment.
Eisenbahnfahrkarte, *f.* railway ticket.
Eisengießerei, *f.* iron-foundry.
Eisenhütte, *f.* iron works.
Eisenwaren, *f.pl.* ironware.
Eiskunstlauf, *m.* figure-skating.
Eisschrank, *m.* refrigerator, fridge.
Eitelkeit, *f.* (~en) vanity.
Eiter, *m.* pus.
Eiweiß, *n.* white of an egg.
ekelhaft, *adj.* disgusting.
elastisch, *adj.* elastic.
Elefant, *m.* (~en, ~en) elephant.
elegant, *adj.* elegant.
elektrisch, *adj.* electric.
Elektrizität, *f.* electricity.
Elektromagnet, *n.* electromagnet.
elektronisch, *adj.* electronic.
Element, *n.* (~e) element.
elend, *adj.* miserable.
Elf, *adj.* eleven.
elfte, *adj.* eleventh.
Ellbogen, *m.* (~) elbow.
Eltern, *pl.* parents *pl.*
Emaille, *f.* enamel.
e-Moll, *n.* e minor.
Empfang, *m.* (⩳e) reception.
empfangen, *v. a.* get; receive.
Empfänger, *m.* (~) receiver.
Empfangsdame, *f.* receptionist.
Empfangstag, *m.* at-home.

empfehlen*, *v. a.* recommend.
Empfehlung, *f.* (~en) recommendation.
empfinden*, feel.
empfindlich, *adj.* sensitive, sensible.
empor, *adv.* upwards.
empören, *v. a.* excite; revolt; *sich* ~ rebel.
Ende, *n.* (~n) end; object; *am* ~ in the end.
enden, *v.a.* end.
endgültig, *adj.* final.
endigen, *v. a. & n.* end.
endlich, *adv.* at last, finally.
Endstation, *f.* terminus.
Endung, *f.* (~en) ending.
Energie, *f.* (~n) energy.
energisch, *adj.* energetic.
eng, *adj.* narrow; tight.
Engel, *m.* (~) angel.
Engländer, *m.* (~) Englishman.
Engländerin, *f.* (~nen) Englishwoman.
englisch, *adj.* English.
Englisch, *n.* English (language).
Enkel¹, *m.* (~) grandson.
Enkel², (~) *m.* ankle.
Enkelin, *f.* (~nen) granddaughter.
enorm, *adj.* great; huge.
entbehren, *v. a.* want; miss; do without.
entdecken, *v. a.* discover.
Entdeckung, *f.* (~en) discovery.
entfalten, *v. a.* develop; unfold.
entfernt, *adj.* distant.
Entfernung, *f.* (~en) distance.
entfliehen*, *v. n.* escape; flee.
Entfroster, *m.* (~) defroster.
entführen, *v.a.* abduct; elope.

entgegen, *prep.* against, towards.
entgegenkommen*, *v. a.* go to meet.
entgegnen, *v.a.* retort; reply.
entgehen*, *v. n.* escape.
enthüllen, *v. a.* reveal.
entkommen*, *v. n.* escape.
entladen*, *v.a.* unload; discharge.
entlang, *adv. & prep.* along.
entlassen*, *v. a.* dismiss; discharge.
Entlastung, *f.* (~en) relief.
Entmutigung, *f.* (~en) discouragement.
Entrüstung, *f.* indignation.
entsagen, *v. n.* resign; abandon.
entschädigen, *v. a. & n.* compensate, indemnify.
Entschädigung, *f.* (~en) indemnity.
entscheiden*, *v. a* decide.
Entscheidung, *f.* (~en) decision.
entschließen*, *v.a.* resolve; decide.
entschlossen, *adj.* resolute.
Entschluß, *m.* (≈e) resolution; decision.
entschuldigen, *v. a.* excuse.
Entsetzen, *n.* horror; terror.
entsetzlich, *adj.* terrible, horrible.
entsprechen*, *v. n.* correspond (to).
entsprechend, *adj.* corresponding.
entstehen*, *v. n.* arise; come into being.
Enttäuschung, *f.* (~en) disappointment.
Entwaffnung, *f.* (~en) disarmamant.

entwässern | **Erklärung**

entwässern, *v.a.* drain.
entweder, *conj.* ~ ... *oder* either ... or.
entweichen*, *v. n.* escape.
entwerfen*, *v.a.* draw up; scatch; plan; draft; outline.
entwickeln, *v. a.* develop.
Entwick(e)lung, *f.* (~en) development; evolution.
Entwicklungsland, *n.* developing country.
entwöhnen, *v.a.* wean.
Entwurf, *m.* (~e) plan; draft.
entziehen*, *v. a.* take away; *sich* ~ withdraw.
entzückend, *adj.* ravishing, charming.
Entzündung, *f.* (~en) ignition; inflammation.
entzwei, *adv.* in two, broken.
er, *pron.* he; ~ *selber* he himself.
erbarmen, *v. a.* pity; move; *sich* ~ take pity on.
erbauen, *v. a.* build, erect; *fig.* edify.
Erbe, *m.* (~n) heir.
erben, *v. a.* inherit.
Erbin, *f.* (~nen) heiress.
erbittern, *v. a.* embitter; exasperate.
erblich, *adj.* hereditary.
erblicken, *v. a.* perceive; see.
Erbschaft, *f.* (~en) inheritance.
Erbse, *f.* (~n) pea.
Erbsünde, *f.* original sin.
Erdbeben, *n.* (~) earthquake.
Erdbeere, *f.* (~n) strawberry.
Erde, *f.* (~n) earth; ground.
erden, *v. a.* earth.
Erdgeschoß, *m.* (-osse) ground-floor, basement.
Erdsatellit, *m.* (~e) earthsatellite.
Erdteil, *m.* continent.
Ereignis, *n.* (~se) event, occurrence.
erfahren*, *v. a.* learn, experience.
erfinden*, *v. a.* invent.
Erfindung, *f.* (~en) invention.
Erfolg, *m.* (~e) success; result; ~ *haben* succeed.
erfolgreich, *adj.* successful.
Erfrischung, *f.* (~en) refreshment.
ergänzen, *v. a.* complete; supplement.
ergeben*, *v.a.* yield; *sich* ~ surrender; *sich* ~ *aus* result from; — *adj.* devoted.
Ergebnis, *n.* (~se) result.
ergreifen*, *v. a.* move; touch.
erhaben, *adj.* exalted.
erhalten*, *v.a.* get; receive, obtain; maintain.
erheblich; *adj.* important; considerable.
Erhöhung, *f.* (~en) elevation; increase.
erholen, *sich* ~ recover.
Erholung, *f.* (~en) recovery; recreation.
erinnern, *v. a.* remember; remind (of).
Erinnerung, *f.* (~en) memory; remembrance.
erkälten: *sich* ~ catch cold.
erkennen*, *v. a.* recognize.
Erkenntnis, *f.* (~se) knowledge.
erklären, *v. a.* explain; declare.
Erklärung, *f.* (~en) ex-

erkranken, *v. a.* fall ill.
erkundigen: *sich* ~ inquire.
erlauben, *v. a.* allow; permit.
Erlaubnis, *f.* (~se) permission.
Erläuterung, *f.* (~en) explanation.
Erlebnis, *n.* (~se) experience.
erledigen, *v. a.* settle.
Erledigung, *f.* (~en) settlement.
erlegen, *v. a.* slay, kill.
Erleichterung, *f.* (~en) relief.
erleiden*, *v. a.* suffer; undergo.
erleuchten, *v. a.* light up; illuminate.
Erlöser, *m.* (~) saviour (dead).
Erlösung, *f.* (~en) deliverance; salvation.
ermächtigen, *v. a.* empower; authorize.
ermahnen, *v. a.* admonish, exhort.
ermäßigen, *v. a.* moderate, reduce.
Ermäßigung, *f.* (~en) reduction.
ermorden, *v.a.* murder.
ermüden, *v.a.* tire, wear out.
ermutigen, *v. a.* encourage.
ernähren, *v. a.* nourish.
Ernährung, *f.* nutrition.
ernennen*, *v. a.* name; appoint.
erneuern, *v. a.* renew.
ernst, *adj.* grave, earnest.
ernsthaft, *adj.* grave, serious.
Ernte, *f.* (~en) harvest.
ernten, *v.a.* harvest, reap.
erobern, *v. a.* conquer.
Eroberung *f.* (~en) conquest.
eröffnen, *v.a.* open; reveal.
erörtern *v.a.* discuss, debate.
Erpressung *f.* (~en) extortion; blackmail.
erraten* *v.a* guess, divine.
erregen *v.a* stir, excite.
Erregung *f.* excitement.
erreichen *v.a* reach.
errichten *v.a.* build, erect.
erröten *v.n* blush.
Ersatz *m.* compensation; substitute.
erschaffen*, *v. a.* create, produce.
erscheinen*, *v. a.* appear.
Erscheinung, *f.* (~en) appearance; vision.
erschießen*, *v.a.* shoot (dead).
erschlagen*, *v.a.* slay, kill.
erschließen*, *v. a.* disclose, infer; conclude.
erschöpfen, *v. a.* exhaust, drain; wear out.
erschrecken*, *v. n.* frighten, terrify.
ersehen*, *v. a.* see; learn (from).
ersetzen, *v. a.* repair, compensate; repay; supply.
Ersparnis, *n.* (~se) savings *pl.*
erst, *adj.* first, leading; — *adv.* firstly; at first.
erstarren, *v. n.* freeze; congeal.
erstatten, *v.n.* refund, compensate; restore; *Bericht* ~ render account.
Erstaufführung, *f.* (~en) first night.
Erstaunen, *n.* surprise, amazement.
erste, *adj. see* erst
Erste, *der, die, das* ~

| erstehen* | 173. | etwas |

the first.
erstehen*, v. a. rise, originate.
ersteigen*, v. a. climb, ascend; mount.
erstens, adv. at first, firstly; first.
ersticken, v. a. choke.
erstklassig, adj. & adv. first-rate, first-class.
erstreben, v. a. strive after.
erstrecken, v. n. (sich) extend.
ersuchen, v. a. request.
erteilen, v. a. assign, give.
ertönen, v. a. ring; (re)sound.
Ertrag, m. (~e) produce; proceeds pl.; profit.
ertragen*, v. a. bear; suffer; endure.
ertränken, v. a. drown; sich ~ drown oneself.
ertrinken*, v. n. & a. be drowned; drown.
erwachen, v. n. wake.
erwachsen, adj. grown up; mature.
erwägen*, v. a. consider; deliberate on, think over.
Erwägung, f. (~en) consideration.
erwählen, v. a. choose.
erwähnen, v. a. mention.
erwähnenswert, adj. worth mentioning.
erwärmen, v. a. heat, warm.
erwarten, v.a. expect; wait for; await.
Erwartung, f. (~en) expectation.
erwecken, v. a. awaken; wake; fig. rouse.
erweisen*, v. a. do; render; prove.
erweitern, v. a. & n. enlarge; extend.
Erweiterung, f. (~en) extension; enlarge-

ment.
Erwerb, m. (~e) acquisition; earnings pl.
erwerben*, v. a. acquire; earn; win.
erwidern, v. a. answer, reply; return.
Erwiderung, f. (~en) answer; reply; return.
erwünscht, adj. desired; desirable; welcome.
Erz, n. (~e) ore.
erzählen, v. a. & n. tell; relate, narrate.
Erzählung, f. (~en) tale; story.
Erzbischof, m. (~e) archbishop.
Erzeugnis, n. (~se) product; production; produce.
Erzeugung, f. manufacture; production.
erziehen*, v. a. bring up; educate.
erzielen, v. a. attain, reach.
erzwingen*, v. a. force, enforce.
es, pron. it; ~ gibt there is.
Esel, m. (~) ass.
Eßbesteck, n. cutlery.
essen*, v.a. eat.
Essen, n. meal; dinner.
Essig, m. vinegar.
Essiggurke, f. pickled cucumber; gherkin.
Eßlöffel, m. table-spoon.
Eßzimmer, n. dining room.
Etage, f. (~n) storey; floor.
Etikette, f. (~n) label; etiquette.
etliche, pron. a few; some.
etwa, adv. about; approximately; perhaps.
etwas, pron. any; some; something.

euch, *pron.* to you; you; yourself.
euer, *pron.* of you; your.
eurig, *pron. der, die, das ~e* yours.
Europäer, *m.* (~); ~in *f.* (~nen) European.
europäisch, *adj.* European.
evangelisch, *adj.* evangelic(al); Protestant.
Evangelium, *n.* (-lien) gospel.
ewig, *adj.* eternal.
Ewigkeit, *f.* eternity.
Examen, *n.* (~) exam(ination); test.
Exemplar, *n.* (~e) copy.
Existenz, *f.* (~en) existence.
existieren, *v. n.* exist; subsist.
exotisch, *adj.* exotic.
expedieren, *v. a.* forward; send.
Experiment, *n.* (~e) experiment.
explodieren, *v. n.* explode.
Explosion, *f.* (~en) explosion.
Export, *m.* (~e) exports.
Exporteur, *m.* (~e) exporter.
Expreßgut, *n.* express goods.
Expreßzug, *m.* express train.
extra, *adv.* extra.
Exzellenz, *f.* (~en) excellency.

F

Fabel, *f.* (~n) fable.
fabelhaft, *adj.* fabulous.
Fabrik, *f.* (~en) factory.
Fabrikant, *m.* (~en; ~en) manufacturer, maker.
Fabrikat, *n.* (~e) product.
Fach, *n.* (~er) compartment; subject; line (of interest); drawer.
Facharzt, *m.* specialist.
Fächer, *m.* (~) fan.
Fachmann, *m.* specialist; expert.
fade, *adj.* flat, stale.
Faden, *m.* (~) thread; filament.
Fadennudeln, *f. pl.* vermicelli.
Fagott, *n.* (~e) bassoon.
fähig, *adj.* able; capable.
Fähigkeit, *f.* (~en) ability; capability; talent.
Fahne, *f.* (~n) flag.
Fahrbahn, *f.* carriageway.
Fähre, *f.* (~n) ferry.
fahren*, *v. a.* drive, ride; go, travel.
Fahrer, *m.* (~) driver.
Fahrgeld, *n.* fare.
Fahrgestell, *n.* chassis.
Fahrkarte, *f.* (~n) ticket.
Fahrkartenausgabe, *f.* booking-office.
Fahrplan, *m.* time-table.
Fahrrad, *n.* bicycle.
Fahrschule, *f.* driving-school.
Fahrstuhl, *m.* lift.
Fahrt, *f.* (~en) drive, journey; voyage; trip.
Fährte, *f.* (~n) track, trail.
Fahrzeug, *n.* vehicle.
Faktur, *f.* (~en) invoice.
Fall, *m.* (~e) fall; case; *auf alle Fälle* at all events; by all means.
Falle, *f.* (~n) trap.
fallen*, *v. n.* drop; fall.
fällig, *adj.* payable, due.
falls, *conj.* if, in case.
Fallschirm, *m.* parachute.
falsch, *adj.* false; wrong.
fälschen, *v. a.* forge.

Faltboot   **175.**   **Fernsehsendung**

Faltboot, *n.* folding-boat.
falten, *v. a.* fold.
Familie, *f.* (~en) family.
Familienname, *m.* surname.
fangen*, *v. a.* seize; catch; take; capture.
Farbe, *f.* (~n) colour.
färben, *v. a.* colour; dye.
Farbfilm, *m.* colour-film.
farbig, *adj.* coloured.
Farbstift, *m.* crayon.
Fasan, *m.* (~en) pheasant.
Faser, *f.* (~n) fiber.
Faß, *n.* (Fässer) vat; barrel; cask.
fassen, *v. a.* hold; contain; seize; take.
Fassung, *f.* (~en) mounting; setting.
fast, *adv.* almost.
fasten, *v. n.* fast.
Fastenzeit, *f.* Lent.
faul, *adj.* lazy; rotten.
Faust, *f.* (~e) fist.
Fäustling, *m.* mitten.
Februar, *m.* (~e) February.
fechten,* *v. n.* fight, fence.
Feder, *f.* (~n) pen; spring; feather; plume.
Federgewicht, *n.* *(sport)* featherweight.
Federmesser, *n.* penknife.
Fee, *f.* (~n) fairy.
Fegefeuer, *n.* purgatory.
Fehlbetrag, *m.* (~e) deficit.
fehlen, *v. n.* err; be wanting; *v.a.* miss.
Fehler, *m.* (~) fault; error.
fehlerhaft, *adj.* faulty.
Fehltritt, *m. fig.* slip; fault.
Feier, *f.* (~n) celebration.
feierlich, *adj.* solemn.
feiern, *v. a.* celebrate.

Feiertag, *m.* holiday; day of rest.
feige, *adj.* cowardly.
Feige, *f.* (~n) fig.
Feigling, *m.* (~e) coward.
feilschen, *v. n.* bargain.
fein, *adj.* fine; elegant.
Feind, *m.* (~e) enemy.
feindselig, *adj.* hostile.
Feld *n.* (~er) field.
Feldbett, *n.* camp-bed.
Feldherr, *m.* general.
Feldmarschall, *m.* marshal.
Feldstecher, *m.* field-glass.
Feldzug, *m.* expedition; campaign.
Fell, *n.* (~e) skin, hide.
Fels, *m.* (~en) rock.
Fenster, *n.* (~) window.
Fensterladen, *m.* shutter.
Fensterscheibe, *f.* (window)pane.
Ferien, *pl.* holidays; vacation.
fern, *adj.* far; distant.
Fernamt, *n.* trunk exchange.
Ferne, *f.* distance.
ferner, *adj. & adv.* farther; further; furthermore.
ferngelenkt, *adj.* remotely controlled.
Ferngespräch, *n.* trunk-call.
Fernmeldetechnik, *f.* telecommunications *pl.*
Fernrohr, *n.* telescope.
Fernschreiber, *m.* teleprinter, telex.
Fernsehapparat Fernsehempfänger *m.* television set.
Fernsehfilm, *m.* telefilm.
Fernsehsender, *m.* television transmitter; tele-station.
Fernsehsendung, *f.* tele-

Fernsprechamt	Flanell
vision broadcasting, telecast.	pl.
Fernsprechamt, n. telephone-exchange.	Feuerwehr, f. fire-brigade.
Fernsprechapparat, m. telephone.	Feuerwerk, n. firework(s).
Fernsprechautomat, m. automatic telephone.	Feuerzeug, n. lighter.
	feurig, adj. fiery; ardent.
Fernsprechdienst, m. telephone-service.	Fiber: (~) f. fibre.
	Fichte, f. (~n) pine-tree).
Fernsprecher, m. telephone.	Fieber, n. (~) fever.
	fieberhaft, adj. feverish.
Fernsprechzelle, call-box; telephone booth.	Figur, f. (~en) figure.
	filet, n. (~s) fillet.
Fernsteuerung, f. remote control.	Film, m. (~e) film.
	Filmatelier, n. studio.
Ferse, f. (~n) heel.	filmen, v. a. & n. film; shoot (a film).
fertig, adj. ready.	
Fertigkeit, f. facility; readiness; skill.	Filmkamera, f. cine-camera.
	Filmleinwand, f. screen.
Fessel, f. (~n) fetter; chain.	Filmstar, m. film-star.
	Filmvorschau, f. trailer.
fest, adj. firm, solid.	Filfer, m. (~) filter.
Fest, n. (~) festival; feast.	filtrieren, v. a. filter.
	Filz, m. (~e) felt.
festhalten*, v. a. & n. hold (on to).	Finanzminister, m. minister of finance; Chancellor of the Exchequer.
festlich, adj. solemn; festive.	
festsetzen, v. a. settle, fix.	finden*, v. a. find.
	Finger, m. (~) finger.
feststellen, v. a. establish; fix, confirm.	Fingerabdruck, m. finger-print.
Festung, f. (~en) fortress.	Fingerhut, m. thimble.
	Finne, m. (~n) Finn(-lander).
Fett, n. (~e) fat; grease.	
fett, adj. fat.	Finnin, f. (~nen) Finn.
Fetzen, m. (~) rag; scrap.	finster, adj. dark, sinister.
feucht, adj. damp.	Finsternis, f. (~se) darkness.
Feuchtigkeit, f. moisture.	
	Firma, f. (Firmen) firm.
Feuer, n. (~) fire.	Fisch, m. (~e) fish.
Feuermelder, m. fire alarm.	fischen, v.a. fish.
feuern, v. a. burn: fire; kindle. v. n. shoot; fire.	Fischhändler, m. fishmonger.
	flach, adj. flat.
Feuerspritze, f. fre-engine.	Fläche, f. (~n) plain; surface.
Feuerversicherung, f. fire-insurance.	Flagge, f. (~n) flag.
	Flamme, f. (~n) flame.
Feuerwaffe, f. fire-arms	Flanell, m. (~e) flannel.

Flanke, *f.* (~n) side.
Flasche, *f.* (~n) bottle.
flattern, *v.n.* flutter.
Flechte, *f.* (~n) plait; tress; lichen.
Fleck *m.* (~en) spot.
fleckenlos, *adj.* spotless.
fleckig, *adj.* spotted.
Fledermaus, *f.* bat.
flehen, *v. a. & n.* implore.
Fleisch, *n.* meat; flesh.
Fleischbrühe, *f.* beef-tea.
Fleischer, *m.* (~) butcher.
Fleiß, *m.* diligence; industry.
fleißig, *adj.* diligent, industrious.
flicken, *v. a. & n.* mend.
Fliege, *f.* (~n) fly.
fliegen*, *v. n.* fly.
Flieger, *m.* pilot, aviator.
Fliegerangriff, *m.* air-raid.
fliehen*, *v. n.* flee; escape.
fließen*, *v. n.* flow; run.
fließend, *adj.* fluent; running.
flink, *adj.* nimble.
Flitterwochen, *f. pl.* honeymoon.
Flocke, *f.* (~n) flake.
Floh, *m.* (~e) flea.
Flosse, *f.* (~n) fin.
Flöte, *f.* (~n) flute.
flott, *adj.* quick; jolly.
Flotte, *f.* (~n) fleet.
Flucht, *f.* (~en) flight.
flüchten, *v. n.* flee; escape.
Flüchtling, *m.* (~e) fugitive, refuge.
Flug, *m.* (~e) flight.
Flugbegleiterin, *f.* airhostess.
Flügel, *m.* (~) wing, blade; grand piano.
Fluggast, *m.* air passenger.
Flughafen, *m.* airport, aerodrome.
Flugkarte, *f.* air-ticket.

Flugplatz, *m.* aerodrome.
Flugschrift, *f.* pamphlet.
Flugwesen, *n.* aviation.
Flugzeug, *n.* aeroplane.
Flugzeugführer, *m.* pilot.
Flur, *f.* (~en) field; passage; hall.
Fluß, *m.* (Flüsse) river;
flüssig, *adj.* liquid.
Flüssigkeit, *f.* (~en) fluid.
flüstern, *v. a. & n.* whisper.
Flut, *f.* (~en) flood; full tide.
Folge, *f.* (~n) consequence.
folgen, *v. n.* follow; succeed; obey.
folgern, *v. a.* conclude, infer.
folglich, *adv.* consequently.
folgsam, *adj.* obedient.
Fonds, *m.* funds *pl.*
förderlich, *adj.* conducive (to); useful.
fordern, *v. a.* demand; ask; require.
fördern, *v. a.* despatch; further, advance.
Forderung, *f.* (~en) demand.
Förderung, *f.* (~en) promotion; help.
Forelle, *f.* (~n) trout.
Form, *f.* (~en) form; figure; mould.
Formel, *f.* (~n) formula.
formell, *adj.* formal.
formen, *v. a.* form; fashion; mould.
formieren, *v. a.* form.
formulieren, *v. a.* formulate.
forschen, *v. a. & n.* search, investigate.
Forscher, *m.* (~) researcher; scholar.
Forschung, *f.* (~en) research; inquiry; investigation.
fort, *adv.* away; off.

Fort | **Frist**

Fort, *n.* (~s) fort.
fortdauern, *v.n.* continue; last.
fortfahren, *v. n.* continue; *v. a.* carry away.
fortgehen*, *v.n.* go on; proceed.
fortpflanzen, *v. a.* propagate.
fortschreiten*, *v.n.* go on, advance; proceed.
Fortschritt, *m.* (~e) advance; progress.
fortsetzen, *v.a.* continue.
Fortsetzung, *f.* (~en) continuation.
fortwährend, *adj.* continual.
Fracht, *f.* (~en) freight.
Frachtbrief, *m.* bill o lading.
Frage, *f.* (~n) question.
Fragebogen, *m.* questionnaire.
fragen*, *v. a.* ask (a question).
fraglich, *adj.* doubtful.
Fraktion, *f.* (~en) fraction.
frankieren, *v. a.* stamp, prepay.
franko, *adv.* post-paid.
Franzose, *m.* (~n) French(man).
Französin, *f.* (~nen) French(woman).
französisch, *adj.* French.
Frau, *f.* (~en) wife; woman.
Fräulein, *n.* (~) miss; young lady.
frech, *adj.* saucy, cheeky.
Frechheit, *f.* (~en) insolence; impertinence.
frei, *adj.* free; vacant; paid; disengaged.
Freie, *f.* n. open air, im ~n in the open.
freien, *v.n.* woo, court.
Freiexemplar, *n.* free copy.
freigebig, *adj.* free; liberal.
Freihafen, *m.* free port.
Freihandel, *m.* free trade.
Freiheit, *f.* freedom, liberty.
Freikarte, *f.* free ticket.
freisinnig, *adj.* liberal.
Freitag, *m.* Friday.
freiwillig, *adj.* voluntary.
fremd, *adj.* strange; foreign.
Fremde¹, *f.* foreign country; distant lands *pl.*
Fremde², *m., f.* (~n) foreigner, stranger.
Fremdenbuch, *n.* visitors' book.
Fremdenführer, *m.* guide.
Fremdenverkehr, *m.* tourist traffic.
Fremdsprache, *f.* foreign language.
fressen*, *v. a. & n.* eat; gorge (of animal).
Freude, *f.* (~n) joy.
freuen, *v.n. sich* ~ be glad; rejoice.
Freund, *m.* (~e) friend.
Freundin, *f.* (~nen) (girl-)friend.
freundlich, *adj.* friendly.
Freundlichkeit, *f.* friendliness; kindness.
Freundschaft, *f.* friendship.
Friede, *m.* (~n) peace.
Friedenspolitik, *f.* peace policy.
Friedensrichter, *m.* justice of the peace.
Friedhof, *m.* cemetery.
friedlich, *adj.* peaceable.
frieren*, *v. n.* be cold; feel cold.
frisch, *adj.* fresh, new; cool.
Friseur, *m.* (~e) hair-dresser.
frisieren, *v. a.* dress sy's hair.
Frist, *f.* (~en) term; pe-

Frisur 179. **Futter**

riod; time-limit.
Frisur, *f.* (~en) hairstyle.
froh, fröhlich, *adj.* glad; joyful; cheerful.
Frohsinn, *m.* mirth.
fromm, *adj.* pious.
Frömmigkeit, *f.* piety.
Front, *f.* (~en) front.
Frosch, *m.* (≈e) frog.
Frost, *m.* (≈e) frost.
Frucht, *f.* (≈e) fruit.
fruchtbar, *adj.* fertile.
früh, *adj.* & *adv.* early.
Frühjahr, *n.* spring.
Frühling, *m.* spring.
Frühstück, *n.* breakfast.
frühstücken, *v. n.* breakfast; have breakfast.
frühzeitig, *adj.* early, premature.
Fuchs, *m.* (≈e) fox.
Fuge, *f.* (~n) joint; *(music)* fugue.
fühlen, *v.a.* feel; *sich wohl* ~ feel well.
führen, *v. a.* lead, guide; conduct.
Führer, *m.* (~) guide; leader; conductor; driver; pilot.
Führung, *f.* (~en) guidance; leadership; management; direction.
Fuhrwerk, *n.* conveyance.
Füllbleistift, *m.* eversharp, propelling pencil.
Fülle, *f.* plenty.
füllen, *v. a.* fill (up).
Füllen, *n.* (~) colt; foal.
Füllfeder, *f.* fountain-pen.
Fund, *m.* (~e) find; discovery.
Fundament, *n.* (~e) base; foundation.
fünf, *adj.* five.
Fünf, *f.* five.
Fünfkampf, *m.* pentathlon.
fünfmal, *adv.* five times.

fünfte, *adj.* (the) fifth.
Fünftel, *n.* (~) fifth part; (the) fifth.
fünfzehn, *adj.* fifteen.
fünfzehnte, *adj.* fifteenth.
fünfzig, *adj.* fifty.
Fünfzig, *f.* fifty.
Fünfziger, *m. (pers)* fifty years old.
Funk, *m.* radio; wireless.
Funke, *m.* (~n) spark.
funkeln, *v. n.* sparkle; glitter.
funken, *v. a.* & *n.* flash; broadcast.
Funkentelegraphie, *f.* wireless telegraphy.
Funker, *m.* (~) wireless operator; signalman.
Funkgerät, *n.* wireless apparatus.
Funkstation, *f.* broadcasting station.
Funktion, *f.* (~en) function.
funktionieren, *v. n.* function; operate.
für, *prep.* for; in behalf of; in favour of.
Furcht, *f.* fear; ~ *haben vor* be afraid of.
furchtbar, *adj.* terrible. dreadful.
fürchten, *v. a.* fear; *sich* ~ be afraid.
fürchterlich, *adj.* frightful, dreadful, terrible.
Fürsorge, *f.* care.
Fürsprache, *f.* intermission.
Fürst, *m.* (~en) prince.
Fürstin, *f.* (~nen) princess.
Fuß, *m.* (≈e) foot; *zu* ~ on foot.
Fußball, *m.* football.
Fußboden, *m.* floor.
Fußbremse, *f.* foot-brake.
Fußgänger, *m.* pedestrian.
Fußtritt, *m.* kick.
Futter, *n.* (~) fodder;

füttern food; lining.
füttern, *v. a.* feed; line.

G

Gabe, *f.* (~n) present.
Gabel, *f.* (~n) fork.
Gabelfrühstück, *n.* lunch; snack.
gähnen, *v.n.* yawn.
Galerie, *f.* gallery.
Galle, *f.* (~n) gall.
Gallert, Gallerte *f.* (~(e)n) jelly, gelatine.
Galopp, *m.* gallop.
Gang, *m.* (~e) walk; pace; course; corridor; gear.
gangbar, *adj.* practicable.
Gans, *f.* (~e) goose.
Gänseblümchen, *n.* daisy.
Gänsebraten, *m.* roast goose.
Gänseklein, *n.* giblets *pl.*
ganz, *adj.* whole, all; quite; ; — *adv.* wholly; entirely; completely.
Ganze(s), *n.* whole.
gänzlich, *adj.* whole, entire; complete.
gar, *adj.* done; — *adv.* quite, entirely; ~ nicht not at all.
Garage, *f.* (~n) garage.
Garantie, *f.* (~n) guarantee.
garantieren, *v. a.* guarantee.
Garde, *f.* (~n) guards *pl.*
Garderobe, *f.* (~n) cloak-room, wardrobe.
Gardine, *f.* (~n) curtain.
gären*, *v. a. & n.* ferment.
Garn, *n.* (~e) yarn; thread.
garnieren, *v.a.* garnish.
Garnison, *f.* (~en) garrison.
Garnitur, *f.* (~en) set; fittings *pl.*
Garten, *m.* (~) garden.
Gärtner, *m.* (~) gardener.
Gas, *n.* (~e) gas.
Gasanstalt, *f.* gas-works.
Gasbeleuchtung *f.* gas-lighting.
Gasbrenner, *m.* gas-burner.
Gasheizung, *f.* gas-heating.
Gasse, *f.* (~n) street; lane.
Gast, (~e) guest.
Gastfreundschaft, *f.* hospitality.
Gastgeber, *m.* host.
Gastgeberin, *f.* (~nen) hostess.
Gasthof, *m.* inn.
gastlich, *adj.* hospitable.
Gastwirt, *m.* host, landlord.
Gastwirtin, *f.* hostess; landlady.
Gastzimmer, *n.* spare-room.
Gatte, *m.* (~n) husband.
Gattin, *f.* (~nen) wife.
Gattung, *f.* (~en) kind; species.
Gaumen, *m.* (~) gum; palate.
G-dur, *n.* G major.
Gebäck, *n.* (~e) pastry.
Gebärde, *f.* (~n) gesture; air.
gebären*, *v. n.* be born; bear, give birth to.
Gebärmutter, *f.* womb.
Gebäude, *n.* (~) building.
geben*, *v. a. & n.* give; present; *es gibt* there is; there are.
Gebet, *n.* (~e) prayer.
Gebiet, *n.* (~e) territory.
gebieten*, *v. a.* command; order.

Gebilde, *n.* formation; structure.
gebildet. *adj.* well-educated.
Gebirge, *n.* (~) mountain; mountain range.
Gebiß, *n.* (-bisse) set of teeth; denture.
geboren, *adj.* born.
Gebot, *n.* (~e) commandment.
gebrauchen, *v. a.* use; employ.
gebräuchlich, *adj.* usual, customary.
Gebühr, *f.* (~en) duty; due; fee.
Geburt, *f.* (~en) birth.
Geburtsschein, *m.* birth-certificate.
Geburtstag, *m.* birthday.
Gebüsch, *n.* (~e) bush.
Gedächtnis, *n.* (~se) memory.
Gedanke, *m.* (~n, ~n) thought.
Gedärme, *m. pl.* intestines *pl.*; bowels *pl.*
Gedeck, *n.* (~e) cover.
gedeihen*, *v. a.* flourish, thrive; prosper.
gedenken*, *v. n.* remember
Gedicht, *n.* (~e) poem.
gediegen, *adj.* solid, pure; sound.
Gedränge, *n.* crowd.
Geduld, *f.* patience.
geduldig, *adj.* patient.
geeignet, *adj.* fit, suitable.
Gefahr, *f.* (~en) danger.
gefährlich, *adj.* dangerous.
Gefährte, *m.* companion, fellow.
gefallen*, *v. n.* please.
Gefallen, *m.* pleasure, liking.
Gefälligkeit, *f.* (~en) favour.
Gefangene, *m., f.* (~n; ~n) prisoner.
gefangennehmen*, *v. a.* captivate, arrest; take prisoner.
Gefangenschaft, *f.* captivity.
Gefängnis, *n.* (~se) prison.
Gefäß, *n.* (~e) vessel.
Geflügel, *n.* fowl, poultry.
Gefolge, *n.* following, suite; attendance.
Gefühl, *n.* (~e) feeling; sentiment.
gegen, *prep.* against; towards.
Gegend, *f.* (~en) countryside.
Gegensatz, *m.* contrast; opposition.
gegenseitig, *adj.* mutual, reciprocal; — *adv.* mutually.
Gegenstand, *m.* subject; object; thing.
Gegenteil, *n.* contrary; *im* ~ on the contrary.
gegenüber, *adv.* opposite.
Gegenwart, *f.* presence.
gegenwärtig, *adj.* present.
gegenzeichnen, *v. a.* countersign.
Gegner, *m.* (~) adversary; opponent.
Gehalt, *m.* (~er) capacity; contents *pl.* salary; pay.
Geheimnis, *n.* (~ses) secret.
geheimnisvoll, *adj.* mysterious.
gehen*, *v. a.* go, walk; *wie geht es?* how are you?
Gehilfe, *m.* (~n; ~n) assistant; helper.
Gehirn, *n.* (~e) brain.
Gehölz, *n.* (~e) forest; wood.
Gehör, *n.* hearing.

gehorchen — **genau**

gehorchen, *v. n.* obey.
gehören, *v. n.* belong.
gehorsam, *adj.* obedient.
Geier, *m.* (~) vulture.
Geige, *f.* (~n) violin.
geigen, *v. a. & n.* play the violin.
Geist, *m.* (~er) spirit; soul.
Geistesgegenwart, *f.* presence of mind.
geistig, *adj.* mental; spiritual.
geistlich, *adj.* spiritual; clerical.
Geistliche, *m.* (~n; ~n) clergyman.
Geiz, *m.* avarice; greediness.
geizig, *adj.* avaricious; mean.
Gelächter, *n.* (~) laughter.
Gelage, *n.* banquet.
Gelände, *n.* (~) ground.
Geländer, *n.* (~) railing.
gelangen, *v. n.* reach; arrive at; get to.
geläufig, *adj.* current; fluent.
gelb, *adj.* yellow.
Geld, *n.* (~er) money; *bares* ~ cash.
Geldanweisung, *f.* postal order; money-order.
Geldschrank, *m.* safe.
Geldsendung, *f.* remittance.
Geldstrafe, *f.* fine.
Geldstück, *n.* coin.
Geldwährung, *f.* currency.
Geldwechsel, *m.* exchange of money.
gelegen, *adj.* opportune; situated.
Gelegenheit, *f.* (~en) opportunity; chance.
gelegentlich, *adj.* occasional.
gelehrt, *adj.* learned.
Gelehrte, *m.* (~n) scholar.

Geleise, *n.* (~) track; rails *pl.*
Gelenk, *n.* (~e) joint; hinge.
Geliebte, *f.* (~n) love, sweetheart; mistress.
Geliebte, *m.* (~n; ~n) lover; sweatheart.
gelingen*, *v. n.* succeed
geloben, *v. n.* vow.
gelten*, *v. n.* be worth; cost; be in force.
Geltung, *f.* value; validity.
Gelübde, *n.* (~) vow.
Gemach, *n.* (⸚er) room; chamber.
gemächlich, *adj.* comfortable, easy.
Gemahl, *m.* (~e) husband.
Gemahlin, *f.* (~nen) wife.
Gemälde, *n.* (~) painting, picture.
gemäß, *adj.* suitable; — *prep.* by; according to.
gemein, *adj.* common; public; mean, base.
Gemeinde, *f.* (~n) community; congregation; parish.
gemeinsam, *adj. & adv.* common; joint(ly).
Gemeinschaft, *f.* (~en) community; congregation.
gemeinschaftlich, *adv.* in common.
Gemenge, *n.*; **Gemisch** *n.* mixture.
Gemurmel, *n.* (~) murmur.
Gemüse, *n.* (~) vegetable.
Gemüsehändler, *m.* greengrocer.
gemütlich, *adj.* comfortable; cosy.
genau, *adj.* accurate; exact.

genehmigen, 183. Geshmack

genehmigen, *v. a.* approve, sanction.
geneigt, *adj.* prone, inclined.
General, *m.* (≈e) general.
Generaldirektor, *m.* general manager.
Generation, *f.* (~en) generation.
genesen*, *v. n.* recover; grow well.
Genick, *n.* (~e) nape.
Genie, *n.* (~s) genius.
genießen*, *v. a.* enjoy, relish.
Genosse, *m.* (~n) companion, comrade.
Genossenschaft, *n.* syndicate; cooperative society.
genug, *adv.* enough.
genügend, *adj.* sufficient; satisfactory.
Genuß, *m.* (-üsse) pleasure; enjoyment.
Geographie, *f.* geography.
Geometrie, *f.* geometry.
Gepäck, *n.* luggage; baggage.
Gepäckaufbewahrung, *f.* cloak-room; left-luggage office.
Gepäcknetz, *m.* luggage-rack.
Gepäckträger, *m.* porter.
Gepäckwagen, *m.* luggage-van.
Gepäckzettel, *m.* label.
gerade, *adj.* even, straight; direct; – *adv.* directly, just; exactly.
Gerät, *n.* (~e) tools *pl.*; implements *pl.*; utensils *pl.*
geraten*, *v. n.* get into; succeed; become.
Geratewohl: *aufs* ~ at random.
Geräusch, *n.* (~e) noise.
geräuschlos, *adj.* noiseless.
gerecht, *adj.* fair; just.
Gerechtigkeit, *f.* justice.
Gericht, *n.* (~e) court of justice; dish.
Gerichtshof, *m.* law-court.
gering, *adj.* a little; small.
gerinnen*, *v. a.* curdle, clot.
Gerippe, *n.* (~) skeleton.
gern, *adv.* gladly, willingly.
Gerste, *f.* (~n) barley.
Geruch, *m.* (~e) smell.
Gerücht, *n.* (~e) rumor.
Gerüst, *n.* (~e) sc ld.
gesamt, *adj.* whole, a .
Gesandte, *m.* (~n) ambassador.
Gesandtschaft, *f.* (~en) embassy.
Gesang, *m.* (≈e) song; singing.
Geschäft, *n.* (~e) business, shop.
geschäftlich, *adj.* commercial.
Geschäftsbrief, *m.* commercial letter.
Geschäftsmann, *m.* (-leute) business-man.
Geschäftsstunden, *pl.* business-hours.
geschehen*, *v. n.* happen, occur; come to pass.
gescheit, *adj.* clever; intelligent.
Geschenk, *n.* (~e) present.
Geschichte, *f.* (~n) story; history.
Geschick, *n.* (~e) fate; skill, aptitude.
geschickt, *adj.* skilful.
Geschirr *n.* (~e) dish; crockery; harness.
Geschlecht, *n.* (~er) sex; gender.
geschlechtlich, *adj.* sexual.
Geschmack, *m.* (≈e)

geschmackvoll | **Gewissensbiß**

taste.
geschmackvoll, *adj.* elegant.
Geschöpf, *n.* (~e) creature.
Geschoß, *n.* (-osse) projectile; story; floor.
Geschrei, *n.* cry, clamour; screams, cries.
Geschütz, *n.* (~e) gun; cannon.
geschwind, *adj.* fast; quick — *adv.* fast; quickly; swiftly.
Geschwindigkeit, *f.* (~en) speed.
Geschwister, *pl.* brother(s) and sister(s).
Geschworene, *m.* (~n; ~n) juryman.
Geselle, *m.* (~n; ~n) companion, fellow; journeyman.
gesellig, *adj.* sociable.
Gesellschaft, *f.* (~en) society; party; company.
Gesellschafter, *m.* (~) companion; partner.
Gesellschaftsvertrag, *m.* contract.
Gesetz, *n.* (~e) law; statute.
gesetzlich, *adj.* lawful.
Gesicht, *n.* (~er) face.
Gesichtskreis, *m.* horizont.
Gesichtspunkt, *m.* point of view.
gesinnt, *adj.* disposed.
Gesinnung, *f.* (~en) disposition; feeling.
Gespann, *n.* (~e) team.
gespannt, *adj.* tense; intent
Gespenst, *n.* (~er) ghost.
Gespräch, *n.* (~e) talks, conversation.
Gestalt, *f.* (~en) figure.
gestalten, *v. a.* form, shape.
Geständnis, *n.* (~se) confession.
gestatten, *v. a.* allow; grant; permit.
gestehen*, *v. a.* confess; grant; admit.
gestern, *adv.* yesterday; ~ *abend* last night.
gestrig, *adj.* yesterday.
Gesuch, *n.* (~e) petition; plea.
gesund, *adj.* healthy; sound.
Gesundheit, *f.* health.
Getränk, *n.* (~e) drink, beverage.
Getreide, *n.* corn, grain, cereals *pl.*
getreu, *adj.* faithful; loyal.
Getriebe, *n.* driving-gear; *fig.* machinery.
getrost, *adj.* confident.
gewahren, *v. a.* perceive.
gewähren, *v. a.* guarantee; warrant; grant.
Gewalt, *f.* (~en) force; power.
gewaltig, *adj.* strong; powerful.
Gewand, *n.* (~̈er) garment; clothes *pl.*
Gewandtheit, *f.* (~en) skill; cleverness.
Gewebe, *n.* (~) weaving; tissue.
Gewehr, *n.* (~e) weapon; gun; rifle.
gewerblich, *adj.* industrial; professional.
Gewerkschaft, *f.* (~en) trade(s)-union.
Gewicht, *n.* (~e) weight; importance.
Gewinn, *m.* (~e) gain; profit.
gewinnen*, *v. a. & n.* win; earn; get; obtain.
gewiß, *adj.* of course; sure, certain; — *adv.* surely, certainly.
Gewissen, *n.* (~) conscience.
Gewissensbiß, *m.* remorse.

gewissermaßen — **Graf**

gewissermaßen, *adv.* to a certain degree.
Gewitter, *n.* (~) storm.
gewöhnen, *v.a.* accustom.
Gewohnheit, *f.* (~en) habit; custom.
gewöhnlich, *adj.* usual, ordinary.
Gewölbe, *n.* (~) vault.
Gewürz, *n.* (~e) spice.
Gicht, *f.* gout.
gierig, *adj.* greedy.
gießen*, *v. n. & a.* pour, cast.
Gift, *n.* (~e) poison.
giftig, *adj.* poisonous.
Gipfel, *m.* (~) summit; top.
Gips, *m.* plaster.
Gis, *n.* G sharp.
Gitarre, *f.* (~n) guitar.
Gitter, *n.* (~) iron bars; grate.
glänzen, *v. n.* shine, glitter.
glänzend, *adj.* bright, brilliant.
Glas, *n.* (⁓er) glass.
glatt, *adj.* even; smooth.
Glaube(n) *m.* faith; belief.
glauben, *v. a. & n.* believe.
gläubig, *adj.* religious; believing.
Gläubiger, *m.* (~) creditor.
gleich, *adj.* like; equal; — *adv.* like.
gleichen*, *v. n.* resemble.
gleichfalls, *adv.* likewise; also.
Gleichgewicht, *n.* equilibrium, balance.
gleichmäßig, *adj.* equal; steady.
Gleichnis, *n.* comparison; simile.
Gleichschaltung, *f.* co-ordination.
Gleichstrom, *m.* direct-current.
Gleichung, *f.* (~en) equation.
gleichwohl, *adv. & conj.* yet, nevertheless; however.
gleichzeitig, *adj.* contemporary; simultaneous.
Gleis, *n.* (~e) track.
gleiten*, *v. n.* glide.
Gleitflug, *m.* glide.
Gletscher, *m.* (~) glacier.
Glied, *n.* (~er) member; limb; link.
Glocke, *f.* (~n) bell.
Glück, *n.* fortune, happiness.
glücken, *v. a.* succeed.
glücklich, *adj.* glad, fortunate.
glücklicherweise, *adj.* fortunately.
Glückwunsch, *m.* congratulation.
Glühbirne, *f.* bulb.
glühen, *v. n.* glow; shine.
Glut, *f.* glow.
g-Moll, *n.* G minor.
Gnade, *f.* (~n) mercy.
gnädig, *adj.* gracious, kind.
Gold, *n.* gold.
golden, *adj.* golden.
Goldwährung, *f.* gold--standard.
Golf¹, *m.* (~) gulf.
Golf², *n.* (~e) golf.
Golfplatz, *m.* golf links *pl.*
gotisch, *adj.* Gothic.
Gott, *m.* (⁓er) God.
Gottesdienst, *m.* divine service.
göttlich, *adj.* divine.
Grab, *n.* (⁓er) grave; tomb.
Graben, *m.* (~) ditch.
graben*, *v. a. & n.* dig.
Grad, *m.* (~e) degree grade.
Graf, *m.* (~en; ~en) count.

Grafik, *f. pl.* graphics.
Gräfin, *f.* (~nen) countess.
Gram, *m.* grief.
Grammatik, *f.* grammar.
Grammophon, *n.* (~e) gramophone.
Grammophonplatte, *f.* grammophone-record.
Granate, *f.* (~n) grenade; shell.
Granit, *m.* (~e) granite.
Gras, *n.* (~er) grass.
gräßlich, *adj.* horrible.
Gräte, *f.* (~n) fish-bone.
gratis, *adv.* gratis, free of charge.
Gratulation, *f.* (~en) congratulation.
grau, *adj.* gray.
grausam, *adj.* cruel.
Grausamkeit, *f.* cruelty.
greifen, * *v. a. & n.* grasp; touch; seize.
Greis, *m.* (~e) old man.
grell, *adj.* shrill; glaring.
Grenze, *f.* (~n) border; frontier.
Grieche, *m.* (~n); -in *f.* (~nen) Greek.
griechisch, *adj.* Greek.
Griff, *m.* (~e) handle.
Grill, *m.* (~e) grill.
Grille, *f.* (~n) cricket; *fig.* whim.
Grippe, *f.* (~n) influenza, flu.
grob, *adj.* coarse, rude.
Gros, *n.* (~se) gross.
groß, *adj.* great; large; big.
großartig, *adj.* grand.
Größe, *f.* (~n) size; greatness.
Großeltern, *pl.* grandparents.
Großhandel, *m.* wholesale trade.
Großmutter, *f.* grandmother.
Großvater, *m.* grandfather.

großzügig, *adj.* generous.
Grube, *f.* (~n) mine, pit.
grün, *adj.* green.
Grund, *m.* (~e) bottom; ground; reason.
Grundbesitz, *m.* property.
gründen, *v.a.* found.
Gründer, *m.* (~) founder.
gründlich, *adj.* thorough.
Grundsatz, *m.* principle.
grundsätzlich, *adj.* on principle.
Grundstück, *n.* real estate.
Gründung, *f.* (~en) foundation; establishment.
Gruppe, *f.* (~n) group.
Gruß, *m.* (~e) greeting; salutation.
grüßen, greet.
G-Schlüssel, *(music)* G clef, treble clef.
gültig, *adj.* valid.
Gültigkeit, *f.* validity.
Gummi, *m.* (India-)rubber.
Gunst, *f.* favour.
günstig, *adj.* favourable.
Gurke, *f.* (~n) cucumber.
Gürtel, *m.* (~) belt; girdle.
gut, *adj.* good; — *adv.* well.
Gut, *n.* (~er) property; estate.
Gutachten, *n.* opinion; judgement.
Güterwagen, *m.* luggage--van; truck.
Güterzug, *m.* goods train.
gütig, *adj.* kind.
Gutsbesitzer, *m.* landowner.
Gymnasium, *n.* grammar-school.

H

Haar, *n.* (~e) hair; *das ~ waschen* shampoo.
Haarbürste, *f.* hair-brush.
haarig, *adj.* hairy.
Haarwaschmittel, *n.*

Habe   187.   **Harfe**

shampoo.
Habe, *f.* property, goods *pl.*
haben*, *v.a.* have; possess; *gern* ~ like; *zu* ~ available.
Hafen, *m.* (~) harbour; port.
Hafendamm, *m.* pier.
Hafer, *m.* oats *pl.*
Haft, *f.* arrest, imprisonment.
haftbar, *adj.* responsible (für).
haften, *v.n.* stick, adhere; ~ *für* be responsible for.
Hagel, *m.* hail.
Hahn, *m.* (~e) cock; tap.
häkeln, *v.a.&n.* crochet.
Haken, *m.* (~) hook.
halb, *adj. & adv.* half; by halves.
Halbbruder, *m.* half-brother.
halbieren, *v.a.* halve.
Halbinsel, *f.* peninsula.
Halbkreis, *m.* semicircle.
Halbmesser, *m.* radius.
Halbmond, *m.* crescent, half-moon.
halbwegs, *adv.* halfway.
Hälfte, *f.* (~n) half.
Halle, *f.* (~n) hall; lounge.
hallen, *v.n.* sound, resound.
Hals, *m.* (~e) neck; throat.
Halsband, *n.* necklace.
Halt, *m.* (~e) hold, stop.
haltbar, *adj.* durable.
halten*, *v.a.* hold, keep; stop; *es* ~ *mit jm* side with; *v.n.* hold; stop.
Haltestelle, *f. (bus, tram)* stop.
Haltung, *f.* (~en) attitude.
Hammel, *m.* (~) mutton.
Hammelfleisch, *n.* mutton (chop).

Hammer, *m.* (~) hammer.
Hand, *f.* (~e) hand.
Handarbeit, *f.* needlework.
Handbuch, *n.* manual.
Handel, *m.*(~)commerce, trade; business.
handeln, *v.n.* act; take action; behave; deal; bargain.
Handelsflotte, *f.* merchant navy.
Handelsgesellschaft, *f.* (trading) company.
Handelsmann, *m.* (-leute) merchant; tradesman.
Handelsschule, *f.* commercial school.
Handelsvertrag, *m.* treaty.
Handfläche, *f.* palm.
Handgelenk, *n.* wrist.
handhaben, *v.a.* handle, manage.
Handkoffer, *m.* suitcase.
Händler, *m.* (~) tradesman.
Handlung, *f.* (~en) action; shop.
Handlungsreisender, *m.* commercial traveller.
Handschrift, *f.* (hand)writing; manuscript.
Handschuh, *m.* gloves *pl.*
Handtasche, *f.* handbag.
Handtuch, *n.* towel.
Handvoll, *f.* handful.
Handwerk, *n.* trade.
Handwerker, *m.* workman; artisan; craftsman.
Handwerkszeug, *n.* tools *pl.*
Hanf, *m.* hemp.
Hängebrücke, *f.* suspension bridge.
Hängematte, *f.* hammock.
hängen*, *v.a.* hang.
Harfe, *f.* (~n) harp.

harmlos — **Heimat**

harmlos, *adj*. harmless.
Harmonie, *f*. (~n) harmony.
Harmonika, *f*. (~s) concertina; accordion.
harmonisch, *adj*. harmonious.
harren, *v. n*. wait; expect.
hart, *adj*. hard.
Härte, *f*. hardness.
härten, *v. a*. temper; harden.
hartnäckig, *adj*. stubborn.
Harz, *n*. (~e) resin.
Hase, *m*. (~n) hare.
Haß, *m*. hate, hatred.
hassen, *v. a*. hate.
häßlich, *adj*. ugly.
Haube, *f*, (~n) cap.
Hauch, *m*. (~e) breath.
hauen*, *v. a. & n*. hew; cut; chop.
Haufen, *m*. (~) heap.
häufen, *v. a. & n*. heap (up); accumulate.
häufig, *adj*. frequent.
Haupt, *n*. (~̈er) head; chief; leader.
Hauptbahnhof, *m*. central railway station; main terminus.
Hauptbuch, *m*. ledger.
Häuptling, *m*. (~e) chief.
Hauptquartier, *n*. headquarters *pl*.
Hauptsache, *f*. the main thing.
hauptsächlich, *adj. & adv*. chief; main; chiefly; mainly; especially.
Hauptstadt, *f*. capital.
Haupttribüne, *f*. grand-stand.
Hauptverkehrsstraße, *f*. thoroughfare.
Hauptwort, *n*. noun.
Haus, *n*. (~̈er) house; zu ~e at home; nach ~ home; im ~e indoors.
Hausbesitzer, *m*. landlord.
hausen, *v. n*. live, dwell.
Hausfrau, *f*. housewife.
Haushalt, *m*. household.
Haushälterin, *f*. housekeeper.
Hausherr, *m*. landlord.
Hausierer, *m*. pedlar.
häuslich, *adj*. domestic.
Hausschuhe, *pl*. slippers *pl*.
Haustier, *s*. domestic animal.
Haustür, *f*. front-door.
Haut, *f*. (~̈e) skin.
H-Bombe, *f*. H-bomb.
Hebel, *m*. (~) lever; jack.
heben*, *v. a*. lift; raise.
Hecke, *f*. (~n) hedge.
Heer, *n*. (~e) army.
Hefe, *f*. (~n) yeast.
Heft, *n*. (~e) handle; copy book.
heftig, *adj*. violent, vehement.
Heftpflaster, *n*. sticking-plaster.
Heftzwecke, *f*. drawing-pin.
hegen, *v. a*. shelter.
Heide[1], *m*. (~n) heathen.
Heide[2], *f*. (~n) heath; moor.
Heidelbeere, *f*. bilberry.
Heil, *n*. welfare, salvation.
Heiland, *m*. Saviour.
Heilanstalt, *f*. sanatorium.
heilbar, *adj*. curable.
heilen, *v. a. & n*. cure; heal.
heilig, *adj*. holy; sacred.
Heilige, *m. f*. (~n) saint.
Heiligenschein, *m*. halo.
Heiligtum, *n*. sanctuary.
Heilmittel, *n*. remedy.
heilsam, *adj*. wholesome, beneficial.
heim, *adv*. home.
Heim, *n*. (~e) home.
Heimat, *f*. (~en) native

heimatlos | **herzlich**

country.
heimatlos, *adj.* homeless.
heimkehren, *v. a.* return home.
heimlich, *adj.* secret; furtive.
heimsuchen, *v. a.* haunt.
Heimweh, *n.* home-sickness.
Heirat, *f.* (~en) marriage.
heiraten, *v. a. & n.* marry.
Heiratsantrag, *m.* proposal.
heiser, *adj.* hoarse.
heiß, *adj.* hot.
heißen*, *v. a.* command; call; *v. n.* be called; signify; *das heißt* that is.
heiter, *adj.* cheerful.
heizen, *v. a. & n.* heat.
Heizkissen, *n.* electric pad.
Heizkörper, *m.* radiator.
Heizung, *f.* (~en) heating.
Held, *m.* (~en; ~en) hero.
heldenhaft, *adj.* heroic.
Heldentat, *f.* exploit.
Heldin, *f.* (~nen) heroine.
helfen*, *v. a.* help; assist.
hell, *adj.* bright; clear; light.
Helm, *m.* (~e) helmet.
Hemd, *n.* (~en) shirt; vest.
Hemmung, *f.* (~en) stopping; inhibition.
Henkel, *m.* (~) handle.
Henne, *f.* (~n) hen.
her, *adv.* here; this way; *lange* ~ long ago.
herab, *adv.* down; downwards.
herabsetzen, *v. a.* reduce; lower.
Herabsetzung, *f.* reduction; degradation.
heran, *adv.* on, near; along.
herauf, *adv.* up; upwards.
heraus, *adv.* out.
herausgeben*, *v. a.* publish.
Herausgeber, *m.* publisher.
herauskommen*, *v. n.* come out; get out.
herausnehmen*, *v. a.* take away.
herbei, *adv.* here; this way; near.
Herberge, *f.* (~n) inn; lodgings *pl.*; shelter.
Herbst, *m.* (~e) autumn.
Herd, *m.* (~e) hearth.
Herde, *f.* (~n) herd; flock.
herein, *adv.* in, inward; ~! come in!.
Hering, *m.* (~e) herring.
Herkunft, *f.* (⸚e) origin.
Hermelin, *n.* (~e) ermine.
hernach, *adv.* afterwards.
Herr, *m.* (~en; ~en) gentleman; master; lord.
Herrenschneider, *m.* tailor.
Herrin, *f.* (~nen) mistress; lady.
herrlich, *adj.* excellent.
herrschen, *v. n.* rule; reign.
Herrscher, *m.* (~) sovereign; ruler.
herstellen, *v. a.* place; produce; make; restore.
Herstellung, *f.* production; manufacture; restoration.
herüber, *adv.* across; over.
herum, *adv.* around.
herunter, *adv.* down; off.
hervor, *adv.* forth; out.
hervorbringen*, *v. a.* bring forth; produce.
hervorgehen*, *v. n.* arise; result (from).
hervorheben*, *v. a.* emphasize.
hervorragend, *adj.* prominent; distinguished.
Herz, *n.* (~ens, ~en) heart.
herzlich, *adj.* cordial;

Herzog		Hochsprung

heartfelt.
Herzog, *m.* (~e) duke.
Herzogin, *f.* (~nen) duchess.
hetzen, *v. a.* hunt.
Heu, *n.* hay.
heulen, *v. n.* howl.
Heuschrecke, *f.* grasshopper.
heute, *adv.* to-day; ~ *abend* tonight.
heutig, *adj.* today.
heutzutage, *adv.* nowadays.
Hexenschuß, *m.* lumbago.
Hieb, *m.* (~e) blow
hier, *adv.* here; in this place.
hieraus, *adv.* out of this, hence.
hierdurch, *adv.* through.
hierher, *adv.* here.
hiesig, *adj.* (of) here.
Hilfe, *f.* (~n) help; assistance.
hilflos, *adj.* helpless.
Hilfsmittel, *n.* remedy.
Himbeere, *f.* raspberry.
Himmel, *m.* (~) sky; heaven.
Himmelfahrt, *f.* Ascension (day).
himmlisch, *adj.* celestial.
hin, *adv.* there; ~ *und her* to and fro.
hinab, *adv.* down.
hinauf, *adv.* up.
hinaus, *adv.* out.
hinausgehen*, *v. n.* go out.
hindern, *v. a.* hinder.
Hindernis, *n.* (~se) obstacle; hindrance.
Hindernisrennen, *n.* steeplechase.
hindurch, *adv.* through.
hinein, *adv.* in, inside, into.
Hingabe, *f.* devotion; abandon.
hingegen, *adv.* & *conj.* (on the) contrary; whereas.
hinlänglich, *adj.* ample; sufficient.
hinreichend, *adj.* sufficient.
hinsichtlich, *adj.* as for; with regard to.
hinten, *adv.* behind, after.
hinter, *adj.* hind, back; — *prep.* behind, after.
hintereinander, *adv.* one after the other.
Hintergrund, *m.* background.
hinterlassen*, *v. n.* leave (behind).
hinterlistig, *adj.* cunning.
Hintertreppe, *f.* backstairs *pl.*
Hintertür, *f.* backdoor.
hinüber, *adv.* over, across.
hinunter, down; downstairs.
Hinweis, *m.* (~e) reference.
hinweisen*, *v. a.* show; point to; refer.
hinzufügen, *v. a.* add (to).
Hirn, *n.* (~e) brain.
Hirsch, *m.* (~e) stag, hart.
Hirt, *m.* (~en. ~en) shepherd.
hissen, *v. a.* hoist.
Historiker, *m.* (~) historian.
historisch, *adj.* historic.
Hitze, *f.* (~n) heat.
hoch, *adj.* high.
hochachten, *v. a.* respect.
Hochachtung, *f.* (~en) respect.
hochachtungsvoll, *adj.* respectful.
Hochbahn, *f.* overhead railway.
Hochdruck, *m.* high pressure.
Hochmut, *m.* pride.
Hochschule, *f.* high--school; university.
Hochsprung, *m.* high

hochstens   **191.**   **ihr**

jump.
höchstens, *adv.* at the most.
Hochverrat, *m.* high treason.
Hochzeit, *f.* (~en) wedding.
Hof, *m.* (~e) court; yard.
hoffen, *v. a. & n.* hope.
hoffentlich, *adv.* it is to be hoped.
Hoffnung, *f.* (~en) hope.
höflich, *adj.* polite.
Höflichkeit, *f.* (~en) politeness.
Höhe, *f.* (~n) height.
Hoheit, *f.* (~en) highness.
hohl, *adj.* hollow.
Höhle, *f.* (~n) cave.
Hohn, *m.* scorn.
hold, *adj.* gracious, lovely.
holen, *v. a.* fetch; ~ *lassen* send for.
Holländer, *m.* (~) Dutch(man).
Holländerin, *f.* (~nen) Dutch(woman).
holländisch, *adj.* Dutch.
Hölle, *f.* (~n) hell.
Holz, *n.* (~̈er) wood.
Honig, *m.* honey.
Honorar, *n.* (~e) fee.
Hörapparat, *m.* hearing aid.
horchen, *v. n.* listen.
hören, *v. a. & n.* hear; ~ *auf* listen to.
Horizont, *m.* (~e) horizon.
Horn, *n.* (~̈er) horn.
Hörsaal, *m.* lecture-room.
Hörspiel, *n.* radio-play.
Hörweite, *f.* earshot.
Hose, *f.* (~n) trousers *pl.*; pants *pl.*
Hosenträger, *m. pl.* braces.
Hotel, *n.* (~s) hotel.
hübsch, *adj.* pretty.
Huf, *m.* (~e) hoof.

Hüfte, *f.* (~n) hip.
Hügel, *m.* (~) hill.
hügelig, *adj.* hilly.
Huhn, *n.* (~̈er) hen.
Hühnerauge, *n.* corn.
Huldigung, *f.* (~en) homage.
Hülse, *f.* (~n) husk.
Hummer, *m.* (~) lobster.
Humor, *m.* humour.
Hund, *m.* (~e) dog.
Hundertjahrfeier, *f.* centenary.
hundertjährig, *adj.* centennial.
hundertmal, *adv.* a hundred times.
Hunger, *m.* hunger.
Hungersnot, *f.* famine.
hungrig, *adj.* hungry.
Hupe, *f.* (~n) hooter.
hüpfen, *v. n.* hop.
Hürdenrennen, *n.* (~) hurdle race.
husten, *v. n.* cough.
Husten, *n.* cough.
Hut¹, *m.* (~̈e) hat.
Hut², *f.* guard; *auf der* ~ *sein* be on one's guard.
hüten, *v. a.* guard.
Hütte, *f.* (~n) cottage.
Hygiene *f.* hygiene.
hygienisch, *adj.* hygienic.
Hypothese, *f.* (~n) hypothesis.
hysterisch, *adj.* hysterical.

I

Ich, *pron.* I; myself.
Ich, *n.* I, self.
Ideal, *n.* (~e) ideal.
Idee, *f.* (~n) idea.
identisch, *adj.* identical.
Idiot, *m.* (~en) idiot.
Idyll, *n.* (~e) idyll.
idyllisch, *adj.* idyllic.
ihm, *pron.* (to) him.
ihr, *pron.* her; you; *ihr*,

Ihr — **interessant**

ihre, ihr her; its; their; your.
Ihr, *n.* your.
illustrieren, *v. a.* illustrate.
Imbiß-Stube, *f.* snack-bar.
immer, *adv.* always; ever; *für ~* for ever.
immerhin, *adv.* still.
immerwährend, *adj.* everlasting.
Immigrant, *m.* (~en) immigrant.
impfen, *v. a.* inoculate; vaccinate.
Import, *m.* (~e) import( ) importation.
Importeur, *m.* (~e) importer.
importieren, *v. a.* import.
imstande, *~ sein* be able (to).
in, *prep.* in, at, within; into, to.
Inbegriff, *m.* (~e) summary; sum total; essence.
indem, *adv. & conj.* as; while.
indes, *adv.* in the meantime; meanwhile; — *conj.* however, yet.
indessen, see **indes.**
indirekt, *adj.* indirect.
indisch, *adj.* Indian.
Individuum, *n.* (-uen) individual.
Industrie, *f.* (~n) industry.
industriell, *adj.* industrial.
Infanterie, *f.* (~n) infantry.
infizieren, *v. a.* infect.
Influenza, *f.* influenza, flu.
infolge,: *~ (von)* in consequence (of).
informieren, *v. a.* inform.
Ingenieur, *m.* (~e) engineer.
Inhaber, *m.* (~) possessor; owner; proprietor.
Inhalt, *m.* (~e) contents; volume.
Inhaltsverzeichnis, *n.* table of contents; index.
Injektion, *f.* (~en) injection.
Inland, *n.* inland; home(land).
Inländer, *m.* (~) native.
inländisch, *adj.* native.
inmitten, *prep.* in the midst of; among.
inne, *adv.* within.
innehalten*, *v. n.* stop.
inner, *adj.* inner, interior, internal.
innere, *adj.* inside.
Innere, *n.* (~n) inside, interior.
innerhalb, *adv. & prep.* within; inside.
innerlich, *adj.* inside.
innig, *adj.* hearty; — *adv.* sincerely.
Insasse, *m.* (~n, ~n) inmate.
insbesondere, *adv.* in particular; above all.
Inschrift, *f.* (~en) inscription.
Insekt, *n.* (~e) insect.
Insel, *f.* (~n) island.
Inserat, *n.* (~e) advertisement.
insofern, *adv.* so far; — *conj.* inasmuch as.
Inspektor, *m.* (~en) inspector.
Instandhaltung, *f.* (~en) maintenance.
Instinkt, *m.* (~e) instinct.
Institut, *n.* (~e) institute, institution.
Instrument, *n.* (~e) instrument.
Instrumentenbrett, *n.* dashboard.
interessant, *adj.* interesting.

Interesse, n. (~n) interest.
interessieren, v. a. interest.
Internat, n. (~e) boarding-school.
international, adj. international.
Invalide, m. (~n; ~n) invalid.
inzwischen, adv. in the meanwhile.
irdisch, adj. earthly.
irgend, adv. any, some.
irgendwie, adv. somehow; anyhow.
irgendwo, adv. somewhere; anywhere.
irisch, adj. Irish.
Irländer, m. (~) Irishman; -in f. (~nen) Irishwoman.
Ironie, f., (~) iron.
ironisch, adj. ironical.
irren, v. a. sich ~ (be) wrong; err.
Irrtum, m. (⁓er) error.
isolieren, v. a. isolate; insulate.
Isotop, n. (~e) isotope.
Italiener, m. (~); -in f. (~nen) Italian.
italienisch, adj. Italian.

J

ja, adv. yes.
Jacht, f. (~en) yacht.
Jacke, f. (~n) coat; jacket; cardigan.
Jagd, f. (~en) hunt.
jagen, v. n. & a. hunt; run.
Jäger, m. (~) hunter.
Jahr, n. (~e) year.
Jahrbuch, n. year-book.
Jahrestag, m. anniversary.
Jahreszeit, f. season.
Jahrhundert, n. century.
jährig, adj. year old.
jährlich, adj. annual; yearly.
Jahrtausend, n. millennium.
jämmerlich, adj. pitiful.
Januar, m. (~e) January.
Japaner, m. (~); -in f. (~nen) Japanese.
japanisch, adj. Japanese.
Jazz, m. jazz.
Jazzkapelle, f. jazz-band.
je, jemals, adv. ever.
jedenfalls, adv. at all events.
jeder, jede, jedes, pron. each, every.
jederzeit, adv. at any time.
jedesmal, adv. (every) time.
jedoch, conj. however, yet.
jemals, adv. ever.
jemand, pron. somebody; anybody.
jener, jene, jenes, pron. former; that.
jenseits, prep. beyond.
jetzt, adv. now.
Joch, n. (~e) yoke.
Jockei, m. (~s) jockey.
jubeln, v. n. rejoice.
Jubiläum, n. (-äen) jubilee.
jucken, v. n. itch.
Jude, m. (~n) Jew.
jüdisch, adj. Jewish; Hebrew.
Jugend, f. youth.
Jugendherberge, f. youth hostel.
jugendlich, adj. youthful; juvenile.
Juli, m. (~s) July.
jung, adj. young.
Junge, m. (~n) boy.
Jungfer, f. (~n) virgin; maid.
Jungfrau, see **Jungfer.**
Junggeselle, m. bachelor.

Jüngling, *m.* (~e) young man, lad.
Juni, *m.* (~s) June.
Junker, *m.* (~) nobleman; squire.
Jurist, *m.* (~en, ~en) lawyer.
Justiz, *f.* justice.
Juwel, *n.* (~en) jewel, gam.
Juwelier, *m.* (~e) jeweller.
Jux, *m.* (~e) oke; fun.

K

Kabale, *f.* (~n) plot; intrigue.
Kabel, *n.* (~) cable.
kabeln, *v. a. & n.* cable.
Kabine, *f.* (~n) cabin.
Kabinett, *n.* (~e) cabinet; closet.
Käfer, *m.* (~) beetle.
Kaffee, *m.* (~s) coffee.
Kaffeehaus, *n.* coffee-house.
Kaffeekanne, *f.* coffee-pot.
Kaffeemühle, *f.* coffee-mill.
Käfig, *m.* (~e) cage.
kahl, *adj.* bald; bare.
Kahn, *m.* (≈e) boat; barge.
Kai, *m.* (~s) quay; wharf.
Kaiser, *m.* (~) emperor.
Kaiserin, *f.* (~nen) empress.
Kajüte, *f.* cabin.
Kakao, *m.* cocoa.
Kalb, *n.* (≈er) calf.
Kalbfleisch, *n.* veal.
Kalbsbraten, *m.* roast veal.
Kalénder, *m.* (~) calendar.
kalt, *adj.* cold.
Kälte, *f.* cold; coldness.

Kamel, *n.* (~e) camel.
Kamera, *f.* (~s) camera.
Kamerad, *m.* (~en, ~en) comrade.
Kameramann, *m.* cameraman.
Kamin, *m.* (~e) chimney; fire-place.
Kamm, *m.* (≈e) comb.
kämmen, *v. a.* comb.
Kammer, *f.* (~n) chamber; room.
Kampf, *m.* (≈e) fight; struggle.
kämpfen, *v. n.* fight.
Kanal, *m.* (≈e) canal.
Kanarienvogel, *m.* canary.
Kandidat, *m.* (~en, ~en), candidate.
Kaninchen, *n.* (~) rabbit.
Kanne, *f.* (~n) can; tankard; jug.
Kanone, *f.* (~n) cannon; gun.
Kante, *f.* (~n) edge.
Kantine, *f.* (~n) canteen.
Kanzel, *f.* (~n) pulpit.
Kanzler, *m.* (~) chancellor.
Kap, *n.* (~s) cap.
Kapazität, *f.* (~en) capacity.
Kapelle, *f.* (~n) chapel; band.
Kapital, *n.* (~e) capital.
Kapitalist, *m.* (~en; ~en) capitalist.
Kapitän, *m.* (~e) captain.
Kapitel, *n.* (~) chapter.
Kaplan, *m.* (~e) chaplain.
Kappe, *f.* (~n) cap.
Kapsel, *f.* (~n) case, box; capsule.
Kaputze, *f.* (~n) hood.
Karaffe, *f.* (~n) decanter.
Karat, *n.* (~e) carat.
Karawane, *f.* (~n) caravan.
Kardinal, *m.* (≈e) cardinal.
Karfreitag, *m.* Good Fri-

karg 195. **Keule**

day.
karg, *adj.* sparing; scanty.
Karikatur, *f.* (~en) caricature.
Karneval, *m.* (~e) carnival.
Karpfen, *m.* (~) carp.
Karriere, *f.* (~n) career.
Karte, *f.* (~n) map; card.
Kartoffel, *f.* (~n) potato.
Karwoche, *f.* Passion Week.
Käse, *m.* (~) cheese.
Kaserne, *f.* (~n) barrack(s).
Kassabuch, *n.* cash-book.
Kasse, *f.* (~n) cash; till; booking-office *(medical)* insurance.
Kassenarzt, *m.* national-health-doctor.
Kasserolle, *f.* saucepan.
Kassierer, *m.* (~) cashier.
Kastanie, *f.* (~n) chestnut.
Kasten, *m.* (~̈) box; chest; case.
Katalog, *m.* (~e) catalogue.
Katarrh, *m.* (~n) catarrh.
Katastrophe, *f.* (~n) catastrophe.
Kategorie, *f.* (~n) category; class.
Kathedrale, *f.* (~n) cathedral.
Katholik, *m.* (~en) Catholic.
katholisch, *adj.* Catholic.
Katze, *f.* (~n) cat.
kauen, *v. a.* chew.
Kauf, *m.* (~̈e) purchase.
kaufen, *v. a.* buy.
Käufer, *m.* (~) buyer.
Kaufhaus, *n.* department store.
Kaufkraft, *f.* purchasing power.
Kaufmann, *m.* tradesman; merchant.
Kaugummi, *m.* chewing-gum.

kaum, *adj.* hardly; scarcely.
Kautschuk, *m.* caoutchouc; rubber.
Kavallerie, *f.* (~n) cavalry.
Kaviar, *m.* (~e) caviar.
keck, *adj.* pert; saucy.
Kegel, *m.* (~) cone; ninepin.
Kehle, *f.* (~n) throat.
kehren, *v. a.* turn; sweep.
Kehricht, *m.* refuse; rubbish.
Keil, *m.* (~e) wedge.
Keim, *m.* (~e) germ; seed.
keimen, *v. n.* germinate.
kein, keiner, keine, keines, *adj.* no; not any; no one; none.
keineswegs, *adv.* (not at) all; by no means.
Keks, *m.* (~e) biscuit.
Kelch, *m.* (~e) cup; chalice.
Keller, *m.* (~) cellar.
Kellner, *m.* (~) waiter.
Kellnerin, *f.* (~nen) waitress.
kennen*, *v. a.* know; be acquainted with.
Kenner, *m.* (~) expert; connoisseur.
Kenntnis, *f.* (~se) knowledge.
Kennzeichen, *n.* distinguishing mark.
Kerbe, *f.* (~n) notch.
Kerl, *m.* (~e) fellow.
Kern, *m.* (~e) kernel; stone; nucleus.
Kernphysik, *f.* nuclear physics.
Kerze, *f.* (~n) candle.
Kessel, *m.* (~) kettle; boiler.
Kette, *f.* (~n) chain.
Kettenbrücke, *f.* suspension-bridge.
keuchen, *v. n.* pant.
Keule, *f.* (~n) leg;

keusch haunch.
keusch, *adj.* chaste.
Kiefer,¹ *m.* (~) jaw.
Kiefer,² *f.* (~n) fir, pine.
Kiel, *m.* (~e) keel.
Kies, *m.* (~e) gravel.
Kind, *n.* (~er) child.
Kinderstube, *f.* nursery.
Kindheit, *f.* (~en) childhood.
kindisch, *adj.* childish.
Kinn, *n.* (~e) chin.
Kino, *n.* (~s) cinema.
Kiosk, *m.* (~e) book-stall.
Kirche, *f.* (~n) church.
Kirchhof, *m.* churchyard.
Kirchturm, *m.* steeple.
Kirsche, *f.* (~n) cherry.
Kirschwasser, *n.* cherry-brandy.
Kissen, *m.* (~) pillow; cushion.
Kiste, *f.* (~n) chest; box; case.
kitzeln, *v. a.* tickle.
Klage, *f.* (~n) complaint; action; lawsuit.
klagen, *v. a. & n.* complain; bewail; sue.
Kläger, *m.* (~) plaintiff.
kläglich, *adj.* lamentable.
Klammer, *f.* (~n) bracket; cramp; peg.
Klang, *m.* (~e) sound.
Klappe, *f.* (~n) flap, cover; valve; key; stop.
klappern, *v.n.* rattle, clatter.
Klappstuhl, *m.* folding-chair.
Klaps, *m.* (~e) clap, slap.
klar, *adj.* clear; obvious.
klären, *v. a.* clear, purify; *v. n. sich* ~ become clear.
Klarinette, *f.* (~n) clarinet.
Klasse, *f.* (~n) class; class-room; school-room.
Klassenzimmer, *n.* class-room.
klassisch, *adj.* classic(al).
Klatsch, *m.* gossip.
klatschen, *v. n.* applaud; gossip.
Klaue, *f.* (~n) claw.
Klausel, *f.* (~n) clause.
Klaviatur, *f.* (~en) keyboard.
Klavier, *n.* (~e) piano.
Klavierspieler, *m.* pianist.
kleben, *v. a. & n.* stick.
klebrig, *adj.* sticky.
Klee, *m.* clover.
Kleid, *n.* (~er) dress.
kleiden, *v. a.* clothe; *sich* ~ dress.
Kleiderbügel, *m.* hanger.
Kleiderbürste, *f.* clothes-brush.
Kleiderschrank, *m.* wardrobe.
Kleidung, *f.* clothes *pl.*
klein, *adj.* little; small.
Kleinauto, *n.* minicar; bubble-car.
Kleine, *n. m. f.* little one; baby.
Kleingeld, *n.* small change.
Kleinhändler, *m.* retailer.
Kleinigkeit, *f.* (~en) trifle.
kleinlich, *adj.* petty; mean.
Kleister, *m.* paste.
klemmen, *v. a.* pinch; squeeze; *v. n. sich* ~ jam; stick.
klettern, *v.n.* climb.
Klient, *m.* (~en; ~en) client.
Klima, *n.* (~te) climate.
Klimaanlage, *f.* air conditioning installation.
Klimatisierung *f.* air conditioning.
Klinge, *f.* (~n) blade.
klingeln, *v.n.* ring (the bell).
klingen*, *v. n.* sound; ring.
Klinik, *f.* (~en) clinic;

Klinke — **Kolonialwarenhändler**

hospital.
Klinke, *f.* (~n) latch.
Klippe, *f.* (~n) cliff; reef.
klirren, *v. a.* clatter.
klopfen, *v. a. & n.* knock, rap.
Klosett, *n.* (~e) water-closet.
Kloster, *n.* (⁓) convent; monastery.
Klotz, *m.* (⁓e) block, log.
Klub, *m.* (~s) club.
klug, *adj.* wise; prudent; clever.
Klugheit, *f.* prudence, cleverness.
Klumpen, *m.* (~) lump.
knabbern, *v. a. & n.* nibble.
Knabe, *m.* (~n) boy.
knacken, *v. a. & n.* crack.
Knall, *m.* (~e) report; explosion.
knapp, *adj.* scanty; scarce.
knarren, *v. n.* creak; grate.
Knecht, *m.* (~e) servant.
kneifen*, *v. a.* pinch.
Kneifzange, *f.* pincers *pl.*
Kneipe, *f.* (~n) tavern, pub(lic house).
kneten, *v. a.* knead, mould.
knicken, *v. a. & n.* crack.
Knicks, *m.* (~) curtsy.
Knie, *n.* (~) knee.
Kniehose, *f.* (~n) breeches *pl.*
knien, *v. n.* kneel.
knirschen, *v. n. & a.* grate.
Knoblauch, *m.* garlic.
Knöchel, *m.* (~) knuckle; ankle.
Knochen, *m.* (~) bone.
knochig, *adj.* bony.
Knopf, *m.* (⁓e) button; knob.
knöpfen, *v. a.* button.
Knopfloch, *n.* buttonhole.
Knospe, *f.* (~n) bud.
knospen, *v. n.* bud.
Knoten, *m.* (~) knot.
Knotenpunkt, *m.* junction.
knüpfen, *v. a.* tie; bind.
knurren, *v. n.* growl.
knusperig, *adj.* crisp.
Koalition, *f.* (~en) coalition.
Koch, *m.* (⁓e) cook.
Kochbuch, *n.* cookery-book.
kochen, *v. n. & a.* cook; boil.
Kocher, *m.* cooker.
Köchin, *f.* (~nen) cook.
Kochgeschirr, *n.* kitchen utensils *pl.*
Kochlöffel, *m.* ladle.
Kochnische, *f.* kitchenette.
Kochrezept, *n.* receipt, recipe.
Köder, *m.* (~) bait.
Koffer, *m.* (~) suit-case; trunk.
Kohl, *m.* cabbage.
Kohle, *f.* (~n) coal.
Kohlenbergwerk, *n.* coal-mine.
Kohlengrube, *f.* coal-mine, coal-pit.
Koje, *f.* (~n) berth.
Kokosnuß, *f.* cocoa-nut.
Koks, *m.* (~e) coke.
Kolben, *m.* (~) butt.
Kolik, *f.* colic.
Kolleg, *n.* (-ien) course of lectures.
Kollege, *m.* (~n; ~n) colleague.
kollektiv, *adj.* collective.
kolonial, *adj.* colonial.
Kolonialwaren, *pl.* groceries *pl.*
Kolonialwarenhändler,

Kolonialwarenhandlung 198. **Konto**

m. grocer.
Kolonialwarenhandlung, f. grocery.
Kolonie, f. (~n) colony.
Kolonist, m. (~en) colonist.
Kolonne, f. (~n) column.
kolossal, adj. great; huge.
kombinieren, v. a. combine.
Kombiwagen, m. station-wagon.
komisch, adj. funny.
Komitee, n. (~s) committee.
Komma, n. (~s) comma.
Kommandant, m. (~en, ~en) commander.
kommandieren, v. a. command; order.
kommen*, v.n. come; arrive; ~ lassen send for.
Kommission, f. (~en) commission.
Kommissionär, m. agent.
Kommode, f. (~n) chest of drawers.
Kommunismus, m. communism.
Komödie, f. (~n) comedy.
Kompagnie, f. (~n) company.
Kompass, m. (~e) compass.
Kompliment, n. (~e) compliment.
kompliziert, adj. complicated.
komponieren, v. a. compose.
Komponist, m. (~en) composer.
Komposition, f. (~en) composition.
Kompott, n. (~e) stewed fruit.
Kondensmilch, f. condensed milk; evaporated milk.
Konditorei, f. (~en) con-

fectioner's shop; café.
kondolieren, v. n. condole.
Konfekt, n. (~e) sweet-(meat)s pl.
Konferenz, f. (~en) conference.
Konfession, f. (~en) confession.
Konfirmation, f. (~en) confirmation.
Kongreß, m. (-resse) congress.
König, m. (~e) king.
Königin, f. (~nen) queen.
königlich, adj. royal.
Königreich, n. kingdom.
Konkurrenz, f. (~en) competition.
Konkurs, m. (~e) bankruptcy; failure.
können*, v. a. & n. can; be able (to); know.
Konossement, n. (~s) bill of lading.
konsequent, adj. consistent.
Konsequenz, f. (~en) consequence; consistency.
konservativ, adj. conservative.
Konserve, f. (~n) conserve; tinned goods pl.
Konstruktion, f. (~en) construction.
Konsulat, n. (~e) consulate.
Konsum, m. consumption; co-operative society.
Konsument, m. (~en) consumer.
Konsumverein, m. co-operative (society).
Kontinent, m. (~e) continent.
kontinental, adj. continental.
Konto, n. (-ten) bank

Kontor — **Krankenwagen**

account.
Kontor, n. (~e) office; counting house.
Kontrakt, m. (~e) contract.
Kontrolle, f. (~n) control; check(ing).
kontrollieren, v. a. control; check.
Konzert, n. (~e) concert.
Konzerthalle, f. music-hall.
Konzession, f. (~en) licence.
Kopf, m. (⁓e) head.
Kopfhörer, m. ear-phone.
Kopfrechnen, n. mental arithmetic.
Kopfsprung, m. header.
Kopfwäsche, f. shampooing.
Kopfweh, n. headache.
Kopie, f. (~n) copy.
kopieren, v.a. copy.
Koralle, f. (~n) coral.
Korb, m. (⁓e) basket.
Kork, m. (~e) cork.
Korkzieher, m. corkscrew.
Korn, n. (⁓er) grain; corn.
Kornblume, f. cornflower.
Körper, m. (~) body.
körperlich, adj. bodily.
Körperschaft, f. corporation.
korrekt, adj. correct.
Korrektur, f. (~en) correction.
Korrespondent, m. (~en) correspondent.
Korrespondenz, f. (~en) correspondence.
Korridor, m. (~e) corridor; passage.
Korsett, n. (~e) corset.
kosmisch, adj. cosmic.
Kost, f. food.
kostbar, adj. valuable; precious.

Kosten, pl. costs pl.; expense(s).
kosten, v. a. cost; taste.
Kostgänger, m. boarder.
köstlich, adj. delicious; exquisite.
Kostüm, n. (~e) costume.
Kot, m. mud; dirt; excrement.
Kotelett, n. (~e) cutlet.
Krach, m. crash; crack; row.
Kraft, f. (⁓e) force; strength; power.
Kraftanlage, f. power-plant.
Kraftbrühe, f. beaf-tea: stock.
Kraftfahrer, m. motorist.
Kraftfahrzeug, n. motor vehicle.
kräftig, adj. strong; vigorous.
kräftigen, v. a. strengthen.
Kraftrad, n. motor-cycle.
Kraftstoff, m. petrol, fuel.
Kraftwagen, m. motor-car.
Kraftwerk, n. power-station.
Kragen, m. (~) collar.
Krähe, f. (~n) crow.
Kralle, f. (~n) claw.
Krampf, m. (⁓e) cramp, spasm.
krank, adj. ill; ~ werden fall ill.
Kranke, m., f. (~n) patient.
kränken, v.n. hurt.
Krankenhaus, n. hospital.
Krankenkasse, f. health-insurance.
Krankenkassenarzt, m. national-health-doctor.
Krankenschwester, f. (hospital) nurse.
Krankenwagen, m. ambulance.

krankhaft *adj.* morbid.
Krankheit, *f.* (~en) disease, illness.
kränklich, *adj.* sickly.
Kranz, *m.* (⁓e) wreath.
Krater, *m.* (~) crater.
kratzen, *v. a.* scratch; scrape.
Kraut, *n.* (⁓er) herb; cabbage.
Krawatte, *f.* (~n) necktie.
Krebs, *m.* (~e) crawfish; crab; cancer.
Kredit, *m.* (~e) credit.
Kreditbrief, *m.* letter of credit.
Kreide, *f.* (~n) chalk.
Kreis, *m.* (~e) circle.
Kreisbahn, *f.* orbit.
kreisen, *v. n.* rotate.
kreisförmig, *adj.* circular.
Kreislauf, *m.* circulation.
Krematorium, *n.* (-rien) crematorium.
Krempe, *f.* (~n) brim.
Kreuz, *n.* (~e) cross.
Kreuzband, *n.* (postal) wrapper; *unter* ~ by book-post.
kreuzen, *v. a.* cross; *v. n.* cruise.
Kreuzigung, *f.* (~en) crucifixion.
Kreuzschmerzen, *pl.* lumbago.
Kreuzung, *f.* (~en) crossing; cross-breading.
Kreuzungspunkt, *m.* junction.
Kreuzverhör, *n.* cross-examination.
Kreuzweg, *m.* cross-road(s).
Kreuzworträtsel, *n.* crossword puzzle
kriechen*, *v. n.* creep; crawl.
Krieg, *m.* (~e) war.
kriegen, *v. a.* get.
Krieger, *m.* (~) warrior.
kriegerisch, *adj.* martial.
Kriegsflotte, *f.* navy.
Kriegsgefangener, *m.* prisoner of war.
Kriegsgericht, *n.* court-martial.
Kriegsschiff, *n.* man-of-war; war-ship.
Kriegsverbrecher, *m.* war criminal.
Kriminalpolizei, *f.* detective force; criminal investigation police.
Kriminalroman, *m.* detective novel.
Krise, *f.* (~n) crisis.
Kristall, *m.* (~e) crystal.
Kritik, *f.* (~en) critique.
Kritiker, *m.* (~) critic.
kritisch, *adj.* critical.
Krokodil, *n.* (~e) crocodile.
Krone, *f.* (~n) crown.
krönen, *v.a.* crown.
Krönung, *f.* (~en) coronation.
Kröte, *f.* (~n) toad.
Krug, *m.* (⁓e) jar; jug; pitcher.
krümmen, *v. a. & n.* bend.
Krümmung, *f.* (~en) curve.
Kruste, *f.* (~n) crust.
Kruzifix, *n.* (~e) crucifix.
Kübel, *m.* (~) bucket; tub.
Küche, *f.* (~n) kitchen.
Kuchen, *m.* (~) cake.
Küchengerät, *n.* kitchen utensils *pl.*
Kücken, *m.* (~) chicken.
Kuckuck, *m.* (~e) cuckoo.
Kugel, *f.* (~n) ball; bullet; globe.
Kugellager, *n.* ball-bearing.
Kugelschreiber, *m.* ball-(point-)pen.

Kuh, *f.* (⁓e) cow.
kühl, *adj.* cool.
kühlen, *v.a.* cool.
Kühlschrank, *m.* refrigerator; fridge.
Kühnheit, *f.* boldness.
Kulisse, *f.* (⁓n) wings *pl.*; *hinter den* ⁓n (behind the) scenes.
Kultur, *f.* (⁓en) culture; civilization.
kulturell, *adj.* cultural.
Kummer, *m.* (⁓) grief.
kümmern; *sich* ⁓ care for; worry about.
Kunde¹, *f.* (⁓n) knowledge; information; science.
Kunde², *m.* (⁓n) customer.
kündigen, *v.a.* (give) notice ;(to).
Kündigung, *f.* (⁓en) notice; warning.
Kundschaft, *f.* (⁓en) custom; customers *pl.*
künftig, *adj.* future.
Kunst, *f.* (⁓e) art.
Kunstgeschichte, *f.* history of art.
Kunstgriff, *m.* trick.
Kunstleder, *n.* leather imitation.
Künstler, *m.* (⁓) artist.
Künstlerin, *f.* (⁓nen) artist.
künstlerisch, *adj.* artistic.
künstlich, *adj.* artificial.
Kunstseide, *f.* rayon.
Kunststoff(e) *m.* plastics *pl.*
Kunststück, *n.* trick.
Kunstwerk, *n.* work of art.
Kupfer, *n.* copper.
Kupferstich, *m.* copperplate engraving.
Kuppel, *f.* (⁓n) dome.
Kur, *f.*(⁓en) cure; course of treatment.
Kürbis, *m.* (⁓se) pumpkin.
Kurfürst, *m.* elector.
Kurort, *m.* wateringplace; spa.
Kurs, *m.* (⁓e) course; exchange.
Kürschner, *m.* (⁓) furrier.
Kursus: *m.* (-se) course.
kurz, *adj.* short; ⁓*adv.* (in) short.
Kürze, *f.* (⁓n) brevity.
kürzlich, *adj.* recently; lately.
Kurzschluß, *m.* short circuit.
kurzsichtig, *adj.* shortsighted.
Kurzwaren, *f. pl.* haberdashery.
Kurzwelle, *f.* shortwave.
Kurzwellensender, *m.* short-wave transmitter.
Kuß, *m.* (Küsse) kiss.
küssen, *v. a.* kiss.
Küste, *f.* (⁓n) coast, beach.
Kutsche, *f.* (⁓n) coach.
Kuvert, *n.* (⁓e) cover, envelope.

L

Laboratorium, *n.* (-rien) laboratory.
lächeln, *v. n.* smile.
lachen, *v. n.* laugh.
lächerlich, *adj.* ridiculous; absurd.
Lachs, *m.* (⁓e) salmon.
laden*, *v. a.* load.
Laden, *m.* (⁓) shop; store; shutter.
Ladung, *f.* (⁓en) load; cargo; charge.
Lage, *f.* (⁓n) position; situation.
Lager, *n.* (⁓) camp; bed.
Lagerhaus, *n.* warehouse.

Lamm, *n.* (⁓er) lamb.
Lampe, *f.* (⁓n) lamp.
Land, *n.* (⁓er) land; country.
Landbau, *m.* agriculture.
Landbesitz, *m.* landed property.
landen, *v. a. & n.* land: disembark.
Landeplatz, *m.* quay, wharf; runway.
Landkarte, *f.* map.
Landmann, *m.* countryman.
Landschaft, *f.* (⁓en) province; landscape.
Landsmann, *m.* compatriot.
Landstraße, *f.* highway.
Landungsbrücke, *f.* pier.
Landwirt, *m.* farmer.
Landwirtschaft, *f.* agriculture, husbandry.
lang, *adj.* long; — *adv.* at full length; long.
Länge, *f.* (⁓n) length; longitude.
langen, *v. n. & a.* reach (after); (be) enough; suffice.
Langeweile, *f.* boredom.
längs, *prep.* along.
langsam, *adj.* slow; ⁓! gently!
Langspielplatte, *f.* long-playing record.
langweilig, *adj.* tiresome; dull.
Lärm, *m.* noise.
lassen*, let; leave; allow; cause; bid.
Last, *f.* (⁓en) load; cargo.
Lastauto, *s.* (motor-)lorry.
Laster, *n.* (⁓) vice.
lästig, *adj.* troublesome.
Lastwagen, *m.* (motor-)lorry.
Laterne, *f.* (⁓n) lantern.
Laub, *n.* foliage.

Lauf, *m.* (⁓e) course, run; race.
Laufbahn, *f.* career.
laufen*, *v. n.* run.
Läufer, *m.* (⁓) runner; *(chess)* bishop; *(football)* half(-back).
Laufmasche, *f.* ladder; run *(in stocking)*.
Laune, *f.* (⁓n) humor.
lauschen, *v. n.* listen.
laut, *adj.* loud.
Laut, *m.* (⁓e) sound.
lauten, *v. n.* sound.
läuten, *v. n.* ring.
lauter, *adj.* clear; — *adv.* clearly.
Lautsprecher, *m.* loudspeaker.
Leben, *n.* (⁓) life.
leben, *v. n.* live.
Lebensalter, *n.* age.
Lebensmittel, *pl.* food; victuals *pl.*
Lebensunterhalt, *m.* livelihood.
Lebensversicherung, *f.* life insurance.
Lebensweise, *f.* way of life, habit.
Leber, *f.* (⁓n) liver.
lebhaft, *adj.* lively.
leblos, *adj.* lifeless.
lecken, *v. a.* lick.
Leder, *n.* (⁓) leather.
ledig, *adj.* unmarried; single.
leer, *adj.* empty.
leeren, *v. a.* drain, empty.
Legat, *n.* (⁓e) legate
legen, *v. a.* lay; place sich ⁓ *(pers)* lie down go to bed; *(wind, etc.)* cease.
legitimieren; legitimize; sich ⁓ prove one's identity.
lehnen, *v. n. & a.* lean (against).
Lehrbuch, *n.* text-book.
Lehre, *f.* (⁓n) lesson doctrine.

| **lehren** | **203.** | **lieben** |

lehren, *v. a.* teach.
Lehrer, *m.* (∼) teacher.
Lehrerin, *f.* (∼nen) teacher.
Lehrling, *m.* (∼e) apprentice.
Leib, *m.* (∼er) body.
Leiche, *f.* (∼n) (dead) body; corpse.
Leichenhaus, *n.* morgue; mortuary.
Leichenschau, *f.* inquest; post mortem.
Leichenverbrennung, *f.* cremation.
Leichenzug, *m.* funeral procession.
Leichnam, *m.* (∼e) (dead) body; corpse.
leicht, *adj.* easy; light; — *adv.* easily.
Leichtathletik, *f.* athletics *pl.*
Leichtgewicht, *n.* light weight.
leichtsinnig, *adj.* thoughtless, frivolous.
Leid, *n.* grief.
leid, *adj.*; *es tut mir* ∼ I am sorry.
leiden*, *v. a. & n.* suffer; endure.
Leidenschaft, *f.* (∼en) passion.
leidenschaftlich, *adj.* passionate.
leider, *adv.* unfortunately.
Leihbibliothek, *f.* circulating library.
leihen*, *v. a.* lend; borrow.
leinen, *adj.* linen.
Leinwand, *f.* linen.
leise, *adj.* soft; low.
Leiste[1], *f.* (∼n) border; ledge.
Leiste[2], *f.* (∼n) groin.
leisten, *v. a.* do; perform; *er kann es sich* ∼ he can afford it.
Leistung, *f.* (∼en) performance.
Leitartikel, *m.* leading article.
leiten, *v. a.* lead; conduct; manage.
Leiter[1], *m.* (∼) leader; guide.
Leiter[2], *f.* (∼n) ladder.
Leitung, *f.* (∼en) guidance; management; line; lead; pipe-line.
Lektüre, *f.* (∼n) reading.
lenken, *v. a.* direct; guide; rule; drive; manage.
Lenkrad, *n.* steering-wheel.
Lerche, *f.* (∼n) lark.
lernen, *v. a. & n.* learn; study.
Lesebuch, *n.* reader.
lesen*, *v. a.* read; lecture; glean.
Leser, *m.* (∼) reader.
letzt, *adj.* last; latest.
leuchten, *v. n.* light; shine.
Leuchter, *m.* (∼) candlestick.
Leuchtturm, *m.* lighthouse.
leugnen, *v. a.* deny.
Leute, *pl.* people.
Leutnant, *m.* (∼e) lieutenant.
Lexikon, *n.* (-ika) lexikon; dictionary.
liberal, *adj.* liberal.
Licht, *n.* (∼er) light.
licht, *adj.* bright; light; clear.
lichten[1], *v. a.* weigh (anchor.)
lichten[2], *v. a.* clear; thin.
Lichtspielhaus, *n.* cinema.
Lid, *n.* (∼er) eye-lid.
lieb, *adj.* dear; *es ist mir* ∼ I am glad (of it).
Liebe, *f.* love.
lieben, *v. a.* love; be fond

of; like.
Liebende, *m.*, *f.* (~n) lover.
liebenswürdig, *adj.* amicable, lovely.
Liebesbrief, *m.* love-letter.
Liebespaar, *n.* (pair of) lovers *pl.*
Liebhaber, *m.* (~) lover; amateur; fan.
Liebhaberei, *f.* (~n) hobby.
lieblich, *adj.* lovely.
Liebling, *m.* (~e) favourite; darling.
Lied, *n.* (~er) song.
Lieferant, *m.* (~en) supplier; purveyor.
liefern, *v. a.* supply; deliver.
liegen*, *v. a.* lie; be situated.
Liegestuhl, *m.* deck-chair.
Limonade, *f.* (~n) lemonade.
Linde, *f.* (~n) linden; lime-tree.
Linie, *f.* (~n) line.
link, *adj.* left.
Linke, *f.* (~n) left.
links, *adv.* to the left; on the left.
Linse, *f.* (~n) lentil; lens.
Lippe, *f.* (~n) lip.
Lippenstift, *m.* lipstick.
List, *f.* (~en) trick; cunning.
Liste, *f.* (~n) list.
listig, *adj.* cunning.
literarisch, *adj.* literary.
Literatur, *f.* (~en) literature.
Lizenz, *f.* (~en) licence.
Lob, *n.* praise.
loben, *v. a.* praise.
Loch, *n.* (~er) hole.
Locke, *f.* (~n) curl.
locken, *v. a.* attract; allure.
locker, *adj.* loose.

Löffel, *m.* (~) spoon.
Loge, *f.* (~n) box.
Logik, *f.* logic.
logisch, *adj.* logical.
Lohn, *m.* (~e) wages *pl*; salary; reward.
lohnen, *v. a.* reward; pay; *sich* ~ pay; *es lohnt sich* it is worth while.
Löhnungstag, *m.* payday.
Lokal, *n.* (~e) locality; premises *pl.*; restaurant; public-house.
Lokomotive, *f.* (~n) locomotive.
Lokomotivführer, *m.* engine-driver.
Lorbeer, *m.* (~en) laurel.
Los, *n.* (~e) lot; (lottery-)ticket; fate; destiny.
los, *adj.* loose; free; — *adv.* on; forward.
löschen*, *v. a.* put out.
losen, *v. n.* draw lots.
lösen, *v. a.* loosen; untie; solve; buy a (ticket)
losgehen*, *v. a.* go off; dash off.
lossprechen*, *v. a.* absolve; acquit.
Lösung, *f.* (~en) solution.
Lotse, *m.* (~n) pilot.
Löwe, *m.* (~n) lion.
Lücke, *f.* (~n) gap.
Luft, *f.* (~e) air.
Luftangriff, *m.* air-raid.
Luftballon, *m.* balloon.
Luftdruck, *m.* atmospheric pressure.
Luftdruckbremse, *f.* atmospheric brake.
lüften, *v. a.* air.
Luftfahrer, *m.* aeronaut.
Lufthafen, *m.* aerodrome; airport.
luftig, *adj.* airy.
luftkrank, *adj.* air-sick.
Luftkrieg, *m.* aerial war-

Luftkühlung — fare.
Luftkühlung, *f.* air-cooling.
Luftpost, *f.* air-mail.
Luftreifen, *m.* pneumatic tyre.
Luftschiffahrt, *f.* aeronautics.
Luftschutz, *m.* anti-aircraft defence.
Luftschutzkeller, *m.* air-shelter.
Luftzug, *m.* draught.
Lüge, *f.* (~n) lie.
lügen*, *v. n.* lie.
Lunge, *f.* (~n) lungs *pl.*
Lungenentzündung, *f.* inflammation of the lungs; pneumonia.
Lupe, *f.* (~n) magnifying glass.
Lust, *f.* (≈e) pleasure; desire; ~ *haben* feel like.
lustig, *adj.* merry; gay.
Lustspiel, *n.* comedy.
Luxus, *m.* luxury.
lynchen, *v. a.* lynch.
Lyrik, *f.* lyric poetry.

M

machen, *v. a.* make; do; cause; manufacture.
Macht, *f.* (≈e) force; power.
mächtig, *adj.* strong; powerful.
Mädchen, *n.* (~) girl; maid; (maid)servant.
Magd, *f.* (≈e) (maid-)servant.
Magen, *m.* (≈) stomach.
Magenbeschwerden, *pl.* indigestion.
mager, *adj. (pers)* thin; lean.
Magnet, *m.* (~e) magnet.
magnetisch, *adj.* magnetic
Magnetophon, *n.* tape recorder.
mähen, *v. a.* mow.
Mäher, *m.* (~) mower.
Mahl, *n.* (~e) meal.
mahlen*, *v. a.* grind.
Mahlzeit, *f.* (~en) meal.
mahnen, *v. a.* warn; remind.
Mahnung, *f.* (~en) warning.
Mai, *m.* (~e) May.
Mais, *m.* maize; (Indian) corn.
Majestät, *f.* (~en) majesty.
Major, *m.* (~e) major.
Mal, *n.* (~e) time; mark; mole.
mal, *adv.* once; *noch* ~ once more.
malen, *v. a.* paint.
Maler, *m.* (~) painter.
Malerei, *f.* (~n) painting.
Mama, *f.* (~s) mamma.
man, *pron.* one; people; we, you.
manch, mancher, *pron.* many (a); some.
mancherlei, *adj.* different; various.
manchmal, *adv.* sometimes.
Mandel, *f.* (~n) almond; *(pers)* tonsil(s).
Mangel, *m.* (~) deficiency; want.
Mann, *m.* (≈er) man; husband.
Männchen, *n.* (~) male; litte man.
mannigfach, mannigfaltig, *adj.* various.
männlich, *adj.* male.
Mannschaft, *f.* (~en) crew; team.
Manöver, *n.* (~) manoeuvre.
Manschette, *f.* (~n) cuff.
Mantel, *m.* (≈) coat; cloak; overcoat.

Manuskript, n. (~e) manuscript.
Märchen, n. (~) fairytale.
Marine, f. (~n) navy.
Mark, n. marrow.
Marke, f. (~n) mark; brand; counter; postage-stamp.
Markt, m. (⸚e) market.
Marmelade, f. (~n) marmalade; jam.
Marmor, m. (~e) marble.
Marsch, m. (⸚e) march.
marschieren, v. n. march.
Marter, f. (~n) torture.
März, m. (~e) March.
Masche, f. (~n) stitch, mesh.
Maschine, f. (~n) machine.
Maschinenbau, m. engineering.
Maschinenschreiber, m., ~in f. typist.
Maschinerie, f. (~n) machinery.
Maske, f. (~n) mask.
Maß, n. (~e) measure; size; *nach* ~ made to measure; *über alle* ~en beyond measure.
Masse, f. (~n) mass; bulk.
maßgebend, adj. standard; authoritative.
massieren, v. a. massage.
mäßigen, v. a. moderate; mitigate.
massiv, adj. massive, solid.
Maßnahme, f. (~n) measure.
Maßregel, f. measure; provision.
Maßstab, m. measure; rule.
Mast, m. (~e) mast.
Material, n. (~ien) material.
Materialismus, m. materialism.

materiell, adj. material; real.
Mathematik, f. mathematics *pl.*
mathematisch, adj. mathematical.
Matratze, f. (~n) mattress.
Matrose, m. (~n) sailor.
matt, adj. faint; weak.
Mauer, f. (~n) wall.
Maul, n. (⸚er) mouth.
Maulesel, m. mule.
maurisch, adj. Moor.
Maus, f. (⸚e) mouse.
Maximum, n. (-ima) maximum.
mechanisch, adj. mechanic(al); — adv. mechanically.
mechanisieren, v. a. mechanize.
Mechanismus, m. (-men) mechanism.
Medizin, f. (~en) medicine.
Meer, n. (~e) sea; ocean.
Meerenge, f. strait.
Meerrettich, m. horseradish.
Mehl, n. flour.
Mehlspeise, f. (~n) pastry; cake.
mehr, adv. & adj. more; *nicht* ~ no longer.
mehrere, adj. several.
mehrfach, adj. manifold; —adv. repeatedly.
Mehrgewicht, n. excess weight.
Mehrheit, f. (~en) majority.
mehrmals, adv. several times.
Mehrzahl, f. majority; plural.
meiden*, v. a. avoid.
Meile, f. (~n) mile.
mein, pron. my; *der, die*

meinen | **Mitarbeiter**

das ~e mine.
meinen, *v. a.* mean; suppose; think.
Meinung, *f.* (~en) opinion; *meiner ~ nach* in my opinion.
meist, *adj.* most; *adv.* mostly; *aufs ~e* at most.
Meister, *m.* (~) master; champion.
Meisterschaft, *f.* championship.
melden, *v. a.* announce; report.
Melodie, *f.* (~n) tune, melody.
Menge, *f.* (~n) amount; quantity.
mengen, *v. a.* mingle; mix.
Mensch, *m.* (~en) man; human being.
Menschheit, *f.* mankind.
menschlich, *adj.* human.
Menschlichkeit, *f.* humanity.
merken, *v. a.* notice; perceive.
Merkmal, *n.* sign; mark.
merkwürdig, *adj.* remarkable; strange.
Messe, *f.* (~n) mass; fair.
messen*, *v. a. & n.* measure.
Messer[1], *n.* (~) knife.
Messer[2], *m.* (~) measuring instrument; meter.
Messing, *n.* brass.
Metall, *n.* (~e) metal.
Meteor, *n.* (~e) meteor.
Meteorologie, *f.* meteorology.
Methode, *f.* (~n) method.
Mieder, *n.* (~) corset.
Mietauto, *n.* taxi.
Miete, *f.* (~n) rent.
mieten, *v. a.* rent; hire; charter.
Mikrobe, *f.* (~n) microbe.

Mikrofilm, *m.* microfilm.
Mikroskop, *n.* (~e) microscope.
Milch, *f.* milk.
mild, *adj.* mild.
mildern, *v. a.* mitigate; soothe.
militärisch, *adj.* military.
Million, *f.* (~en) million.
Millionär, *m.* (~e) millionaire.
minder, *adj. & adv.* less; minor.
Minderheit, *f.* (~en) minority.
mindestens, *adv.* (at) least.
Mineral, *n.* (~ien) mineral.
Miniatur, *f.* (~en) miniature.
Minister, *m.* (~) minister; Secretary of State.
Ministerium, *n.* (-rien) ministry.
Ministerpräsident, *m.* prime minister.
Minute, *f.* (~n) minute.
mischen, *v. a.* mix.
Mischung, *f.* (~en) mixture.
mißfallen*, *v. a.* displease.
Mißgeschick, *n.* misadventure.
mißhandeln, *v. a.* illtreat.
Mission, *f.* (~en) mission.
Missionar, *m.* (~e) missionary.
mißtrauen, *v. n.* mistrust.
Mißverständnis, *n.* misunderstanding.
Mist, *m.* (~e) dung; rubbish.
mit, *adv.* together; — *prep.* with; by; in; at; on.
Mitarbeiter, *m.* fellow

worker; collaborator.
Mitbewerber, *m.* competitor; rival.
mitbringen*, *v. a.* bring along.
miteinander, *adv.* together.
Mitgift, *f.* dowry.
Mitglied, *n.* member.
Mitlaut, *m.* consonant.
Mitleid, *n.* pity.
mitmachen, *v. a.* take part in.
mitnehmen*, *v. a.* take along with.
Mittag, *m.* (~e) noon, midday; *zu ~ essen* (have) lunch.
mittags, *adv.* at noon.
Mitte, *f.* (~n) center; middle.
mitteilen, *v. a.* communicate; inform.
Mitteilung, *f.* (~en) information; communication.
Mittel, *n.* (~) means.
Mittelalter, *n.* middle ages *pl.*
mittelmäßig, *adj.* mediocre.
Mittelpunkt, *m.* center.
mittels, *prep.* with; by means of.
Mittelstürmer, *m.* centre forward.
mitten, *adv.* in the midst of; among.
Mitternacht, *f.* midnight.
mittler(e), *adj.* middle; average.
Mittwoch, *m.* (~e) Wednesday.
mitunter, *adv.* sometimes.
mitwirken, *v. n.* co-operate.
Mitwirkung, *f.* (~en) assistance; co-operation.
Möbel, *n.* (~) furniture.
mobil, *adj.* mobile; movable.
mobilisieren, *v.a.* mobilize.
Mode, *f.* (~n) fashion.
Modell, *n.* (~e) model.
modern, *adj.* modern.
modisch, *adj.* fashionable.
Modistin, *f.* (~nen) milliner.
mögen*, *v. n.* be able; be possible; like; wish; want; may; *ich möchte gern...* I should like; to...
möglich, *adj.* possible.
Möglichkeit, *f.* (~en) possibility.
Mohrrübe, *f.* carrot.
Molkerei, *f.* (~en) dairy.
Moll, *n.* minor (key).
Moment, *m.* (~e) moment.
momentan, *adj.* momentary.
Momentaufnahme, *f.* snap-shot.
Monarchie, *f.* (~n) monarchy.
Monat, *m.* (~e) month.
monatlich, *adj.* monthly.
Monatschrift, *f.* monthly (journal).
Mönch, *m.* (~e) monk.
Mond, *m.* (~e) moon.
Mondschein, *m.* moonlight.
Monitor, *m.* (-oren) monitor.
Monographie, *f.* (~n) monograph.
Monolog, *m.* (~e) monologue; soliloquy.
Monopol, *n.* (~e) monopoly.
monopolisieren, *v. a.* monopolize.
Montag, *m.* (~e) Monday.
moralisch, *adj.* moral.
Mord, *m.* (~e) murder.
Mörder, *m.* (~) murderer.
Morgen, *m.* (~) morning;

morgen

guten ~ good morning.

morgen, *adv.* tomorrow; ~ *früh* tomorrow morning; *heute* ~ this morning.

Morgenrock, *m.* dressing-gown.

Most, *m.* (~e) cider.

Motor, *m.* (~en) motor.

Motorboot, *n.* motor-boat.

motorisieren, *v. a.* mechanize.

Motorrad, *n.* motor bicycle.

Motorroller, *m.* scooter.

Motte, *f.* (~n) moth.

Mücke, *f.* (~n) mosquito.

müde, *adj.* tired.

Muff, *m.* (~e) muff.

Mühe, *f.* (~n) trouble; pains *pl.*; *sich* ~ *geben* take pains.

Mühle, *f.* (~n) mill.

mühsam, *adj.* troublesome.

Müll, *m.* refuse; rubbish.

Müller, *m.* (~) miller.

multiplizieren, *v. a.* multiply.

Mund, *m.* (⁓er) mouth.

Mündel, *m.* (~) ward.

münden, *v.n.* run into; fall into.

mündlich, *adj.* oral; — *adv.* orally.

Mündung, *f.* (~en) mouth.

Mundvorrat, *m.* provisions *pl.*

Munition, *f.* (~en) ammunition.

munter, *adj.* merry; cheerful.

Münze, *f.* (~n) coin; change; medal.

murmeln, *v. n.* murmur.

Muselmann, *m.* Mussulman.

Museum, *n.* (-seen) museum.

Musik, *f.* music.

musikalisch, *adj.* musical.

Musiker, *m.* (~) musician.

Muskel, *m.* (~) muscle.

Muße, *f.* leisure.

müssen*, *v.n.* be obliged (to); have to; *ich muß* I must; *müßte* ought (to).

müßig, *adj.* idle.

Muster, *n.* (~) example; model; sample.

Mut, *m.* courage.

mutig, *adj.* brave; courageous.

mutmaßen, *v.a.* presume; suppose.

Mutter, *f.* (⁓) mother.

mütterlich, *adj.* motherly, maternal.

Muttersprache, *f.* mother-tongue.

Mütze, *f.* (~n) cap.

mystisch, *adj.* mystic.

N

Nabel, *m.* (~) navel.

nach, *adv.* after; behind; ~ *und* ~ gradually; by and by; —*prep.* towards, to; for; according to.

Nachahmung, *f.* (~en) imitation.

Nachbar, *m.* (~n) neighbour.

Nachbarschaft, *f.* (~en) neighbourhood.

nachdem, *adv.* after; to.

nachdenken*, *v. n.* meditate (on).

nachdrücklich, *adj.* energetic; emphatic.

nacheinander, *adv.* one after the other.

Nachfolger, *m.* (~) successor.

Nachfrage, *f.* demand; inquiry.

nachgeben — Nebenhandlung

nachgeben, *v. a. & n.* give up; yield.
nachher, *adv.* afterwards.
Nachkomme, *m.* (~n) descendant.
nachlassen*, *v. a. & n.* leave behind; slacken, decrease.
Nachlässigkeit, *f.* (~en) negligence.
nachmachen, *v. a.* imitate.
Nachmittag, *m.* afternoon.
Nachmittagsvorstellung, *f.* matinée.
Nachschlagebuch, *n.* book of reference.
Nachschrift, *f.* postscript; dictation.
nachsehen*, *v. n.* look after; see to; *v. a.* revise; examine.
nächst, *adv.* next; nearest; — *prep.* next to; close by.
Nächste, *m.* (~n) fellow-creature.
nächstens, *adv.* shortly.
Nacht, *f.* (~̈e) night.
Nachteil, *m.* disadvantage.
Nachtigall, *f.* (~en) nightingale.
Nachtisch, *m.* dessert.
nächtlich, *adj.* nightly; —*adv.* at night.
Nachtportier, *m.* night-porter.
Nachweis, *m.* proof; reference.
nachweisen*, *v. a.* establish; prove; show; point out.
Nachwelt, *f.* posterity.
Nacken, *m.* (~) neck; nape.
nackt, *adj.* bare; naked.
Nadel, *f.* (~n) needle; pin.

Nagel, *m.* (~) nail.
Nagelbürste, *f.* nail-brush.
nageln, *v. a.* nail.
nagen, *v. a.* gnaw.
nah, nahe, *adj. & adv.* near; close.
Nähe, *f.* (~n) proximity neighbourhood; *in der* ~ near by.
nähen, *v. a.* sew.
nähern: *v. n. sich* ~ approach.
Nähmaschine, *f.* sewing-machine.
nähren, *v. a.* nourish.
Nahrung, *f.* (~en) food.
Nahrungsmittel, *pl.* foodstuffs *pl.*; victuals *pl.*
Name, *m.* (~n) name.
nämlich, *adv.* namely; that is to say.
Narbe, *f.* (~n) scar.
Narr, *m.* (~en; ~en) fool.
Nase, *f.* (~n) nose.
naß, *adj.* wet.
Nässe, *f.* humidity.
Nation, *f.* (~en) nation.
national, *adj.* national.
Nationalität, *f.* (~en) nationality.
Natur, *f.* (~en) nature.
Naturalisierung, *f.* (~en) naturalization.
Naturgeschichte, *f.* natural history.
natürlich, *adj.* natural; — *adv.* naturally; of course.
Naturwissenschaft, *pl.* natural sciences.
Nebel, *m.* (~) fog.
neben, *prep.* beside; near; next to; by.
nebenbei, *adv.* near by; by the way.
Nebenbuhler, *m.* rival.
nebeneinander, *adv.* side by side.
Nebenfluß *m.* tributary.
Nebenhandlung *f.* episode;

Nebenprodukt 211. **Notbremse**

suborüinate action.
Nebenprodukt, *n.* byprodukt.
nebst, *prep.* with; together with.
Neffe, *m.* (~n; ~n) nephew.
Negative, *n.* (~n) negative (photo)
Neger, *m.* (~) negro.
nehmen*, *v. a.* take; capture.
neidisch, *adj.* envious.
Neigung, *f.* (~en) inclination.
nein, *adv.* no.
Nelke, *f.* (~n) clove; carnation.
nennen*, *v. a.* name; call.
Neonbeleuchtung, *f.* strip-lighting.
Nerv, *m.* (~en) nerve.
nervös, *adj.* nervous; nervy.
Nest, *n.* (~er) nest.
nett, *adj.* neat; nice.
netto, *adv.* net.
Netz, *n.* (~e) net, network; rack.
neu, *adj.* new; late; modern.
Neudruck, *m.* reprint.
neuerdings, *adv.* lately.
Neuerung, *f.* (~en) innovation.
neugeboren, *adj.* newborn.
neugierig, *adj.* curious.
Neugkeit, *f.* (~en) novelty.
Neujahr, *n.* New-Year.
neulich, *adj.* recent; — *adv.* recently.
neun, *adj.* nine.
neunte, *adj.* ninth.
neunzehn, *adj.* nineteen.
neunzig, *adj.* ninety.
neutral, *adj.* neutral.
nicht, *adv.* not; ~ *mehr* no more; *auch* ~ neither.
Nichte, *f.* (~n) niece.

Nichtraucher, *m.* nonsmoker.
nichts, *pron.* nothing; ~ *als* nothing but.
nicken, *v. n.* nod.
nie, *adv.* never.
nieder, *adj.* low; inferior; — *adv.* down; low.
Niedergang, *m.* decline.
Niederlage, *f.* defeat.
niederländisch, *adj.* Dutch.
niederlegen, *v. a.* lay down; *sich* ~ go to bed; lie down.
niederreißen*, *v.a.* demolish; pull down.
Niederschlag, *m.* precipitation; sediment.
niedlich, *adj.* neat; pretty.
niedrig, *adj.* low.
niemals, *adv.* never.
niemand, *pron.* nobody; no-one.
Niere, *f.* (~n) kidney.
niesen, *v.n.* sneeze.
nimmer, *adv.* never; no more.
nimmermehr, *adv.* never(more).
nirgends, *adv.* nowhere.
Niveau, *n.* (~s) level.
noch, *adv.* besides; in addition; still; *weder* ... ~ neither ... nor ... — *conj.* nor.
nochmals, *adv.* again, once more.
Nonne, *f.* (~n) nun.
Norden, *m.* north.
nordisch, *adj.* northern.
nördlich, *adj.* northern.
Nordwesten, *m.* northwest.
normal, *adj.* normal.
Not, *f.* (~e) necessity; want.
Notar, *m.* (~e) notary.
Notausgang, *m.* emergency exit.
Notbremse, *f.* *(Eisenbahn)* communication cord.

Note — **Ökonomie**

Note, *f.* (~n) note.
Notfall, *m.* emergency.
notieren, *v.a.* note.
nötig, *adj.* necessary.
Notiz, *f.* (~en) notice.
Notizbuch, *n.* note-book.
Nottreppe, *f.* fire-escape.
notwendig, *adj.* necessary.
Novelle, *f.* (~n) short story.
November, *m.* (~) November.
nüchtern, *adj.* sober.
Nudeln, *pl.* vermicelli; noodles.
Null, *f.* (~en) nought; zero.
Nummer, *f.* (~n) number.
Nummerschild, *n.* number-plate.
nun, *adv.* now; von ~ an henceforth; — *conj.* then.
nunmehr, *adv.* now.
nur, *adv.* only; but; merely.
Nuß, *f.* (Nüsse) nut.
Nutzen, *m.* use, profit.
nützen, *v. n.* be of use; *v. a.* make use of.
nützlich, *adj.* useful.
nutzlos, *adj.* useless.
Nylon, *n.* nylon.
Nylonstrümpfe, *pl.* nylons

O

Oase, *f.* (~n) oasis.
ob, *conj.* if; whether.
oben, *adv.* above; on; upstairs.
ober, *adj.* upper; higher.
Ober, *m.* (~) head-waiter.
Oberarm, *m.* upper-arm.
Oberfläche, *f.* surface.
oberhalb, *adv.* above.
Oberleitungsbus, *m.* trolley-bus.
Oberschule, *f.* grammar school.
Oberst, *m.* (~en) colonel; chief.
obgleich, *conj.* although.
obig, *adj.* above-mentioned.
Objekt, *n.* (~e) object.
Objektive, *n.* Lens.
Oboe, *f.* (~n) oboe.
Obrigkeit, *f.* (~en) authority.
obschon, *conj.* although.
Observatorium, (-rien) observatory.
Obst, *n.* fruit.
Obstbaum, *m.* fruit-tree.
Obstgarten, *m.* orchard.
Obus, *m.* trolley-bus.
obwohl, *conj.* although.
Ochse, *m.* (~n) ox.
Ochsenfleisch, *n.* beef.
Ochsenschwanz, *m.* ox-tail.
öde, *adj.* deserted.
Öde, *f.* (~n) desert.
oder, *conj.* or; else.
Ofen, *m.* (~) stove, oven; furnace.
offen, *adj.* open.
offenbar, *adj.* evident.
Offenheit, *f.* frankness.
Offensive, *f.* (~n) offensive.
öffentlich, *adj.* public.
Öffentlichkeit, *f.* public; publicity.
offerieren, *v.a.* offer.
Offerte, *f.* (~n) offer.
offiziell, *adj.* official.
Offizier, *m.* (~e) officer.
öffnen, *v. a.* open.
Öffnung, *f.* (~en) opening.
oft, öfter(s); oftmals *adv.* often.
ohne, *prep.* without.
ohnehin, *adv.* besides.
ohnmächtig, *adj.*: ~ werden faint.
Ohr, *n.* (~en) ear.
Ohrfeige, *f.* box on the ear.
Ökonomie, *f.* (~n) econ-

ökonomisch — **Parlament**

omy.
ökonomisch, *adj.* economic.
Oktober, *m.* (~) October.
Öl, *n.* (~e) oil.
Omnibus, *m.* (-busse) bus.
Onkel, *m.* (~) uncle.
Oper, *f.* (~n) opera; operahouse.
Operation, *f.* (~en) operation.
Operette, *f.* (~n) operetta; musical comedy.
operieren, *v.a.* operate.
Opfer, *n.* (~) sacrifice; victim.
Opposition, *f.* (~en) opposition.
Optiker, *m.* (~) optician.
Optimist, *m.* (~en) optimist.
optimistisch, *adj.* optimistic.
optisch, *adj.* optic.
Orange, *f.* (~n) orange.
Oratorium, *n.* (-rien)
Orchester, *n.* (~) orchestra.
Orden, *m.* (~) medal; order; decoration.
ordentlich, *adj.* neat; orderly.
ordnen, *v. a.* (put in) order; arrange.
Ordnung, *f.* (~en) order.
Organ, *n.* (~e) organ.
organisieren, *v. a.* organize.
Organismus, *m.* (-men) organism.
Organist, *m.* (~en) organist.
Orgel, *f.* (~n) organ.
Orient, *m.* Orient; East.
originell, *adj.* original.
Ort, *m.* (~e) place.
örtlich, *adj* local.
Örtlichkeit, *f.* (~en) locality.
Ortschaft, *f.* (~en) place; village.

Ortsgespräch, *n.* local call.
Ortsverkehr, *m.* local traffic.
Ost(en), *m.* east.
Ostern, *pl.* Easter.
Österreicher *m.* (~); -in *f.* (~nen) Austrian.
österreichisch, *adj.* Austrian.
östlich, *adj.* eastern.
Ozean, *m.* (~e) ocean.

P

paar: *ein* ~ (a) few; — *adj.* matching.
Paar, *n.* (~e) pair.
Pacht, *f.* (~en) lease.
packen, *v.a.* seize; pack (up).
Packung, *f.* (~en) packing.
Packwagen, *m.* luggage-van.
Paddelboot, *n.* canoe.
Paket, *n.* (~e) parcel.
Palast, *n.* (~e) palace.
Palmsonntag, *m.* Palm-Sunday.
Panne, *f.* (~n) break-down; burst tire.
Pantoffel, *m.* (~) slipper.
Papa, *m.* (~s) papa.
Papagei, *m.* (~en) parrot.
Papier, *n.* (~e) paper.
Papierhandlung, *f.* stationers's (shop).
Papst, *m.* (~e) pope.
Paradies, *n.* (~e) paradies.
parallel, *adj.* parallel.
Parfüm, *n.* (~e) perfume; scent.
Park, *m.* (~e) park.
parken, *v. a.* & *n.* park.
Parkett, *n.* (~e) parquetry; stalls *pl.*
Parkmeter, *m.* parking-meter.
Parkplatz, parking-place.
Parlament, *n.* (~e) parliament.

parlamentarisch   214.   **Picknick**

parlamentarisch, *adj.* parliamentary.
Partei, *f.* (~en) party.
Parterre, *s.* (~s) ground-floor; pit.
Partitur, *f.* (~en) score.
Paß, *m.* (Pässe) pass(port).
Passagier, *m.* (~e) passenger.
passen, *v. a. & n.* fit; suit.
passieren, *v. n.* happen; come to pass.
Passion, *f.* (~en) passion.
Paßkontrolle, *f.* passport examination.
Pastille, *f.* (~n) tablet; lozenge.
Pastor, *m.* (~en) pastor.
Pate, *m., f.* (~n) godfather; godmother.
Patenkind, *n.* god-child.
Patent, *n.* (~e) patent.
Patient, *m.* (~en; ~en) patient.
Patriot, *m.* (~en; ~en) patriot.
Patrone, *f.* (~n) cartridge.
Pause, *f.* (~n) pause; interval.
Pavillon, *n.* (~s) pavilion.
Pech, *n.* (~e) bad luck.
Pein, *f.* pain; agony; torture.
peinlich, *adj.* painful; distressing.
Peitsche, *f.* (~n) whip.
Pelz, *m.* (~e) fur.
Pelzmantel, *m.* fur-coat.
Pendelverkehr, *m.* shuttle-service.
Penicillin, *n.* (~e) penicillin.
Pension, *f.* board; boarding-house; pension.
Pensionär, *m.* (~e) pensioner; boarder.
Pensionat, *n.* (~e) boarding-school.
Periode, *f.* (~n) period.

Perle, *f.* (~n) pearl, bead.
Person, *f.* (~en) person.
Personal, *n.* staff.
Personalausweis, *m.* identity card.
persönlich, *adj.* personal.
Persönlichkeit, *f.* (~en) personality.
pessimistisch, *adj.* pessimistic.
Petersilie, *f.* (~n) parsley.
Petroleum, *n.* petroleum.
Pfad, *m.* (~e) path.
Pfanne, *f.* (~n) frying pan.
Pfarrer, *m.* (~) clergyman.
Pfeffer, *m.* (~s) pepper.
Pfeife, *f.* (~en) pipe; whistle.
Pfeil, *m.* (~e) arrow.
Pferd, *m.* (~e) horse.
Pfingsten, *n. pl.* Whitsuntide.
Pfirsich, *m.* (~e) peach.
Pflanze, *f.* (~n) plant.
pflanzen, *v. a.* plant.
Pflanzung, *f.* (~en) plantation.
Pflaster, *n.* pavement; elastoplast.
Pflaume, *f.* (~n) plum.
Pflege, *f.* (~n) care; nursing.
pflegen*, *v. a.* nurse; *v. n.* be in the habit of; *(past)* used to.
Pflicht, *f.* (~en) duty.
Pflug, *m.* (~e) plow.
Pförtner, *m.* (~) porter.
Pfote, *f.* (~n) paw.
Phantasie, *f.* (~n) fancy.
phantastisch, *adj.* fantastic.
Phase, *f.* (~n) phase.
Philosophie, *f.* (~n) philosophy.
Photographie, *f.* (~n) photograph.
Phrase, *f.* (~n) sentence.
Physik, *f.* physics.
Picknick, (~e) picnic.

Pille   215.   **Probe**

Pille, *f.* (~n) pill.
Pilotenkabine, *f.* cockpit.
Pilz, *m.* (~e) mushroom; fungus.
Pinsel, *m.* (~) brush.
Pionier, *m.* (~e) pioneer.
Pistole, *f.* (~n) pistol.
plagen, *v. a.* torment; *v. n. sich ~* toil.
Plakat, *n.* (~e) poster.
Plan, *m.* (~e) plan.
planen, *v. a.* plan.
Planet, *m.* (~en; ~en) planet.
plastisch, *adj.* plastic.
Platin, *m.* platinum.
platt, *adj.* flat.
Platte, *f.* (~n) plate; platter.
Platz, *m.* (~e) place; square, space; seat; *~ nehmen* sit down.
plaudern, *v. n. & a.* chat.
plötzlich, *adv.* sudden(ly).
Pneumatik, *m.* (~s) pneumatics; pneumatic tyre.
pochen, *v. n.* knock.
Poesie, *f.* (~n) poetry; poem.
poetisch, *adj.* poetic.
Pol, *m.* (~e) pole.
Pole, *m.* (~n) Pole.
Police, *f.* (~n) policy.
Politik, *f.* (~) politic(s); policy.
politisch, *adj.* political.
Polizei, *f.* (~en) police; police department.
Polizeiwache, *f.* police-station.
Polizist, *m.* (~en; ~en) policeman.
polnisch, *adj.* Polish.
Polster, *m.* (~) cushion; bolster.
Pony, *m., n.* (~s) pony.
populär, *adj.* popular.
Porto, *n.* (~s) postage.
Porträt, *n.* (~s) portrait.
Portugiese, *m.* (~n); -in

f. (~nen) Portuguese.
portugiesisch, *adj.* Portuguese.
Porzellan, *n.* china.
positiv, *adj.* positive.
Posse, *f.* (~n) farce.
Post, *f.* (~en) post; post-office.
Postanweisung, *f.* money-order; postal-order.
Postkarte, *f.* postcard.
postlagernd, *adj.* to be called for.
Postschiff, *n.* mail-boat.
Pracht, *f.* splendour.
prächtig, prachtvoll, *adj.* splendid.
prahlen, *v. n.* boast.
praktisch, *adj.* practical.
Prämie, *f.* (~n) prize; premium.
Präposition, *f.* (~en) preposition.
präsentieren, *v. a.* present.
Präsident, *m.* (~en) president; chairman.
Praxis, *f.* practice.
predigen, *v. a.* preach.
Predigt, *f.* (~en) sermon.
Preis, *m.* (~e) price; prize.
Preisangabe, *f.* quotation.
preisen*, *v. a.* praise.
Preisliste, *f.* price-list.
Premierminister, *m.* premier; prime minister.
Presse, *f.* (~n) press.
pressen, *v. a.* press.
Preuße, *m.* (~n); -in *f.* (~nen) Prussian.
preußisch, *adj.* Prussian.
Priester, *m.* (~) priest.
Prinz, *m.* (~en; ~en) prince.
Prinzessin, *f.* (~nen) princess.
Prinzip, (~ien) principle.
Prinzipal, *m.* (~e) chief; master; head.
privat, *adj.* private.
Probe, *f.* (~n) test; trial;

probieren — **Rabatt**

sample; rehearsal.
probieren, *v. a.* try.
Problem, *n.* (~e) problem.
Produkt, *n.* (~e) product.
Produktion, *f.* (~en) production.
produzieren, *v. a.* produce.
Professor, *m.* (~en) professor.
Profil, *n.* (~e) profile.
Programm, *n.* (~e) program.
Project, *n.* (~e) project; scheme.
Projectil, *n.* (~e) projectile; missile.
Projectionsapparat, *m.*; **Projector,** *m.* (~en) projector.
Prosa, *f.* prose.
Prospekt, *m.* (~e) prospectus.
Protest, *m.* (~e) protest.
Protestant, *m.* (~en) Protestant.
protestieren, *v. n.* protest.
Protokoll, *n.* (~e) minutes *pl.*; protocol.
Proviant, *m.* provisions *pl.*
Provinz, *f.* (~en) province.
Prozent, *n.* (~e) per cent.
Prozeß, *m.* (-esse) process; law-suit.
prüfen, *v. a.* examine.
Prüfung, *f.* (~en) examination.
prügeln, *v. a.* beat.
Psalm, *m.* (~e) psalm.
Psychologie, *f.* psychology.
Publication, *f.* (~en) publication.
Publikum, *n.* public.
Puder, *m.* (~) powder.
Puls, *m.* (~e) pulse.
Pulver, *n.* (~) powder.
Pumpe, *f.* (~n) pump.
Punkt, *m.* (~e) point.
pünktlich, *adj.* punctual.
Puppe, *f.* (~n) doll; puppet.
purzeln, *v. n.* tumble.
putzen, *v. a.* polish.
Putzmacherin, *f.* (~nen) milliner.
Pyramide, *f.* (~n) pyramid.

Q

Quadrat, *n.* (~e) square.
Qual, *f.* (~en) torment.
quälen, *v. a.* torment; torture.
Qualification, *f.* (~en) qualification.
Qualität, *f.* (~en) quality.
Quantität, *f.* (~en) amount.
Quantum, *n.* (~s) quantity.
Quark, *m.* courd; cottage-cheese.
Quartett, *n.* (~e) quartet.
Quartier, *n.* (~e) quarter(s).
Quecksilber, *n.* mercury.
Quelle, *f.* (~n) spring; well.
quer, *adv.* across; — *adj.* cross; transverse.
Querschnitt, *m.* cross-section.
Querstraße, *f.* crossroad.
Quintett, *n.* (~en) quintette.
Quittung, *f.* (~en) receipt.
Quiz, *n.* (~e) quiz.
Quote, *f.* (~n) quota.
quotieren, *v. a.* quote (prices).

R

Rabatt, *m.* (~e) discount.

| Rabbiner | 217. | Reaktion |

Rabbiner, *m.* (~) rabbi.
Rache *f.* (~n) revenge.
Rachen *m.* (~) throat.
rächen, *v. a.* avenge.
Rad, *n.* (≈er) wheel.
Radar, *n.* (~s) radar.
radfahren*, *v. n.* ride a bicycle; cycle; bike.
Radfahrer, *m.* cyclist.
Radiergummi, *m.* India rubber; eraser.
Radieschen, *n.* (~) radish.
Radio, *n.* (~s) radio.
radioaktiv, *adj.* radioactive.
Radioapparat, *m.* wireless set; radio.
Radiogramm, *n.* radiogram.
Radiosendung, *f.* broadcast.
Radiotelegraphie, *f.* wireless telegraphy.
Radius, *m.* (-ien) radius.
Radreifen, *m.* tire; tyre.
Rahm, *m.* cream.
Rahmen, *m.* (~) frame(work)
Rakete, *f.* (~n) rocket.
Raketenantrieb, *m.* rocket-propulsion.
Raketenflugzeug *n.* jet-plane.
Rampenlicht, *n.* footlights *pl.*
Rand, *m.* (≈er) edge; margin.
Rang, *m.* (≈e) rank.
Rarität, *f.* (~en) rarity.
rasch, *adj.* quick, swift.
rasen, *v. n.* rage; rave; rush.
Rasen, *m.* (~) lawn; turf.
Rasierapparat, *m.* (safety) razor; shaver.
Rasiercreme *f.*, shaving-cream.
rasieren, *v. a. & n.* shave.
Rasierklinge, *f.* razor-blade.
Rasiermesser, *n.* razor.
Rasierseife, *f.* shaving stick; shaving-soap.
Rasse, *f.* (~) race; breed.
Rast, *f.* (~en) rest.
rasten, *v. n.* rest; repose.
Raststätte, *f.* motel.
Rat, *m.* (≈e) advice; council.
Rate, *f.* (~n) instalment.
raten*, *v. a.* advise; counsel; guess.
Rathaus, *n.* town hall.
ratifizieren, *v. a.* ratify.
Ratschlag, *m.* advice.
Rätsel, *n.* (~) riddle.
Ratsherr, *m.* alderman.
Ratte, *f.* (~n) rat.
Raub, *m.* (~e) robbery; prey.
Rauben, *v. a.* rob.
Räuber, *m.* (~) robber.
Raubtier, *n.* beast of prey.
Rauch, *m.* smoke.
rauchen, *v. a. & n.* smoke.
Raucherabteil, *n.* smoker; smoking compartment.
rauh, *adj.* rough; harsh.
Raum, *m.* (≈e) place; room, space.
Raumanzug, *m.* spacesuit.
räumen, *v. a.* clear; remove; evacuate.
Raumfahrer, *m.* space-man.
Raumkapsel *f.* space capsule.
Räumlichkeit, *f.* (~en) locality.
Raumschiff, *n.* spaceship.
Raupenschlepper, *m.* caterpillar-tractor.
Rausch, *m.* (~e) intoxication.
rauschen, *v. n.* rustle.
reagieren, *v. n.* react.
Reaktion, *f.* (~en) re-

Reaktor 218. **Reingewinn**

action.
Reaktor, *m.* (~en) reactor.
Rebe, *f.* (~n) vine.
Rebell, *m.* (~en; ~en) rebel.
Rechenautomat, *m.* computer.
Rechenschaft, *f.* account; ~ *ablegen von* account for.
rechnen, *v. a. & n.* count; calculate.
Rechnung, *f.* (~en) account; bill; invoice.
recht, *adj. & adv.* right; correct.
Recht, *n.* (~e) right; law; justice; ~ *haben* be right.
Rechteck, *n.* rectangle.
rechtfertigen, *v.a.* justify.
Rechtfertigung, *f.* justification.
rechtmäßig, *adj.* legal.
rechts, *adv.* on the right; to the right.
Rechtsanwalt, *m.* solicitor; barrister.
rechtzeitig, *adj.* timely; seasonable.
Redakteur, *m.* (~e) editor.
Rede, *f.* (~n) speech; *eine* ~ *halten* deliver a speech.
reden, *v. a. & n.* speak; talk.
Redner, *m.* (~) speaker; orator.
Referenz, *f.* (~en) reference.
Reform, *f.* (~en) reform.
Reformation, *f.* (~en) reformation.
reformieren, *v.a.* reform.
Regal, *n.* (~e) bookshelf.
Regel, *f.* (~n) rule.
regelmäßig, *adj.* regular.
regeln, *v. a.* regulate.
Regen, *m.* (~) rain.
Regenmantel, *m.* waterproof raincoat; mackintosh.
Regenschirm, *m.* umbrella.
regieren, *v. a. & n.* rule; govern.
Regierung, *f.* (~en) government; reign.
Regiment, *n.* (~e) regiment.
Regisseur, *m.* (~e) producer; stage manager.
Register, *n.* (~) record; register.
Registrierapparat, *m.* recorder.
Registrierkasse, *f.* cash-register.
regnen, *v. n.* rain.
regnerisch, *adj.* rainy.
regulieren, *v. a.* regulate.
reiben*, *v. a. & n.* rub.
Reibung, *f.* (~en) friction.
reich, *adj.* rich.
Reich, *n.* (~e) empire; kingdom.
reichen, *v.n.* reach; suffice; *v.a.* reach; hand; present.
reichlich, *adj.* plentiful.
Reichtum, *m.* (~̈er) wealth; richess.
reif, *adj.* ripe.
Reife, *f.* maturity.
Reifen, *m.* tire; tyre; hoop.
Reifenpanne, *f.* puncture.
Reihe, *f.* (~n) row; line; series.
Reihenfolge, *f.* succession.
Reim, *m.* (~e) rhyme.
rein, *adj.* clean; pure.
Reingewinn, *m.* net profit.

Reinheit — **Rindsbraten**

Reinheit, *f.* purity.
reinigen, *v. a.* clean.
Reinigungsmittel, *n.* detergent.
reinlich, *adj.* cleanly.
Reis, *m.* rice.
Reise, *f.* (~n) journey; voyage.
Reisebureau, *n.* travel(ing) agency; tourists' office.
Reiseführer, *m.* guide-book.
Reisegeschwindigkeit, *f.* cruising speed.
Reisegrammophon *n.* portable (record-player).
Reisehandbuch, *n.* guidebook.
reisen, *v. n.* travel.
Reisende, *m.; f.* (~n) traveller; passenger.
Reisepaß, *m.* passport.
Reisescheck, *m.* traveller's cheque.
reißen*, *v. a.* tear.
Reißverschluß, *m.* zipper; zip-fastener.
reiten*, ride.
Reiter, *m.* (~) horseman.
Reiz, *m.* (~e) attraction; grace; charm.
reizend, *adj.* charming.
Reklame, *f.* (~n) publicity; advertisement.
reklamieren, *v. a.* protest; claim.
Rekord, *m.* (~e) *(sport)* record.
Rektor, *m.* (~en) rector; headmaster.
Relais, *n.* (~) relay.
Relief, *n.* (~s) relief.
Religion, *f.* (~en) religion.
religiös, *adj.* religious.
Rennbahn, *f.* race-course.
rennen*, run; race.
Rennreiter, *m.* jockey.
Renntier, *n.* (~e) reindeer.

rentabel, *adj.* profitable.
Rente, *f.* (~n) pension.
reorganisieren, *v.a.* reorganize.
Reparatur, *f.* (~en) repair.
Reporter, *m.* reporter.
Republik, *f.* (~en) republic.
reservieren, *v. a.* reserve.
Residenz, *f.* (~en) residence.
Respect, *m.* (~e) respect.
Rest, *m.* (~e) rest; remainder.
Restaurant, *n.* (~s) restaurant.
Resultat, *n.* (~e) result; outcome.
retten, *v.a.* save.
Rettich, *m.* (~e) radish.
Rettungsboot, *n.* lifeboat.
Rettungsgürtel, *m.* lifebelt.
Reue, *f.* remorse; repentance.
Revolution, *f.* (~en) revolution.
Revolver, *m.* (~) revolver.
Rezept, *n.* (~e) prescription; receipe.
Rheumatismus, *m.* rheumatism.
Rhythmus, *m.* (-men) rhythm.
richten, *v. a.* direct; judge.
Richter, *m.* (~) judge.
richtig, *adj.* right; correct.
Richtung, *f.* (~en) direction.
riechen*, smell.
Riegel, *m.* (~) bolt.
Riese, *m.* (~n) giant.
riesig, *adj.* gigantic, huge.
Rind, *n.* (~er) cattle.
Rinde, *f.* (~n) bark.
Rindfleisch, *n.* beef.
Rindsbraten, *m.* roast beef.

Ring 220. **Rundreise**

Ring, *m.* (~e) circle; ring.
ringen*, *v. n.* fight; wrestle.
Ringkämpfer, *m.* wrestier.
rings, *adv.* around.
ringsum, ringsherum, *adv.* round about.
rinnen*, flow; leak.
Risiko, *n.* (~s) risk.
Riß, *m.* (Risse) rent; split.
Ritt, *m.* (~e) ride.
ritterlich, *adj.* chivarous.
Rock, *m.* (~e) skirt.
Rodel, *m.* (~) toboggan.
roh, *adj.* raw; rude.
Rohr, *n.* (~e) reed; tube; pipe.
Röhre, *f.* (~n) pipe, tube; valve.
Rolle, *f.* (~n) roller; pulley; *(theater)* part.
rollen, *v. a.* roll.
Roller, *m.* (~) scooter.
Rolltreppe, *f.* escalator.
Roman, *m.* (~e) novel.
romantisch, *adj.* romantic.
römisch, *adj.* Roman.
Röntgenaufnahme, *f.* X-ray picture; radiograph.
Röntgenbehandlung, *f.* X-ray treatment.
Röntgenstrahlen, *pl.* X-rays.
rosa, *adj.* pink.
Rose, *f.* (~n) rose.
Rosenkohl, *m.* Brussels sprouts *pl.*
Roß, *n.* (Rosse) horse.
Rost, *m.* rust.
Rostbraten, *m.* grill; roast joint.
rosten, *v. n.* rust.
rösten, *v.a. & n.* roast; toast; grill.
rot, *adj.* red.

Röte, *f.* (~n) blush.
Rübe, *f.* (~n) turnip; beetroot.
Rubin, *m.* (~e) ruby.
rücken, *v. n.* move; proceed; *v. a.* move; push.
Rücken, *m.* (~) back.
Rückfahrt, *f.* return journey.
Rückgrat, *n.* backbone; spine.
Rückkehr, *f.* return.
Rucksack, *m.* haversack, knapsack.
Rücksicht, *f.* regard; consideration.
rückständig, *adj.* backward.
rückwärts, *adv.* back(wards).
Rückzug, *m.* return, retreat.
Ruder, *n.* (~) oar.
rudern, *v. n.* row.
Ruf, *m.* (~e) call; cry; reputation.
rufen*, *v. n. & a.* call, cry.
Ruhe, *f.* (~n) rest.
ruhen, *v. n.* rest.
ruhig, *adj.* quiet.
Ruhm, *m.* fame; glory.
rühmen, *v. a.* praise; boast.
Rührei, *n.* scrambled eggs.
rühren, *v. a.* stir; touch.
Ruine, *f.* (~n) ruin.
ruinieren, *v. a.* ruin.
Rumpf, (~e) trunk; hull.
rund, *adj.* round; circular.
Rundfunk, *m.* broadcasting.
Rundfunkgerät, *n.* wireless set; radio.
Rundfunkstation, *f.* broadcasting station.
Rundfunkübertragung, *f.* broadcast.
Rundreise, *f.* circular tour; round trip.

Rundschau, *f.* review.
runzeln, *v. a.* frown; wrinkle.
Ruß, *m.* soot.
Russe, *m.* (~n) Russian.
Russin, *f.* (~nen) Russian.
russisch, *adj.* Russian.
rüsten, *v. a. & n.* arm.
rutschen, *v. n.* glide, slide.
rütteln, *v. a.* shake.

S

Saal, *m.* (Säle) hall; room.
Saat, *f.* (~en) seed(s); sowing.
Säbel, *m.* (~) sword; saber.
Sache, *f.* (~n) thing; case.
sächsisch, *adj.* Saxon.
Sachverständige, *m.* expert.
Sack, *m.* (~e) bag; sack.
säen, *v.a.* sow.
Saft, *m.* (~e) sap; juice.
saftig, *adj.* juicy.
Säge, *f.* (~n) saw.
sagen, *v.a.* say; tell.
Sahne, *f.* cream.
Saite, *f.* (~n) string.
Sakristei, *f.* (~en) vestry.
Salat, *m.* (~e) salad; lettuce.
Salbe, *f.* (~n) ointment.
Saldo, *m.* (-di) balance.
Salm, *m* (~e) salmon.
Salon, *m.* (~s) drawing-room.
Salz, *n.* (~e) salt.
salzen*, *v. a.* salt.
Samen, *m.* (~) seed.
sammeln, *v.a.* gather, collect, pluck.
Sammlung, *f.* (~en) collection; assembly.
Samstag, *m.* (~e) Saturday.

samt, *adv. & prep.* with.
sämtlich, *adj. & adv.* all; all together.
Sand, *m.* (~e) sand.
Sandale, *f.* (~n) sandal.
sanft, *adj.* soft; gentle.
Sang, *m.* (~e) song.
Sänger, *m.* (~) singer.
Sankt, *adj.* saint.
Sanktion, *f.* (~en) sanction.
Saphir, *m.* (~e) sapphire.
Sardelle, *f.* (~n) anchovy.
Sardine, *f.* (~n) sardine.
Sarg, *m.* (~e) coffin.
sarkastisch, *adj.* sarcastic.
Satellit, *m.* (~en; ~en) satellite.
Satire, *f.* (~n) satire.
satt, *adj.* satisfied.
Satz, *m.* (~e) sentence; leap; sediment; composition.
Satzung, *f.* (~en) statute.
sauber, *adj.* clean.
Sauce, *f.* (~n) sauce; gravy.
sauer, *adj.* sour.
saugen*, *v. a.* suck(le).
Säugling, *m.* (~e) baby; infant.
Säule, *f.* (~n) column.
Saum, *m.* (~e) seam, hem.
Säure, *f.* (~n) acid.
Schach, *n.* chess.
Schachbrett, *n.* chessboard.
Schachmatt, *n.* checkmate.
Schachtel, *f.* (~n) box.
Schädel, *m.* (~) skull.
Schaden, *m.* (~) damage, harm.
schaden, *v. n.* hurt, harm, damage.
Schadenersatz, *m.* indemnity.
schädlich, *adj.* injurious.

Schaf, *n.* (~e) sheep.
schaffen*, *v. a.* create; do; make.
Schaffner, *m.* (~) guard; conductor.
Schale, *f.* (~n) shell, peel; bowl; dish.
schälen, *v. a.* peel.
schallen, *v. n.* sound.
Schallplatte, *f.* (gramophone) record.
Schaltbrett, *n.* switch-board.
Schalter, *m.* (~) booking-office; ticket window; switch.
Schaltjahr, *n.* leap-year.
Scham, *f.* shame.
schämen, *sich* ~ be ashamed.
Schampun, *n.* (~s) shampoo.
schampunieren, *v. a.* shampoo.
Schande, *f.* (~n) shame; disgrace.
scharf, *adj.* sharp; keen.
scharfsinnig, *adj.* shrewd.
Scharlach, *n..* scarlet.
Schatten, *m.* (~) shade.
schattig, *adj.* shady.
Schatz, *m.* (~e) treasure.
schätzen, *v. a.* value; esteem.
Schau, *f.* (~en) show; display.
schaudern, *v. n.* shudder.
schauen, *v. a. & n.* look (at); see; behold.
Schauer, *m.* (~) shower, thrill; awe.
Schaufel, *f.* (~n) spade.
Schaufenster, *n.* shop-window.
schaukeln, *v.a.& n.* swing, rock.
Schaum, *m.* foam.
schäumen, *v. n.* foam.
Schaumgummi, *m.* foam-rubber.
Schauplatz, *m.* scene.

Schauspiel, *n.* play.
Schauspieler, *m.*; ~in *f.* actor; actress.
Scheck, *m.* (~s) cheque.
Scheckbuch, *n.* cheque-book.
Scheibe, *f.* (~n) pane; slice; disk.
scheiden*, *v. a. & n.* separate; divorce; *sich ~ von* divorce sy.
Scheidung, *f.* (~en) divorce, separation.
Schein, *m.* (~e) light, appearance.
scheinen*, *v.n.* appear; seem; look.
Scheitel, *m.* (~) crown; parting.
scheitern, *v.n.* founder; fail; miscarry.
schelten*, *v. a. & n.* scold.
schenken, *v. a.* give; present.
Schenkwirt, *m.* publican.
Schere, *f.* (~n) scissors *pl.*
Scherz, *m.* (~e) joke.
scheu, *adj.* shy.
scheuern, *v.a.* scour.
Scheune, *f.* (~n) barn.
scheußlich, *adj.* hideous; abominable.
Schi, *m.* (~er) ski; ~ *laufen* ski.
Schicht, *f.* (~en) shift; layer.
schicken, *v.a.* send.
schicklich, *adj.* fit, becoming.
Schicksal, *n.* (~e) fate; destiny.
schieben*, *v. a.* push.
Schiedsrichter, *m.* umpire; referee.
schief, *adj.* oblique.
schielen, *v.n.* squint.
Schiene, *f.* (~n) rail.
schießen*, *v. n.* shoot.
Schießpulver, *n.* gunpowder.
Schießscheibe, *f.* target.

Schiff, *n.* (~e) ship; vessel.
Schiffahrt, *f.* (~en) navigation.
schiffbar, *adj.* navigable.
Schiffbau, *m.* shipbuilding.
Schiffer, *m.* (~) sailor; seaman.
Schiffsmannschaft, *f.* crew.
Schiffszug, *m.* boat-train.
Schild¹, *n.* (~er) sign(board).
Schild², *m.* (~e) shield.
schildern, *v. a.* describe.
Schilderung, *f.* (~en) description.
Schildkrötensuppe, *f.* turtle-soup.
schimmern, *v. n.* glitter.
schimpfen, *v.a. & n.* abuse, insult.
schinden*, *v.a.* skin; *fig.* vex; harass.
Schinken, *m.* (~) ham.
Schirm, *m.* (~e) umbrella; screen.
Schlacht, *f.* (~en) battle.
schlachten, *v. a.* slaughter; slay.
Schlachtfeld, *n.* (battle)field.
Schlaf, *m.* sleep.
Schlafanzug, *m.* pyjamas *pl.*
Schläfe, *f.* (~n) temple.
schlafen*, *v. n.* sleep.
Schlafkoje, *f.* bunk.
Schlafmittel, *n.* sleeping-pill.
schläfrig, *adj.;* ~ *sein* be sleepy.
Schlafrock, *m.* dressing-gown.
Schlafsack *m.* sleepingbag.
Schlafwagen, *m.* sleeping-car.
Schlafzimmer, *n.* bedroom.
Schlag, *m.* (⸚e) blow; apoplexy.
Schlagbaum, *m.* turnpike.
schlagen*, *v.n.* strike, beat; *sich* ~ fight; *v.a.* beat, strike; knock down.
Schlager, *m.* (~) hit; best-seller.
Schläger, *m.* (~) racket; bat.
Schlagsahne *f.* whipped cream.
Schlagwort, *n.* catchword.
Schlamm, *m.* mud; mire.
Schlange, *f.* (~n) serpent; queue; ~ *stehen* queue up.
schlank, *adj.* slim.
schlau, *adj.* clever, sly.
schlecht, *adj.* bad; wicked.
schleichen*, *v. n.* creep.
Schleife, *f.* (~n) loop; bow.
schleifen¹, *v. n. & a.* drag.
schleifen²*, *v.a.* grind; sharpen.
Schleim, *m.* mucus.
Schleppe, *f.* (~n) train.
schleppen, *v.a.* drag, tow.
Schlepper, *m.* (~) tug(boat).
schleunig, *adj.* quick; speedy.
schlicht, *adj.* simple.
schließen*, *v.a.* close; shut; conclude.
schließlich, *adj.* final; — *adv.* eventually.
schlimm, *adj.* bad.
Schlitten, *m.* (~) sledge.
Schlittschuh, *m.* skate; ~ *laufen* skate.
Schloß, *n.* (-össer) castle; lock.
Schlosser, *m.* (~) locksmith.

Schlucht | **schrauben**

Schlucht, *f.* (~en) gorge; ravine.
schluchzen, *v. n.* sob.
schlüpfen, *v. n.* slip.
Schlupfwinkel, *m.* hiding-place.
Schluß, *m.* (Schlüsse) end; close; conclusion.
Schlüssel, *m.* (~) key; *music)* clef.
Schlüsselbein, *n.* collar-bone.
schmachten, *v.n.* languish.
schmal, *adj.* narrow.
Schmalfilm, *m.* narrow film.
Schmalz, *n.* lard; dripping.
schmecken, *v. a.* taste.
schmeicheln, *v.n.* flatter.
schmeißen, *v. a.* throw.
schmelzen, *v. n.* melt.
Schmerz, *m.* (~en) pain.
schmerzlich, *adj.* painful.
Schmetterling, *m.* (~e) butterfly.
Schmied, *m.* (~e) blacksmith.
schmieren, *v. a.* spread; grease.
Schminke, *f.* (~n) make-up.
schmoren, *v. a.* & *n.* stew; roast.
Schmuck, *m.* (~e) jewel.
schmücken, *v.a.* adorn; decorate.
schmuggeln, *v. a.* & *n.* smuggle.
Schmutz, *m.* dirt.
schmutzig, *adj.* dirty.
Schnabel, *m.* (~) beak, bill.
Schnaps, *m.* (~e) brandy.
Schnecke, *f.* (~n) snail.
Schnee, *m.* snow.
Schneeball, *m.* snow-ball.
Schneekette, *f.* non-skid chain (motor-car).
Schneeschuhlaufen, *n.* skiing.
schneiden*, *v.a.* cut; carve.
Schneider, *m.* (~) tailor.
Schneiderin, *f.* (~nen) dressmaker.
schneien, *v. n.* snow.
schnell, *adj.* fast.
Schnellstraße, *f.* speedway.
Schnellzug, *m.* express (train).
Schnitt, *m.* (~e) cut.
Schnitte, *f.* (~n) slice; steak.
Schnittmuster, *n.* pattern.
Schnitzel, *n.* (~) cutlet.
Schnupfen, *m.* (~) cold (in the head).
Schnur, *f.* (~e) string, cord, rope.
Schnurrbart, *m.* moustache.
Schokolade, *f.* chocolate.
schon, *adv.* already.
schön, *adj.* fine, fair.
Schönheit, *f.* (~en) beauty.
Schönheitspflege, *f.* cosmetic, beauty culture.
schöpfen, *v.a.* draw (water); ladle.
Schöpfer, *m.* (~) creator.
Schoß, *m.* (~e) lap.
Schote, *f.* (~n) pod, husk; ~n *pl.* green peas.
Schotte, *m.* (~n) Scotsman.
schottisch, *adj.* scottish.
schräg, *adj.* oblique.
Schrank, *m.* (~e) cupboard; wardrobe; *eingebauter* ~ built-in wardrobe.
Schranke, *f.* (~n) bar(rier); limit; bound.
Schraube, *f.* (~n) screw.
schrauben, *v. a.* & *n.*

Schraubenschlüssel screw.

Schraubenschlüssel, *m.* spanner.

Schraubenzieher, *m.* screw-driver.

Schrecken, *m.* (~) fright.

schrecklich, *adj.* terrible.

Schrei, *m.* (~e) cry.

schreiben*, *v. a. & n.* write.

Schreiber, *m.* (~) writer; clerk.

Schreibmaschine, *f.* typewriter.

Schreibtisch, *m.* (writing) desk.

Schreibwaren, *pl.* stationary.

schreien*, *v. n.* cry; scream.

schreiten*, *v. n.* step; go; proceed.

Schrift, *f.* (~en) writing; script.

schriftlich, *adj. & adv.* written; in writing.

Schriftsteller, *m.* (~) author.

Schriftstück, *n.* document.

Schritt, *m.* (~e) step.

Schrittmacher, *m.* pace-maker.

schrumpfen, *v. n.* shrink.

Schublade, *f.* (~n) drawer.

schüchtern, *adj.* shy; timid.

Schuh, *m.* (~e) shoe.

Schuhanzieher, *m.* shoe-horn.

Schuhmacher, *m.* shoe-maker; boot-maker.

Schuhnummer, *f.* size (in shoes); *ich habe* ~ *39* I take size 39 in shoes.

Schuhputzer, *m.* shoe-black.

Schulaufgabe, *f.* homework, prep.

Schulbuch, *n.* schoolbook.

Schuld, *f.* (~en) debt; guilt; *wer ist schuld?* whose fault is it?

schulden, *v. a.* owe.

schuldig, *adj.* guilty; owing, due, to be blamed; *sich ~ bekennen* plead guilty; *~ sein* owe (sy).

Schuldner, *m.* (~) debtor.

Schuldschein, *m.* promissory note; IOU.

Schule, *f.* (~n) school.

Schüler, *m.* (~) school-boy, school-girl; pupil, scholar.

Schuljahr, *n.* scholastic year.

Schulter, *f.* (~n) shoulder.

Schuß, *m.* (Schüsse) shot.

Schußwaffe, *f.* fire-arm.

Schuster, *m.* (~) shoemaker.

schütteln, *v. a.* shake.

schütten, *v. a.* pour.

Schutz, *m.* shelter; protection; defence.

Schutzbrille, *f.* goggles; sun-glasses.

schützen, *v. a.* protect; defend.

Schutzherrschaft, *f.* protectorate.

Schutzmann, *m.* policeman.

schwach, *adj.* weak.

Schwäche, *f.* (~n) weakness.

schwächen, *v. a.* weaken.

Schwager, *m.* (~) brother-in-law.

Schwägerin, *f.* (~nen) sister-in-law.

Schwalbe, *f.* (~n swallow.

Schwamm, *m.* (~e) sponge; mushroom.

Schwan, m. (⁓e) swan.
Schwanger, adj. pregnant.
schwanken, v. n. stagger.
Schwanz, m. (⁓e) tail.
Schwarm, m. swarm.
schwärmen, v. n. swarm; be enthusiastic.
schwarz, adj. black.
schwatzen, v.n. & a. chat; gossip.
schweben, v. n. hang; hover; soar.
Schwede, m. (⁓n; ⁓n) Swede.
Schwedin, f. (⁓nen) Swede.
schwedisch, adj. Swedish.
Schweif, m. (⁓e) tail.
schweigen*, v.a. be silent.
Schwein, n. (⁓e) pig; swine.
Schweinebraten, m. roast-pork.
Schweinefleisch, n. pork.
Schweiß, m. sweat; perspiration.
Schweizer, m. (⁓); ⁓in f. (⁓nen) Swiss.
schweizerisch, adj. Swiss.
Schwelle, f. (⁓n) threshold; sleeper.
schwellen*, v.n. swell.
schwenken, v.a. swing; rinse.
schwer, adj. heavy; difficult.
Schwere, f. weight; gravity.
schwerfällig, adj. clumsy; slow.
schwerlich, adj. hardly; scarcely.
Schwerpunkt, m. centre of gravity.
Schwert, n. (⁓er) sword.
Schwester, f. (⁓n) sister; nurse.
Schwiegermutter, f. mother-in-law.
Schwiegersohn, m. son-in-law.
Schwiegertochter, f. daughter-in-law.
Schwiegervater, m. father-in-law.
schwierig, adj. hard; difficult.
Schwierigkeit, f. (⁓en) difficulty.
Schwimmanstalt, f.; Schwimmbad, n. swimming-bath.
schwimmen*, v. n. swim.
Schwindel, m. (⁓) giddiness; swindle.
schwinden*, v. n. disappear; diminish.
Schwindler, m. (⁓) swindler.
Schwingung, f. (⁓en) swinging; vibration; oscillation.
schwitzen, v. n. sweat; perspire.
schwören*, v. a. & n. swear; take an oath.
Schwur, m. (⁓e) oath.
Schwurgericht, n. jury
sechs, adj. six.
sechste, adj. sixth.
sechzehn, adj. sixteen.
sechzig, adj. sixty.
See¹, m. (⁓n) lake.
See², f. (⁓n) sea.
Seebad, n. seaside resort.
Seekrankheit, f. sea sickness.
Seele, f. (⁓n) soul.
Seemann, m. seeman; mariner; sailor.
Seereise, f. voyage.
Seeschaden, m. average; loss suffered at sea.
Segel, n. (⁓) sail.
Segelflugzeug, n. glider.
segeln, v. n. sail.
segnen, v. a. bless.
sehen*, v. a. & n. see; look at.
Sehenswürdigkeit, f. sights pl.

Sehne, *f.* (~n) sinew.
Sehnsucht, *f.* longing.
sehr, *adj.* very.
Seide, *f.* (~n) silk.
Seife, *f.* (~n) soap.
Seil, *n.* (~e) rope.
Seilbahn, *f.* cable-railway, funicular railway.
sein[1], *pron.* sein, seine, seines his, its, his.
sein*[2], *v. n.* be; exist.
Sein, *n.* being; existence.
seinige, *pron. der, die, das* ~ his (own).
seit, *prep.* since; for; ~ wann? since when; — *conj.* since.
seitdem, *adv.* since.
Seite, *f.* (~n) side; page.
Seitenschiff, *n.* aisle.
seither, *adv.* since then.
seitwärts, *adv.* aside; sideways.
Sekretär, *m.* (~e) secretary.
Sekt, *m.* (~e) champagne.
Sekunde, *f.* (~n) second.
selber, selbst *adj.* self; — *adv.* even.
selbständig, *adj.* independent.
Selbstbedienung, *f.* self-service.
Selbstbeherrschung, *f.* selfcontrol.
Selbstfahrer, *m.* ownerdriver.
Selbstfertigung, *f.* automation.
Selbstmord, *m.* suicide.
Selbstsucht, *f.* selfishness; egoism.
selbstverständlich, *adj.* of course.
selig, *adj.* blessed.
Sellerie, *f.* celery.
selten, *adj.* rare; — *adv.* rarely; seldom.
seltsam, *adj.* strange.
Seminar, *n.* (~e) training college.
Semmel, *f.* (~n) roll.
Senat, *m.* (~e) senate.
Senator, *m.* (~en) senator.
senden*, *v. a.* send; broadcast; transmit.
Sender, *m.* (~) sender; transmitter; broadcasting station.
Sendung, *f.* (~en) consignment; transmission.
Senf, *m.* mustard.
senken, *v. a.* lower; sich ~ sink.
senkrecht, *adj.* vertical.
September, *m.* (~) September.
Septime, *f.* seventh (music).
Serie, *f.* (~n) serial.
servieren, *v. a. & n.* serve.
Serviette, *f.* (~n) napkin.
Sessel, *m.* (~) seat.
setzen, *v. a.* set; place; put; lay.
seufzen, *v. a. & n.* sigh.
Seufzer, *m.* (~) sigh.
sexuell, *adj.* sexual.
sich, *pron.* himself, herself, itself; themselves; each other; one another.
sicher, *adj.* safe; sure; certain.
Sicherheit, *f.* safety; security.
Sicht, *f.* sight; auf ~ at sight.
sichtbar, sichtlich, *adj.* visible.
Sichtvermerk, *n.* visa.
sie, *pron.* she, her, it; they, them; *Sie* you.
sieben[1], *adj.* seven.
sieben[2], *v. a.* strain.
siebente, *adj.* seventh.
siebzehn, *adj.* seventeen.
siebzig, *adj.* seventy.

Siedler — **spannen**

Siedler, *m.* (∼) settler.
Sieg, *m.* (∼e) victory.
Siegel, *m.* (∼) seal.
siegen, *v. n.* conquer.
Sieger, *m.* (∼); ∼in *f.*; (∼nen) victor; conqueror.
Signal, *n.* (∼e) signal.
Silbe, *f.* (∼n) syllable.
Silber, *n.* silver.
Silvesterabend, *m.* New Year's Eve.
singen*, *v. a.* sing.
sinken*, *v. n.* sink.
Sinn, *m.* (∼e) mind; sense.
sinnen*, *v. a.* meditate.
sinnlich, *adj.* sensual.
Sitte, *f.* (∼n) custom.
Sittlich, *adj.* moral.
Sitz, *m.* (∼e) seat.
sitzen*, *v. a.* sit; fit (of clothes).
Sitzung, *f.* (∼en) sitting.
Skala, *f.* (∼len) *(music)* gamut; scale.
Skandal, *m.* (∼e) scandal.
Skelett, *n.* (∼e) skeleton.
Skizze, *f.* (∼n) sketch.
Smaragd, *m.* (∼e) emerald.
Smoking, *m.* (∼s) dinner-jacket.
so, *adv.* so; thus; therefore; ∼ ... *wie* as...as; *nicht* ∼ *wie* not so ... as; ∼ *bald als* as soon as.
sobald, *conj.* as soon as.
Socke, *f.* (∼n) sock(s).
Sodawasser, *n.* soda-water.
Sodbrennen, *n.* heartburn.
Sofa, *n.* (∼s) couch; sofa.
sofern, *conj.* as far as; provided that.
sogar, *adv.* even.
Sohle, *f.* (∼n) sole.
Sohn, *m.* (∼e) son.
Soldat, *m.* (∼en; ∼en) soldier.
Solist, *m.* (∼en, ∼en) soloist; solo singer.
Soll, *n.* debit; target.
sollen*, *v. a.* shall; to be to; be obliged (to).
Sommer, *m.* (∼) summer.
Sommerfrische, *f.* summer resort.
Sommersprosse, *f.* freckle.
Sonate, *f.* (∼n) sonata.
sonderbar, *adj.* strange.
Sonnabend, *m.* Saturday.
Sonne, *f.* (∼n) sun.
Sonnenaufgang, *m.* sunrise.
Sonnenschein, *m.* sunshine.
Sonnenschirm, *m.* sunshade; parasol.
Sonnenstich, *m.* sunstroke.
Sonnenuntergang, *m.* sunset.
sonnig, *adj.* sunny.
Sonntag, *m.* Sunday.
sonst, *conj.* & *adv.* else; ∼ *noch etwas?* anything else?
sonstig, *adv.* other.
Sopran, *m.* (∼e) soprano.
Sorge, *f.* (∼n) care.
sorgen, *v. n.* (take) care; care (about).
Sorte, *f.* (∼n) sort.
soweit, *conj.* as far as; — *adv.* so far.
Sowjet, *m.* (∼s) soviet.
sowohl, *conj.* ∼ *als* as well as.
sozial, *adj.* social.
Sozialdemokrat, *m.* (∼en) social democrat.
spähen, *v. a.* & *n.* spy.
Spalte, *f.* (∼n) cleft; crack.
Spanier, *m.* (∼); ∼in *f.* (∼nen) Spaniard.
spanisch, *adj.* Spanish.
spannen, *v. a.* stretch.

Spannung 229. **Spritze**

Spannung, *f.* (~en) tension; suspense.
sparen, *v.a.* save (up).
Spargel, *m.* asparagus.
Sparkasse, *f.* savings-bank.
sparsam, *adj.* economical.
Spaß, *m.* (⁓e) joke; fun.
spaßhaft, *adj.* funny.
spät, *adj. & adv.* late.
Spaten, *m.* (~) spade.
später, *adv.* later (on).
spätestens, *adv.* at the latest.
Spatz, *m.* (~en) sparrow.
Spaziergang, *m.* walk.
Speck, *m.* bacon.
Spediteur, *m.* (~e) forwarding agent.
Speerwerfen, *n. (sport)* throwing the javelin.
speien, *v. a. & n.* spit.
Speise, *f.* (~n) food.
Speiseeis, *n.* ice-cream.
Speisekammer, *f.* pantry.
Speisekarte, *f.* bill of fare.
speisen, *v. n.* dine; eat.
Speisesaal, *m.* dining-room.
Speisewagen, *m.* restaurant-car.
Speisezimmer, *n.* dining-room.
spenden, *v. a.* contribute.
Sperling, *m.* (~e) sparrow.
Sperrsitz, *m.* stall(s).
Spesen, *pl.* expenses.
Spezialarzt, *m.* specialist.
Spezialist, *m.* (~en; ~en) specialist.
Spezialität, *f.* (~en) speciality.
speziell, *adj.* special.
Spiegel, *m.* (~) mirror; looking-glass.
Spiegelei, *n.* fried egg.

Spiel, *n.* (~e) play; game.
spielen, *v. a. & n.* play; gamble; act; perform.
Spielkarte, *f.* playing-card(s).
Spielleiter, *m.* stage-manager.
Spielplatz, *m.* playground.
Spielsache, *f.;* **Spielzeug** *n.* plaything; toy.
Spinat, *m.* spinach.
Spinne, *m.* (~n) spider.
spinnen*, *v. a. & n.* spin.
Spion, *m.* (~e) spy.
Spirituosen, *pl.* spirits.
Spiritus, *m.* methylated spirits.
Spital, *n.* (⁓er) hospital.
Spitze, *f.* (~n) point; top; tip; lace.
Spitzname, *m.* nickname.
splitterfrei, *adj.* shatter-proof.
Sport, *m.* (~e) sport; ~ *treiben* go in for sports.
sportlich, *adj.* sportsmanlike.
spotten, *v. a.* mock; scoff.
Sprache, *f.* (~n) language.
sprechen*, *v. a. & n.* speak; talk.
Sprecher, *m.* spokesman; speaker.
Sprechstunde, *f.* consultation hour.(s).
Sprechzimmer, *n.* consulting room; surgery.
sprengen, *v.a.* burst; sprinkle.
Sprengstoff, *m.* explosive.
Sprichwort, *n.* (⁓er) proverb.
Springbrunnen, *m.* fountain.
springen*, *v.n.* spring; jump.
Spritze, *f.* (~n) syringe; injection; fire-engine.

spritzen	staunen

spritzen, *v. a. & n.* splash; spurt; sprinkle.
Sproß, *m.* (Sprossen) shoot; sprout; offspring.
Sprosse, *f.* (~n) rung.
Spruch, *m.* (≈e) sentence; saying.
sprudeln, *v. n.* bubble.
Sprung, *m.* (≈e) jump; leap.
Sprungbrett, *n.* springboard.
Sprungschanze, *f.* ski-jump.
spülen, *v. a. & n.* rinse.
Spur, *f.* (~en) trace; track; clue.
spüren, *v. a. & n.* feel; trace; smell; perceive.
Staat, *m.* (~en) state.
staatenlos, *adj.* without nationality.
staatlich, *adj.* state.
Staatsangehörigkeit, *f.* nationality; citizenship.
Staatsanwalt, *m.* public prosecutor.
Staatsbeamter, *m.* civil servant.
Staatsbürger, *m.* citizen.
Staatsmann, *m.* statesman.
Staatsminister, *m.* Secretary of State; Minister of State.
Staatssekretär, *m.* Secretary of State.
Staatswirtschaft, *f.* political economy.
Stab, *m.* (≈e) staff; stick; rod.
Stabhochsprung, *m.* pole-jump.
Stachel, *m.* (~) prickle, prick; thorn.
Stadion, *n.* (sport) stadium.
Stadt, *f.* (≈e) town; city.
Stadtbahn, *f.* metropolitan railway.

städtisch, *adj.* municipal of a town.
Staffelei, *f.* (~n) easel.
Stahl, *m.* (~e) steel.
stählen, *v. a.* steel; temper.
Stall, *m.* (≈e) stable.
Stamm, *m.* (≈e) stem; trunk (of tree); tribe; race.
Stammbaum, *m.* family tree; pedigree.
stampfen, *v. a. & n.* trample.
Stand, *m.* (≈e) stand; condition; rank.
Ständchen, *n.* (~) serenade.
Standesamt, *n.* registrar's office.
Standesbeamte, *m.* registrar.
standhaft, *adj.* firm.
ständig, *adj.* constant; permanent.
Standpunkt, *f.* point of view.
Stange, *f.* (~n) pile; rod; bar.
Staniol, *n.* (~e) tinfoil.
stark, *adj.* strong.
stärken, *v. a.* strengthen.
starr, *adj.* stiff; rigid.
Station, *f.* (~en) station.
Statistik, *f.* statistics.
statistisch, *adj.* statistical.
statt *adv.* instead.
Statt, *f.* place; stead.
Stätte, *f.* place.
stattfinden, *v.a.* take place.
Statthalter, *m.* (~s) governor.
stattlich, *adj.* grand; stately.
Statue, *f.* (~n) statue.
Staub, *m.* dust.
Staubsauger, *m.* vacuum-cleaner.
staunen, *v.n.* be

stechen*, *v. a. & n.* sting, prick.
Steckdose, *f.* wall-socket.
stecken*, *v. a.* put; stick; pin.
Steckenpferd, *n.* hobby(-horse).
Stecknadel, *f.* pin.
stehen*, *v. n.* stand, suit (sg).
stehenbleiben, *v. n.* stop.
stehlen*, *v. a.* steal; rob.
steif, *adj.* stiff; rigid.
Steigbügel, *m.* stirrup.
steigen*, *v. n.* ascend; mount, go up.
steigern, *v. a.* raise; increase.
steil, *adj.* steep.
Stein, *m.* (~e) stone.
steinern, *adj.* (of) stone; stony.
Stelldichein, *n.* rendezvous.
Stelle, *f.* (~n) place; situation; opening.
stellen, *v. a.* place; put; set.
Stellung, *f.* (~en) place; position; posture.
Stellvertreter, *s.* substitute; representative.
Stempel, *m.* (~) stamp; seal.
Stengel, *m.* (~) stalk.
Stenograph, *m.* (~en; ~en) stenographer.
Stenographie, *f.* (~) stenography; shorthand.
Stenotypistin, *f.* stenotypist; shorthand-typist.
sterben*, *v. n.* die.
Sterblichkeit, *f.* mortality.
steril, *adj.* sterile.
sterilisieren, *v. a.* sterilize.
Stern, *m.* (~e) star.
Sternwarte, *f.* observatory.
stet, *adj.* fixed; stable.
stetig, *adj.* continual.
stets, *adv.* always; constantly.
Steuer,[1] *n.* (~) helm; rudder; steering-wheel.
Steuer[2] *f.* (~n) tax.
steuern, *v. a.* steer; control.
Steuerrad, *n.* steering-wheel.
Steuerung, *f.* (~en) steering gear; control.
Stich, *m.* (~e) prick; sting; stitch.
stichhaltig, *adj.* valid.
Stichwort, *n.* cue; catchword.
sticken, *v. a.* embroider.
Stickerei, *f.* (~en) embroidery.
Stiefel, *m.* (~) bo
Stiefmutter, *f.* stepmother.
Stiefvater, *m.* stepfather.
Stiege, *f.* (~n) stairs *pl.*; staircase.
Stiel, *m.* (~e) handle.
Stier, *m.* (~e) bull.
stiften, *v. a.* found.
Stil, *m.* (~e) style.
still, *adj.* still; silent.
stillen, *v. a.* quench; appease; quel.
Stimme, *f.* (~n) voice; vote; part.
stimmen, *v. n.* agree; vote; *v. a.* tune.
Stimmenmehrheit, *f.* majority (of votes).
Stimmrecht, *n.* suffrage.
Stimmung, *f.* (~en) humour; disposition; atmosphere.
stinken*, *v. n.* stink.
Stirn, *f.* (~en) forehead.
Stock, *m.* (~e) stick.
stocken, *v. n.* stop; stagnate.
Stockwerk, *n.* floor.

Stoff, *m.* (~e) matter; stuff; material.
stöhnen, *v. a. & n.* groan.
stolpern, *v.n.* stumble.
Stolz, *m.* pride.
stolz, *adj.* proud.
stopfen, *v. a.* stuff; fill; darn.
Stöpsel, *m.* (~) stopper.
Storch, *m.* (~e) stork.
stören, *v. a.* disturb; trouble.
Stoß, *m.* (~e) shock; blow; jolt.
stoßen*, *v. a.* push; thrust; strike; jostle.
strafbar, *adj.* punishable.
Strafe, *f.* (~n) punishment; fine.
strafen, *v. a.* punish; fine.
Strahl, *m.* (~en) ray; jet.
strahlen, *v. a. & n.* radiate; shine; beam (with).
Strahlturbine, *f.* turbo-jet (engine).
Strand, *m.* (~e) beach.
Straße, *f.* (~n) street.
Straßenbahn, *f.* tram(way).
Straßenübergang, *m.* crossing.
Strauß¹, *m.* (~e) bunch; nosegay; fight; combat.
Strauß², *m.* (~e) ostrich.
streben, *v. n.* strive (for).
Strecke, *f.* (~n) distance; line.
strecken, *v. a.* stretch; extend.
Streich, *m.* (~e) stroke.
streicheln, *v. a.* stroke; caress.
streichen*, *v. a.* paint; spread.
Streichholz, *n.* match.
Streichinstrument, *n.* string instrument.
Streifen, *m.* (~) strip; stripe.

treik, *m.* (~s) strike.
streiken, *v. n.* strike.
Streit, *m.* (~igkeiten) quarrel; fight.
streiten*, *v. n.* quarrel; fight.
streng, *adj.* severe.
Strich, *m.* (~e) stroke, line.
Strick, *m.* (~e) rope.
stricken, *v. a. & n.* knit.
Striptease, *n.* strip-tease.
Stroh, *n.* straw.
Strom, *m.* (~e) river; current.
stromabwärts, *adv.* downstream.
stromaufwärts, *adv.* upstream.
strömen, *v. n.* flow; stream.
Stromkreis, *m.* circuit.
Strömung, *f.* current.
Strumpf, *m.* (~e) stocking.
Strumpfband, *n.* garter.
Strumpfhalter, *m.* suspender(s).
Stube, *f.* (~n) room.
Stück, *n.* (~e) piece.
Student, *m.* (~en; ~en) student.
Studie, *f.* (~n) study.
studieren, *v. a. & n.* study.
Studium, *n.* (-ien) study.
Stufe, *f.* (~n) step, degree.
Stuhl, *m.* (~e) chair.
stumm, *adj.* dumb.
Stunde, *f.* (~n) hour; lesson.
Stundenplan, *m.* time-table.
Sturm, *m.* (~e) storm.
stürmen, *v.n.* rage; storm; *v. a.* take by storm.
Sturz, *m.* (~e) fall; decline; slump.
stürzen, *v. n.* fall; tumble; rush; *v. a.* overthrow.
Sturzflug, *m.* nose-dive.
Sturzhelm, *m.* crash-helmet.
Stütze, *f.* (~n) support;

stutzen | **Tätlichkeit**

prop.
stutzen, *v. a.* bob; clip; trim.
Subskribent, *m.* (~en) subscriber.
Substanz, *f.* (~en) substance; matter.
suchen, *v.a.* seek; look for.
Süd(en) *m.* south.
Südfrüchte, *pl.* tropical fruit.
südlich, *adj.* southern.
Südwest(en), *m.* southwest.
Sühne, *f.* atonement.
Summe, *f.* (~n) sum; amount.
summen, *v. n.* buzz; hum.
Sumpf, *m.* (≈e) marsh; mire.
Sünde, *f.* (~n) sin.
Suppe, *f.* (~n) soup.
Suppenlöffel, *m.* soupspoon.
Suppenschüssel, *f.* tureen.
süß, *adj.* sweet.
Süßigkeiten, *pl.* sweets.
Süßwasser, *n.* freshwater.
Symbol, *n.* (~e) symbol.
symmetrisch, *adj.* symmetrical.
Sympathie, *f.* sympathy.
Symphonie, *f.* (~n) symphony.
synchronisieren, *v. a.* synchronize; dub.
synthetisch, *adj.* synthetic.
System, *n.* (~e) system.
Szene, *f.* (~n) scene; setup.

T

Tabak, *m.* (~e) tobacco.
Tabakhändler, *m.* tobacconist.
Tabelle, *f.* (~n) table; index.
tadeln, *v. a.* blame.
Tafel, *f.* (~n) table; board; slate.
Tag, *m.* (~e) day; *guten* ~ good morning.
Tageblatt, *n.* daily paper.
Tagelohn, *n.* daily wages *pl.*
Tagesbericht, *m.* bulletin.
Tageslicht, *n.* daylight.
Tagesordnung, *f.* agenda.
täglich, *adj.* daily.
Taille, *f.* (~n) waist.
Takt, *m.* (~e) measure; time; *fig.* tact.
Tal, *n.* (≈er) valley.
Talar, *m.* (~e) gown; cassock.
Talent, *n.* (~e) talent.
Tank, *m.* (~s) tank.
Tankstelle, *f.* petrol station.
Tanne, *f.* (~n) pine; fir.
Tante, *f.* (~n) aunt.
Tanz, *m.* (≈e) dance.
tanzen, *v. a. & n.* dance.
Tanzmusik, *f.* dance-music.
Tapete, *f.* (~n) wallpaper.
tapfer, *adj.* brave.
Tapferkeit, *f.* courage.
Tarif, *m.* (~e) tariff.
Tasche, *f.* (~en) pocket; bag.
Taschenbuch, *n.* notebook.
Taschendieb, *m.* pickpocket.
Taschengeld, *n.* pocket money; allowance.
Taschentuch, *n.* handkerchief.
Tasse, *f.* (~n) cup.
Taste, *f.* (~n) key.
Tat, *f.* (~en) act; action.
Täter, *m.* (~) culprit, perpetrator.
Tätigkeit, *f.*(~en) activity.
Tätlichkeit, *f.* (~en) violence; assault.

Tatsache | **Textbuch**

Tatsache, *f.* (~n) fact.
tatsächlich, *adj,* real; actual; – *adv.* as a matter of fact.
Tatze, *f.* (~n) paw.
Tau¹, *m.* dew.
Tau², *n.* (~e) cable; rope.
taub, *adj.* deaf.
Taube, *f.* (~n) dove; pigeon.
Tauchboot, *n.* submarine.
tauchen, *v. n. & a.* dive.
Taucher, *m.* (~) diver.
tauen, *v. n.* thaw.
Taufe, *f.* (~n) baptism.
Taufname, *m.* Christian name.
Taugenichts, *m.* good-for-nothing.
tauglich, *adj.* useful; fit; able.
Tausch, *m.* (~e) exchange.
täuschen, *v.a.* deceive; disappoint.
tausend, *adj.* (a, one) thousand.
Tausend, *f.* (~e) thousand.
Taxe, *f.* (~n) tax; tariff.
Taxenhalteplatz, *m.* taxi rank.
Technik, *f.* technics *pl.;* engineering.
technisch, *adj.* technical.
Tee, *m.* tea.
Teekanne, *f.* tea-pot.
Teich, *m.* (~e) pond.
Teig, *m.* (~e) dough.
Teil, *m.* (~e) part; share.
teilen, *v. a.* divide; share.
teilnehmen, *v.n.* take part (in).
Teilnehmer, *m.* (~) participant.
Teilpension, *f.* half board.
teils, *adv.* partly.
Teilung, *f.* (~en) division.
Teilzahlung, *f.* instalment.
Teint, *m.* (~s) complexion.

Telegramm, *m.* (~e) telegram; wire.
Telegrammformular, *n.* telegraph-form.
Telegraph, *m.* (~en) telegraph.
telegraphieren, *v. a.* telegraph; wire.
Teleobjektiv, *n.* telephoto (lens).
Telephon, *n.* (~e) (tele)phone.
Telephonamt, *n.* exchange.
Telephonbuch, *n.* directory.
Telephongespräch, *n.* telephone conversation.
telephonieren, *v. a. & n.* (tele)phone; ring up.
Telephonzelle, *f.* call-box.
Telephonzentrale, *f.* exchange.
Teleskop, *n.* (~e) telescope.
Teller, *m.* (~) plate.
Tempel, *m.* (~) temple.
Temperatur, *f.* (~en) temperature.
Tempo, *n.* (~s) pace; time.
Tendenz, *f.* (~en) trend; tendency.
Tennis, *n.* tennis.
Tennisplatz, *m.* tennis court.
Tennisschläger, *m.* racket.
Tenor, *m.* (~̈e) tenor.
Tenorist, *m.* (~en; ~en) tenor (singer).
Teppich, *m.* (~e) carpet.
Termin, *m.* (~e) term.
Terrain, *n.* (~s) ground.
Terrasse, *f.* (~en) terrace.
Testament, *n.* (~e) will; testament.
teuer, *adj.* dear; expensive.
Teufel, *m.* (~) devil.
Text, *m.* (~e) text.
Textbuch, *n.* text-book, libretto.

Theater, Transitvisum

Theater, n. (~) theatre.
Theaterkasse, f. box-office.
Thema, n. (-men) theme; subject.
Theologie, f. theology; divinity.
theoretisch, adj. theoretical.
Theorie, f. (~n) theory.
Thermometer, n. (~) thermometer.
thermonuklear, adj. thermonuclear.
Thermosflasche, f. thermos, vacuum flask.
Thron, m. (~e) throne.
tief, adj. deep.
Tier, n. (~e) animal; beast.
Tierarzt, m. veterinary surgeon; vet.
Tiger, m. (~) tiger.
tilgen, v.a. extinguish; erase; cancel (debt).
Tinte, f. (~n) ink.
Tip, m. (~s) tip.
Tisch, m. (~e) table.
Tischgebet, n. grace.
Tischler, m. (~) joiner.
Tischtennis, n. table-tennis.
Tischtuch, n. table-cloth.
Titel, m. (~) title.
Toast, m. (~e) toast.
toben, v. n. rage; rave.
Tochter, f. (≈) daughter.
Tod, m. death.
Todesanzeige, f. obituary (notice).
Todesfall, m. death; casualty.
tödlich, adj. mortal, fatal.
Toilette, f. (~n) lavatory.
Toilettenpapier, n. toilet-paper.
toll, adj. mad.
Tomate, f. (~n) tomato.
Ton¹, m. (≈e) sound.
Ton², m. (≈e) clay.
Tonabnehmer, m. pick-up.

Tonart, f. tone; key.
Tonaufnahme, f. sound recording.
Tonband, n. (magnetic) tape.
Tonband(aufnahme)gerät, n. tape-recorder.
tönen, v. n. sound.
Tonne, f. (~n) barrel; ton; cask.
Topf, m. (≈e) pot.
Tor¹, n. (~e) gate.
Tor², m. (~en, ~en) fool.
Torheit, f. (~en) folly.
Tormann, m. goal-keeper.
Torte, f. (~n) tart; cake.
tot, adj. dead.
Tote, m.; f. (~n) dead; deceased.
töten, v. a. kill.
Totenschein, m. certificate of death.
Tourist, m. (~en; ~en) tourist.
Tracht, f. (~en) costume.
trächtig, adj. pregnant.
Tragbahre, f. stretcher.
tragbar, adj. portable.
träge, adj. idle.
tragen*, v. a. bear; carry; take; *(clothes)* wear v. n. bear; carry.
tragisch, adj. tragic.
Tragödie, f. (~n) tragedy.
Tragweite, f. range; *fig.* importance.
trainieren, v. n. & a. train, coach.
Traktor, m. (-toren) tractor.
Träne, f. (~n) tear.
Trank, m. (≈e) beverage, drink.
transatlantisch, adj. transatlantic.
Transfusion, f. (~en) transfusion.
Transistor, m. (~en) transistor.
Transitvisum, n. transit

Transmission   236.   **über**

visa.
Transmission, *f.* (~en) transmission.
Transport, *m.* (~e) transport.
Traube, *f.* (~n) grapes *pl.*
trauen, *v. a.* marry; *v. n.* trust.
Trauer, *f.* mourning.
Traum, *m.* (~e) dream.
träumen, *v. a. & n.* dream.
traurig, *adj.* sad.
Trauring, *m.* wedding-ring.
Trauung, *f.* wedding; marriage.
Treff, *n.* (~e) club.
treffen*, *v. a. & n.* meet; hit.
Treffen, *m.* (~) meeting; encounter.
treiben*, *v. a.* drive; do; carry on.
Treibstoff, *m.* fuel.
trennen, *v. a.* separate.
Trennung, *f.* (~en) separation.
Treppe, *f.* (~n) stairs *pl.*
Treppenhaus, *n.* staircase.
treten*, *v. n.* tread; walk.
treu, *adj.* faithful.
Tribüne, *f.* (~n) platform; stand.
Trieb, *m.* (~e) impulse.
triefen, *v. n.* drip.
Trikot, *n.* (~s) tights *pl.*; stockinet, hosiery. knitted goods *pl.*
trillern, *v. a. & n.* shake; warble *(of birds).*
trinken*, *v. a. & n.* drink.
Trinkgeld, *n.* tip.
Tritt, *m.* (~e) kick.
Triumph, *m.* (~e) triumph.
trocken, *adj.* dry.
trocknen, *v. a. & n.* dry.
Trommel, *f.* (~n) drum.
Trompete *f.* (~n) trumpet.
Tropen, *pl.* tropics.
Tropfen, *m.* (~) drop.
Trost, *m.* comfort.

trösten, *v.a.* comfort; console.
Trottel, *m.* (~) idiot.
trotz, *prep.* in spite of.
Trotz, *m.* defiance.
trotzdem, *adv.* notwithstanding.
trüb, *adj.* troubled, dismal.
trüben, *v. a.* trouble.
trügen*, *v. a.* deceive.
Trümmer, *pl.* ruins.
Trumpf, *m.* (~e) trump.
Trunk, *m.* (~e) drink.
Truppe, *f.* (~n) troop.
Tuch, *n.* (~er) cloth.
Tuchhändler, *m.* draper.
tüchtig, *adj.* able.
Tugend, *f.* (~en) virtue.
tun*, *v. a. & n.* do; perform; make; pretend to do; put, lay.
Tunke, *f.* (~n) sauce.
Tunnel, *m.* (~s) tunnel.
Tür, *f.* (~en) door.
Turbine, *f.* (~n) turbine.
Turbostrahltriebwerk, *n.* tu Do-jet (engine).
Türke, *m.* (~) Turk.
türkisch, *adj.* Turkish.
Turm, *m.* (~e) tower.
turnen, *v. n.* do gymnastics.
Turnhalle, *f.* gymnasium.
Turnier, (~e) tournament.
Tüte, *f.* (~n) paper bag.
Typ, *m.* (~e) type.
typisch, *adj.* typical.
Tyrann, *m.* (~en; ~en) tyrant.

U

übel, *adj.* bad; evil; — *adv.* ill; badly.
Übel, *n.* evil.
Übelkeit, *f.* sickness.
übelnehmen, *v.a.* take amiss.
üben, *v. a. & n.* exercise; practise.
über, *adv.* over; — *prep.*

überall   237.   **um**

over; above; *fig.* on; about.
überall, *adv.* everywhere.
überaus, *adv.* very; extremely.
überbelichten, *v. a.* overexpose.
Überblick, *m.* (~e) survey.
überdies, *adv.* besides.
übereinkommen*, übereinstimmen, *v. n.* agree.
überfahren*, *v.a.* run over.
Überfahrt, *f.* passage.
Überfall, *m.* attack; raid.
überflüssig, *adj.* superfluous.
überführen, *v. a.* convict.
Übergabe, *f.* (~n) delivery; surrender.
Übergang, *m.* crossing; passage.
übergeben*. *v. a.* deliver; yield; *sich* ~ vomit.
Übergewicht, *n.* overweight.
überhaupt, *adv.* in general.
überholen. *v* overtake.
überhören, *v. a.* overhear.
überlassen*, *v.a.* leave.
Überlebende, *m. f.* survivor.
Überlegenheit, *f.* superiority.
Überlegung, *f.* (~en) reflection; consideration.
überliefern, *v. a.* deliver.
Überlieferung, *f.* tradition.
Übermacht, *f.* superiority.
übermäßig, *adj.* extreme; excessive.
Übermittlung, *f.* transmission
übermorgen, *adv.* day after tomorrow.
Übermut, *m.* insolence.
übernachten, *v. n.* pass the night.
übernatürlich, *adj.* supernatural.
übernehmen*, *v. a.* receive; take over; undertake.
Überraschung, *f.* (~en) surprise.
überreichen, *v.a.* hand over; present.
Überrest, *m.* rest; remains pl.
überschreiten*, *v. a.* exceed.
Überschuß, *m.* (-schüsse) surplus.
übersehen*, *v. a.* overlook.
Übersetzen, *v.a.* translate.
Übersetzung, *f.* (~en) translation.
Übersicht, *f.* survey; view.
Überstunden, *pl.* overtime.
übertragen*, *v.a.* carry over; transmit; relay; translate.
übertreffen, *v. a.* surpass.
übertreiben*, *v. a.* exaggerate; overdo.
überwältigen, *v.a.* overcome.
überweisen*, *v.a.* transfer; remit.
Überzeugung, *f.* conviction.
üblich, *adj.* usual, customary.
U-Boot, *n.* submarine.
übrigens, *adv.* as for the rest.
Übung, *f.* (~en) exercise; practice.
Ufer, *n.* (~) bank; shore.
Uhr, *f.* (~en) clock; watch; *wieviel* ~ *ist es?* what is the time?
Uhrmacher, *m.* watchmaker.
Uhrwerk, *n.* clockwork.
ultraviolett, *adj.* ultraviolet.
um, *adv.* past; *prep.* ~...

| umarmen | 238. | unentschlossen |

herum around; about; — *conj.* ~ ... *zu* to; in order to.
umarmen, *v. a.* embrace.
Umarmung, *f.* (~en) embrace.
umdrehen; *sich* ~ turn round.
Umfang, *f.* extent; range-
umfassend, *adj.* comprehensive; overall.
Umgang, *m.* going round or abouth with.
umgeben*, *v. a.* surround.
Umgebung, *f.* (~en) neighbourhood; environs *pl.*
umgehend, *adj.* by return of post.
umgekehrt, *adj.* contrary; vice-versa.
umher, *adv.* about, all around.
umkehren, *v.n.* turn back. return; *v. a.* turn; overturn; invert.
umkreisen, *v. a.* orbit.
Umlauf, *m.* revolution; rotation; circulation.
Umleitung, *f.* roundabout.
Umrechnungskurs, *m.* rate of exchange.
Umriß, *m.* (-isse) outline
Umsatz, *m.* (~e) turnover.
umschalten, *v.a.* switch (over).
Umschlag, *m.* (~e) envelope; wrapper; compress.
Umsicht, *f.* circumspection.
umsonst, *adv.* free (of charge); in vain.
Umstand, *m.* (~e) circumstance.
umsteigen*, *v.n.* change (for).
umtauschen, *v. a.* exchange.
Umwandlung, *f.* (~en) change.
Umwandlungsanlage, *f.* reactor.
Umweg, *m.* (~e) détour.
umwenden*, *v.a.* turn round.
Umzäunung, *f.* (~en) enclosure.
unabhängig, *adj.* independent.
Unabhängigkeit, *f.* independence.
unangenehm, *adj.* unpleasant.
unbeachtet, *adj.* unnoticed.
unbedeutend, *adj.* insignificant.
unbedingt, *adj.* unconditional; absolute.
unbefangen, *adj.* unprejudiced; simple.
unbefugt, *adj.* incompetent.
unbegreiflich, *adj.* incomprehensible.
unbekannt, *adj.* unknown.
unbemerkt, *adj.* unnoticed; unseen.
unbequem, *adj.* inconvenient; uncomfortable.
unbestimmt, *adj.* vague; undecided.
unbeweglich, *adj.* immovable.
unbewohnt, *adj.* unoccupied.
unbewußt, *adj.* unconscious.
unbezahlt, *adj.* unpaid.
unbrauchbar, *adj.* useless.
und, *conj.* and.
undankbar, *adj.* ungrateful.
undeutlich, *adj.* indistinct.
unendlich, *adj.* endless.
unentbehrlich, *adj.* indispensable.
unentschieden, *adj.* undecided.
unentschlossen, *adj.* irresolute.

unerfahren, *adj.* inexperienced: unskilled.
unerhört, *adj.* unprecedented; unheard of.
unerklärlich, *adj.* inexplicable.
unermüdlich, *adj.* untiring; indefatiguable.
unerwartet, *adj.* unexpected.
unfähig, *adj.* unable; incapable.
Unfall, *m.* (~e) accident.
unfrankiert, *adj.* not prepaid.
unfruchtbar, *adj.* barren; sterile.
ungar, *adj.* underdone.
Ungar, *m.* (~n); -in *f.* (~nen) Hungarian.
ungarisch, *adj.* Hungarian.
ungebildet, *adj.* uneducated.
ungebraucht, *adj.* unused.
ungeduldig, *adj.* impatient.
ungefähr, *adj.* about; almost.
ungeheuer, *adj.* great; enormous.
ungehörig, *adj.* improper; undue.
ungehorsam, *adj.* disobedient.
ungemütlich, *adj.* uncomfortable.
ungenügend, *adj.* insufficient.
ungerecht, *adj.* unjust.
Ungerechtigkeit, *f.* injustice.
ungeschickt, *adj.* awkward.
ungesetzlich, *adj.* illegal.
ungesund, *adj.* unhealthy; unwholesome.
ungewiß, *adj.* uncertain; vague.
ungewöhnlich, *adj.* unusual.
Ungeziefer, *n.* (~) vermin.
ungezogen, *adj.* rude; naughty.
unglaublich, *adj.* incredible.
ungleich, *adj.* unequal.
Unglück, *n.* (~e) misfortune; accident.
unglücklich, *adj.* unhappy; unfortunate.
Unglücksfall, *m.* accident.
ungünstig, *adj.* unfavourable.
Unheil, *n.* mischief.
unheilbar, *adj.* incurable.
unhöflich, *adj.* impolite.
Uniform, *f.* (~en) uniform.
Universität, *f.* (~en) university.
Unkosten, *pl.* expenses.
Unkraut, *n.* weeds *pl.*
unlängst, *adv.* recently; lately.
unmenschlich, *adj.* inhuman.
unmerklich, *adj.* imperceptible.
unmittelbar, *adj.* direct; — *adv.* directly.
unmöglich, *adj.* impossible.
Unmöglichkeit, *f.* impossibility.
unnötig, *adj.* unnecessary.
unordentlich, *adj.* disorderly; untidy.
Unordnung, *f.* disorder.
unparteiisch, *adj.* impartial.
unpassend, *adj.* unsuitable; improper.
unpraktisch, *adj.* unpractical.
Unrecht, *n.* wrong; unjust.
unregelmäßig, *adj.* irregular.
Unregelmäßigkeit, *f.* irregularity.

unrentabel, *adj.* unprofitable.
unruhig, *adj.* restless; uneasy; worried.
uns, *pron.* us; ourselves.
unschädlich, *adj.* harmless.
unschuldig, *adj.* innocent.
unser, *pron.* us; *pl.* our; ours; *der, die, das ~e* ours.
Unsicherheit, *f.* doubt; uncertainty.
unsichtbar, *adj.* invisible.
Unsinn, *m.* nonsense.
unsportlich, *adj.* unsportsmanlike.
unsterblich, *adj.* immortal.
unten, *adv.* below; down; downstairs.
unter, *prep.* under; below; during; among; between.
Unterarm, *m.* forearm.
unterbelichten, *v.a.* underexpose.
unterbrechen, *v.a.* interrupt.
Unterbrechung, *f.* (~en) interruption; break.
unterbringen, *v.a.* shelter; lodge.
unterdessen, *adv.* meanwhile, in the meantime.
unterdrücken, *v.a.* suppress.
untere, *adj.* under, lower; inferior.
untereinander, *adv.* mutually.
unterentwickelt, *adj.* underdeveloped.
unterernährt, *adj.* underfed.
Untergang, *m.* fall; ruin.
Untergebene, *m.* subject.
untergehen,* *v.n.* sink; perish.
Untergestell, *n.* undercarriage.
Untergrundbahn, *f.* underground (railway); tube.
Unterhalt, *m.* maintenance.
unterhalten, *v.a.* keep up; maintain; entertain; *sich ~ mit* converse with.
Unterhandlung, *s.* negotiation.
Unterholz, *n.* brushwood.
Unterhose, *f.* pants *pl.*
Unterjacke, *f.* vest.
Unterkleidung, *f.* underclothes *pl.*
Unterkunft, *f.* accommodation.
unterlassen,* *v.a.* leave off; omit.
Unterleib, *m.* abdomen.
unterliegen,* *v.n.* succumb.
Unternehmen, *n.* (~) undertaking.
Unternehmer, *m.* (~) contractor.
Unterredung, *f.* (~en) conversation.
Unterricht, *m.* instruction; lessons *pl.*
unterrichten, *v.a.* instruct.
untersagen, *v.a.* forbid.
unterscheiden,*, distinguish.
unterschreiben, *v.a.* sign.
Unterseeboot, *n.* submarine.
Unterstützung, *f.* support; relief.
untersuchen, *v.a.* examine; explore.
Untersuchung, *f.* (~en) examination; inquiry.
Untertan, *m.* (~en) subject.
untertauchen, *v.a. & n.* dive; immerse; dip.
Unterwäsche, *see* Unter-

unterwegs 241. **Vaterland**

kleidung.
unterwegs, *adv.* on the way.
Unterwerfung, *f.* submission.
unterzeichnen, *v. a.* sign.
untreu, *adj.* faithless; unfaithful.
ununterbrochen, *adj.* uninterrupted.
unverändert, *adj.* unchanged.
unverantwortlich, *adj.* irresponsible.
unverdient, *adj.* undeserved.
unvereinbar, *adj.* incompatible.
Unverfrorenheit, *f.* impertinence.
unvergeßlich, *adj.* unforgettable.
unvergleichlich, *adj.* incomparable.
unverheiratet, *adj.* unmarried.
unvermeidlich, *adj.* inevitable.
unvermutet, *adj.* unexpected.
unvernünftig, *adj.* unreasonable.
unveröffentlicht, *adj.* unpublished.
unverschämt, *adj.* impertinent, impudent.
unversehrt, *adj.* unhurt.
unverständlich, *adj.* incomprehensible.
unvorsichtig, *adj.* careless; imprudent.
unwahr, *adj.* untrue; false.
unwahrscheinlich, *adj.* improbable.
unweit, *adj.* not far.
Unwetter, *n.* (∼) bad weather; storm.
unwiderruflich, *adj.* irrevocable.
unwiderstehlich, *adj.* irresistible.
unwillkommen, *adj.* unwelcome.
unwillkürlich, *adj.* involuntary.
unwissend, *adj.* ignorant.
unwohl, *adj.* unwell, indisposed.
unwürdig, *adj.* unworthy.
unzählig, *adj.* countless.
unzertrennlich, *adj.* inseparable.
Unzufriedenheit, *f.* discontent.
unzugänglich, *adj.* inaccessible.
unzuverlässig, *adj.* unreliable.
unzweifelhaft, *adj.* undoubted.
üppig, *adj.* luxurious.
uralt, *adj.* very old.
Uraufführung, *f.* first night.
Urgroßvater, *m.* great--grandfather.
Urheber, *m.* (∼) author; originator.
Urkunde, *f.* (∼n) document.
Urlaub, *m.* leave.
Urne, *f.* (∼n) urn.
Ursache, *f.* (∼n) cause; reason.
ursprünglich, *adj.* original.
Urteil, *n.* (∼e) judgement; sentence.
urteilen, *v. a.* judge.
Utensilien, *pl.* utensils

V

Valuta, *f.* (-ten) currency.
Varieté, *n.* (∼s) variety- (-theatre), music-hall.
Vase, *f.* (∼n) vase.
Vater, *n.* (∼) father.
Vaterland, *n.* native country.

| Vaterlich | 242. | Vergleich |

väterlich, *adj.* paternal.
Vegetation, *f.* (~en) vegetation.
Veilchen, *n.* (~) violet.
Ventilation, *f.* (~en) ventilation.
Ventilator, *m.* (~ren) ventilator.
Verabredung, *f.* (~en) agreement; appointment.
Verachtung, *f.* scorn.
Veranlassung, *f.* (~en) occasion.
veranstalten, *v. a.* organize.
verantwortlich, *adj.* responsible.
Verantwortlichkeit, *f.* responsibility.
verbannen, *v.a.* banish.
verbergen*, *v. a.* hide; conceal.
verbeugen, *v.n. sich ~* bow.
verbieten*, *v. a.* forbid.
verbinden*, *v.a.* join; connect; dress; oblige.
Verbindung, *f.* (~en) connection.
Verbot, *n.* (~e) prohibition.
Verbrauch, *m.* consumption.
verbrauchen, *v.a.* consume; use (up).
Verbrechen, *n.* (~) crime.
verbreiten, *v.a.* spread.
verbrennen*, *v.a.* burn.
Verbrennungsmotor, *m.* internal combustion engine.
verbringen*, *v. a.* spend.
Verbündete, *m.* (~n) ally.
Verdacht, *m.* (~e) suspicion.
verdächtig, *adj.* suspicious.
verdammen, *v. a.* damn.
verdanken, *v. a.* owe.
Verdauung, *f.* digestion.
verderben*, *v. a.* spoil.

verdienen, *v.a.* earn; deserve.
Verdienst, *m.* (~e) earnings *pl.*
verdoppeln, *v. a.* double.
Verehrer, *m.* (~) admirer.
Verein, *n.* (~e) society; club.
vereinbaren, *v. a.* agree on (sg).
Vereinbarung, *f.* (~en) agreement.
vereinigen, *v. a.* unite.
vereiteln, *v. a.* frustrate.
Verfahren, *n.* (~) process; proceeding.
Verfall, *m.* destruction; decay.
verfallen*, *v. n.* decay; — *adj.* decayed; due.
Verfasser, *m.* (~) author.
Verfassung, *f.* (~en) constitution.
verfehlen, *v. a.* miss.
verfeinern, *v. a.* refine.
verfertigen, *v.a.* manufacture; make.
verfließen*, *v. n.* pass; expire.
verfolgen, *v.a.* pursue; persecute.
verfrachten, *v. a.* freight; ship.
verfügen, *v.a.* dispose (of).
verführen, *v.a.* seduce.
Vergangenheit, *f.* (~en) past.
Vergaser, *m.* (~) carburetter.
vergeben*, *v. a.* pardon.
vergeblich, *adj.* vain; fruitless; — *adv.* in vain.
vergehen*, pass; *v.n. sich ~* commit an offence.
Vergehen, *n.* (~) offence.
vergessen*, *v.a.* forget.
vergiften, *v. a.* poison.
Vergiftung, *f.* (~en) poisoning.
Vergleich, *m.* (~e) comparison.

vergleichen*, *v. a.* compare.
Vergnügen, *n.* (~) pleasure.
Vergnügungsfahrt, *f.* cruise; pleasure-trip.
vergrößern, *v. a.* enlarge; magnify.
Vergrößerungsglas, *n.* magnifying glass.
vergüten, *v. a.* indemnify.
verhaften, *v. a.* arrest.
Verhältnis, *n.* (~se) relation(ship); connection; proportion.
verhältnismäßig, *adj.* proportional.
verhandeln, *v. n.* negotiate.
verheiraten, *v. a.* marry.
verhindern, *v. a.* prevent.
verirren; *sich* ~ loose one's way.
Verkauf, *m.* (~e) sale.
verkaufen, *v. a.* sell.
Verkäufer, *m.* seller; salesman; shop assistant.
Verkehr, *m.* trade; traffic.
Verkehrszeichen, *n.* traffic-sign.
verkehrt, *adj.* wrong.
Verkleidung, *f.* (~en) disguise.
verkünden, *v. a.* announce.
Verlag, *m.* (~e) publication; publisher; *pl.*; *in* ~ *nehmen* publish.
Verlagsrecht, *n.* copyright.
verlangen, *v. a.* demand.
verlängern, *v. a.* extend; prolong.
verlassen*, *v. a.* leave; forsake; *sich* ~ *auf* rely on.
Verlauf, *m.* course.
verlegen, *v. a.* misplace; remove; publish; postpone.
Verlegenheit, *f.* (~en) embarassment; *in* ~ *setzen* embarrass.
Verleger, *m.* (~) publisher.
verleihen,* *v. a.* grant, lend.
verlernen, *v. a.* forget.
verletzen, *v. a.* hurt.
verleugnen, *v. a.* deny.
verlieben: *sich* ~ fall in love (with).
verlieren*, *v. a.* lose.
verlobt, *adj.* engaged (to be married.)
Verlobte, *m.* fiancé.
Verlobte, *f.* fiancée.
Verlobung, *f.* (~en) engagement.
Verlobungsring, *m.* engagement ring.
verloren, *adj.* lost.
Verlust, *m.* (~e) loss.
vermachen, *v. a.* leave; bequeath.
Vermächtnis, *n.* (~se) legacy.
vermählen, *v. a.* marry.
vermeiden*, *v. a.* avoid.
vermieten, *v. a.* let; rent.
vermischen, *v. a.* mix.
vermitteln, *v. a.* mediate.
Vermittlung, *f.* (~en) mediation.
Vermögen, *n.* (~) wealth; fortune.
vermuten, *v. a.* suppose.
vermutlich, *adj.* probable.
vernachlässigen, *v. a.* neglect.
vernehmen*, *v. a.* perceive; hear.
Vernehmung, *f.* (~en) hearing; examination.
verneinen, *v. a.* deny.
vernichten, *v. a.* annihilate.
vernünftig, *adj.* reasonable.
veröffentlichen, *v. a.* publish.

Verordnung, f. (~en) order; decree.
verpacken, v. a. pack up.
verpflichten, v. a. engage, oblige.
Verrat, m. treason.
verraten*, v. a. betray.
verreisen, v. n. go on a journey.
Verrenkung, f. (~en) sprain.
verrosten, v. n. rust.
Vers, m. (~e) verse.
versagen, v. a. refuse.
versammeln, v. n. assemble.
Versammlung, f. (~en) meeting.
verschaffen, v. a. procure.
verschenken, v. a. give away.
verschicken, v. a. forward, send.
verschieben*, v. a. put off; delay.
verschieden, adj. different.
verschiffen, v. a. ship; export.
verschlagen, adj. cunning.
verschließen*, v. a. lock up.
Verschluß, m. (-schlüsse) lock.
verschnupft; ~ sein have a cold.
verschweigen*, v. a. hide; keep secret.
verschwenden, v. a. waste; squander.
Verschwörung, f. (~en) conspiracy.
Versehen, n. (~) mistake; oversight.
versenden*, v. a. send; forward.
versichern, v. a. assure; insure.
Versicherung, f. (~en) insurance.
Versicherungsgesellschaft, f. insurance company.
versinken, v. a. & n. sink.
versöhnen, v. a. reconcile.
versorgen, v. a. supply.
versprechen*, v. a. promise.
Verstaatlichung, f. (~en) nationalization.
Verstand, m. (~e) understanding.
verständig, adj. reasonable.
verstärken, v. a. strengthen.
verstecken, v. a. hide.
verstehen*, v. a. understand.
verstellen, v. a. block; sich ~ dissemble.
verstimmt, adj. out of tune; cross.
Verstopfung, f. constipation.
verstorben, adj. deceased.
verstoßen*, v. n. offend; v. a. cast off; repudiate.
Versuch, m. (~e) attempt.
versuchen, v. a. try; taste; tempt.
Versuchung, f. (~en) temptation.
vertagen, v. a. adjourn.
vertauschen, v. a. exchange.
verteidigen, v. a. defend.
verteilen, v. a. distribute.
Vertrag, m. (~e) treaty.
vertragen, v. a. bear; sich ~ agree.
Vertrauen, n. confidence.
vertreten*, v. a. represent.
Vertreter, m. (~) representative.
verunglücken, v. n. meet with an accident.
verursachen, v. a. cause.
verurteilen, v. a. condemn.
vervielfältigen, v. a. multiply.
verwahren, v. a. preserve.

| verwalten | 245. | voran |

verwalten, *v.a.* manage; administer.
Verwaltung, *f.* (~en) administration; management.
verwandeln, *v.a.* transform.
Verwandlung, *f.* (~en) transformation.
Verwandte, *m.*, *f.* (~n) relative.
Verwandtschaft, *f.* relation(ship).
verwechseln, *v.a.* confound.
verwegen, *adj.* daring.
verweigern, *v. a.* refuse.
verweisen*, *v.a.* reprimand; refer (to).
verwelken, *v. n.* fade.
verwenden*, use; employ.
verwerfen, *v. a.* reject.
verwerten, *v. a.* turn to account.
verwickeln, *v. a.* entangle.
verwirklichen, *v.a.* realize.
Verwirklichung, *f.* realization.
verwirren, *v. a.* confuse.
verwöhnen, *v. a.* spoil.
verwunden, *v. a.* wound.
Verwunderung, *f.* astonishment.
verwünschen, *v. a.* curse.
verzehren, *v. a.* consume.
Verzeichnis, *n.* (~se) list.
verzeihen*, *v.a.* pardon.
verzerren, *v. a.* distort.
verzichten, *v.n.* renounce; resign.
Verzögerung, *f.* (~en) delay.
verzollen, *v. a.* pay duty; *nichts zu* ~ nothing to declare.
Verzug, *m.* delay.
verzweifeln, *v. n.* despair.
verzweigen, *v. n.* branch off.
Veto, *n.* (~s) veto.

Vetter, *m.* (~n) cousin.
Vieh, *n.* cattle.
Viehzucht, *f.* cattle-breeding.
viel, *adj.* much; *pl.* many; *sehr* ~ a great deal (of); ~*e pl.* a great many; — *adv.* much.
vielleicht, *adv.* perhaps.
vielmals, *adv.* many times.
vier, *adj.* four.
viereckig, *adj.* square.
vierte, *adj.* fourth.
Viertel, *n.* (~) quarter.
vierzehn, *adj.* fourteen.
vierzig, *adj.* forty.
Villa, *f.* (-len) country house; villa.
Violine, *f.* (~n) violin.
Violinist, *m.* (~en); -in *f.* (~nen) violinist.
Violoncell, *n.* (~e) violoncello.
Visitenkarte, *f.* visiting card.
Visum, *n.* (-sa) visa.
Vitamin, *n.* (~e) vitamin.
Vogel, *m.* (~) bird.
Volk, *n.* (~er) people; nation.
Volkslied, *n.* folk-song.
volkstümlich, *adj.* popular.
Volkswirtschaft, *f.* political economics.
voll, *adj.* full.
vollbringen*, *v. a.* carry out.
völlig, *adj.* full; complete.
vollkommen, *adj.* complete.
Vollmacht, *f.* full power; authority.
Volt, *n.* volt.
von, *prep.* from; of; by; ~ *nun an* (from) now on.
vor, *prep.* ago; before; in front of.
voran, *adv.* before; in

vorangehen*   **Vorsteher**

front.
vorangehen*, *v.n.* precede.
voraus, *adv.* advance; *im* ~ in advance.
voraussetzen, *v. a.* presume.
voraussichtlich, *adj.* probable.
vorbehalten*, *v.a.* reserve.
vorbei, *adv.* past; by; over.
vorbereiten, *v. a.* prepare.
Vorbereitung, *f.* (~en) preparation.
Vorbild, *n.* model.
vorder, *adj.* fore, front.
Vordergrund, *m* foreground.
Vordersitz, *m.* front seat.
Vorderteil, *m.* front part.
voreilig, *adj.* rash.
vorfabriziert, *adj.* prefabricated.
Vorfahr, *m.* (~en) ancestor.
vorfahren*, *v.n.* drive up.
Vorfahrtsrecht, *n.* priority.
Vorfall, *m.* event.
Vorgang, *m.* event.
Vorgänger, *m.* (~) predecessor.
vorgehen*, *v.n.* advance; proceed; be fast.
Vorgesetzte, *m.* superior.
vorgestern, *adv.* the day before yesterday.
vorhanden; ~ *sein* exist.
Vorhang, *m.* (≈e) curtain.
vorher, *adv.* before; previously.
vorhin, *adv.* just now.
vorig, *adj.* preceding; former.
vorkommen*, *v. a.* happen; occur.
Vorladung, *f.* (~en) summons *pl.*
vorläufig, *adj.* for the present.
vorlesen*, *v. a.* read.
Vorlesung, *f.* lecture.
vorletzt, *adj.* last but one.
Vorliebe, *f.* predilection.
vorliegend, *adj.* in question.
Vormittag, *m.* morning.
Vormund, *m.* (~e) guardian.
vorn, *adv.* before; in front of.
Vorname, *m.* Christian name.
vornehm, *adj.* distinguished.
vornehmen: *sich* ~ intend.
Vorort, *m.* suburb.
Vorrat, *m.* stock.
Vorrecht, *n.* privilege.
Vorrede, *f.* preface
Vorrichtung, *f.* apparatus.
vorrücken, *v. n.* advance.
Vorsatz, *m.* intention.
Vorschlag, *m.* proposition.
vorschlagen*, *v. a.* propose.
Vorschrift, *f.* instruction; prescription.
Vorschuß, *m.* advance.
Vorsehung, *f.* (~en) providence.
Vorsicht, *f.* precaution.
vorsichtig, *adj.* cautious.
Vorsitz, *m.* chair.
Vorsitzende, *m.* president; chairman.
Vorspeise, *f.* entrée.
Vorspiel, *n.* prelude.
vorsprechen*, *v. n.* call on.
Vorsprung, *m.* start; advantage.
Vorstadt, *f.* suburb.
Vorsteher, *m.* (~) director; manager; superior.

vorstellen, *v.a.* present; introduce; *sich ~ imagine*; fancy.
Vorstellung, *f.* (~en) introduction; performance.
Vorteil, *m.* advantage.
vorteilhaft, *adj.* advantageous.
Vortrag, *m.* (⁓e) lecture.
vortragen*, *v.a.* recite.
vortrefflich, *adj.* excellent.
vortreten*, *v.n.* step forward.
vorüber, *adv.* past, by; over.
vorübergehen*, *v. a.* pass.
Vorurteil, *n.* prejudice.
Vorverkauf, *m.* booking (in advance).
Vorwand, *m.* (⁓e) pretext.
vorwärts, *adv.* forward.
Vorwort, *n.* preface.
Vorwurf, *m.* reproach.
vorzeitig, *adj.* premature.
vorziehen*, prefer.
Vorzimmer, *n.* antechamber.
Vorzug, *m.* (⁓e) preference.
vorzüglich, *adj.* excellent.
vorzugsweise, *adv.* preferably.
Vulkan, *m.* (~e) volcano.

W

Waage, *f.* (~n) balance.
Waagerecht, *adj.* horizontal.
Wache, *f.* (~n) guard.
wachen, *v. n.* be awake; sit up.
wachsen*, *v. n.* grow; increase; *sie ist ihm gewachsen* she is equal to him.
Wächter, *m.* (~) watchman.
wacker, *adj.* brave.
Waffe, *f.* (~n) arm.
Waffenstillstand, *m.* armistice.
wagen, *v.a.* dare; risk.
Wagen, *m.* (~) car; carriage.
Wahl, *f.* (~en) choice; election.
wählen, *a. v.* choose; vote.
Wähler, *m.* (~) voter.
Wahlrecht, *n.* franchise.
Wahnsinn, *m.* madness.
wahr, *adj.* true.
währen, *v. n.* last.
während, *prep.* during; — *conj.* while.
wahrhaft, *adj.* true; genuine.
Wahrheit, *f.* truth.
wahrnehmen*, *v. a.* perceive.
wahrscheinlich, *adj.* probable.
Wahrscheinlichkeit, *f.* probability.
Währung, *f.* (~en) currency.
Waise, *f.* (~n) orphan.
Wald, *m.* (⁓er) wood; forest.
Walnuß, *m.* (-nüsse) walnut.
Walze, *f.* (~n) cylinder.
wälzen, *v. a.* roll.
Walzer, *m.* (~) waltz.
Wand, *f.* (⁓e) wall.
wandern, *v. n.* walk; hike.
Wandtafel, *f.* blackboard.
Wange, *f.* (~n) cheek.
wann: *adv.* when; *bis ~?* how long?
Wanne, *f.* (~n) tub.
Wappen, *n.* (~) coat of arms.
Ware, *f.* (~n) merchandise; goods *pl.*
Warenhaus, *n.* department store.

| Warenlager | Wellenlänge |

Warenlager, n. warehouse.
Warenzeichen, n. trade-mark.
warm, adj. warm.
Wärme, f. heat.
Wärmflasche, f. hot-water-bottle.
warnen, v. a. warn.
warten, v. n. wait.
Wartezimmer, n. waiting-room.
warum, adv. why.
was, pron. what; which.
waschbar, adj. washable.
Wäsche, f. washing; linen.
waschen*, v. . & n. wash.
Wäscherin, f. (~nen) laundress.
Waschmaschine, f. washing-machine.
Wasser, n. water.
Wasserfall, m. waterfall.
Wasserflugzeug, n. hydroplane.
wässern, v. a. water; irrigate.
Wasserstoff, m. hydrogen.
Wasserwerk, n. water-works.
Watt, n. (~) watt.
Watte, f. cotton-wool.
weben*, v. a. weave.
Wechsel, m. exchange; bill of exchange.
wechseln, v. a. change.
Wechselstrom, m. alternating current.
wecken, v. a. wake;
Wecker, m. (~) alarm-clock.
weder, conj. ~ ... noch neither ... nor.
weg, adv. away; off.
Weg, m. (~e) way; road.
wegen, prep. because of; owing to.
weggehen*, v. n. go away.
weglassen*, v. a. omit.
wegnehmen*, v. a. take away.
Wegweiser, m. (~) signpost.
wegwerfen*, v. a. throw away.
weh, adj. sore; ~tun hurt ache.
wehen, v. n. blow.
wehren, v. a. defend.
Weib, n (~er) woman; wife.
weiblich, adj. female; feminine.
weich, adj. soft.
Weide, f. (~n) willow; pasture.
weigern: sich ~ refuse.
weihen, v. a. consecrate.
Weihnachten, pl. Christmas.
Weihnachtsabend, m. Christmas Eve.
Weihnachtsbaum, m. Christmastree.
Weihrauch, m. incense.
weil, conj. because.
weilen, v. n. stay; sojourn.
Wein, m. (~e) wine.
Weinberg, m. vineyard.
weinen, v. n. cry; weep.
Weinkarte, f. wine list.
Weinlese, f. (~n) vintage.
Weise, f. (~n) manner; way.
weisen*, v. a. direct; show.
Weisheit, f. wisdom.
weiß, adj. white.
Weisung, f. (~en) direction.
weit, adj. far; und so ~er etc.; and so on.
Weite, f. width.
weitergehen*, v. n. go on.
Weizen, m. wheat.
welcher; weiche, welches pron. what; which; who; that.
welken, v. n. wither.
Welle, f. (~n) wave; axle.
Wellenlänge, f. (radio) wave-length.

Welt   249.   **Wimper**

Welt, f. (~en) world.
Weltausstellung, f. world exhibition.
Weltfriede(n), m. world peace.
Weltkrieg, m. World-War.
weltlich, adj. worldly.
Weltmacht, f. world-power.
Weltraumfahrer, m. spaceman.
Weltraumflug, m. space-flight.
Weltteil, m. continent.
wenden*, v. a. & n. turn; sich ~ an apply to.
Wendung, f. (~en) turn.
wenig, adj. little; ~er less; ~ste least; ~stens at least.
wenn, conj. when; if; ~ auch although.
wer, pron. who; ~ immer whoever.
werben*, v. n. court; woo; recruit.
werden*, v. n. become, grow; turn; (future) shall; will.
werfen*, v. a. throw.
Werft, f. (~en) wharf.
Werk, n. (~e) work.
Werkstatt, f. workshop.
Werkzeug, n. tool.
Wermut, m. vermouth.
Wert, m. (~e) value; ~ sein be worth.
wertlos, adj. worthless.
Wertpapiere, pl. securities pl.
wertvoll, adj. valuable.
wesentlich, adj. essential.
Wespe, f. (~n) wasp.
wessen, pron. whose.

West(en), m. west.
westlich, adj. western.
wetten, v. n. & a. bet.
Wetter, n. (~) weather.
Wetterbericht, m. weather-forecast.
Wetterkunde, f. meteorology.
Wettkampf, m. contest.
wichtig, adj. important.
Wichtigkeit, f. importance.
wickeln, v. a. wind; wrap up.
wider, prep. against.
widerfahren*, v. a. happen, occur.
widerlegen, refute; disprove.
Widerrede, f. contradiction.
widersprechen*, v. n. contradict.
Widerspruch, m. contradiction.
Widerstand*, m. resistance.
Widerwille, m. disgust.
widmen, v. a. dedicate.
widrig, adj. adverse.
wie, adv. how; — conj. as, like; so ... ~ as (good) as.
wieder, adv. again.
wiedergeben*, v. a. give back; return.
wiederholen, v. a. repeat.
wiederkommen*, v. n. return.
Wiedersehen, n. auf ~ farewell.
Wiegenlied, n. lullaby.
Wiese, f. (~n) meadow.
wieviel, how much?
wild, adj. wild.
Wild, n. game.

Wildbret, n. venison.
Wildnis, f. (~se) wilderness.
Wille, m. (~n) will.
willig, adj. (be) willing.
willkommen, v. a. & n. welcome.
willkürlich, adj. arbitrary.
wimmeln, v. n. teem.
Wimper, f. (~n) eyelash.

Wind, *m.* (~e) wind.
Winde, *f.* (~n) winch.
Windel, *f.* (~n) diaper, nappy.
winden, *v. a.* wind, twist.
windig, *adj.* windy.
Wink, *n.* (~e) hint.
Winkel, *m.* (~) angle.
Winker, *m.* (~) indicator.
Winter, *m.* (~) winter.
wir, *pron.* we.
Wirbelsäule, *f.* spine.
Wirbelwind, *m.* whirlwind.
wirken, *v. n.* act; *v. a.* work; weave.
wirklich, *adj.* real.
wirksam, *adj.* working; efficient.
Wirkung, *f.* (~en) effect.
Wirt, *m.* (~e) landlord; host.
Wirtin, *f.* (~nen) landlady; hostess.
Wirtschaft, *f.* husbandry; household; economy.
wirtschaftlich, *adj.* economical.
Wirtshaus, *n.* public-house; tavern.
wischen, *v. a.* wipe.
wissen*, *v. a. & n.* know
Wissen, *n.* knowledge.
Wissenschaft, *f.* (~en) science.
wissenschaftlich, *adj.* scientific.
wissentlich, *adj.* willful.
Witterung, *f.* scent; weather.
Witwe, *f.* (~n) widow.
Witwer, *m.* (~) widower.
Witz, *m.* (~e) joke.
witzig, *adj.* witty.
wo, *adv.* where.
Woche, *f.* (~n) week.
Wochenblatt, *n.* weekly (paper).
Wochentag, *m.* weekday.
wöchentlich, *adj.* weekly; — *adv.* every week.
wodurch, *pron.* by what; by which.
wofür, *pron.* for which; *adv.* why.
wogegen, *pron.* against which; — *conj.* whereas.
woher, *adv.* whence, from where.
wohin, *adv.* where.
wohl, *adv.* well.
Wohl, *n.* welfare.
wohlbekannt, *adj.* well-known.
Wohlgefallen, *n.* pleasure.
wohlhabend, *adj.* well-to-do.
Wohlstand, *m.* prosperity.
Wohltat, *f.* benefit.
Wohltäter, *m.* benefactor.
wohlwollend, *adj.* benevolent.
wohnen, *v. n.* live; dwell.
Wohnhaus, *n.* dwelling-house.
Wohnort, *m.* (place of) residence.
wohnsitz, *m.* domicile.
Wohnung, *f.* (~en) flat; lodgings *pl.*; residence.
Wohnzimmer, *n.* sitting-room.
Wolf, *m.* (~e) wolf.
Wolke, *f.* (~n) cloud.
Wolle, *f.* wool; *aus* ~ woolen.
wollen*, *v. a. & n.* want, wish.
Wonne, *f.* (~n) bliss.
woran, *adv.* at what.
worauf, *adv.* upon which.
woraus, *adv.* where from.
worin, *adv.* in what.
Wort, *n.* (~er) word.
Wörterbuch, *n.* dictionary.
Wortführer, *m.* spokesman.

Wortlaut, *m.* wording.
wörtlich, *adj.* verbal; — *adv.* literally.
Wortwechsel, *m.* dispute.
wovon, *adv.* of what.
wozu, *adv.* why; for what.
Wuchs, *m.* growth.
wund, *adj.* sore.
Wunde, *f.* (~n) wound.
Wunder, *n.* (~) wonder.
wunderbar, *adj.* wonderful.
wundern: *sich* ~ wonder; be astonished (at).
wundervoll, *adj.* wonderful.
Wunsch, *m.* (⸚e) wish; desire.
wünschen, *v. a.* desire.
Würde, *f.* dignity.
würdig, *adj.* worthy.
Wurf, *m.* (⸚e) throw.
Würfel, *m.* (~) cube; dice.
Wurfgeschoß, *n.* missile; projectile.
würgen, *v. a.* choke; strangle.
Wurm, *m.* (⸚er) worm.
Wurst, *f.* (⸚e) sausage.
Würze, *f.* (~n) spice.
Wurzel, *f.* (~n) root.
würzen, *v. a.* season.
Wüste, *f.* (~n) desert.
Wut, *f.* rage.

X

X-beine, *pl.* knock-knees.
X-Strahl, *m.* X-ray.

Z

zaghaft, *adj.* timid.
zäh(e), *adj.* tough.
Zahl, *f.* (~en) number; figure.
zahlbar, *adj.* payable.
zahlen, *v. a.* pay.
zählen, *v. a.* count.
zahllos, *adj.* countless.
zahlreich, *adj.* numerous.
Zahltag, *m.* pay-day.
Zahlung, *f.* (~en) payment.
Zahlungsanweisung, *f.* cheque.
Zahlungsmittel, *n.* (legal) tender.
zähmen, *v. a.* tame.
Zahn, *m.* (⸚e) tooth.
Zahnarzt, *m.* dentist.
Zahnbürste, *f.* toothbrush.
Zahnfleisch, *n.* gums.
Zahnpasta, *f.* tooth-paste.
Zahnrad, *n.* cog-wheel.
Zahnradbahn, *f.* rack-railway
Zahnstocher, *m.* toothpick.
Zahnweh, *n.* toothache.
Zange, *f.* (~n) tongs.
Zapfen, *m.* (~) peg; pin.
zart, *adj.* tender; delicate.
Zärtlichkeit, *f.* (~en) tenderness; caresses *pl.*
Zauber, *m.* (~) charm.
Zauberer, *m.* magician.
zaudern, *v. n.* hesitate.
Zaun, *m.* (⸚e) fence.
Zebra, *n.* (~s) zebra.
Zeche, *f.* (~n) score; bill.
Zehe, *f.* (~n) toe.
zehn, *adj.* ten.
zehnte, *adj.* tenth.
Zeichen, *n.* (~) sign.
zeichnen, *v. a. & n.* mark; draw; sign.
Zeichnung, *f.* (~en) drawing.
Zeigefinger, *m.* index finger.
zeigen, *v. a. & n.* show; point out.
Zeiger, *m.* (~) hand.
Zeile, *f.* (~n) line.

Zeit	zornig
Zeit, *f.* (~en) time.	become, be suitable.
Zeitalter, *n.* age.	ziemlich, *adj.* fit; suitable; — *adv.* rather.
zeitig, *adj.* early.	
zeitlich, *adj.* temporal.	zieren, *v.a.* decorate adorn.
Zeitpunkt, *m.* date.	
Zeitschrift, *f.* periodical.	zierlich, *adj.* graceful.
Zeitung, *f.* (~en) newspaper.	Ziffer, *f.* (~n) figure; number.
Zeitvertreib, *m.* pastime.	Zifferblatt, *n.* dial.
zeitweilig, *adj.* temporary.	Zigarette, *f.* (~n) cigarette.
zeitweise, *adv.* at times; from time to time.	Zigarre, *f.* (~n) cigar.
Zeitwort, *n.* verb.	Zigeuner, *m.* (~) gypsy.
Zelle, *f.* (~n) cell.	Zimmer, *n.* (~) room.
Zelt, *n,* (~e) tent.	Zimmergast, *m.* lodger.
Zement, *m.* cement.	Zimmermädchen, *n.* chambermaid.
Zentralheizung, *f.* central heating.	Zimmernummer, *f.* room-number.
zentralisieren, *v. a.* centralize.	Zimt, *m.* cinnamon.
Zentrum, *n.* (-tren) centre.	Zink, *n.* zinc.
	Zinn, *n.* tin.
Zepter, *m.* (~) sceptre.	Zins, *m.* (~e) interest; rent.
zerbrechen*, break (in pieces); shatter.	Zinsfuß, *m.* rate of interest.
zerfallen*, *v. n.* fall to pieces.	Zirkel, *m.* compasses *pl.*
zerlegen, *v. a.* carve.	Zirkus, *m.* (~se) circus.
zerreißen*, *v.a.* rend; tear.	Zitat, *n.* (~e) quotation.
zerstören, *v. a.* destroy.	zitieren, *v. a.* quote.
Zerstörung, *f.* (~en) destruction.	Zitrone, *f.* (~n) lemon.
zerstreuen, *v. a.* scatter; disperse; distract.	zittern, *v.n.* tremble; vibrate.
Zerstreuung, *f.* (~en) diversion.	zivilisieren, *v.a.* civilize.
Zettel, *m.* (~) bill; note; label.	Zivilist, *m.* (~en; ~en) civilian.
Zeug, *n.* (~e) stuff; nonsense.	zögern, *v. n.* hesitate.
Zeuge, *m.* (~n) witness.	Zögling, *m.* (~e) pupil.
zeugen, *v. a.* testify; beget.	Zoll, *m.* duty; custom; inch.
Zeugnis, *n.* (~se) certificate.	Zollabfertigung, *f.* customs-clearance.
Ziege, *f.* (~n) goat.	Zollbeamte, *m.* customs-officer.
Ziegel, *m.* (~) brick.	
ziehen*, *v. a.* pull; draw.	zollfrei, *adj.* free of duty.
Ziel, *n.* (~e) aim; destination.	Zoo, *m.* (~s) zoo.
	Zopf, *m.* (~̈e) pigtail, plait.
zielen, *v. a.* aim.	Zorn, *m.* anger.
ziemen, *v.n. sich* ~	zornig, *adj.* angry.

zu, *adv.* too; towards, to; shut; — *prep.* to; unto; at; ~ *Hause* at home; *um* ... ~ in order to.

zubereiten, *v. a.* prepare.

zubringen*, *v. a.* pass, spend (time).

Zucht, *f.* (~en) breeding; rearing (of cattle.)

züchten, *v. a.* breed.

Zuchthaus, *n.* prison.

zucken, *v. a.* shrug; *v. n.* move, stir.

Zucker, *m.* (~) sugar.

Zuckerbäcker, *m.* confectioner.

zudem, *adv.* besides; (in) addition.

zudringlich, *adj.* importunate.

zuerst, *adv.* (at) first.

Zufall, *m.* chance; accident.

zufällig, *adj.* by chance accidental(ly).

Zuflucht, *f.* refuge.

Zufluß, *m.* tributary.

zufolge, *prep.* in consequence of.

zufrieden, *adj.* contented.

Zufriedenheit, *f.* satisfaction.

zufügen, *v. a.* add; cause.

Zufuhr, *f.* (~en) supply.

Zug, *m.* (⸚e) train; traction; feature; draught.

Zugang, *m.* (⸚e) entrance.

zugänglich, *adj.* accessible.

zugeben*, *v. a.* admit; grant; add.

zugegen, *adv.* present.

zugehen*, *v. n.* happen; come about, go.

Zügel, *m.* (~) bridle.

zügellos, *adj.* unbridled.

zugestehen*, *v. a.* admit; grant.

Zugführer, *m.* conductor; (chief) guard.

zugleich, *adv.* at the same time.

zuhören, *v. n.* listen.

Zuhörer, *m.* (~) audience; listener; hearer.

Zukunft, *f.* future.

zukünftig, *adj.* future.

zulangen, *v. n.* suffice; *v. a.* reach, hand.

zulassen*, *v. a.* admit; allow.

zulässig, *adj.* admissible.

zuletzt, *adv.* at last.

zumachen, *v. a.* shut; close.

zumal, *adv.* especially; — *conj.* the more so.

zumeist, *adv.* mostly.

zunächst, *prep.* next to; *adv.* first of all; at first.

Zunahme, *f.* (~n) increase.

zünden, *v. a.* kindle; *v. n.* catch fire.

Zünder, *m.* (~) fuse; lighter.

Zündkerze, *f.* sparking-plug.

Zündmagnet, *m.* magneto.

Zündung, *f.* ignition.

zunehmen*, *v. n.* increase; put on weight.

Zuneigung, *f.* (~en) affection.

Zunge, *f.* (~n) tongue.

zürnen, *v. n.* be angry.

zurück, *adv.* back; backwards.

zurückbleiben*, *v. n.* remain behind.

zurückbringen*, *v. a.* bring back.

zurückgeben*, *v. a.* give back; return.

zurückgehen*, *v. n.* go back.

zurückhalten*, *v. a.* keep back.

Zurückhaltung, *f.* re-

zurückkommen*, *v.n.* come back.

zurücklegen, *v. a.* leave behind; cover (a distance).

zurückweisen*, *v. a.* reject.

Zuruf, *m.* (~e) call.

zusagen, *v.a.* assent.

zusammen, *adv.* together.

zusammenarbeiten, *v. n.* cooperate; collaborate.

zusammenbrechen*, *v. n.* break down; collapse.

Zusammenfassung, *f.* summary.

zusammengesetzt, *adj.* complex.

Zusammenhang, *m.* connection.

Zusammenkunft, *f.* meeting.

Zusammensetzung, *f.* (~en) composition; combination.

zusammenstellen, *v.a.* combine.

Zusammenstoß, *m.* collision; clash.

Zusammentreffen, *n.* meeting.

zusammenzählen, *v.a.* add up; sum up.

Zusatz, *m.* addition; supplement.

Zuschauer, *m.* (~) spectator; viewer.

Zuschlag, *m.* addition(al payment).

zuschreiben*, *v. a.* attribute.

Zuschrift, *f.* (~en) letter.

zusehen*, *v. n.* watch, look on.

zusenden*, *v. a.* send.

Zustand, *m.* (~e) condition.

zuständig, *adj.* competent; belonging to.

zustehen*, *v. n.* belong; serve.

zustimmen, *v. n.* agree; consent.

Zustimmung, *f.* (~en) consent; assent.

zustoßen*, *v. a. & n.* befall, happen (to).

zutrauen, *v. a.* trust; give credit for.

Zutritt, *m.* (~e) access.

zuverlässig, *adj.* reliable.

zuvor, *adv.* previously.

zuvorkommen*, *v. n.* anticipate.

zuvorkommend, *adj.* obliging.

Zuwachs, *m.* increment.

zuweilen, *adv.* sometimes.

zuweisen*, *v. a.* assign (to).

zuwenden*, *v. a.* turn to.

zuwider, *prep.* contrary to.

zuziehen*, *v. a.* draw; *sich* ~ catch *(cold ect.)*.

Zwang, *m.* constraint.

zwanzig, *adj.* twenty.

Zwanzig, *f.* (~en) (number) twenty.

zwanzigste, *adj.* twentieth.

zwar, *adv.* indeed.

Zweck, *m.* (~e) aim; purpose.

zweckmäßig, *adj.* suitable.

zwei, *adj.* two.

Zweifel, *m.* (~) doubt; *ohne* ~ without doubt.

zweifelhaft, *adj.* doubtful.

Zweig, *m.* (~e) branch.

zweimal, *adv.* twice.

Zwerg, *m.* (~e) dwarf.

Zwetch(g)e, *f.* (~n) plum.

Zwieback, *m.* biscuit.

Zwiebel, *f.* (~n) onion.

Zwielicht, *n.* twilight.

Zwietracht, *m.* discord.

Zwilling, *m.* (~e) twin(s).

zwingen*, *v. a.* force; compel.

Zwirn, *m.* (~e) thread. **zwischen**, *prep.* between; among. **Zwischenraum**, *m.* interval.	**zwölf**, *adj.* twelve. **zwölfte**, *adj.* twelfth. **Zylinder**, *m.* (~) cylinder; top-hat. **Zypresse**, *f.* (~n) cypress.